Abortion Bibliography

for 1981

Compiled by
Polly T. Goode

Abortion Bibliography

for 1981

Compiled by
Polly T. Goode

The Whitston Publishing Company
Troy, New York
1983

TABLE OF CONTENTS

PREFACE

Abortion Bibliography for 1981 is the twelth annual list of books and articles surrounding the subject of abortion in the preceding year. It appears serially each fall as a contribution toward documenting in one place as comprehensively as possible the literature of one of our central social issues. It is an attempt at a comprehensive world bibliography.

Searches in compiling this material have covered the following sources: *Abstracts on Criminology & Penology; Abstracts on Police Science; Access; Air University Library Index to Military Periodicals; Alternative Index, America: History and Life; American Humanities Index; American Reference Books Annual; Applied Science & Technology Index; Art Index; Bibliographic Index; Biological Abstracts; Biological & Agricultural Index; British Humanities Index; Business Periodicals Index; Canadian Education Index; Canadian Periodicals Index; Catholic Periodical & Literature Index; Communication Abstracts; College Student Personnel Abstracts; Completed Research in Health, Physical Education, & Recreation; Criminal Justice Abstracts; Criminal Justice Periodical Index; Cumulated Index Medicus; Cumulative Book Index; Cumulative Index to Nursing and Allied Health Literature; Current Index to Journals in Education; Dissertation Abstracts International: A. Social Sciences & Humanities; Dissertation Abstracts International: B. The Sciences & Engineering; Education Index; Environment Abstracts; Environment Index; Essay & General Literature Index; Hospital Literature Index; Human Resources Abstracts; Humanities Index; Index to Jewish Periodicals; Index to Legal Periodicals; Index to Periodical Articles Related to Law; International Nursing Index; Masters Abstracts; Media Review Digest; Monthly Periodical Index; Music Index; New Periodicals Index; PAIS;*

PAIS Foreign Language Index; Psychological Abstracts; Psychopharmacology Abstracts; Readers Guide to Periodical Literature; Religion Index One: Periodicals (from: Index to Religious Periodical Literature); Sage Urban Studies Abstracts; Social Sciences Index; Social Work Research & Abstracts; Sociolgocial Abstracts; and *Women's Studies Abstracts.*

The Bibliography is divided into two sections: a title section in alphabetical order; and a subject section. Thus, if the researcher does not wish to observe the subject heads of the compiler, he can use the title section exclusively. The subject heads have been allowed to issue from the nature of the material indexed rather than being imposed from Library of Congress subject heads or other standard lists.

The Book section includes Government Publications and Monographs.

The Subject Head Index includes page numbers.

Polly T. Goode
Troy, New York

LIST OF PERIODICALS CITED

AFER: Africal Ecclesial Review
AMB: Revista da Associacao Medica Brasileira
Acta Bio-Medica de l'Ateneo Parmense
Acta Cytologica
Acta Endocrinologica
Acta Europaea Fertilitatis
Acta Gastroenterologica Belgica
Acta Haematologica
Acta Medicinae Legalis et Socialis
Acta Morphologica Academiae Scientiarum Hungaricae
Acta Obstetricia et Gynecologica Scandinavica
L'Actualite
Adolescence
Africa
Akusherstvo i Ginekologiia
Alberta Report
Allergologia et Immunopathologia
America
American Annals of the Deaf
American Baby
American Bar Association Journal
American Criminal Law Review
American Druggist
American Heart Journal
American Journal of Clinical Nutrition
American Journal of Diseases of Children
American Journal of Epidemiology
American Journal of Family Therapy
American Journal of Forensic Medicine and Pathology
American Journal of Human Genetics
American Journal of Jurisprudence
American Journal of Law and Medicine

American Journal of Maternal Child Nursing
American Journal of Medical Genetics
American Journal of Obstetrics and Gynecology
American Journal of Optometry & Physiological Optics
American Journal of Orthopsychiatry
American Journal of Orthopsychology
American Journal of Pharmaceutical Education
American Journal of Proctology, Gastroenterology and Colon &
    Rectal Surgery
American Journal of Psychiatry
American Journal of Public Health
American Journal of Trial Advocacy
American Medical News
American Spectator
Anaesthesie-Intensivtherapie-Notfallmedizin
Andrologia
Anesthesia and Analgesia
Anesthesiology
Anglo-American Law Review
Annales Medico-Psychologiques
Annales Universitatis Mariae Curie-Sklodowska
Annali di Ostetricia Ginecologia, Medicina Perinatale
Annals of the Academy of Medicine, Singapore
Annals of Clinical and Laboratory Science
Annals of Emergency Medicine
Annals of Internal Medicine
Annals of Ophthalmology
Annual Survey of American Law
Archives d'Anatomie et de Cytologie Pathologique
Archives des Maladies du Coeur et des Vaisseaux
Archives Francaises de Pediatrie
Archives of Dermatology
Archives of General Psychiatry
Archives of Gynecology
Archives of Pathology & Laboratory Medicine
Archives of Sexual Behavior
Archivio di Ostetricia e Ginecologia
Arkhiv Anotomii, Gistologii i Embriologii
Arquivos de Gastroenterologia
Arthritis and Rheumatism
Artery
Arzneimittel Forschung

Atherosclerosis
Atlantic Insight
Australasian Nurses Journal
Australasian Radiology
Australian Family Physician
Australian Journal of Social Issues
Australian Paediatrics Journal
Australian Veterinary Journal

Bangladesh Development Studies
Baylor Law Review
Beitraege zur Gerichtlichen Medizin
Bijdragen
Bilten za Hematologiju i Transfuziju
Biochemical Medicine
Biochemical Pharmacology
Bioethics Quarterly
Biomedical Mass Spectrometry
Black Law Journal
Bolletino della Societa Italiana di Biologia Sperimentale
Boston
Bratislavske Lekarske Listy
BRIEFS
Brigham Young University Law Review
British Journal of Anaesthesia
British Journal of Anaesthesology
British Journal of Clinical Pharmacology
British Journal of Clinical Practice
British Journal of Hospital Medicine
British Journal of Obstetrics and Gynaecology
British Journal of Urology
British Journal of Venereal Diseases
British Medical Journal
Bulletin de l'Academie Nationale de Medicine
Bulletin of the Atomic Scientists
Bulletin of the Menninger Clinic
Business Insurance

Canada and the World
Canadian Journal of Comparative Medicine

Canadian Journal of Public Health
Canadian Journal of Surgery
Canadian Medical Association Journal
Cancer
Cancer Detection and Prevention
Cancer Reports
Cancer Research
Case Western Reserve Law Review
Catholic Digest
Catholic Lawyer
Catholic Mind
Ceskoslovenska Gynekologie
Ceskoslovenska Neurologie a Neurochirurgio
Ceylon Medical Journal
Changing Times
Chatelaine
Chemical and Engineering News
Chemical Weekly
Chemistry and Industry
Children's Health Care
China Quarterly
Chinese Medical Journal
Chirurgia Italiana
Christian Century
Christianity and Crisis
Christianity Today
Chung Hua Fu Chan Ko Tsa Chih
Church and Society
Ciba Foundation Symposium
Circulation
Cleveland State Law Review
Clinica Chimica Acta
Clinical and Experimental Hypertension
Clinical Chemistry
Clinical Genetics
Clinica Terapeutica
Clinical Neurology and Neurosurgery
Clinical Nuclear Medicine
Clinical Obstetrics and Gynecology
Clinical Pediatrics
Clinical Pharmacology and Therapeutics
Clinical Research

Clinical Science
Clinical Therapeutics
Commonweal
Community Medicine
Comprehensive Psychiatry
Concepte
Congressional Monitor
Congressional Monthly
Congressional Quarterly Weekly Report
Connecticut Medicine
Contemporary Review
Contraception
Creighton Law Review
Crime and Delinquency
Crime and Social Justice
Criminal Law Reporter: Court Decisions and Proceedings
Criminal Law Reporter: Supreme Court Proceedings
Criminal Law Reporter: Text Section
The Criminal Law Review
Cross-reference on Human Resources Management
Current
Current History
Current Medical Research and Opinion
Currents in Theology and Mission
Cutis
Cytogenetics and Cell Genetics

Daily Telegraph
Danish Medical Bulletin
Demography
Das Deutsche Gesundheitswesen
Deutsche Medizinische Wochenschrift
Developmental Medicine and Child Neurology
Diabetes Care
Diagnostic Gynecology and Obstetrics
Dialogos
Die Suid-Afrikaanse Tyclskrif vir Sosiologie
Discussion
Dissertation Abstracts International
La Documentation Catholique
Draper Fund Report

Drug Intelligance and Clinical Pharmacy
Drug Topics
Drugs
Duodecim

EMT Journal: National Aossciation of Emergency Medical
    Technicians. Journal
East African Medical Journal
Eastern Anthropologist
Economic Development and Cultural Change
The Economist
Educational Broadcasting International
Egyptian Journal of Psychiatry
Encore
Endokrinologie
Environment
Environment News
Essence
European Journal of Obstetrics, Gynecology and Reproductive
    Biology
Evaluation Review
Executive
Experimental and Molecular Pathology

FDA Consumer
Family Coordinator
Family Health
The Family Law Reporter: Court Opinions
Family Planning Perspectives
Family Relations
Far Eastern Ecomonic Review
Fel'dsher i Akusherka
Feminist Studies
Fertility and Sterility
Finance and Development
Florida State University Law Review
Folia Haematologica
Folia Medica Cracoviensia
Forbes
The Forensic Science Gazette

Fortschritte der Medizin
Forum
From the State Capitals: Juvenile Delinquency and Family
    Relations
Furrow
Futurist

Gaceta Medica de Mexico
Gastroenterology
Geburtshilfe und Frauenheilkunde
Gene
Georgia Law Review
Ginekologia Polska
Ginecologia y Obstetricia de Mexico
Giustizia Penal
Glamour
Glendale Law Review
Good Housekeeping
Gregorianum
Guardian
Gynaekologische Rundschau
Gynecologic and Obstetric Investigation
Gynecologie

Haematologia
Haematologica
Harefuah
Harper's Bazaar
Hastings Constitutional Law Quarterly
Health
Health and Social Service Journal
Health and Social Work
Health Bulletin
Health Education
Health Law Vigil
Health Visitor
Hecate
Hepatogastroenterology
Homemaker's Magazine
Homiletic and Pastoral Review

Hormone and Metabolic Research
Hospital and Community Psychiatry
Hospital Formulary
Hospital Progress
Hospital Supervisors Bulletin
Hospitals
Houston Law Review
Human Biology
Human Genetics
Human Life Review
Human Pathology
Humanist

IRCS (International Research Communications System) Medical
    Science: Library Compendium
Indian Journal of Adult Education
International Journal of Epidemiology
Indian Journal of Experimental Biology
Indian Journal of Medical Research
Indian Journal of Pharmaceutical Sciences
Indian Journal of Public Health
Indian Journal of Social Work
Indiana Law Journal
Indian Philosophical Quarterly
Infirmiere Francaise
Interfaces
International Archives of Occupational and Environmental
    Health
International Family Planning Perspectives
International Journal of Andrology
International Journal of Clinical Pharmacology, Therapy and
    Toxicology
International Journal of Epidemiology
International Journal of Fertility
International Journal of Gynaecology and Obstetrics
International Journal of Health Education
International Journal of Health Services
International Journal of Middle Eastern Studies
International Journal of Nursing Studies
International Journal of Social Economics
International Library Review

International Ophthalmology Clinics
International Social Work
International Statistical Institute Review
International Surgery
Irish Journal of Medical Science
Irish Medical Journal
Irish Nursing Newsletter
Issues in Health Care of Women

JAMA: Journal of the American Medical Association
JNE: Journal of Nursing Education
JOGN Nursing: Journal of Obstetric, Gynecologic and Neonatal
    Nursing
JPMA: Journal of the Pakistan Medical Association
Josanpu Zasshi
Journal de Chirurgie
Journal de Gynceologie, Obstetrique et Biologie de la Reproduc-
    tion
Journal des Maldies Vasculaires
Journal of the American Academy of Dermatology
Journal of the American College Health Association
Journal of the American Dental Association
Journal of Analytical Toxicology
Journal of the Arkansas Medical Society
Journal of Biological Science
Journal of Biosocial Science
Journal of Church and State
Journal of Clinical Endocrinology and Metabolism
Journal of Clinical Pathology
Journal of Clinical Psychology
Journal of Communication
Journal of Community Psychology
Journal of Comparative and Physiological Psychology
Journal of Computor Assisted Tomography
Journal of Consumer Research
Journal of Counseling Psychology
Journal of Criminal Law and Criminology
Journal of the Egyptian Medical Association
Journal of the Egyptian Public Health Association
Journal of Endocrinology
Journal of Endocrinological Investigation

Journal of Toxicology and Environmental Health
Journal of Tropical Pediatrics and Environmental Child Health
Journal of Urology
Journal of Youth and Adolescence
Jugoslavenska Ginekologija i Opstetricija
Juvenile Law Digest

Katilolehti
Keio Journal of Medicine
Kentucky Law Journal
Klinische Monatsblaetter fur Augenheilkunde

Laboratornoe Delo
Ladies Home Journal
Lakartidningen
Lancet
Law and Policy Quarterly
Law Enforcement News
Lebensversicherungsmedizin
Life and Health
Life Sciences
Liguorian
Lille Medical
Linacre Quarterly
Loyola Law Review
Loyola University Law Journal

MMW: Muenchener Medizinishe Wochenschrift
MMWR
McCalls
Maclean's
Mademoiselle
Maine Law Review
Marketing
Maroc Medical
Marriage
Media Asia
Medical Journal of Australia
Medical Journal of Malaysia

Medical Journal of Zambia
Medical Times
Medical World News
Meditsinskaia Parazitologiia i Parazitarnyė Bolezni
Medizinische Klinik
Medizinische Monatsschrift fur Pharmazeuten
Medizinische Welt
Mental Retardation
Metabolism
Michigan Hospitals
Michigan Medicine
Middle Eastern Studies
Midwife, Health Visitor and Community Nurse
Minerva Anestesiologica
Minerva Ginecologia
Minerva Medica
Minnesota Medicine
Modern Law Review
Month
Mother Jones
Ms Magazine
Mutation Research

Nation
National Catholic Reporter
National Institute on Drug Abuse Research Monograph Series
National Review
Nature
Nederlands Tijdschrift voor Geneeskunde
The Netherlands Journal of Sociology
Neurology
Neuropsychobiology
Neurosurgery
New Covenant
New Directions for Women
New England Journal of Medicine
New England Journal of Prison Law
New Humanist
New Republic
New Scientist
New Society

New Statesman
New York
New York Review of Books
New York State Journal of Medicine
New Zealand Medical Journal
New Zealand Nursing Forum
Newsweek
Nippon Rinsho
Nippon Sanka Fujinka Gakkai Zasshi
Nordisk Medicin
North Carolina Law Review
North Carolina Medical Journal
Northwestern University Law Review
Notas de Población
Nouvelle Presse Medicale
Nurses Drug Alert
Nursing Focus
Nursing Journal of India
Nursing Law and Ethics
Nursing Mirror
Nursing News
Nursinglife

OR
Observer
Obstetrics and Gynecology
Oeffentliche Gesundheitswesen
Off Our Backs
Oklahoma Observer
Omni
Opthalmology
Oral Surgery
Orient
Origins
Orvosi Hetilap
Our Sunday Visitor

Pacific Affairs
Paediatrie und Paedologie
Parents

Pastoral Psychology
Pathologie Biologie
Patient Counselling and Health Education
Pediatric Clinics of North America
Pediatrics
People
Peperdine Law Review
Philosophy and Public Affairs
Phoenix
Pielegniarka i Polozna
Playboy
Policy Report
Policy Studies Journal
Politica del Diritto
Polski Tygodnik Lekarski
Population
Population and Development Review
Population and Environment
Population Bulletin
Population et Famille
Population Reports
Population Studies
Population Trends
Populi
Postgraduate Medical Journal
Practitioner
Praxis
Primary Care
Proceedings of the Society for Experimental Biology and
    Medicine
Progress in Clinical and Biological Research
Progressive
Prostaglandins and Medicine
Psychology of Women Quarterly
Psychopharmacology
Psychophysiology
Public Health Reports
Public Welfare
Publius

Queen's Law Review

RN
RNACB News
Radical American
Radical Religion
Radical Science Journal
Radiologe
Recombinant DNA Technical Bulletin
Reformatio: Evangelische Zeitschrift fur Kultur and Politik
Refractory Girl
Relations
Religion in Life
Reproduction
Review and Exposition
Review of Politics
Review of Public Data Use
Revista Chilena de Obstetricia y Ginecologia
Revista Chilena de Pediatria
Revue d' Epidemiologie et de Sante Publique
Revue de Medecine Interne
Revue Medicale de Liege
Rinsho Ketsueki
Rivista Internazionale di Filosofia del Diritto
Rivista Italiana di Ginecologia
Rolling Stone

SPM: Salud Publica de Mexico
Saint Anthony Messenger
St. Mary Law Journal
Same-Day Surgery
San Francisco Freeman
Scandinavian Journal of Infectious Diseases Supplement
Scandinavian Journal of Urology and Nephrology
Scandinavian Journal of Work, Environment and Health
Science
Science Digest
Science News
Scientific American
SciQuest
Scottish Medical Journal
Schweizerische Medizinische Wochenschrift
Semaines des Hopitaux de Paris

Seminars in Perinatology
Seton Hall Law Review
Seventeen
Sexually Transmitted Diseases
Sign
Signs
Singapore Medical Journal
Social and Economic Studies
Social Biology
Social Justice Review
Social Praxis
Social Science and Medicine
Social Thought
Society and Culture
Society and Welfare
Sociological Analysis
Sociologija Sela
Sociology and Social Research
Soldiers
South African Medical Journal
Southern Economic Journal
Southern Medical Journal
Srpski Arhiv za Celokupno Lekarstvo
Stanford Law Review
Stimmen der Zeit
Studies in Family Planning
Studies in Short Fiction
Suffolk University Law Review
Supervisor Nurse
Supplément
The Surgical Technologists

THESA Journal
Tablet
Technology and Culture
Technology Review
Teratology
Texas Tech Law Review
Therapeutic Recreation Journal
Therapeutische Umschau
Therapie

Therapie der Gegenwart
Tidsskrift for den Norske Laegeforening
Tijdschrift voor Diergeneeskunde
Tijdschrift voor SocialeWetenschappen
Tijdschrift vor Ziekenverpleging
Time
Times Higher Educational Supplement
Times Literary Supplement
Today
Toxicology
Transactions of the Royal Society of Tropical Medicine and
    Hygiene
Trial

UCLA Law Review
US Catholic
US News and World Report
USA Today
Ugeskirft for Laeger
Union Medicale du Canada
University of Dayton Law Review
University of Detroit Journal of Urban Law
University of Toronto Law Journal
University of Western Ontario Law Review
Urologic Clinics of North America
Urology

Valparaiso University Law Review
Values, Ethics and Health Care
Vardfacket
Vasa
Vestnik Akademii Meditsinskikh Nauk SSSR
The Village Voice
Vital Health Statistics
Vogue
Voprosy Okhrany Materinstva i Detstva

Wall Street Journal
Washington University Law Quarterly

West Indian Medical Journal
West Virginia Law Review
Western Folklore
Whittier Law Review
Wiadomosci Lekarskie
Wiener Klinische Wochenschrift
Witness
Woman's Day
Women and Health
Women's Rights Law Reporter
Women's Studies International Quarterly
Working Women
World Health
World of Irish Nursing
World Press Review
Worldwatch Paper

Yao Hsueh Hsueh Pao; Acta Pharmaceutica Sinica
Yonsei Medical Journal
Youth Alternatives
Youth and Society

Zdravookhraneniye Belorussii
Zeitschrift fur Aerztliche Fortbildung
Zeitschrift fur die Gesamte Innere Medizin
Zeitschrift fur Geburtschilfe und Perinatologie
Zentralblatt fur Chirurgie
Zentralblatt fur Gynaekologie
Zhurnal Mikrobiologii, Epidemiologii i Immunobiologii
Zhurnal Nevropatologii i Psikhiatrii

SUBJECT HEADING INDEX

BOOKS, GOVERNMENT PUBLICATIONS, AND MONOGRAPHS

ABORTION BIBLIOGRAPHY FOR 1978. Troy, New York: Whitston, 1980.

ACTES DU COLLOQUE NATIONAL SUR LA DÉMOGRAPHIE FRANÇAISE, PARIS, 23-24-25 JUIN 1980. Paris: Presses Universitaires de France, 1981.

American Neurological Association. Committee for the investigation of Eugenical Sterilization. EUGENICAL STERILIZATION. New York: Arno Press, 1980.

Anderson, T. L. and P. J. Hill. THE BIRTH OF A TRANSFER SOCIETY. Stanford, California: Hoover Institution Press, c. 1981.

Balis, A. WHAT ARE YOU USING? New York: Dial Press, 1981.

Basson, Marc, et al. ETHICS, HUMANITIES AND MEDICINE. New York: Liss, 1981.

BIRTH CONTROL AND CONTROLLING BIRTH. Humana Press, 1980.

Blake, J., et al. FAMILY STRUCTURE IN JAMAICA. Westport, Connecticut: Greenwood Press, 1980.

Bondestam, Lars and Staffan Bergström, editors. POVERTY AND POPULATION CONTROL. New York: Academic Press, 1980.

Bonitz, D. THE PSYCHOLOGY OF ABORTION, COMPARING

LEGAL WITH ILLEGAL ABORTIONS. Gottingen: Verlag
fur Medizinische Psychologie, Verlag Vandenhveck and
Rupprecht, 1979.

Brennan, W. MEDICAL HOLOCAUSTS I. Belmont, Massachusetts: Nardland, 1980.

Briggs, Michael. ANIMAL MODELS AND THE CARCINO-
GENICITY OF CONTRACEPTIVE STEROIDS. New York:
Raven Press, 1980,

Chandrasekhar, S. A DIRTY, FILTHY BOOK. Berkeley:
University of California Press, 1981.

Charbit, Yves and Henri Leridon. TRANSITION DÉMO-
GRAPHIQUE ET MODERNISATION EN GUADELOUPE
ET EN MARTINIQUE. Paris: Presses Universitaires de
France, 1980.

FERTILITY CONTROL, BIOLOGIC AND BEHAVIORIAL
ASPECTS. New York: Harper & Row, 1980.

Fotherby, K., et al. ANIMAL MODELS FOR THE DEVELOP-
MENT OF LONG-ACTING INJECTABLE CONTRACEP-
TIVES. New York: Raven Press, 1980.

Gosney, E. S. STERILIZATION FOR HUMAN BETTERMENT.
New York: Arno Press, 1980.

Grassian, Victor. MORAL REASONING: ETHICAL THEORY
AND SOME CONTEMPORARY MORAL PROBLEMS.
Englewood Cliffs, New Jersey: Prentice-Hall, 1981.

Hauerwas, Stanley. A COMMUNITY OF CHARACTER:
TOWARD A CONSTRUCTIVE CHRISTIAN SOCIAL
ETHIC. Notre Dame, Indiana: Notre Dame University
Press, 1981.

Hilgers, Thomas W. and Dennis J. Haran, editors. ABORTION
AND SOCIAL JUSTICE. Thaxton, Virginia: Sun Life, 1980.

Hunter, J. F. M. THINKING ABOUT SEX AND LOVE. New

York: St. Martin's Press, 1980.

IMMUNOLOGICAL ASPECTS OF REPRODUCTION AND
FERTILITY CONTROL. Baltimore: University Park Press,
1980.

INDUCED ABORTIONS IN OREGON, JANUARY-DECEM-
BER, 1979. Portland, Oregon: Center for Health Statistics,
1980.

L'INTERRUPTION VOLONTAIRE DE GROSSESSE DANS
L'EUROPE DES NEUF; JOURNÉE D'ÉTUDE DU 23
OCTOBRE 1979. Paris: Presses Universitaires de France,
1981.

Jackson, M. VAGINAL CONTRACEPTION. Boston: G. K. Hall
& Co., 1981.

Jaffe, Frederick S., et al. ABORTION POLITICS: PRIVATE
MORALITY AND PUBLIC POLICY [UNITED STATES].
New York: McGraw-Hill, 1981.

Keller, A. SCANDALOUS LADY. New York: Atheneum
Publishers, 1981.

Khan, M. E. and C. V. S. Prasad. FERTILITY CONTROL IN
INDIA. Manohar Publishers, 1980.

Leathard, Audrey. FIGHT FOR FAMILY PLANNING: THE
DEVELOPMENT OF FAMILY PLANNING SERVICES IN
BRITAIN, 1921-1974. London: Macmillan, 1980.

Lieberman, E. J. and E. Peck. SEX AND BIRTH CONTROL.
Revised edition. New York: Harper & Row, 1981.

Lightbourne, Robert E. URBAN-RURAL DIFFERENTIALS
IN CONTRACEPTIVE USE. International Statistics Institute, 1980.

Londis, J. J. ABORTION—MERCY OR MURDER? Nashville:
Southern Publishing Association, 1980.

3

McDonough, Peter and Amaury DeSouza. THE POLITICS OF POPULATION IN BRAZIL: ELITE AMBIVALENCE AND PUBLIC DEMAND. Austin, Texas: University of Texas Press, 1981.

Mukherjee, Bishwa Nath. PREDICTION OF FAMILY PLANN- ING AND FAMILY SIZE FROM MODERNITY VALUE ORIENTATIONS OF INDIAN WOMEN. East-West Popula- tion Institute, 1979.

New Jersey. General Assembly. Institutions, Health and Welfare Committee. Public hearing before [a] subcommittee, on A-1155 and A-1592 (ABORTION: PARENTAL NOTIFICA- TION AND INFORMED CONSENT): held: Elizabeth, New Jersey, October 1, 1980. Trenton, New Jersey: The Assembly, 1980.

NEW PERSPECTIVES OF HUMAN ABORTION. Washington: University Publications of America, 1981.

Nortman, Dorothy L. and Ellen Hopfstatter. POPULATION AND FAMILY PLANNING PROGRAMS: A COMPENDIUM OF DATA THROUGH 1978. New York: Population Council, 1980.

Porter, Cedric W. and Ronald S. Waife. INTRAUTERINE DE- VICES: CURRENT PERSPECTIVES. New York: Pathfinder, 1978.

PSYCHOLOGY AND HUMAN REPRODUCTION. New York: Macmillan, 1980.

Reed, James. FROM PRIVATE VICE TO PUBLIC VIRTUE: THE BIRTH CONTROL MOVEMENT AND AMERICAN SOCIETY SINCE 1830. New York: Basic Books, 1978.

Risdon, E. E. ABORTION ON DEMAND. Los Angeles: Reality Publishing, 1980.

Sandoval A, Guillermo. LOS PROGRAMAS DE POBLACIÓN Y LA ASAMBLEA LEGISLATIVA. Heredia, Costa Rica: Instituto de Estudios Sociales en Pollacion, Universidad

Nacional, 1980.

Scheidegger, Elisabeth. POBLACIÓN Y DESARROLLO: LA
EVOLUCIÓN DEMOGRÁFICA Y EL DESARROLLO
ECONÓMICO Y SOCIAL DE AMERICA LATINA. Geneva:
International Institute for labor studies, 1980.

Serio, Mario and Luciano Martini, editors. ANIMAL MODELS
IN HUMAN REPRODUCTION. New York: Raven Press,
1980.

Stark, R. THE BOOK OF APHRODISIACS. Briarcliff Manor,
New York: Stein & Day, 1981.

Sumner, L. W. ABORTION AND MORAL THEORY. Princeton:
Princeton University Press, 1981.

Tietze, Christopher. INDUCED ABORTION. 1979. 3rd edition.
New York: Population Council, 1979.

United States. House. Committee on Foreign Affairs. CHINA'S
POPULATION POLICIES AND POPULATION DATE:
REVIEW AND UPDATE. Washington: Library of Congress
Congressional Research Service, 1981.

—. Senate. Committee on Foreign Relations. WORLD POPULA-
TION TRENDS: HEARINGS, APRIL 29 AND JUNE 5,
1980, ON U.S. POPULATION POLICY AND PROGRAMS.
Washington: GPO, 1980.

Valentine, S. R. ALL SHALL LIVE. Richmond, Indiana: Friends
United Press, 1980.

Walling, R. WHEN PREGNANCY IS A PROBLEM. St. Meinerod,
Indiana: Abbey Press, 1980.

Welch, W. THE ART OF POLITICAL THINKING. Totawa, New
Jersey: Littlefield, Adams & Co., 1981.

Wilson, John. LOVE, SEX AND FEMINISM. New York: Praeger,
1980.

THE WORLD POPULATION CRISIS. Westport, Connecticut: Greenwood Press, 1980.

Zimmermann, W. CONDEMNED TO LIVE. Memphis: Vita Press, 1981.

PERIODICAL LITERATURE

TITLE INDEX

APHA: renew Title X, lift ban on radio, TV contraceptive ads. FAMILY PLANNING PERSPECTIVES 13:47-48, January-February, 1981.

A-nor steroids as post-coital contraceptives in the hamster with special reference to the transport and degernation of eggs, by Z. Gu, et al. CONTRACEPTION 20(6):549-557, December, 1979.

"Abhorrent and offensive": from the witness chair, Sandra O'Connor said that about abortion, by Beth Spring. CHRISTIANITY TODAY 25:52-53, October 23, 1981.

Abortion, by H. Jung. ZEITSCHRIFT FUR GEBURTSHILFE UND PERINATOLOGIE 184(2):83-93, April, 1980.

Abortion [Helms-Hyde bill], by E. Switzer. WORKING WOMEN 6:32+, July, 1981.

Abortion, 1954, by S. Matulis. PROGRESSIVE 45:66, August, 1981.

The abortion activists . . . the National Abortion Rights Action League and the National Right to Life Committee, by D. Granberg. FAMILY PLANNING PERSPECTIVES 13:157-163, July-August, 1981.

Abortion alternatives leader up for U.S. job, by Mary B. Papa. NATIONAL CATHOLIC REPORTER 17:6, February 27,

1981.

Abortion and American population politics, by J. M. Ostheimer. THE POLICY STUDIES JOURNAL 6(2):216-223, 1977.

Abortion and the casual theory of names, by J. A. Nelson, PhD. DAI 41(7-8), 1981.

Abortion and civil disobedience, by D. Morris. OUR SUNDAY VISITOR 70:6-7, September 6, 1981.

Abortion and coalition politics: whose survival? [Failure of Mobilization for Survival, anti-nuclear and pro-disarmament coalition, to take a stand on abortion.], by T. Dejanikus. OFF OUR BACKS 11:2+, April, 1981.

Abortion and Criminal law, by H. R. S. Ryan. QUEEN'S LAW JOURNAL 6:362-371, Spring, 1981.

Abortion and the elections: a statement, by H. S. Medeiros. CATHOLIC MIND 79:8-9, January, 1981.

Abortion and infant mortality before and after the 1973 U. S. Supreme Court decision on abortion, by L. S. Robertson. JOURNAL OF BIOSOCIAL SCIENCE 13:275-280, July, 1981.

Abortion and judicial review: of burdens and benefits, hard cases and some bad law, by R. W. Bennett. NORTHWESTERN UNIVERSITY LAW REVIEW 75:978-1017, February, 1981.

Abortion and the limitations of science, by B. G. Zack. SCIENCE 213:291, July 17, 1981.

Abortion and the "right-to-life": facts, fallacies, and fraud, by J. Prescott. THE HUMANIST 38(4):18-24, July-August, 1978.

—. II., by J. Prescott. THE HUMANIST 38(6):36-42, November-December, 1978.

Abortions—Appeals. THE FAMILY LAW REPORTER: COURT OPINIONS 7(8):2119, December 23, 1980.

Abortion: are men there when women need them most? by
C. L. Mithers. MADEMOISELLE 87:230-231+, April, 1981.

Abortion as Fatherhood Lost: Problems and reforms, by A.
Shostak. THE FAMILY COORDINATOR 28(4):569-574,
October, 1979.

Abortion as holocaust: a colloquy. pt. 1: A crippling analogy, by
E. J. Fisher; pt. 2: The victims of rhetoric, by B. Brickner.
CONGRESSIONAL MONTHLY 48:13-15, January, 1981.

Abortion—attorney's fees. THE FAMILY LAW REPORTER:
COURT OPINIONS 6(46):2889, September 30, 1980.

Abortion bill praised, hit by Catholics. NATIONAL CATHOLIC
REPORTER 18:18, November 13, 1981.

Abortion chic, by L. Savan. VILLAGE VOICE 26:32, February 4, 1981.

Abortion committees in Israel—a reflection of a social dilemma—
from the viewpoint of social workers (Hebrew), by N. Laron,
et al. SOCIETY AND WELFARE 3(3):334-347, 1980.

Abortion, the Constitution, and the human life statute, by F. J.
Flaherty. COMMONWEAL 108:586-593, October 23, 1981.

Abortion—constitutional rights—religion—due process. THE
FAMILY LAW REPORTER: COURT OPINIONS. 7(9):2136,
January 6, 1981.

The abortion controversy: an overview, by D. Granberg. HU-
MANIST 41:28-38, July-August, 1981.

The abortion decision—perspective: counseling, by C. Dornblaser.
MINNESOTA MEDICINE 64(1):45-47, January, 1981.

Abortion: 1. Definitions and implications [editorial], by B. M.
Dickens. CANADIAN MEDICAL ASSOCIATION JOURNAL
124(2):113-114, January 15, 1981.

—. 2. Fetal status and legal representation [editorial], by B. M.

Dickens. CANADIAN MEDICAL ASSOCIATION JOURNAL
124(3):253-254, February 1, 1981.

—. 3. Therapeutic abortion committees and third parties [edi-
torial] , by B. M. Dickens. CANADIAN MEDICAL ASSOCIA-
TION JOURNAL 124(4):362-363, 384, February 15, 1981.

Abortion: Dr. Koop and Mr. Hyde. ECONOMIST 278:25+,
March 28, 1981.

Abortion—due process. THE FAMILY LAW REPORTER:
COURT OPINIONS 6(49):2939, October 21, 1980.

Abortion: an epidemiologic study at Ramathibodi Hospital,
Bangkok, by K. Chaturachinda, et al. STUDIES IN FAMILY
PLANNING 12:257-261, June-July, 1981.

Abortion, euthanasia and the pluralist society, by D. J. Ryan.
OR (8):672, February 23, 1981.

Abortion facilities and the risk of death, by D. A. Grimes, et al.
FAMILY PLANNING PERSPECTIVES 13:30-31, January-
February, 1981.

Abortion foe tags move an ouster. NATIONAL CATHOLIC
REPORTER 17:3, January 9, 1981.

Abortions for minors after Bellotti II (Bellotti v. Baird, 99 S Ct
3035): an analysis of state law and a proposal. ST. MARY
LAW JOURNAL 11:946-997, 1980.

Abortion from the ethical point of view, by W. Vossenkuhl.
MMW 123(6):198-200, February 6, 1981.

Abortion-funding issue: a study in mixed constitutional cues, by
T. E. Yarbrough. NORTH CAROLINA LAW REVIEW 59:
611-627, March, 1981.

Abortion funding ruling: the controversy rages, by M. Middleton.
AMERICAN BAR ASSOCIATION JOURNAL 66:945,
August, 1980.

Abortion: hell's fury. ECONOMIST 279:22, May 30, 1981.

Abortion: an important decision. TABLET 234:1115-1116, November 15, 1980.

Abortion—in an action seeking declaratory and injunctive relief, several provisions of the 1979 Missouri statute regulating abortions were found unconstitutional. JOURNAL OF FAMILY LAW 19:342-350, March, 1981.

Abortion in American teenagers, 1972-1978, does race matter? by D. Kramer. AMERICAN JOURNAL OF EPIDEMIOLO-GY 112(3):433, 1980.

Abortion in Israel: Social demand and political responses, by Y. Yisai. THE POLICY STUDIES JOURNAL Winter, 1978.

Abortion in Italy, by J. Emanuel. TABLET 235:547-548, June 6, 1981.

Abortion in the nineteenth century Maori: a historical and ethnopsychiatric review, by L. K. Gluckman. NEW ZEA-LAND MEDICAL JOURNAL 93(685):384-386, June 10, 1981.

Abortion in Odessa is trashy business, Texans learn, by M. Mawyer. OUR SUNDAY VISITOR 69:7, January 18, 1981.

Abortion in proportion, by M. G. Gregory. JOURNAL OF THE TENNESSEE MEDICAL ASSOCIATION 73(7):518-519, July, 1980.

Abortion in the 2d trimester by extra-amniotic infusion. Descrip-tion of 149 cases, by M. Blum. MINERVA GINECOLOGICA 33(2-3):253-256, February-March, 1981.

Abortion in the United States, 1978-1979, by S. Henshaw, et al. FAMILY PLANNING PERSPECTIVES 13:6-18, January-February, 1981.

Abortion incidence following fallopian tube repair, by R. P. Jansen. OBSTETRICS AND GYNECOLOGY 56(4):499-502,

October, 1980.

The abortion law that could divide America, by P. Levi. DAILY TELEGRAPH p15, March 18, 1981.

Abortion laws, religious beliefs and the First Amendment, by S. L. Skahn. VALPARAISO UNIVERSITY LAW REVIEW 14:487-526, Spring, 1980.

Abortion lives. ECONOMIST 279:50, May 23-29, 1981.

Abortion: the modern temptation, by B. B. Morton. ST. ANTHONY MESSENGER 88:24-27, May, 1981.

Abortion: the new facts of life, by B. M. Campbell. ESSENCE 12:86-87+, September, 1981.

Abortion 1980: the debate continues, by J. M. Healey. CONNECTICUT MEDICINE 44(9):605, September, 1980.

Abortion 1981: the search for perspective [editorial], by J. M. Healey. CONNECTICUT MEDICINE 45(7):467, July, 1981.

Abortion on demand: policy and implementation, by M. Cohen, et al. HEALTH AND SOCIAL WORK 6:65-72, February, 1981.

Abortion, or the way to a social technique, by W. Becker. CONCEPTE 16(9):6-13, 1980.

Abortion—parental notification. THE CRIMINAL LAW REPORTER: SUPREME COURT PROCEEDINGS 28(4):4049-4050, October 22, 1980.

An abortion perspective: legal considerations, by F. A. Lyon. MINNESOTA MEDICINE 63(9):659-661, September, 1980.

Abortion policy: ideology, political cleavage and the policy process, by H. A. Palley. THE POLICY STUDIES JOURNAL 7(2):224-233, Winter, 1978.

Abortion policy in 1978: A follow-up analysis, by D. Stewart.

12

PUBLIUS 9(1):161-168, 1979.

Abortion Politics and family life: an interpretation, by P. T. Lynch, PhD. DAI 41(3-4), 1981.

Abortion politics: Italian style, by M. Bosworth. REFRACTORY GIRL (22):25-26, May, 1981.

Abortion1, Pope 0 [John Paul II's support of unsuccessful referendum to tighten abortion laws, by T. Sheehan. COMMONWEAL 108:357-359, June 19, 1981.

Abortion practices in the rural areas around Najafgarh, by T. Verghese, et al. NURSING JOURNAL OF INDIA 71(6):153-154, June, 1980.

The abortion problem from the ophthalmologist's point of view, by L. Mewe. KLINISCHE MONATSBLAETTER FUR AUGENHEILKUNDE 178(3):219-223, Marcy, 1981.

Abortion prompts emotional lobbying, by N. Cohodas. CONGRESSIONAL QUARTERLY WEEKLY REPORT 39:384-387, February 28, 1981.

Abortion rate and chromosomal abnormality [letter], by R. J. Gardner. LANCET 2(8244):474-475, August 29, 1981.

Abortion regulation: the circumscription of state intervention by the doctrine of informed consent. GEORGIA LAW REVIEW 15:681-713, Spring, 1981.

Abortion-related mortality—United States, 1977. THE FORENSIC SCIENCE GAZETTE 10(3):5-6, July-September, 1979.

Abortion: religious differences and public policy, by H. Siegman. CONGRESSIONAL MONTHLY 48:3-4, June, 1981.

Abortion rights group to sue three dioceses. NATIONAL CATHOLIC REPORTER 16:3+, October 3, 1980.

Abortion rights group sues nation's Catholic bishops. OUR SUNDAY VISITOR 69:7, March 1, 1981.

13

Abortion rights: taking the offensive, by N. Weisstein. MS
MAGAZINE 10:36+, September, 1981.

Abortion: a severe testing. COMMONWEAL 108:643, November 20, 1981.

Abortion—state statutes—informed consent—waiting period. THE
CRIMINAL LAW REPORTER: COURT DECISIONS AND
PROCEEDINGS 27(22):2492, September 3, 1980.

Abortion-sterilization by abdominal hysterectomy [letter].
AMERICAN JOURNAL OF OBSTETRICS AND GYNECOL-
OGY 139(1):115-117, January, 1981.

Abortion—strict limitations on federal Medicaid reimbursements
for abortions imposed by the Hyde amendment held permissible. Participating states held not obligated to fund medically necessary abortions not federally funded. JOURNAL OF
FAMILY LAW 19:335-341, March, 1981.

The abortion struggle in Mexico, by E. Haley. HECATE 7(1):78-
87, 1981.

Abortion surveillance—United States, 1978. MMWR 30(19):222-
225, May 22, 1981.

Abortion threatens political parties, by R. Gustaitus. OKLA-
HOMA OBSERVOR 13:15, January 25, 1981.

Abortion: torchlight marchers condemn abortions [Dublin,
Ireland] ; Spain; Mexico; Soviet Union. OFF OUR BACKS
11:4, April, 1981.

Abortion: toward developing a policy in a Catholic social service
agency, by D. C. Dendinger, et al. SOCIAL THOUGHT 6:
33-46, Fall, 1980.

Abortion voting reveals deep change in Italy, by E. Grace.
CHRISTIANITY AND CRISIS 41:212-213, July 20, 1981.

Abortion weights [letter] , by C. B. Goodhart. LANCET
1(8235):1429, June 27, 1981.

Abortion: will we lose our right to choose? by J. Coburn. MADEMOISELLE 87:32, July, 1981.

Abortions for the poor. AMERICA 145:134, September 19, 1981.

Abortive activity of mimosine and its prevention, by J. Perea-Sasiain, et al. REPRODUCTION 5(2):113-118, April-June, 1981.

Accidental pregnancy: why do some women play sexual roulette? by F. Maynard. CHATELAINE 57(37):61-64+, March, 1981.

Activist pro-life priest ousted: board defends actions, by F. Franzonia. OUR SUNDAY VISITOR 69:8, December 28, 1980.

Acute ischemic lesions in young women taking oral contraceptives. A report on 5 cases, by R. K. Danis, et al. JOURNAL DES MALADIES VASCULAIRES 5(4):273-276, 1980.

Acute kidney insufficiency after septic abortion according to data from the Pirogov RNPISMP, by P. Petrov, et al. AKUSHERSTVO I GINEKOLOGIIA 19(4):304-309, 1980.

Adjuvant anticoagulant therapy in repeated fetal loss, by R. Langer, et al. HAREFUAH 99(3-4):65-67, August, 1980.

The adolescent and contraception: issues and controversies, by A. Rosenfield. INTERNATIONAL JOURNAL OF GYNAECOLOGY AND OBSTETRICS 19(1):57-64, March, 1981.

Adolescent contraception, by A. K. Kreutner. PEDIATRIC CLINICS OF NORTH AMERICA 28(2):455-473, May, 1981.

Adolescent girls and contraception, by R. Frydman, et al. ARCHIVES FRANCAISES DE PEDIATRIE 37(Suppl 1):XXV-XXVIII, 1980.

Adolescent health services and contraceptive use, by E. Mudd. AMERICAN JOURNAL OF ORTHOPSYCHIATRY 48(3):

495-504, July, 1978.

Adolescent pregnancy, by P. J. Goldstein. JOURNAL OF THE INTERNATIONAL ASSOCIATION OF PUPIL PERSONNEL WORKERS 25(2):124-129, Spring, 1981.

Adolescent sexuality and pregnancy, by N. J. Burton. ISSUES IN HEALTH CARE OF WOMEN 2:43-51, April, 1980.

Adopters and non-adopters of family planning in an Indian village: a case study, by S. A. S. C. Mouli, et al. JOURNAL OF FAMILY WELFARE 27:30-38, March, 1981.

Advances in the research of the contraceptive action of LH-RH analogs, by Y. Pardo, et al. HAREFUAH 99(8):229-231, October 15, 1980.

Adverse effects of oral contraceptives, by H. J. Engel. MEDIZINISCHE MONATSSCHRIFT FUR PHARMAZENTEN 2(7):199-204, July, 1979.

Advertisements for contraceptives as commercial speech in the broadcast media. CASE WESTERN RESERVE LAW REVIEW 31:336-362, Winter, 1981.

After a decade, Respect Life program is still growing, by J. Castelli. OUR SUNDAY VISITOR 70:6, October 4, 1981.

Aftermath of abortion: Anniversary depression and abdominal pain, by J. Cavenar, et al. BULLETIN OF THE MENNINGER CLINIC 42(5):433-438, September, 1978.

The age at first birth and timing of the second in Costa Rica and Guatemala, by A. R. Pebley. POPULATION STUDIES 35: 387-397, November, 1981.

Aggregate mortality, socio-demographic factors and attitudes toward abortion and euthanasia, by S. Steele, PhD. DAI 41: 11-12, 1981.

Alcohol and spontaneous abortion [letter], by R. J. Sokol. LANCET 2(8203):1079, November 15, 1980.

All freedoms are not free: the tab for abortions should be picked up by those who want them, by B. Amiel. MACLEANS 94: 11, July 27, 1981.

Allylestrenol: three years of experience with Gestanon in threatened abortion and premature labor, by J. Cortés-Prieto, et al. CLINICAL THERAPEUTICS 3(3):200-208, 1980.

An alternative contraceptive method: fertility awareness, by E. A. Magenheimer. ISSUES IN HEALTH CARE OF WOMEN (6):39-50, 1979.

Alternatives in midtrimester abortion induction, by J. Robins, et al. OBSTETRICS AND GYNECOLOGY 56(6):716-722, December, 1980.

Alternatives to adolescent pregnancy: a discussion of the contraceptive literature from 1960 to 1980, by D. E. Greydanus. SEMINARS IN PERINATOLOGY 5(1):53-90, January, 1981.

Amenorrhea following oral contraception, by N. Smiljanić, et al. ACTA OBSTETRICIA ET GYNECOLOGICA SCANDINAVICA 59(3):261-264, 1980.

—. Pathophysiological problems, by G. Schaison. NOUVELLE PRESSE MEDICALE 9(41):3083-3086, November 1, 1980.

Anaesthesia for termination of pregnancy, by I. S. Grant. BRITISH JOURNAL OF ANAESTHESOLOGY 52(8):711-713, August, 1980.

Analgesia with buprenorphin (Temgesic) in abortions with sulproston (PGE2 derivative), by S. Heinzl, et al. GYNAEKOLOGISCHE RUNDSCHAW 20(Suppl 1):69-71, June, 1980.

Analysis of attitudes of Oklahomans of voting age toward sex education, teen contraception, and abortion, by N. L. Turner. DAI 42(5), 1981.

Analysis of serum-mediated immunosuppression in normal pregnancy, abortion and contraception, by B. Masset, et al.

17

ALLERGOLOGIA ET IMMUNOPATHOLOGIA 8(5):569-578, September-October, 1980.

Anatomic and chromosomal anomalies in 639 spontaneous abortuses, by T. Kajii, et al. HUMAN GENETICS 55(1):87-98, 1980.

Anesthesiological problems and choice in operations for the termination of pregnancy. A study of 1500 cases, by G. B. Paolella, et al. MINERVA ANESTESIOLOGICA 47(1-2): 37-40, January-February, 1981.

Anesthetic gases and occupational hazard [letter], by C. J. Göthe, et al. SCANDINAVIAN JOURNAL OF WORK, ENVIRONMENT AND HEALTH 6(4):316, December, 1980.

Angiography of cerebrovascular accidents in patients taking contraceptive pills. An analysis of 85 cases, by S. Hardy-Godon, et al. JOURNAL OF NEURORADIOLOGY 6(3): 239-254, 1979.

Another barrier to pregnancy. TIME 117:57, January 26, 1981.

Another blast at spermicide ads. CHEMICAL WEEKLY 123:26+, January 14, 1981.

Another violation of N1H guidelines [news], by D. Dickson. NATURE 286(5774):649, August 14, 1980.

Anovulation syndrome in nulligravidae following intake of hormonal contraceptives, by R. Müller, et al. ZENTRAL-BLATT FUR GYNAEKOLOGIE 102(1):33-41, 1980.

Antecedents affecting contraceptive behavior of teenage females, by C. R. Griffin, PhD. DAI 41(11), 1981.

Anti-abortion, anti-birth control, anti-woman, by S. Dawson. OFF OUR BACKS 11:17, March, 1981.

Antiabortion, antifeminism, and the rise of the New Right, by R. P. Petchesky. FEMINIST STUDIES 7:206-246, Summer, 1981.

Anti-abortion Congress members blast hit list, by C. P. Winner. NATIONAL CATHOLIC REPORTER 17:6+, June 19, 1981.

Anti-abortion groups spar over amendment tactic [news]. CHRISTIANITY TODAY 25:84, February 6, 1981.

Anti-abortionists: the right takes aim. ECONOMIST 277:27+, October 4, 1980.

Antibiotic-oral contraceptive interaction? by R. C. Andersen, et al. DRUG INTELLIGENCE AND CLINICAL PHARMACY 15:280, April, 1981.

Antibiotic peritoneal lavage in acute peritonitis resulting from septic abortion or a ruptured pyosalpinx, by H. Nel. SOUTH AFRICAN MEDICAL JOURNAL 57(4):114-116, January 26, 1980.

Antibiotics and oral contraceptives [letter], by D. F. Rubin. ARCHIVES OF DERMATOLOGY 117(4):189, April, 1981.

Anti-choice forces gain, by B. Hurwitz. NEW DIRECTIONS FOR WOMEN 10:3+, May-June, 1981.

Antifertility activity of DMA in hamsters: protection with a luteotropic complex, by W. L. Miller, et al. PROCEEDINGS OF THE SOCIETY FOR EXPERIMENTAL BIOLOGY AND MEDICINE 166(2):199-204, February, 1981.

Antifertility activity of Lygodium flexosum, by B. B. Gaitonde, et al. INDIAN JOURNAL OF MEDICAL RESEARCH 72: 597-204, October, 1980.

Antifertility activity of Montana tomentosa (Zoapatle), by D. W. Hahn, et al. CONTRACEPTION 23(2):133-140, February, 1981.

Antifertility activity of N-protected glycine activated esters, by J. H. Drew, et al. JOURNAL OF PHARMACEUTICAL SCIENCE 70(1):60-63, January, 1981.

Antifertility effects of luteinizing hormone-releasing hormone

analog in male rats and dogs, by J. Sandow, et al. INTERNA-
TIONAL JOURNAL OF FERTILITY 25(3):213-221, 1980.

Antifertility properties of Embelia ribes: (embelin), by M.
Krishnaswamy, et al. INDIAN JOURNAL OF EXPERIMEN-
TAL BIOLOGY 18(11):1359-1360, November, 1980.

An anti-spermatozoan contraceptive, the ST film. JOSANPU
ZASSHI 35(2):138-142, February, 1981.

Appeals Courts decision reverses former minors' contraceptive
position, by A. S. Kerr. MICHIGAN MEDICINE 79(17):331,
June, 1980.

An applicator for the Hulka fallopian tube clip, by P. Renou.
AMERICAN JOURNAL OF OBSTETRICS AND GYNE-
COLOGY 139(6):665-668, March 15, 1981.

Are contraceptive pills teratogenic? by A. Czeizel. ACTA MOR-
PHOLOGICA ACADEMIAE SCIENTIARUM HUNGARI-
CA 28(1-2):177-188, 1980.

Artificial interruption of pregnancy after a course of treatment
for gonorrhea, by V. P. Zherebtsov. AKUSHERSTVO I
GINEKOLOGIIA (3):57-58, March, 1981.

As the abortion furor flares again in Washington, two doctors
lead an emotional debate [views of J. Willke and G. Ryan],
by G. Breu. PEOPLE 16:47-48+, September 21, 1981.

As annual march nears, pro-lifers focus on amendment, by F.
Franzonia. OUR SUNDAY VISITOR 69:3, January 18, 1981.

Ask a doctor, by C. Carver. CHATELAINE 54:33, September,
1981.

Ask a doctor (barrier methods), by C. Carver. CHATELAINE
54:24, February, 1981.

Ask a doctor: what are my chances of having a miscarriage? by
C. Carver. CHATELAINE 54:26, June, 1981.

Aspects of abortion: Clarity can be confusing, by W. S. Coffin. CHRISTIANITY AND CRISIS 41(274):284-286, October 19, 1981.

—: What happens at conception? by G. H. Ball. CHRISTIANITY AND CRISIS 41(274):286-288, October 19, 1981.

Aspects of female sterilization, by P. Bhatia. EASTERN ANTHROPOLOGIST 32(2):107-115, 1979.

Assessment of an intervention program for partners of abortion patients, by A. J. Lubman. DAI 41(8).

Atheromatous mesenteric occlusion associated with oral contraceptives and cigarette smoking, by W. R. Carlisle, et al. SOUTHERN MEDICAL JOURNAL 74(3):369-370, March, 1981.

Attack on abortion, by D. M. Alpern, et al. NEWSWEEK 97: 38+, April 6, 1981.

The attack on women's rights, by L. Cooper. CRIME AND SOCIAL JUSTICE 15:39-41, 1981.

Attitude towards introduction of abortion as a method of family planning in Bangladesh, by S. K. C. Bhuyan. JOURNAL OF FAMILY WELFARE 27:46, March, 1981.

Attitudes, knowledge and the extent of use of artificial contraception in social classes IV and V in Ireland, by A. Moore, et al. IRISH MEDICAL JOURNAL 73(9):342-347, September, 1980.

Attitudes of Catholic and Protestant clergy on euthanasia and abortion, by M. H. Nagi, et al. PASTORAL PSYCHOLOGY 29:178-190, Spring, 1981.

Attitudes of medical practitioners towards abortion: a Queensland study, by M. C. Sheehan, et al. AUSTRALIAN FAMILY PHYSICIAN 9(8):565-570, August, 1980.

Attitudes of 110 married men towards family planning, by J. T.

Arokiasamy. MEDICAL JOURNAL OF MALAYSIA 35(1):
22-27, September, 1980.

Attitudes of patients after 'genetic' termination of pregnancy, by
P. Donnai, et al. BRITISH MEDICAL JOURNAL 282(6264):
621-622, February 21, 1981.

Attitudes of women in Britain to abortion: trends and changes,
by C. M. Langford. POPULATION TRENDS p11-13, Winter,
1980

Attitudes towards and practice of contraception in Indore and
surrounding villages, by S. Deshpande, et al. JOURNAL OF
FAMILY WELFARE 27:25-30, December, 1980.

Attitudes towards legislation of abortion among a cross-section
of metropolitan Dacca, by R. H. Chaudhury. JOURNAL OF
BIOSOCIAL SCIENCE 12(4):417-428, October, 1980.

Aussie doctor Evelyn Billings promotes a new birth control
device—a woman's own body, by J. Dunn. PEOPLE 16:83-
84, October 12, 1981.

Autoantibodies from vasectomized guinea pigs inhibit fertilization in vitro, by T. T. Huang, Jr., et al. SCIENCE 213(4513):
1267-1269, September 11, 1981.

Automatic assay of circulating immune complexes induced by
oral contraceptives, by J. C. Buxtorf, et al. PATHOLOGIE
BIOLOGIE 29(1):62-64, January, 1981.

Autosomal translocation in an apparently normospermic male
as a cause of habitual abortion, by M. Granat, et al. JOUR-
NAL OF REPRODUCTIVE MEDICINE 26(1):52-55, January, 1981.

The availability of birth control: Victoria, 1971-1975, by K.
Betts. AUSTRALIAN JOURNAL OF SOCIAL ISSUES 15:
1, February 17-29, 1980.

Bacterial infection from actinoymces, though rare, is found to
be a problem among some IUD users. FAMILY PLANNING

PERSPECTIVES 12:306-307, November-December, 1980.

Bacteriological colonisation of uterine cavity: role of tailed intrauterine contraceptive device, by R. A. Sparks, et al. BRITISH MEDICAL JOURNAL 6271:1189-1191, April 11, 1981.

A balanced translocation 5(4;9) (q35;112) with a breakpoint within the heterochromatic region of chromosome 9 in a woman with recurrent abortion, by G. Neri, et al. CLINICAL GENETICS 18(4):239-243, October, 1980.

Balanced translocations in the karyotype as the cause of spontaneous abortion and reproductive disorders, by S. Adžič, et al. SRPSKI ARHIV ZA CELOKUPNO LEKARSTVO 108 (1):1-10, January, 1980.

Balneological treatment of spontaneous habitual abortion caused by the uterine factor or hormonal deficiency, by K. Marzinek, et al. GINEKOLOGIA POLSKA 51(6):545-549, June, 1080.

Barnstorming on feminist Air Force One [organizing Project 13 to override an antiabortion amendment] , by G. Steinem. MS MAGAZINE 10:79-80+, December, 1981.

Barrier contraception and breast cancer, by A. N. Gjorgov. CANCER DETECTION AND PREVENTION 3(1), 1980.

Barrier contraception: a comprehensive overview, by H. J. Tatum, et al. FERTILITY AND STERILITY 36(1):1-12, July, 1981.

Barriers to acceptance of genetic counseling among primary care physicians, by R. Weitz. SOCIAL BIOLOGY 26:189-197, Fall, 1979.

Barriers to birth control, by M. Potts. NEW SCIENTIST 88 (1224):221, October 23, 1980.

Basilar artery occlusion, two angiographically demonstrated cases in young women using oral contraceptives, by W. A. Nolen. CLINICAL NEUROLOGY AND NEUROSURGERY

82(1):31-36, 1980.

The Battle over abortion. TIME 117(14):20, April 6, 1981.

Behavior of Butanol-extractable jodine in serum, during and after long-time application of hormonal contraceptives, by G. Klinger, et al. ZENTRALBLATT FUR GYNAEKOLOGIE 103(1):31-35, 1981.

Behavior of maternal serum immunoglobulins in abortion, by A. Tolino, et al. ARCHIVIO DI OSTETRICIA E GINE-COLOGIA 85(1-2):45-51, January-April, 1980.

Behavioral response to vasectomy, by R. L. Vaughn. ARCHIVES OF GENERAL PSYCHIATRY 36(7):815-821, 1979.

Behavioral-social aspects of contraceptive sterilization, by S. H. Newman, et al. HEALTH p217-268, 1978.

The benefit of the classification of oral contraceptives. Studies of 525 women taking oral contraceptives, by J. M. Wenderlein. MMW 123(23):957-961, June 5, 1981.

Benign hepatic tumours and oral contraception. Pathophysiology, by H. Bondue. ACTA GASTROENTEROLOGICA BELGICA 43(7-8):278-284, 1980.

Benign tumours of the liver and oral contraceptives, by F. Lesbros, et al. SEMAINES DES HOPITAUX DE PARIS 56 (43-44):1823-1830, November 18-25, 1980.

Beyond proof and disproof, by J. Garvey. COMMONWEAL 108: 360-361, June 19, 1981.

Beyond the stereotypes, by J. R. Kelley. COMMONWEAL 108: 654-656+, November 20, 1981.

Bill Baird abortion survey misleading, anti-Catholic. OUR SUNDAY VISITOR 69:7, January 25, 1981.

Bill Baird's holy war [member of pro-choice movement], by A. Merton. ESQUIRE 95:25-31, February, 1981.

Bill to ban abortions [views of S. Galebach]. CHRISTIANITY
TODAY 25:14-15, May 8, 1981.

Bill would give legal person status to unborn babies. OUR SUN-
DAY VISITOR 69:6, February 22, 1981.

Bill would make abortion illegal, by T. Dejanikus. OFF OUR
BACKS 11:11, August-September, 1981.

Billboards censored. MARKETING 86:1, March 2, 1981.

The Billings method: natural family planning that works, by C. M.
Anthony. OUR SUNDAY VISITOR 70:3, July 19, 1981.

Billings method of contraception in adolescents [letter], by T. J.
Silber. PEDIATRICS 66(4):645-646, October, 1980.

Biochemical-hormonal bases for the selection of contraceptives
for oral use, by V. Cortés-Gallegos. GACETA MEDICA DE
MEXICO 116(7):323-326, July, 1980.

Biodegradable drug delivery systems based on aliphatic polyesters:
application to contraceptives and narcotic antagonists, by
C. G. Pitt, et al. NATIONAL INSTITUTE ON DRUG ABUSE
RESEARCH MONOGRAPH SERIES 28:232-253, 1981.

Biodegradable microsphere contraceptive system, by L. R. Beck,
et al. ACTA EUROPAEA FERTILITATIS 11(2):139-150,
June, 1980.

Biological action and half life in plasma or intramuscular sulprostone for termination of second trimester pregnancy, by
R. C. Briel, et al. PROSTAGLANDINS AND MEDICINE 6
(1):1-8, January, 1981.

Birth control, by J. Selby. JOURNAL OF NURSING 1(16):701-
703, August, 1980.

Birth control and the fertility of the U.S. black population, 1880-
1980, by J. A. McFalls, et al. JOURNAL OF FAMILY
HISTORY 6:104-106, Spring, 1981.

Birth control ban [Pope John Paul II, December 15, 1981; news]. CHRISTIAN CENTURY 98:1361-1362, December 30, 1981.

Birth control controversy, continued [Catholic Church]. AMERICA 145:66-68, August 15-22, 1981.

Birth control effects on ethanol pharmacokinetics, acetaldehyde, and cardiovascular measures in Caucasian females, by P. S. Keg, et al. PSYCHOPHYSIOLOGY 17(3):294, 1980.

Birth control—Guatemala [letters]. NATIONAL CATHOLIC REPORTER 17:11, November 14, 1980.

Birth control in China: local data and their reliability, by L. Bianco. CHINA QUARTERLY 85:119-137, March, 1981.

Birth control in the year 1001, by C. Djerassi. BULLETIN OF THE ATOMIC SCIENTISTS 37(3):24, March, 1981.

Birth control—medical practices-torts-wrongful birth. THE FAMILY LAW REPORTER: COURT OPINIONS 7(12): 2184, January 27, 1981.

Birth control methods: the choice is yours. AMERICAN BABY 34:37-38+, May, 1981.

Birth control: the new findings, by S. Dillon. MCCALLS 108:57-58, April, 1981.

Birth control, personalism, and the Pope, by R. Modras. CURRENTS IN THEOLOGY AND MISSION 8:283-290, October, 1981.

Birth control: the safety story now, by M. L. Schildkraut. GOOD HOUSEKEEPING 193:215-216, August, 1981.

Birth planning in Cuba: a basic human right, by J. M. Swanson. INTERNATIONAL JOURNAL OF NURSING STUDIES 18 (2):81-88, 1981.

Birth weight before and after a spontaneous abortion, by E. Alberman, et al. JOURNAL OF OBSTETRICS AND GYNAE-

COLOGY 87(4):275-280, April, 1980.

Bishops' aide: Congress lacks human life bill authority. OUR SUNDAY VISITOR 69:7, April 26, 1981.

The bishops and the abortion amendment. AMERICA 145:312-313, November 21, 1981.

Bishops support Hatch amendment; Capitol Hill testimony, by J. R. Roach. ORIGINS 11:359+, November 19, 1981.

Black genocide [view that abortion is a means of genocide against blacks], by D. L. Cuddy. AMERICA 145:181, October 3, 1981.

Blocking family planning, by J. I. Rosoff. FAMILY PLANNING PERSPECTIVES 13(3):125-131, May-June, 1981.

Blood groups and histocompatibility antigens in habitual abortion, by L. E. de Carapella, et al. HAEMATOLOGIA 13(1-4): 105-111, 1980.

Blood pressure changes and oral contraceptive use: a study of 2676 black women in the southeastern United States, by B. A. Blumenstein, et al. AMERICAN JOURNAL OF EPIDEMIOLOGY 112(4):539-552, October, 1980.

Boost for birth control and fertility studies, by L. Cohen. TIMES HIGHER EDUCATIONAL SUPPLEMENT 427:5, January 9, 1981.

Breast cancer and oral contraceptives: findings in Oxford-Family Planning Association contraceptive study, by M. P. Vessey, et al. BRITISH MEDICAL JOURNAL 282(6282):2093-2094, June 27, 1981.

Breast cancer and oral contraceptives: findings in Royal College of General Practitioners' study. BRITISH MEDICAL JOURNAL 282(6282):2089-2093, June 27, 1981.

Breast cancer and the pill [letter], by P. L. Diggory. LANCET 1(8227):995, May 2, 1981.

Breast cancer and the pill—a muted reassurance. BRITISH
MEDICAL JOURNAL 6282:2075-2076, June 27, 1981.

Breast cancer in women who have taken contraceptive steroids,
by P. N. Matthews, et al. BRITISH MEDICAL JOURNAL
6266:774-776, March 7, 1981.

Breast-feeding and contraception. PEDIATRICS 68(1):138-140,
July, 1981.

Breast feeding and contraceptive patterns postpartum—a study
in South Lebanon, by H. Zurayk. STUDIES IN FAMILY
PLANNING 12:237, May, 1981.

Breast feeding and oral contraceptives, by P. E. Treffers. NEDER-
LANDS TIJDSCHRIFT VOOR GENEESKUNDE 125(11):
425-427, March 14, 1981.

Breast is best; for birth control. NEW SCIENTIST 88:416,
November 13, 1980.

Brief note on rubber technology and contraception: the diaphragm and the condom, by V. L. Bullough. TECHNOLOGY
AND CULTURE 22:104-111, January, 1981.

Brigade zaps Senate hearings: Protest leads to arrest, 1; Activist
set cornerstone for abortion rights [interview with Julie Huff,
who in 1971 as Mary Doe was plaintiff in abortion case in
Washington, D.C.], by E. Soldinger. NEW DIRECTIONS
FOR WOMEN 10:4+, July-August, 1981.

Bringing surgical sterilization, the number one contraceptive
method for married couples, to a low income rural population, by C. N. Wells. JOURNAL OF THE ARKANSAS MED-
ICAL SOCIETY 77(6):226-228, November, 1980.

British pill studies stress importance of relation between progestogen content and vascular disease. FAMILY PLANNING
PERSPECTIVES 12(5):262-264, September-October, 1980.

Budd-Chiari syndrome and oral contraceptives. Report of a case
and review of the literature, by J. P. Lima, et al. ARQUIVOS

DE GASTROENTERELOGIA 17(3):135-140, July-September, 1980.

Budd-Chiari syndrome following intake of oral contraceptives, by H. Gstöttner, et al. ZENTRALBLATT FUR GYNAEKOLOGIE 102(3):146-150, 1980.

Budd-Chiari syndrome in women taking oral contraceptives, by S. H. Tsung, et al. ANNALS OF CLINICAL AND LABORATORY SCIENCE 10(6):518-522, November-December, 1980.

But is it a person? [human life bill], by J. Adler, et al. NEWSWEEK 99:44, January 11, 1982.

'But that's no longer necessary nowadays?!', by H. Doppenberg. TIJDSCHRIFT VOR ZIEKENVERPLEGING 34(13):575-580, June 23, 1981.

CDC's surveillance of surgical sterilization: objectives and methods of data collection, by J. C. Smith. PUBLIC HEALTH REPORTS 96:357-362, July-August, 1981.

The Calabar Rural Maternal and Child Health/Family Planning Project. STUDIES IN FAMILY PLANNING 12(2):47, February, 1981.

Campaign for pro-life amendment to the constitution . . . Ireland. WORLD OF IRISH NURSING 10:2, July-August, 1981.

The campaign to encourage family planning in Tunisia and some responses at village level, by K. L. Brown. MIDDLE EASTERN STUDIES 17:64-84, January, 1981.

Can a fetus be murdered? [case of R. L. Hollis indicted for murder in successful effort to abort his wife's fetus]. NEWSWEEK 98:72, August 24, 1981.

Can Joel Wells be wrong on contraception, by W. E. May. OUR SUNDAY VISITOR 69:5, December 28, 1980.

Can parents of a daughter under legal age oppose pregnancy interruption?, by G. H. Schlund. GEBURTSHILFE UND

FRAUENHEILKUNDE 40(9):834-835, September, 1980.

Canadian Catholics: at odds on abortion, by T. Sinclair-Faulkner. CHRISTIAN CENTURY 98:870-871, September 9, 1981.

Carbohydrate metabolism with three months of low-estrogen contraceptive use, by W. N. Spellacy, et al. AMERICAN JOURNAL OF OBSTETRICS AND GYNECOLOGY 138(2): 151-155, September 15, 1980.

Cardinal's view on abortion fails to defeat liberals, by J. W. Michaels. NATIONAL CATHOLIC REPORTER 16:1, September 26, 1980.

Cardiovascular side-effects of oral contraceptives with special regard to metabolism, lipoproteins and their role in the pathogenesis of vascular complications, by H. Ludwig. PRAXIS 70(13):549-553, March 24, 1981.

Case and comment: abortion, by R. Williams, et al. THE CRIMI-NAL LAW REVIEW p169-170, March, 1981.

The case for a human life amendment. ORIGINS 11:360-372, November 19, 1981.

A case of multiple cerebrovascular and migraine episodes caused by the use of oral contraceptives, by G. Moretti, et al. ACTA BIO-MEDICA DE L'ATENEO PARMENSE 52(1):25-29, 1981.

Case of the unborn patient, by G. F. Will. NEWSWEEK 97:92, June 22, 1981.

Catecholamines and dopamine-beta-hydroxylase activity during therapeutic abortion induced by sulprostone, by S. Saari-koski, et al. PROSTAGLANDINS 20(3):487-492, September, 1980.

Catholic liberals and abortion, by M. Meehan. COMMONWEAL 108:650-654, November 20, 1981.

Cerebral circulatory disorders while taking contraceptives, by D.

Khadzhiev, et al. ZHURNAL NEVROPATOLOGII I PSI-KHIATRII 81(1):64-67, 1981.

Cerebral thrombosis in woman receiving oral contraceptives: report of two cases, by I. Maruyama, et al. RINSHO KET-SUEKI 21(6):822-827, June, 1980.

Cerebral vein thrombosis and the contraceptive pill in paroxysmal nocturnal naemoglobinuria, by M. L. Stirling, et al. SCOTTISH MEDICAL JOURNAL 25(3):243-244, July, 1980.

Cerebrovascular complications following intake of oral contraceptives (review of the literature apropos of a case), by K. Bouraoui, et al. UNION MEDICALE DU CANADA 109(2): 284-288, February, 1980.

The cervical cap: an alternative contraceptive, by P. A. Canavan, et al. JOGN NURSING 10:271-273, July-August, 1981.

—: past and current experience, by B. Fairbanks, et al. WOMEN AND HEALTH 5:61-80, Fall, 1980.

Cervical caps—the perfect, untested contraceptive, by J. Willis. FDA CONSUMER 15:20-21, April, 1981.

Cervical cerclage, by I. A. McDonald. CLINICAL OBSTETRICS AND GYNAECOLOGY 7(3):461-479, December, 1980.

Cesarean hysterectomy for sterilization [letter], by N. D. Diebel. AMERICAN JOURNAL OF OBSTETRICS AND GYNECOLOGY 140(3):351-352, June 1, 1981.

Challenge of pluralism [Humanae vitae], by C. E. Curran. COMMONWEAL 108:45-46, January 30, 1981.

Changes in attitudes toward abortion in a large population of Canadian university students between 1968 and 1978, by F. M. Barrett. CANADIAN JOURNAL OF PUBLIC HEA HEALTH 71(3):195-200, May-June, 1980.

Changes in insulin receptors during oral contraception, by R.

31

De Pirro, et al. JOURNAL OF CLINICAL ENDOCRINOLO-
GY AND METABOLISM 52(1):29-33, January, 1981.

Changes in the N1H Guidelines for Recombinant DNA Research
(Appendix 3: September 1979-April 1980), by W. Szybalski.
GENE 10(4):375-377, September, 1980.

Changes in serum beta-thromboglobulin levels during oral contraception, cardiac valve disease and pulmonary emoblism, by
J. Conrad, et al. NOUVELLE PRESSE MEDICALE 10(16):
1327-1329, April 11, 1981.

Changing attitudes to birth control, by I. Allen. NEW SOCIETY
p15-16, April 2, 1981.

Changing profile of IUD users in family planning clinics in rural
Bangladesh, by S. Bhatia, et al. JOURNAL OF BIOSOCIAL
SCIENCE 13:169-178, April, 1981.

Changing the system to meet the needs of patient and nurse, by
V. L. Derby, et al. AMERICAN JOURNAL OF MATERNAL
CHILD NURSING 6:225-226+, July-August, 1981.

Changing tactics in the war on abortion [Helms-Hyde bill redefining the beginning of life] , by M. Kramer. NEW YORK 14:
28+, April 27, 1981.

Chapman would cut rapists off at the pass. LAW ENFORCE-
MENT NEWS 7(4):4, February 23, 1981.

Characteristics of contraceptive acceptors in rural Zaire, by J.
E. Brown, et al. STUDIES IN FAMILY PLANNING 11:378-
384, December, 1980.

Characteristics of the course of periodic disease in women who
use hormonal contraceptives, by K. B. Akunts, et al. A-
KUSHERSTVO I GINEKOLOGIIA(9):44-46, September,
1980.

Characteristics of lipoprotein metabolic disorders during treatment with oral contraceptives, by V. N. Titov, et al. FARMA-
KOLOGIYA I TOKSIKOLOGIYA 43(3):345-348, May-

June, 1980.

Characteristics of special groups of abortion patients from one
health district, by J. R. Ashton. JOURNAL OF BIOSOCIAL
SCIENCE 13(1):63-69, January, 1981.

The childless marriage: a moral observation, by J. A. Selling.
BIJDRAGEN 42:158-173, 1981.

Children born to women denied abortion: an update, by H. P.
David, et al. FAMILY PLANNING PERSPECTIVES 13(1):
32-34, January-February, 1981.

China cracks down. WORLD PRESS REVIEW 28:58, February,
1981.

China. Family planning. Interpersonal communication, by A.
Goonesekera. MEDIA ASIA 7(2):105-109, 1980.

China progresses with male contraceptive. CHEMISTRY AND
INDUSTRY p630, August 16, 1980.

China's people at bay, by P. G. Andrews. TABLET 235:360-361,
April 11, 1981.

Choice in the womb [abortion performed on mongoloid fetus
while preserving life of the healthy twin], by M. Clark, et
al. NEWSWEEK 97:86, June 29, 1981.

The choice of a method of contraception during adolescence, by
U. Gaspard. REVUE MEDICALE DE LIEGE 35(9):377-390,
May 1, 1980.

Cholestatic jaundice after triacetyloleandomycin and oral contraceptives. The diagnostic value of gamma-glutamyl transpeptidase, by I. Haber, et al. ACTA GASTROENTEROLOGICA
BELGICA 43(11-12):475-482, November-December, 1980.

Chorea induced by oral contraceptives [letter], by P. M. Green.
NEUROLOGY 30(10):1131-1132, October, 1980.

Choriocarcinoma presenting as a complication of elective first

trimester abortion, by F. A. Lyon, et al. MINNESOTA MED-
ICINE 63(10):733-735, October, 1980.

Chromosomal analysis of couples with repeated spontaneous
abortions, by L. J. Sant-Cassia, et al. BRITISH JOURNAL
OF OBSTETRICS AND GYNAECOLOGY 88(1):52-58,
January, 1981.

Chronic treatment with the gonadotropin-releasing hormone
agonist D-Ser(TBU)6-EA10-LRH for contraception in women
and men, by S. J. Nillius, et al. INTERNATIONAL JOUR-
NAL OF FERTILITY 25(3):239-246, 1980.

Cigarette smoking, oral, contraceptives and serum lipid and
lipoprotein in children of a total community, by G. S. Berenson. CIRCULATION 62(3):III-270, 1980.

Circulating antiprothrombinase anticoagulant, thrombosis and
spontaneous abortions; a new syndrome [letter], by L.
Gabriel, et al. NOUVELLE PRESSE MEDICALE 9(31):2159,
August 30-September 6, 1980.

The circus come to town, by A. Soueif. OBSERVER p38, June
28, 1981.

Clinical and ultrasonic aspects in the diagnosis and follow-up of
patients with early pregnancy failure, by P. Jouppila. ACTA
OBSTETRICIA ET GYNECOLOGICA SCANDINAVICA 59
(5):405-409, 1980.

A clinical double-blind study on the effect of prophylactically
administered single dose tinidazole on the occurrence of
endometritis after first trimester legal abortion, by L.
Westrom, et al. SCANDINAVIAN JOURNAL OF INFEC-
TIOUS DISEASES [SUPPLEMENT] 26:104-109, 1981.

Clinical evaluation of injectable biodegradable contraceptive
system, by L. R. Beck, et al. AMERICAN JOURNAL OF
OBSTETRICS AND GYNECOLOGY 140(7):799-806,
August 1, 1981.

Clinical experience from transervical intra-amnionic hypertonic saline instillation for termination of pregnancy in second trimester, by E. Ehrig, et al. ZENTRALBLATT FUR GYNAEKOLOGIE 102(22):1288-1293, 1980.

Clinical experiences with a new gel for intracervical application of prostaglandin E2 before therapeutic abortion or induction of term labor, by U. Ulmsten, et al. PROSTAGLANDINS 20(3):533-546, September, 1980.

Clinical observations on 201 cases of mid-term abortion induced by Yuanhuacine. CHUNG HUA FU CHAN KO TSA CHIH 14(4):287-289, 1979.

Clinical performance and endocrine profiles with contraceptive vaginal rings containing a combination of estradiol and D-norgestrel, by S. Mehta, et al. CONTRACEPTION 23(3): 241-250, March, 1981.

A clinical trial of Neo Sampoon vaginal contraceptive tablets, by S. F. Begum, et al. CONTRACEPTION 22(6):573-582, December, 1980.

Clip sterilization [letter], by C. S. Vear. MEDICAL JOURNAL OF AUSTRALIA 2(2):96, July 26, 1980.

Clomipramine and oral contraceptives: an interaction study— clinical findings, by M. Gringras, et al. JOURNAL OF INTER-NATIONAL MEDICAL RESEARCH 8(Suppl 3):76-80, 1980.

A cluster of septic complications associated with illegal induced abortions, by J. Gold, et al. OBSTETRICS AND GYNECOL-OGY 56(3):311-315, September, 1980.

Coagulation studies in Asian women using injectable progestogen for contraception, by F. H. Tsakok, et al. INTERNATIONAL JOURNAL OF GYNAECOLOGY AND OBSTETRICS 18(2): 105-108, September-October, 1980.

The coagulation system in Rivanol-induced abortion, by A. Olund, et al.ZENTRALBLATT FUR GYNAEKOLOGIE 102(9):507-512, 1980.

Coalitions can end sterilization abuse, by H. Rodriquez-Trias. WITNESS 64:10-13+, January, 1981.

Coercive and noncoercive abortion deterrence policies: a comparative state analysis, by C. A. Johnson, et al. LAW AND POLICY QUARTERLY 2:106-108, January, 1980.

Cohort consistency in family size preferences: Taiwan, 1965-1973. STUDIES IN FAMILY PLANNING 12(5):229, May, 1981.

The coil and the law, by C. Brewer. GUARDIAN p11, February 18, 1981.

Colo-uterine fistula. An unusual case report and a literature review, by F. R. Kaban, et al. AMERICAN JOURNAL OF PROCTOLOGY, GASTROENTEROLOGY AND COLON AND RECTAL SURGERY 32(7):36-37, 40, July, 1981.

Combination of the ovulation method with diaphragm, by J. F. Cattanach. MEDICAL JOURNAL OF AUSTRALIA 2(9): 511-512, November 1, 1980.

Commentary on Rosner's "Induced abortion and Jewish morality", by R. B. Reeves, Jr. VALUES, ETHICS AND HEALTH CARE 1:225-226, Spring, 1976.

Common outpatient procedures represent malpractice 'gold mine', by R. Lucas. SAME DAY SURGERY 4(12):126-127, December, 1980.

The community health nurse and family planning, by N. Stockton. NURSING NEWS 3:7, August, 1980.

Comparative blood coagulation studies in PGF2a- and 15-methyl-PGF2a-induced therapeutic abortion, by R. During, et al. FOLIA HAEMATOLOGICA 107(3):502-507, 1980.

Comparative evaluation of two methods of natural family planning in Columbia, by J. E. Medina, et al. AMERICAN JOURNAL OF OBSTETRICS AND GYNECOLOGY 138(8):1142-1147, December 15, 1980.

Comparative morbidity following tubal ligation by abdominal and vaginal routes, by I. Gupta, et al. INDIAN JOURNAL OF MEDICAL RESEARCH 72:231-235, August, 1980.

Comparative popularity of vasectomy and tubectomy, by S. D. R. Devi. JOURNAL OF FAMILY WELFARE 26:79-93, June, 1980.

Comparative risks of rhesus autoimmunisation in two different methods of mid-trimester abortion, by C. Brewer, et al. BRITISH MEDICAL JOURNAL 282(6280):1929-1930, June 13, 1981.

Comparative studies of the human chorionic gonadotropin levels in threatened abortion by the passive hemagglutination inhibition and Gravindex tests in the first and second trimesters of pregnancy, by B. Berliński, et al. WIADOMOSCI LEKARSKI 33(23):1887-1889, December 1, 1980.

A comparative study of standard-dose and low-dose oral contraceptives in rural Bangladesh, by R. Bairagi, et al. INTERNATIONAL JOURNAL OF GYNAECOLOGY AND OBSTETRICS 18(4):264-267, 1980.

Comparative value of biophysical and biochemical parameters in threatened abortion, by A. Tolino, et al. ARCHIVIO DI OSTETRICIA E GINECOLOGIA 85(1-2):13-20, January-April, 1980.

A comparison of the efficacy and acceptability of the Copper-7 intrauterine device following immediate or delayed insertion after first-trimester therapeutic abortion, by P. G. Gillett, et al. FERTILITY AND STERILITY 34(2):121-124, August, 1980.

Comparison of laparoscopic sterilization via spring-loaded clip and tubal ring, by G. Argueta, et al. INTERNATIONAL JOURNAL OF BYNAECOLOGY AND OBSTETRICS 18 (2):115-118, September-October, 1980.

Comparison of minors' and adults' pregnancy decisions, by C. C. Lewis. AMERICAN JOURNAL OF ORTHOPSYCHOLO-

GY 50:446-453, July, 1980.

Comparison of two intramuscular prostaglandin analogs for inducing abortion in the first pregnancy trimester, by B. Schüssler, et al. GYNAEKOLOGISCHE RUNDSCHAU 20 (2):102-109, 1980.

A comparison of two stable prostaglandin E analogues for termination of early pregnancy and for cervical dilatation, by M. Bygdeman, et al. CONTRACEPTION 22(5):471-483, November, 1980.

A comparison of unwed pregnant teenagers and nulligravid sexually active adolescents seeking contraception, by L. A. DeAmicis, et al. ADOLESCENCE 16(61):11-20, Spring, 1981.

Complete abortion of early ectopic pregnancy, by G. Ohel, et al. INTERNATIONAL JOURNAL OF GYNAECOLOGY AND OBSTETRICS 17(6):596-597, May-June, 1980.

Compliance and the state legislature: an empirical analysis of abortion and aid to non-public schools in Illinois and Minnesota, by C. Neal, PhD. DAI 41(11-12), 1981.

Complications after the premature termination of an unwanted pregnancy as an etiological factor in spontaneous abortions and the motives for abortions on demand, by I. Vasileva. AKUSHERSTVO I GINEKOLOGIIA 19(4):300-303, 1980.

Complications from induced abortion in Bangladesh related to types of practitioner and methods, and impact on mortality, by A. R. Measham, et al. LANCET 1(8213):199-202, January 24, 1981.

Complications in sterilized women in Ljubljana, by D. Kos-Gril. JUGOSLAVENSKA GINEKOLOGIJA I OPSTETRICIJA 20 (3-4):145-147, May-August, 1980.

Complications of abortion in developing countries. POPULATION REPORTS Series F(7):105-155, July, 1980.

Complications of abortion in developing countries. POPULA-
TION REPORTS 8(4):1, July, 1980.

Complications of laparoscopic sterilisation [letter], by M. D.
Birnbaum. LANCET 1(8210):43, January 3, 1981.

A comprehensive review of injectable contraception with special
emphasis on depot medroxyprogesterone acetate, by I. S.
Fraser, et al. MEDICAL JOURNAL OF AUSTRALIA 1
(1 Suppl):3-19, January 24, 1981.

Computerized patient-flow analysis of local family planning
clinics, by J. L. Graves, et al. FAMILY PLANNING PER-
SPECTIVES 13:164-170, July-August, 1981.

The concept of a person in the context of abortion, by S. Sherwin. BIOETHICS QUARTERLY 3:21-24, Spring, 1981.

Conception and misconception. TIMES LITERARY SUPPLI-
MENT p1253, October 30, 1981.

Concerning abortion: an attempt at a rational view, by C. Hartshorne. CHRISTIAN CENTURY 98:41-45, January 21, 1981.

Concise report on the monitoring of population policies [pre-
pared by the U.N. Secretariat for the World Population Plan
of Action]. POPULATION BULLETIN (12):20-40, 1979.

Condoms and foam: traditional forms of contraception still
going strong, by V. Wirth. ISSUES IN HEALTH CARE OF
WOMEN 1(5):29-36, 1979.

Conference examines proposed human life amendment; report
of the human life amendment conference, St. Louis. HOS-
PITAL PROGRESS 62:22-23, October, 1981.

Congress and the zygote [Helms-Hyde Human Life bill], by H.
Kohn. ROLLING STONE p13, June 11, 1981.

Congress to reexamine antiabortion amendment [news], by C.
Holden. SCIENCE 213(4506):421, July 24, 1981.

Congress turns a serious eye toward Human Life bill, by R. B. Shaw. OUR SUNDAY VISITOR 69:8, March 29, 1981.

Congressional confusion over "conception" [Helms-Hyde bill], by J. L. Marx. SCIENCE 212:423, April 24, 1981.

Conocimiento y uso de métodos anticonceptivos: un análisis comparativo con datos de los informes de países en América Latina [Colombia, Costa Rica, the Dominican Republic, Panama and Peru], by E. Taucher. NOTAS DE POBLACIÓN 8:9-43, December, 1980.

Conservatives and Liberals on prolife issues, by C. DeCelles. AMERICA 144:365-368, May 2, 1981.

Conservatives, liberals back Denton's chastity bill. OUR SUNDAY VISITOR 70:7, October 11, 1981.

Constitutional law—abortion funding and the demise of maternal health consideration. SUFFOLK UNIVERSITY LAW REVIEW 15:285-305, April, 1981.

Constituional law—health law—constitutionality of the Hyde amendment—medically necessary abortions need not be funded by the state or federal government under Medicaid. WHITTIER LAW REVIEW 3:381-408, 1981.

Constitutional law—Supreme Court upholds validity of Hyde amendment—states need not fund all abortions under Medicaid. CREIGHTON LAW REVIEW 14:607-628, 1981.

Constitutional rights—birth control. THE FAMILY LAW REPORTER: COURT OPINIONS 7(1):2010, November 4, 1980.

Consultant gynaecologists and attitudes towards abortion, by A. Chamberlain. JOURNAL OF BIOSOCIAL SCIENCE 12(4): 407-415, October, 1980.

Consumer demand and marketing action plans for family planning in Bangladesh, by R. I. Molla, et al. JOURNAL OF MANAGEMENT STUDIES 18:219-230, April, 1981.

Contemporary attitudes toward sex, by M. Shivanandan. MAR-
RIAGE 63:18+, November, 1981.

Content of blood group A and B factors in sera of placental and
abortive blood, their fractions at different stages of alcoholic
fractionation and in immunoglobulin preparations, by E. V.
Volevach, et al. ZHURNAL MIKROBIOLOGII, EPIDEMI-
OLOGII I IMMUNOBIOLOGII (10):63-67, October, 1980.

Un contexte nouveau por l'enseignement sur la contraception, by
J. R. Quinn. LA DOCUMENTATION CATHOLIQUE 77:
1054-1058, November 23, 1980.

Continuous monitoring of uterine contractions to control intra-
amniotic administration of prostaglandin F2 alpha for therapeutic and missed abortion, by C. J. Roux, et al. SOUTH
AFRICAN MEDICAL JOURNAL 59(23):819-821, May 30,
1981.

Contraception, by C. Lane, et al. PRIMARY CARE 8(1):45-53,
March, 1981.

Contraception-abortion lifeline, by G. E. Richardson. HEALTH
EDUCATION 12(2):37, March-April, 1981.

Contraception after the act. NURSES DRUG ALERT 5:23,
March, 1981.

Contraception and abortion in Poland, by D. P. Mazur. FAMILY
PLANNING PERSPECTIVES 13:195-198, July-August,
1981.

Contraception and adolescent pregnancy, by C. A. Burbach.
JOGN NURSING 9(5):319-323, September-October, 1980.

Contraception and the etiology of pelvic inflammatory disease:
new perspectives, by P. Senanayake, et al. AMERICAN
JOURNAL OF OBSTETRICS AND GYNECOLOGY 138
(7 Pars 2):852-860, 1980.

Contraception and female sterilization, by A. J. Penfield. NEW
YORK STATE JOURNAL OF MEDICINE 81(2):255-258,

February, 1981.

Contraception and the 'high-risk' woman, by S. K. Khoo, et al. MEDICAL JOURNAL OF AUSTRALIA 1(2):60-68, January 24, 1981.

Contraception and liberal medical acts. The results of a national enquiry carried out by INSERM 1974-1975, by B. Garros, et al. JOURNAL DE GYNECOLOGIE OBSTETRIQUE ET BIOLOGIE DE LA REPRODUCTION 9(8):835-841, 1980.

Contraception and pelvic inflammatory disease, by P. Senanayake, et al. SEXUALLY TRANSMITTED DISEASES 8(2): 89-91, April-June, 1981.

Contraception and the under-16s [news] . BRITISH MEDICAL JOURNAL 281(6235):318, July, 1980.

Contraception breakthroughs. HARPER'S BAZAAR 114:90+, September, 1981.

Contraception: burdens impossible, by J. P. Breen. NATIONAL CATHOLIC REPORTER 17:38, February 13, 1981.

Contraception by female sterilisation [letter] , by A. F. Wright. BRITISH MEDICAL JOURNAL 280(6231):1618-1619, June 28, 1980.

Contraception by progestational agents administered in sequential form, by J. Barrat, et al. NOUVELLE PRESSE MEDICALE 9(21):1491-1494, May 10, 1980.

Contraception for the insulin-dependent diabetic woman: the view from one clinic, by J. M. Steel, et al. DIABETES CARE 3(4):557-560, July-August, 1980.

Contraception in adolescence, by R. Gagné, et al. UNION MEDICALE DU CANADA 110(3):197-200, March, 1981.

Contraception in China, by G. Perkin. POPULI 7(4):16-25, 1980.

Contraception in the eighties, by J. Klein. WORKING WOMEN

6:32+, February, 1981.

Contraception in the light of immunological studies, by A. Bromboszcz, et al. WIADOMOSCI LEKARSKIE 33(14): 1141-1143, July 15, 1980.

Contraception in a new context, by J. M. Russell. AMERICA 145:182-183, October 3, 1981.

Contraception in risk patients. Discussion, by K. Detering, et al. MEDIZINISCHE WELT 31(49):1805-1806, December 5, 1980.

Contraception: a proposal for the Synod, by J. R. Quinn. CATHOLIC MIND 79:25-34, February, 1981.

Contraception with Monogest in young women, by M. Chalupa. CESKOSLOVENSKA GYNEKOLOGIE 46(4):300-301, May, 1981.

Contraception with subcutaneous capsules containing ST-1435. Pituitary and ovarian function and plasma levels of ST-1435, by P. Lähteenmäki, et al. CONTRACEPTION 23(1):63-75, January, 1981.

Contraceptive attitudes and practices; a comparison of nonpregnant college females and those with problem pregnancies, by K. E. Lelm, et al. HEALTH EDUCATION 11:39-41, September-October, 1980.

Contraceptive availability. POPULATION REPORTS 9(3):M-176, May-June, 1981.

Contraceptive ban on under 16s in care condemned, by D. Spencer. TIMES EDUCATIONAL SUPPLEMENT 3369: 3, January 16, 1981.

Contraceptive behavior in adolescence: a decision-making perspective, by M. J. Rogel, et al. JOURNAL OF YOUTH AND ADOLESCENCE 9:491-506, December, 1980.

Contraceptive behavior of vasectomy acceptors, by S. S. R.

Grover. JOURNAL OF FAMILY WELFARE 27:3-15, March, 1981.

Contraceptive behaviour and fertility patterns in an inner London group practice, by P. C. Stott. JOURNAL OF THE ROYAL COLLEGE OF GENERAL PRACTITIONERS 30 (215):340-346, June, 1980.

Contraceptive choices for lactating women: suggestions for postpartum family planning. STUDIES IN FAMILY PLANNING 12(4):156, April, 1981.

Contraceptive distribution in Bangladesh: some lessons learned, by M. Rahman, et al. STUDIES IN FAMILY PLANNING 11 (6):191-201, June, 1980.

The contraceptive effect of breastfeeding. STUDIES IN FAMILY PLANNING 12(4):125, April, 1981.

Contraceptive effects of an agonist of luteinizing hormone releasing hormone: a long-term study on the female stumptailed monkey, by H. M. Fraser. JOURNAL OF ENDOCRINOLOGY 85(2):1-13, 1980.

Contraceptive efficacy among married women aged 15-44 years, by B. Vaughan, et al. VITAL HEALTH STATISTICS 23(5): 1-62, May, 1980.

Contraceptive efficacy: the significance of method and motivation, by E. F. Jones, et al. STUDIES IN FAMILY PLANNING 11(2):39-50, February, 1980.

Contraceptive embarrassment and contraceptive behavior among young single women, by E. S. Herold. JOURNAL OF YOUTH AND ADOLESCENCE 10:233-242, June, 1981.

Contraceptive foams and birth defects. SCIENCE NEWS 119: 229, April 11, 1981.

Contraceptive habits in women between thirty and fifty years of age. A comparison of two periods, 1967-1969 and 1972-1974, by E. Bostofte, et al. ACTA OBSTETRICIA ET GYNE-

COLOGICA SCANDINAVICA 59(3):237-243, 1980.

Contraceptive knowledge: antecedents and implications, by R. O. Hansson, et al. THE FAMILY COORDINATOR 28(1): 29-34, January, 1979.

Contraceptive pills and thrombosis [letter] , by K. Helweg-Larsen, et al. UGESKRIFT FOR LAEGER 143(4):220, January 19, 1981.

Contraceptive prevalence surveys: a new source of family planning data. POPULATION REPORTS Series M(5):M162-200, May-June, 1981.

Contraceptive research [letter] . FAMILY PLANNING PER-. SPECTIVES 13(1):5+, January-February, 1981.

Contraceptive risk-taking in a population with limited access to abortion, by D. R. Horowitz, et al. JOURNAL OF BIOLOG- ICAL SCIENCE 12(4):373, October, 1980.

Contraceptive services for adolescents: an overview, by J. G. Dryfoos, et al. FAMILY PLANNING PERSPECTIVES 10 (4):223-233, 1978.

Contraceptive use. POPULATION REPORTS 9(3):M-167, May- June, 1981.

Contraceptive use among family planning clinic personnel. FAM- ILY PLANNING PERSPECTIVES 13(1):22, January- February, 1981.

Contraceptive use of cervical caps [letter] , by K. P. Zodhiates, et al. NEW ENGLAND JOURNAL OF MEDICINE 304(15): 915, April 9, 1981.

Contraceptive utilization: United States, by K. Ford. VITAL HEALTH STATISTICS 23(2):1-48, September, 1979.

—, 1976, by W. D. Mosher. VITAL HEALTH STATISTICS 23(7):1-58, March, 1981.

Contraceptive vaccine research: still an art [news] , by E. R. González. JAMA 244(13):1414-1415, September 26, 1980.

Contraceptives. DRUG TOPICS 124:50, June, 1980.

—. DRUG TOPICS 125:82, July 3, 1981.

Contraceptives and cancer. SCIQUEST 54:4, January, 1981.

Contraceptives in sickle cell disease, by H. W. Foster, Jr. . SOUTHERN MEDICAL JOURNAL 74(5):543-545, May, 1981.

Contraceptives: the latest news on how to choose, by S. Connelly. LADIES HOME JOURNAL 98:56+, March, 1981.

Contraceptives—return of the condom, by A. Benoist. INFIRMI-ERE FRANCAISE (219):27, November, 1980.

Contraindications to the pill [letter] , by S. J. Emans. PEDIA-TRICS 66(4):643-644, October, 1980.

Controversy destined to dog Supreme Court's heels, by R. B. Shaw. OUR SUNDAY VISITOR 70:5, July 26, 1981.

Coping with contraception: a cognitive behavioral approach to prevention of unwanted teenage pregnancy, by L. D. Gil-christ, PhD. DAI 41(1-2), 1981.

Coping with a miscarriage, by H. Pizer, et al. AMERICAN BABY 43:42+, September, 1981.

The costs and benefits of government expenditures for family planning programs, by M. Chamie, et al. FAMILY PLAN-NING PERSPECTIVES 13:117-118+, May-June, 1981.

Counselling for vasectomy, by B. Spencer, et al. PATIENT COUNSELLING AND HEALTH EDUCATION 2:47-50, 1980.

Counselling needs of women seeking abortions, by M. J. Hare, et al. JOURNAL OF BIOSOCIAL SCIENCE 13:269-274, July,

1981.

Court case: should your conscience be your guide? NURSING-
LIFE 1(1):15, July-August, 1981.

Court ruling suggests justices seeking pro-family label, by R. B.
Shaw. OUR SUNDAY VISITOR 69:6, April 12, 1981.

Court upholds Utah law requiring preabortion notice of minor's
parents, by P. Geary. HOSPITAL PROGRESS 62:22-23,
May, 1981.

Criminal abortion. Fact or fiction? by D. A. Bowen. AMERICAN
JOURNAL OF FORENSIC MEDICINE AND PATHOLOGY
1(3):219-221, September, 1980.

Criminal liability of physicians: an encroachment on the abortion
right? AMERICAN CRIMINAL LAW REVIEW 18:591-615,
Spring, 1981.

Critique of the abortion funding decisions: on private rights in
the public sector, by L. F. Goldstein. HASTINGS CONSTI-
TUTIONAL LAW QUARTERLY 8:313-342, Winter, 1981.

A critique of the pro-choice argument, by W. J. Voegeli, Jr.
REVIEW OF POLITICS 43:560-571, October, 1981.

A cross-cultural study of menstruation: implications for contraceptive development and use. STUDIES IN FAMILY PLAN-
NING 12:3-16, January, 1981.

The crossing of swords on abortion, by C. Gerster. PHOENIX
p15-18, November, 1980.

Crusader under attack [effect of Pope John Paul II's proclamations on referendum to tighten abortion laws in Italy. TIME
117:54, May 18, 1981.

The cultural context of condom use in Japan, by S. Coleman.
STUDIES IN FAMILY PLANNING 12(1):28, January, 1981.

Customized cervical cap: evolution of an ancient idea, by C.

Arthur. JOURNAL OF NURSE-MIDWIFERY 25:33-34, November-December, 1980.

Cystic disease, family history of breast cancer and use of oral contraceptives, by D. V. Vakil, et al. CANCER DETECTION AND PREVENTION 3(1):No pagination, 1980.

Cytochemical studies of the vaginal squamous epithelial cells in pregnancy and threatened abortion, by V. S. Tolmachev. LABORATORNOE DELO (2):72-74, 1981.

Cytogenetic analysis of conceptus material of Korean women at first trimester, by K. Y. Kim, et al. YONSEI MEDICAL JOURNAL 20(2):113-126, 1979.

Cytogenetic findings in habitual abortion. Chromosomal analysis in 123 couples, by P. Husslein, et al. WIENER KLINISCHE WOCHENSCHRIFT 92(16):575-578, August 29, 1980.

Cytogenetic findings in 122 couples with recurrent abortions, by C. Stoll. HUMAN GENETICS 57(1):101-103, 1981.

A cytogenetic study of repeated spontaneous abortions, by T. J. Hassold. AMERICAN JOURNAL OF HUMAN GENETICS 32(5):723-730, September, 1980.

Cytologic findings in postpartum and postabortal smears, by T. K. Kobayashi, et al. ACTA CYTOLOGICA 24(4):328-334, July-August, 1980.

Cytologic smear findings in oral contraceptive users: population screening in Jewish women, by A. E. Schachter, et al. ACTA CYTOLOGICA 25(1):40, 1981.

Cytological studies in women using different types of hormonal contraceptives, by A. D. Engineer, et al. JOURNAL OF THE INDIAN MEDICAL ASSOCIATION 74(5):88-91, March 1, 1980.

Czech women, burdened by their dual roles, rely on contraception, abortion to keep families small. FAMILY PLANNING PERSPECTIVES 13:189-190, July-August, 1981.

DNA guidelines: bowing out [news] , by D. Dickson. NATURE 288(5791):529-530, December 11, 1980.

DNA guidelines for further attenuation [news] , by D. Dickson. NATURE 290(5704):281, March 26, 1981.

DNA guidelines. More relaxation [news] , by D. Dickson. NATURE 287(5781):380-381, October 2, 1980.

DNA recombination forces resignation [news] , by D. Dickson. NATURE 287(5779):179-180, September 18, 1980.

Dalkon Shields are out. FDA CONSUMER 15:31, May, 1981.

Damages for wrongful conception: Doiron v. Orr, by J. E. Bickenbach. UNIVERSITY OF WESTERN ONTARIO LAW REVIEW 18:493-503, December, 1980.

The dead baby joke cycle, by A. Dundes. WESTERN EUROPE 38(3):145-157, 1979.

Death loses its race with birth. ECONOMIST 278:69, March 28, 1981.

Deaths following female sterilization with unipolar electrocoagulating devices. MMWR 30(13):149-151, April 10, 1981.

The decision for male versus female sterilization, by M. P. Clark, et al. THE FAMILY COORDINATOR 28(2):250-254, April, 1979.

Decision making by single women seeking abortion, by M. Quinn. NEW ZEALAND NURSING FORUM 8(2):4-7, 1980.

The decline of unwanted fertility, 1971-1976, by C. F. Westoff. FAMILY PLANNING PERSPECTIVES 13:70-72, March-April, 1981.

The declining length of hospitalization for tubal sterilization, by P. M. Layde, et al. JAMA 245(7):714-718, February 20, 1981.

Degree of perinatal pathology risk in a history of threatened abortion, by L. V. Moissenko. AKUSHERSTVO I GINE-KOLOGIIA (7):20-21, July, 1980.

Delay, limited access found key factors in septic abortion deaths. FAMILY PLANNING PERSPECTIVES 13:46-47, January-February, 1981.

La demande d'interruption volontaire de grossesse, by E. Zucker-Rouvillois. POPULATION ET FAMILLE 3(45):47-75, 1978.

Demographic impact of family welfare programme in the area covered by Rural Health Training Centre, Harsola Indore (Madhya Pradesh), by R. K. Patodi, et al. INDIAN JOURNAL OF PUBLIC HEALTH 24(1):32-34, January-March, 1980.

Demographic transition in the Middle East and North Africa, by J. Allman. INTERNATIONAL JOURNAL OF MIDDLE EASTERN STUDIES 12:277-301, November, 1980.

Depo-provera: a critical analysis, by S. Minkin. WOMEN AND HEALTH 5:49-69, Summer, 1980.

Depo-provera: new developments in a decade-old controversy, by R. B. Gold, et al. FAMILY PLANNING PERSPECTIVES 13:35-39, January-February, 1981.

Desacralization of Venus [Catholic Church], by C. Derrick. AMERICA 145:106-109, September 12, 1981.

The design of a stress management program for Stanford intensive care nurses, by J. T. Bailey, et al. JOURNAL OF NURSING EDUCATION 19(6):26-29, June, 1980.

Destructive operations, by G. P. Dutta, et al. JOURNAL OF INDIAN MEDICAL ASSOCIATION 74(1):1-5, January 1, 1980.

Detection of N-acetylneuraminic acid with long-time application of hormonal contraceptives, by G. Klinger, et al. ZENTRALBLATT FUR GYNAEKOLOGIE 103(1):36-40, 1981.

Determinants of fertility differential in Korea, by E. H. Shin, et al. SOCIOLOGY AND SOCIAL RESEARCH 65(2):211-225, January, 1981.

Determinants of fertility in Guatemala, by J. E. Anderson, et al. SOCIAL BIOLOGY 27:20-35, Spring, 1980.

Determination of trace elements in serum (Fe, Cu, Zn) and urine (Fe, Cu, Za, Mn) as well as carrier proteins in hormonal contraception, by G. Klinger, et al. ZEITSCHRIFT FUR AERZTLICHE FORTBILDUNG 74(22):1077-1084, November 15, 1980.

The devastating costs of professional burnout, by R. Vessell. THERAPEUTIC RECREATION JOURNAL 14(3):11-14, 3d Quarter, 1980.

Developing countries. Family planning. Latin America. Media, by F. Risopatin, et al. JOURNAL OF COMMUNICATION 30 (4):81-89, Autumn.

Developing print materials in Mexico for people who do not read, by A. Leonard. EDUCATIONAL BROADCASTING INTERNATIONAL 13(4):168-173, December, 1980.

Development of contraceptive prevalence surveys. POPULATION REPORTS 9(3):M-163, May-June, 1981.

Diagnosis and management of post-pill amenorrhea, by R. Roias-Walsson, et al. JOURNAL OF FAMILY PRACTICE 13(2): 165-169, August, 1981.

Diagnosis of septic abortion in dairy cows, by R. Higgins, et al. CANADIAN JOURNAL OF COMPARATIVE MEDICINE 45(2):159-166, April, 1981.

Diagnostic ultrasound in threatened abortion and suspected ectopic pregnancy, by C. Jörgensen, et al. ACTA OBSTETRICIA ET GYNECOLOGIA SCANDINAVICA 59(3):233-235, 1980.

The diagnostic value of maternal pregnancy-specific beta 1-

glyoprotein in threatened abortion, by N. J. Karg, et al. ZEITSCHRIFT FUR GEBURTSCHILFE UND PERINATOLOGIE 185(1):38-40, February, 1981.

Diaphragm use instruction: time of insertion before coitus, by A. Mariella. JOURNAL OF NURSE MIDWIFERY 25(6):35-36, November-December, 1980.

Diet and oral contraceptive induced changes in bile acid pools in healthy women, by C. Williams. GASTROENTEROLOGY 78(5 Part 2):1327, 1980.

Diet supplements lead to more mouths to feed [diet, breast feeding, and natural birth control]. NEW SCIENTIST 86:193, April 24, 1980.

Differences between women who begin pill use before and after first intercourse: Ontario, Canada, by E. S. Herold, et al. FAMILY PLANNING PERSPECTIVES 12:304-305, November-December, 1980.

Dilatation of the cervix prior to vacuum aspiration by single vaginal administration of 15-methyl-PGF2 alpha methyl ester, by O. Frankman, et al. CONTRACEPTION 21(6):571-576, June, 1980.

Dilation and evacuation: a preferred method of midtrimester abortion, by K. I. Cadesky, et al. AMERICAN JOURNAL OF OBSTETRICS AND GYNECOLOGY 139(3):329-332, February 1, 1981.

Diploidy in second trimester prostaglandin E2 induced abortuses, by K. H. Sit, et al. AUSTRALIAN PAEDIATRICS JOURNAL 16(3):201-204, September, 1980.

Dire warnings by pro-abortionists found in error. OUR SUNDAY VISITOR 70:7, August 23, 1981.

Disagreement over proposed human life bill. ORIGINS 11:100-105, July 2, 1981.

Discontinued intrauterine device use and spontaneous abortion,

by D. W. Kaufman, et al. AMERICAN JOURNAL OF EPI-
DEMIOLOGY 112(3):434, 1980.

Discussion of 'Laparoscopic sterilization in a community hospital
with a two-year follow-up' given by Dr. Joshua Tayloe, by A.
C. Christakos. NORTH CAROLINA MEDICAL JOURNAL
41(9):583-584, September, 1980.

The distribution of contraceptives to unemancipated minors:
does a parent have a constitutional right to be notified? by
J. L. Rue. KENTUCKY LAW JOURNAL 69(2):436-452,
1980-1981.

Distribution of lipoproteins triglyceride and lipoprotein cholesterol in an adult population by age, sex, and hormone use—
The Pacific Northwest Bell Telephone Company health survey, by P. W. Wahl, et al. ATHEROSCLEROSIS 39(1):111-
124, April, 1981.

Distributions of amenorrhoea and anovulation, by R. G. Potter,
et al. POPULATION STUDIES 35:85-99, March, 1981.

Dizziness associated with discontinuation of oral contraceptives
in Bangladesh, by A. R. Measham, et al. INTERNATIONAL
JOURNAL OF GYNAECOLOGY AND OBSTETRICS 18
(2):109-112, September-October, 1980.

Do OTC vaginal contraceptives face FDA? DRUG TOPICS 125:
16, January 16, 1981.

Doctor ordered to disclose copies of public aid patients' ID
cards. THE CRIMINAL LAW REPORTER: COURT DECI-
SIONS AND PROCEEDINGS 29(7):2140-2141, May 13,
1981.

Doctor's dilemma over abortion, by A. Veitch. GUARDIAN p8,
July 13, 1981.

Doe v. Irwin. AMERICAN JOURNAL OF TRIAL ADVOCACY
4:470-473, Fall, 1980.

Does the career woman face infertility? by A. B. Kapstrom.

SUPERVISOR NURSE 12:54-55+, July, 1981.

Does your contraceptive fit your personality? by G. A. Bachman. MADEMOISELLE 87:52-53, June, 1981.

Does the 'pill' promote the development of tumors? by C. Lauritzen. MEDIZINISCHE KLINIK 75(16):6-7, August 1, 1980.

Dosage of antighrombin III in women taking oral contraceptives, by N. Agoumi, et al. MAROC MEDICAL 2(3):309-315, October, 1980.

A double blind study of the treatment of threatened abortion with fenoterol hydrobromide, by E. Ruppin, et al. GEBURT-SCHILFE UND FRAUENHEILKUNDE 41(3):218-221, March, 1981.

Doubts about vasectomies. TIME 117:63, February 9, 1981.

Down's syndrome, amniocentesis, and abortion: prevention or elimination? by J. D. Smith. MENTAL RETARDATION 19(1):8-11, February, 1981.

Dr Koop and Mr Hyde. ECONOMIST 278:25+, March 28-April 3, 1981.

Drop in pill sales may have lead to increase in Denmark's abortion rate. FAMILY PLANNING PERSPECTIVES 12:313-314, November-December, 1980.

Dublin students defy birth control curbs, by J. Walshe. TIMES HIGHER EDUCATION SUPPLEMENT 419:6, November 14, 1980.

Dutch get tough [news], by J. Becker. NATURE 290(5806): 436, April 9, 1981.

Early and late complications in induced abortions of primigravidae (including suggested measures), by H. Kreibich, et al. ZEITSCHRIFT ZUR AERZTLICHE FORTBILDUNG 74(7): 311-316, April 1, 1980.

Early inflammatory complications in induction of abortion by means of intrauterine extra-amnial administration of prostaglandin F 2 alpha in primigravidae, by G. Koinzer, et al. ZEITSCHRIFT ZUR AERZTLICHE FORTBILDUNG 73 (21):1007-1009, November 1, 1979.

Early reproductive loss and the factors that may influence its occurrence, by P. S. Weathersbee. JOURNAL OF REPRODUCTIVE MEDICINE 25(6):315-318, December, 1980.

East Asia review, 1978-1979, by J. J. Clinton, et al. STUDIES IN FAMILY PLANNING 11:311-350, November, 1980.

—. Hong Kong, by P. Lam, et al. STUDIES IN FAMILY PLANNING 11(11):316-320, November, 1980.

—. Indonesia, by S. Surjaningrat, et al. STUDIES IN FAMILY PLANNING 11(11):320-324, November, 1980.

—. Introduction, by J. J. Clinton, et al. STUDIES IN FAMILY PLANNING 11(11):311-316, November, 1980.

—. Malaysia, by N. L. Aziz, et al. STUDIES IN FAMILY PLANNING 11(11):330-334, November, 1980.

—. The Philippines, by M. B. Concepción. STUDIES IN FAMILY PLANNING 11(11):335-340, November, 1980.

—. Republic of Korea, by T. I. Kim, et al. STUDIES IN FAMILY PLANNING 11(11):324-330, November, 1980.

—. Singapore, by S. Devi, et al. STUDIES IN FAMILY PLANNING 11(11):341-342, November, 1980.

—. Thailand, by S. Varakamin, et al. STUDIES IN FAMILY PLANNING 11(11):347-350, November, 1980.

Ectopic pregnancy after correct application of Hulka-Clemens clips [letter], by G. O'Neill, et al. MEDICAL JOURNAL OF AUSTRALIA 2(10):573, November 15, 1980.

Ectopic pregnancy and tubal ligation [letter], by N. H. Wright, et al. AMERICAN JOURNAL OF OBSTETRICS AND GYNE-COLOGY 139(5):611-612, March 1, 1981.

The effect of abortion method on the outcome of subsequent pregnancy, by P. E. Slater, et al. JOURNAL OF REPRODUCTIVE MEDICINE 26(3):123-128, March, 1981.

Effect of age, sex, oral contraceptive steroids and liver disease on the disposition of caffeine, by R. Patwardhan. CLINICAL RESEARCH 27(4):684A, 1979.

The effect of artificial and spontaneous abortions on the secondary human sex ratio, by G. D. Golovachev, et al. HUMAN BIOLOGY 52(4):721-729, December, 1980.

Effect of chemical sterilization on the sexual functions of male mosquitoes, by N. F. Zakharova, et al. MEDITSINSKAIA PARAZITOLOGIIA I PARAZITARNYE BOLEZNI 50(3): 56-62, May-June, 1981.

Effect of a combined oral contraceptive preparation on the dental pulp of experimental animals, by A. Cowie, et al. ORAL SURGERY 51(4):426-433, April, 1981.

The effect of condom use on squamous cell cervical intraepithelial neoplasia, by A. C. Richardson, et al. AMERICAN JOURNAL OF OBSTETRICS AND GYNECOLOGY 140(8):909-913, August 15, 1981.

Effect of contraceptive steroids on serum levels of sex hormone binding globulin and caeruloplasmin, by S. Limpongsanurak, et al. CURRENT MEDICAL RESEARCH AND OPINION 7(3):185-191, 1981.

Effect of a controlled exercise program on serum lipoprotein levels in women on oral contraceptives, by T. P. Wynne, et al. METABOLISM 29(12):1267-1271, December, 1980.

The effect of a 15(S)-15-methyl prostaglandin F2 alpha (methyl ester) suppository upon termination of early pregnancy, by J. F. Roux, et al. CONTRACEPTION 22(1):57-61, July, 1980.

Effect of HR (O-(beta-hydroxyethyl)-rutosides) on the impaired venous function of young females taking oral contraceptives. A strain guage plethysmographic and clinical open controlled study, by S. Forconi, et al. VASA 9(4):324-330, 1980.

Effect of halothane vapors on the course of pregnancy, by F. Kolasa, et al. GINEKOLOGIA POLSKA 51(10):931-933, October, 1980.

Effect of legalized abortion on wrongful life actions. FLORIDA STATE UNIVERSITY LAW REVIEW 9:137-156, Winter, 1981.

Effect of long-term use of intra-uterine contraception on the form of the uterine cavity and on the patency of the uterine tubes, by E. V. Derankova. VOPROSY OKHRANY MA-TERINSTVA I DETSTVO 24(6):69, 1979.

Effect of a low dose estrogen-progestogen oral contraceptive on lipids and lipoproteins, by H. Taggart, et al. IRISH JOUR-NAL OF MEDICAL SCIENCE 150(1):13-14, January, 1981.

Effect of oral contraceptive cycle on dry socket (localized alveolar osteitis), by J. E. Catellani, et al. JOURNAL OF THE AMERICAN DENTAL ASSOCIATION 101(5):777-780, November, 1980.

Effect of an oral contraceptive on uterine tonicity in women with primary dysmenorrhea, by O. Lalos, et al. ACTA OB-STETRICIA ET GYNECOLOGICA SCANDINAVICA 60 (3):229-232, 1981.

Effect of oral contraceptives on the circulatory system, by T. Stasiński, et al. POLSKI TYGODNIK LEKARSKI 35(19): 713-715, May 12, 1980.

The effect of oral contraceptives on serum lipids gamma-glutamyl transpeptidase, and excretion of d-glucaric acid, by P. Hajós, et al. INTERNATIONAL JOURNAL OF CLINICAL PHAR-MACOLOGY, THERAPY AND TOXICOLOGY 19(3):117-123, March, 1981.

JOURNAL OF INTERNATIONAL MEDICAL RESEARCH
8(Suppl 3):88-95, 1980.

Effects of angiotensin II analog on blood pressure, renin and aldosterone in women on oral contraceptives and toxemia, by T. Saruta, et al. GINECOLOGIA Y OBSTETRICIA DE MEXICO 12(1):11-20, 1981.

Effects of child mortality on fertility in Thailand, by M. Hashimoto, et al. ECONOMIC DEVELOPMENT AND CULTURAL CHANGE 29:781-794, July, 1981.

Effects of contraceptive agents on the biochemical and protein composition of human endometrium, by K. Umapathysivam, et al. CONTRACEPTION 22(4):425-440, October, 1980.

Effects of d-norgestrel-releasing intracervical devices in the non-human primate, Erythrocebus patas, by G. E. Dagle, et al. CONTRACEPTION 22(4):409-423, October, 1980.

Effects of D-tryptopha n6-proline-9-N-ethyl luteinizing hormone on reproductive functions in the male rat, by C. Rivier, et al. INTERNATIONAL JOURNAL OF FERTILITY 25(3): 145-150, 1980.

The effects of hormonal contraceptives on lactation: current findings, methodological considerations, and future priorities. STUDIES IN FAMILY PLANNING 12(4):134, April, 1981.

Effects of hormonal contraceptives on parameters of lipid metabolism, by W. Carol, et al. ZENTRALBLATT FUR GYNAEKOLOGIE 102(22):1273-1282, 1980.

Effects of an intra-epididymal and intra-scrotal copper device on rat spermatozoa, by N. J. Chinoy, et al. INTERNATIONAL JOURNAL OF ANDROLOGY 3(6):719-737, December, 1980.

Effects of oestro-progestogenic oral contraceptives on blood coagulation, fibrinolysis, and platelet aggregation, by F. Ghezzo, et al. HAEMATOLOGICA 65(6):737-745, December, 1980.

Effects of oral contraceptive agents on copper and zinc balance in young women, by M. G. Crews, et al. AMERICAN JOURNAL OF CLINICAL NUTRITION 33:1940-1945, September, 1980.

Effects of oral contraceptive steroids on the thickness of human cornea, by P. S. Soni. AMERICAN JOURNAL OF OPTOMETRY AND PHYSIOLOGICAL OPITCS 57(11):825-834, November, 1980.

Effects of oral contraceptives containing 50 microgram estrogen on blood coagulation in non-Caucasian women, by F. H. Tsakok, et al. CONTRACEPTION 21(5):505-527, May, 1980.

The effects of oral contraceptives in inducing changes in blood pressure in the African green monkey; the role of the renin-angiotensin system, by F. F. Vickers, PhD. DAI 42(5), 1981.

Effects of oral contraceptives on erythrocytic porphyrins, by J. G. Aurora. INDIAN JOURNAL OF MEDICAL RESEARCH 70:632-635, October, 1979.

Effects of oral contraceptives on the liver [letter], by A. T. Coopland. CANADIAN JOURNAL OF SURGERY 23(6): 511, November, 1980.

Effects of prostaglandin-F2 alpha and a plant protein 'Trichosanthin', on 10-day pregnant rabbits, by S. K. Saksena, et al. PROSTAGLANDINS AND MEDICINE 5(5):383-390, November, 1980.

Effects of restricted public funding for legal abortions: a second look, by R. M. Selik, et al. AMERICAN JOURNAL OF PUBLIC HEALTH 71(7):77-81, January, 1981.

The effects of school sex education programs: a review of the literature, by D. Kirby. JOURNAL OF SCHOOL HEALTH 50(10):559-563, December, 1980.

The effects of sterilisation: a comparison of sterilised women with the wives of vasectomised men, by E. Alder, et al. CONTRACEPTION 23(1):45-54, January, 1981.

Effects of subjects' sex, and intake of tobacco, alcohol and oral contraceptives on plasma phenytoin levels, by E. A. De Leacy, et al. BRITISH JOURNAL OF CLINICAL PHARMA-COLOGY 8(1):33-36, July, 1979.

L'Église anglicane et la contraception, by C. Vaillant. SUPPLÉ-MENT 138:434-455, September, 1981.

An elective course in fertility control, by J. B. Modrak. AMERI-CAN JOURNAL OF PHARMACEUTICAL EDUCATION 44(3):266-269, August, 1980.

Elective sterilization in childless women, by L. Benjamin, et al. FERTILITY AND STERILITY 34(2):116-120, August, 1980.

Electrocardiographic changes induced by suction curettage for elective termination of pregnancy, by L. M. Mabee, Jr., et al. AMERICAN JOURNAL OF OBSTETRICS AND GYNE-COLOGY 138(2):181-184, September 15, 1980.

Elevated prolactin levels in oral contraceptive pill-related hyper-tension, by P. Lehtovirta, et al. FERTILITY AND STERILI-TY 35(4):403-405, April, 1981.

Embryo-maternal transfusions in 100 therapeutic induced abor-tions, by P. Spelina, et al. GYNAEKOLOGISCHE RUND-SCHAU 20(Suppl 1):113-116, June, 1980.

Endocrine, cardiovascular, and psychological correlates of olfactory sensitivity changes during the human menstrual cycle, by R. L. Doty, et al. JOURNAL OF COMPARATIVE AND PHYSIOLOGICAL PSYCHOLOGY 95:45-60, Febru-ary, 1981.

Endocrinology of sexual function, by J. Bancroft. CLINICAL OBSTETRICS AND GYNAECOLOGY 7(2):253-282, 1980.

Endometriosis and the development of tuboperitoneal fistulas after tubal ligation, by J. A. Rock, et al. FERTILITY AND STERILITY 35(1):16-20, January, 1981.

Endoscopic tubal ligation, by M. Oliver. SURGICAL TECH-NOLOGISTS 13:21-25, September-October, 1981.

Enigma of when personhood begins generates lively legislative fight, by E. E. Plowman. CHRISTIANITY TODAY 25:30, May 29, 1981.

Enzyme picture in the use of oral contraceptives, by R. Lorenz. ZFA 56(32):2237-2240, November 20, 1980.

Epidemiology of human fertility [editorial] , by D. Schwartz. REVUE D'EPIDEMIOLOGIE ET DE SANTE PUBLIQUE 28(1):7-12, April 30, 1980.

Epidemiology of voluntary abortion in the region of Emilia Romagna and in Italy, by M. Filicori, et al. ACTA EURO-PAEA FERTILITATIS 11(2):157-165, June, 1980.

Epidural morphine analgesia in second-trimester induced abor-tion, by F. Magora, et al. AMERICAN JOURNAL OF OB-STETRICS AND GYNECOLOGY 138(3):260-262, Octo-ber 1, 1980.

Erythema nodosum and oral contraception. Demonstration of an anti-ethinyl estradiol antibody [letter] , by J. L. Touboul, et al. NOUVELLE PRESSE MEDICALE 10(9):712, February 28, 1981.

'Escape' ovulation in women due to the missing of low dose combination oral contraceptive pills, by V. Chowdhury, et al. CONTRACEPTION 22(3):241-247, September, 1980.

Establishing linkages between women's literacy programmes, status issues and access to family planning, by R. Chhabra. INDIAN JOURNAL OF ADULT EDUCATION 41(4):6-9, April 24, 1980.

Establishing regulatory control over contraception, by C. Djerassi. USA TODAY 109:7-8, April, 1981.

Estimating the need for subsidized family planning in the U.S.: obtaining imput from a special tabulation of the 1970 census, by J. Dryfoos. REVIEW OF PUBLIC DATA USE 1(4):1-9, October, 1973.

The estimation of costs and effectiveness of community-based family planning services [experience in the Grampian Health Board Area, Scotland], by A. Chamberlain. INTERNATIONAL JOURNAL OF SOCIAL ECONOMICS 7(5)::260-272, 1980.

Estradiol implants for conception control, by C. Nezhat, et al. AMERICAN JOURNAL OF OBSTETRICS AND GYNECOLOGY 138(8):1151-1156, December 15, 1980.

Estrogen and lipid regulation in normal rats, by J. N. Wilson, et al. CLINICAL RESEARCH 28(1):27A, 1980.

Estrogen regimen of women with endometrial carcinoma. A retrospective case-control study at Radiumhemmet, by A. Obrink, et al. ACTA OBSTETRICIA ET GYNECOLOGICA SCANDINAVICA 60(2):191-197, 1981.

Ethnic differences in family planning acceptance in rural Guatemala, by J. Bertrand. STUDIES IN FAMILY PLANNING 10(8-9):238-245, August-September, 1979.

Etiology of pelvic infections treated by the gynecologic service of the Kasturba Hospital, Delhi, India, by M. Kochar. AMERICAN JOURNAL OF OBSTETRICS AND GYNECOLOGY 138(7 Part 2):872-874, 1980.

The etiology, physiopathology and clinical aspects of habitual abortion, by G. B. Candiani, et al. ANNALI DI OSTETRICIA, GINECOLOGIA, MEDICINA PERINATALE 101(5):295-318, September-October, 1980.

Eugenic sterilization: great for what ails the poor, by R. Fleming. ENCORE 9:17-19, June, 1980.

An evaluation of an adolescent family planning program, by N. Ralph. AMERICAN JOURNAL OF EPIDEMIOLOGY 112

(3):434-435, 1980.

Evaluation of hormonal treatment of threatened abortion, by Z.
Skolicki. FOLIA MEDICA CRACOVIENSIA 22(1):137-149,
1980.

Evaluation of the prognosis of threatened abortion by the determination of HCG in serum and urine, by O. Reiertsen, et
al. TIDSSKRIFT FOR DEN NORSKE LAEGEFORENING
100(34-36):2038-2040, December 10, 1980.

Evaluation of therapeutic results of gestagen preparations in
imminent abortion and preterm deliveries, by J. Vierik, et al.
BRATISLAVSKE LEKARSKE LISTY 74(3):347-353,
September, 1980.

Evaluation of threatened abortion by human chorionic gonado-
tropin levels and ultrasonography, by H. A. Sande, et al.
INTERNATIONAL JOURNAL OF GYNAECOLOGY AND
OBSTETRICS 18(2):123-127, September-October, 1980.

Every child a wanted child, by C. Sevitt. CANADA AND THE
WORLD 46:18, January, 1981.

Evolution of Margaret Sanger's Family limitation pamphlet,
1914-1921, by J. M. Jensen. SIGNS 6:548-555, Spring, 1981.

Examination of abortuses [letter], by A. J. Barson. BRITISH
MEDICAL JOURNAL 280(6220):1055, April 12, 1980.

Excerpts from a National Conference on Recombinant DNA
and the Federal Government. Department of Health and
Human Services perspective [news], by L. T. Harmison.
RECOMBINANT DNA TECHNICAL BULLETIN 4(2):49-
51, July, 1981.

Exercise, blood clots, and the pill [work of S. Pizzo], by G. B.
Kolata. SCIENCE 211:913, February 27, 1981.

Exercise ECG and serum enzymes in women using oral contraceptives, by K. Ziesenhenn, et al. ZEITSCHRIFT FUR DIE
GESAMTE INNERE MEDIZIN 35(15):619-623, August 1,

1980.

Exogenous estrogens and carcinoma of the endometrium: a critical analysis of the literature, by S. Franceschi, et al. ANNALI DI OSTETRICIA GINECOLOGIA, MEDICINA PERINATALE 101(6):397-403, November-December, 1980.

Experience in a series of fimbriectomies, by S. Oskowitz, et al. FERTILITY AND STERILITY 34(4):320-323, October, 1980.

Experience with and remarks 1 year's application of the abortion law 194, by A. Benedetti, et al. MINERVA GINECOLOGIA 33(4):377-379, April, 1981.

Experiences with a tampon-spermicide device, by E. W. Page. CONTRACEPTION 23(1):37-44, January, 1981.

Experiences with 3120 outpatients sterilized by laparoscopic tubal bipolar coagulation, by H. J. Lindemann, et al. GEBURTSHILFE UND FRAUENHEILKUNDE 41(7):500-503, July, 1981.

Experimental studies of intra-amniotic pargyline and/or reserpine for termination of midterm pregnancy, by M. Q. Zheng. CHUNG HUA FU CHAN KO TSA CHIH 15(2):105-107, 1980.

The experts rate important features and outcomes of sex education programs, by D. Kirby. JOURNAL OF SCHOOL HEALTH 50(9):497-502, November, 1980.

Exploring risks and benefits of the birth control pill . . . teaching ideas, by D. A. Dunn. HEALTH EDUCATION 12:35, January-February, 1981.

Extra-amniotic instillation of rivanol in the management of patients with missed abortion and fetal death, by A. Olund. ACTA OBSTETRICIA ET GYNECOLOGICA SCANDINAVICA 60(3):313-315, 1981.

Extraovular instillations of normal saline for termination of midtrimester pregnancy, by A. Rofé, et al. INTERNATIONAL JOURNAL OF GYNAECOLOGY AND OBSTETRICS 18 (5):351-353, 1980.

Extrauterine pregnancy after sterilization, by S. Ulbak, et al. UGESKRIFT FOR LAEGER 143(5):276, January 26, 1981.

Factors influencing birth control habits in Victoria, by T. Selwood, et al. AUSTRALIAN FAMILY PHYSICIAN 10(2): 96-101, February, 1981.

Factors influencing morbidity in termination of pregnancy, by C. R. Harman, et al. AMERICAN JOURNAL OF OBSTETRICS AND GYNECOLOGY 139(3):333-337, February 1, 1981.

Factors influencing the outcome of vasectomy reversal, by H. A. Bagshaw, et al. BRITISH JOURNAL OF UROLOGY 52(1): 57-60, February, 1980.

Facts of life in Thailand, by M. Ho. TECHNOLOGY REVIEW 83:60-61, November-December, 1980.

Failure of an Irving tubal sterilization, by A. C. Wittich. OBSTETRICS AND GYNECOLOGY 57(6 Suppl):50S-51S, June, 1981.

Failure of oral contraceptive with rifampicin, by K. C. Gupta, et al. MEDICAL JOURNAL OF ZAMBIA 15(1):23, December 1980-January, 1981.

A familial t(9;13) balanced translocation associated with recurrent abortion. Repository identification No. GM2492, by A. Serra, et al. CYTOGENETICS AND CELL GENETICS 27(4): 269, 1980.

Family building: a social psychological study of fertility decisions, population and environment. POPULATION AND ENVIRONMENT 3(3-4):210, Fall-Winter, 1980.

Family history and oral contraceptives: unique relationships in breast cancer patients, by M. M. Black, et al. CANCER 46

(12):2747-2751, December 15, 1980.

Family planning [letter], by E. Elliott. BRITISH MEDICAL
JOURNAL 281(6250):1287-1288, November 8, 1980.

Family planning and immigrants, by P. Thornton. NURSING
1(16):704-708, August, 1980.

Family planning and tuberculosis, by M. Prasad, et al. INDIAN
JOURNAL OF PUBLIC HEALTH 24(2):92-98, April-June,
1980.

Family planning: a cautionary tale, by M. Norman. HEALTH
VISITOR 54:61-62, February, 1981.

Family planning centers strong in drug stores, by E. Cheney.
AMERICAN DRUGGIST 181:78+, March, 1980.

Family planning: helping men ask for help, by B. M. Rappaport.
PUBLIC WELFARE 39:22-27, Spring, 1981.

Family planning in Africa: a 1981 People wallchart. PEOPLE
8:1 folded insert no. 1, 1981.

Family planning in Bangladesh, by S. Saito. JOSANPU ZASSHI
35(3):181-185, March, 1981.

Family planning in Finland in the 1970s, by O. Riihinen, et al.
KATILOLEHTI 86(1):8-14, January, 1981.

Family planning in the 1980's: challenges and opportunities;
recommendations of the International Conference on Family
Planning in the 1980's, Jakarta, Indonesia, 26-30 April 1981.
STUDIES IN FAMILY PLANNING 12:251-256, June-July,
1981.

Family planning in Pakistan: an analysis of some factors constraining use, by I. Sirageldin, et al. STUDIES IN FAMILY
PLANNING 7(5):144-154, May, 1976.

Family planning in the People's Republic of China, by Z. F.
Zhang, et al. INTERNATIONAL JOURNAL OF GYNAE-

COLOGY AND OBSTETRICS 18(5):345-347, 1980.

Family planning in the postpartum period, by W. E. Fuller. CLINICAL OBSTETRICS AND GYNECOLOGY 23(4): 1081-1086, December, 1980.

Family planning in the year 2000, by T. Standley, et al. WORLD HEALTH p10, February-March, 1981.

Family planning knowledge, attitude and practice in the rural areas of Sarawak, by C. K. Lam. JOURNAL OF BIOSOCIAL SCIENCE 11(3):315-323, July, 1979.

Family planning—the pill or natural method of birth control, by H. Janisch. WIENER KLINISCHE WOCHENSCHRIFT 92 (16):555-558, August, 1980.

Family planning practices among Anglo and Hispanic women in U. S. counties bordering Mexico, by R. W. Rochat, et al. FAMILY PLANNING PERSPECTIVES 13:176-180, July-August, 1981.

Family planning programs and fertility decline [based on a World Bank study of 63 developing nations], by R. Cuca. FI-NANCE AND DEVELOPMENT 17:37-39, December, 1980.

Family planning programs and fertility decline [developing countries], by R. Cuca. JOURNAL OF SOCIAL AND POLITICAL STUDIES 5:183-190, Winter, 1980.

Family planning realities in the third world. PEOPLE 7(4):12, 1980.

Family planning services in the United States, 1978-1979, by A. Torres, et al. FAMILY PLANNING PERSPECTIVES 13:132-141, May-June, 1981.

A family planning survey, by C. J. Carr. IRISH MEDICAL JOURNAL 73(9):340-341, September, 1980.

Family size and family planning in Kenya: continuity and change in metropolitan and rural attitudes, by T. E. Dow, Jr., et al.

STUDIES IN FAMILY PLANNING 12(6-7):272, June-July, 1981.

Family size and sex preference of children: a biracial comparison, by V. V. Ruo, et al. ADOLESCENCE 16(62):385-401, Summer, 1981.

Family-size limitation and birth spacing: the fertility transition of African and Asian immigrants in Israel. POPULATION AND DEVELOPMENT REVIEW 6(4):581, December, 1980.

Fatal ectopic pregnancy after attempted legally induced abortion, by G. L. Rubin, et al. JAMA 244(15):1705-1708, October 10, 1980.

Fatal septic abortion in the United States, 1975-1977, by D. A. Grimes, et al. OBSTETRICS AND GYNECOLOGY 57(6): 739-744, June, 1981.

Fathers and birth control, by D. Spangler. AMERICAN BABY 43:20+, September, 1981.

Federal abortion. AMERICA 145:232-233, October 24, 1981.

Female sterilization, by J. M. Emens. PRACTITIONER 224 (1349):1177-1183, November, 1980.

—: a centennial conference, by D. Wulf. FAMILY PLANNING PERSPECTIVES 13:24-29, January-February, 1981.

— no more tubal coagulation [letter], by M. Sutton, et al. BRITISH MEDICAL JOURNAL 281(6254):1564, December 6, 1980.

—: the nurse's role, by M. T. Stone. ISSUES IN HEALTH CARE OF WOMEN 1(5):45-60, 1979.

Female work status and fertility in urban Latin America, by M. Davidson. SOCIAL AND ECONOMIC STUDIES 27:481-506, December, 1978.

Feminists disrupt anti-abortion hearings in U.S. Senate, by T.

69

Dejanibus, et al. OFF OUR BACKS 11:2-3+, June, 1981.

Fertility and abortion inside and outside marriage, by J. Thompson. POPULATION TRENDS 5:5-8, Autumn, 1976.

Fertility and contraception in 12 developed countries. FAMILY PLANNING PERSPECTIVES 13(2):93, March-April, 1981.

Fertility following abortion, using Boero's method, by S. Lembrych, et al. ZENTRALBLATT FUR GYNAEKOLOGIE 103(3):154-156, 1981.

Fertility impairment in females—present status, by M. Prashad, et al. ENDOKIRNOLOGIE 76(2):192-201, May, 1980.

Fertility status of men following vaso-vasostomy, by M. L. Mehrotra, et al. INDIAN JOURNAL OF MEDICAL RESEARCH 73:33-40, January, 1981.

Fetal loss after implantation. A prospective study, by J. F. Miller, et al. LANCET 2(8194):554-556, September 13, 1980.

Fetal personhood threat [Helms-Hyde bill]. MS MAGAZINE 9: 19, June, 1981.

Fetal viability and individual autonomy: resolving medical and legal standards for abortion. UCLA LAW REVIEW 27:1340-1364, August, 1980.

Feto-placentopathies in practice, by E. Philippe. ARCHIVES D'ANATOMIE ET DE CYTOLOGIE PATHOLOGIQUE 28 (5):286-293, 1980.

Fibrinolytic response and oral contraceptive associated thromboembolism, by S. V. Pizzo, et al. CONTRACEPTION 23(2): 181-186, February, 1981.

Films for family planning programs. POPULATION REPORTS (23):J493-522, January-February, 1981.

First FDA medical device regulations will effect development of many experimental contraceptives. FAMILY PLANNING

Effect of oral contraceptives on tryptophan and tyrosine availability: evidence for a possible contribution to mental depression, by S. E. Moller. NEUROPSYCHOBIOLOGY 7(4):192-200, 1981.

Effect of prolonged administration of oral contraceptives and psychotropic drugs on some ovarian adrenocortical functions, by M. T. Abdel-Aziz, et al. JOURNAL OF THE EGYPTIAN MEDICAL ASSOCIATION 61(11-12):703-709, 1978.

Effect of selected progestational hormones used for the protection of high-risk pregnancy on the clinical course, morphological changes and proliferative activity of the trophoblast, by Z. Papierowski. GINEKOLOGIA POLSKA 52(3):298-303, 1981.

Effectiveness and side-effects of intracervical application of prostaglandin F2-alpha-gel in the early weeks of pregnancy, by U. Neeb. GEBURTSHILFE UND FRAUENHEILKUNDE 40(10):901-903, October, 1980.

The effectiveness of different methods of laparoscopic tubal sterilization, by H. Frangenheim. GEBURTSHILFE UND FRAUENHEILKUNDE 40(10):896-900, October, 1980.

Effectivity and acceptability of oral contraceptives containing natural and artificial estrogens in combination with a gestagen. A controlled double-blind investigation, by J. Serup, et al. ACTA OBSTETRICIA ET GYNECOLOGICA SCANDINAVICA 60(2):203-206, 1981.

Effect of silver nitrate on pregnancy termination in cynomolgus monkeys, by N. H. Dubin, et al. FERTILITY AND STERILITY 36(1):106-109, July, 1981.

Effects and side effects of hormonal contraceptives, by W. Carol, et al. ZEITSCHRIFT FUR AERZTLICHE FORTBILDUNG 74(3):97-104, February 1, 1980.

Effects of age, cigarette smoking and the oral contraceptive on the pharmacokinetics of clomipramine and its desmethyl metabolite during chronic dosing, by V. A. John, et al.

PERSPECTIVES 12:212-213, July-August, 1980.

First trimester termination of pregnancy. The value of treating the cervix pre-operatively in the primigravid patient by extra-amniotic administration of a single dose of F2-alpha prostaglandin gel, by P. De Grandi, et al. JOURNAL DE GYNE-COLOGIE OBSTETRIQUE ET BIOLOGIE DE LA REPRODUCTION 9(5):587-594, 1980.

Fitting of diaphragms, by E. Weisberg. MEDICAL JOURNAL OF AUSTRALIA 2(5):250-253, September 6, 1980.

Flower intrauterine contraceptive device, by L. Zilan. CHINESE MEDICAL JOURNAL 93(8):528-530, 1980.

Focal hemorrhagic necrosis of the liver. A clinicopathological entity possibly related to oral contraceptives, by E. Z. Zafrani, et al. GASTROENTEROLOGY 79(6):1295-1299, December, 1980.

Focal nodular hyperplasia of the liver and hepatic cell adenoma in women on oral contraceptives, by I. Bartók, et al. HEPATOGASTROENTEROLOGY 27(6):435-440, December, 1980.

Foetus compressus, by B. Prasad, et al. JOURNAL OF THE INDIAN MEDICAL ASSOCIATION 74(8):154-155, April 16, 1980.

Folding -approximating clamp to simplify microvasovasostomy, by B. Strauch. UROLOGY 16(3):295-296, September, 1980.

Follow-up of 375 sterilised women—the view from a general practice, by A. F. Wright. HEALTH BULLETIN 38(5):194-198, September, 1980.

Follow-up study of mid-term abortion induced by five different methods, by X. X. Zhong. CHUNG HUA FU CHAN KO TSA CHIH 15(4):216-218, October, 1980.

For life—against abortion, by M. F. Jefferson. ENCORE 10:18-19, October, 1981.

For the pro-life movement, it's a matter of Time, by R. McMunn. OUR SUNDAY VISITOR 69:5, April 19, 1981.

For women aged 35 and under, little or no risk of circulatory disease death found from pill use. FAMILY PLANNING PERSPECTIVES 13:142-146, May-June, 1981.

Four years of experience with the TCu 380A intrauterine contraceptive device, by I. Sivin, et al. FERTILITY AND STERILITY 36(2):159-163, August, 1981.

Free choice [Catholics for a free choice]. HUMANIST 41:57, January-February, 1981.

Free thyroxine and free thyroxine index in women taking oral contraceptives, by M. A. Swanson, et al. CLINICAL NUCLEAR MEDICINE 6(4):168-171, April, 1981.

From the NIH: the 'pill' recieves mixed reviews in latest report of Walnut Creek study. JAMA 246(10):1071-1072, September 4, 1981.

Funding of abortions under the Medicaid program—constitutionality of the Hyde amendment. AMERICAN JOURNAL OF TRIAL ADVOCACY 4:708-717, Spring, 1981.

Further analyses of mortality in oral contraceptive users. Royal College of General Practitioners' Oral Contraception Study. LANCET 1(8219):541-546, March 7, 1981.

Further studies of an intravasal copper device in rats, by R. K. Ahsan, et al. JOURNAL OF REPRODUCTIVE FERTILITY 59(2):341-345, July, 1980.

Gallstone risk, by J. Labreche. CHATELAINE 53:38, December, 1980.

Gap between law and moral order: an examination of the legitimacy of the Supreme Court abortion decisions, by L. D. Wardle. BRIGHAM YOUNG UNIVERSITY LAW REVIEW 1980:811-835, 1980.

Genetic compatibility may explain recurrent spontaneous abortions [news], by C. Yarbrough. JAMA 246(4):315-316, July 24-31, 1981.

Good news about the pill, by J. E. Rodgers. MADEMOISELLE 87:107-109, May, 1981.

Gooley v. Moss [(Ind) 398 N E 2d 1314]. NEW ENGLAND JOURNAL OF PRISON LAW 6:321-323, Summer, 1980.

Government barriers against the cervical cap. OFF OUR BACKS 11:12, January, 1981.

Government funding for elective abortions. PROGRESS IN CLINICAL AND BIOLOGICAL RESEARCH 50:213-243, 1981.

Grady, in re (NJ) 405 A 2d 851. SETON HALL LAW REVIEW 10:757-758, 1980.

The great abortion battle of 1981, by R. Kramer. VILLAGE VOICE 26:1, March 11, 1981.

Group prods pro-life, peace work; interview by Thomas C. Fox, by J. Loesch. NATIONAL CATHOLIC REPORTER 18:2, December 4, 1981.

The growing queue for the ultimate alternative, by I. Allen. GUARDIAN p12, October 28, 1981.

Gynaecological sequelae of induced abortion, by M. Brudenell. PRACTITIONER 224(1347):893-898, September, 1980.

Gynaecology: piercing pains . . . a woman admitted to hospital in an attempt to remove her intrauterine device, by E. Hawkes. NURSING MIRROR 152:41, April 2, 1981.

HCG, progesterone and 17-beta-estradiol levels during extraamniotically induced early abortion by a new prostaglandin derivative (Sulprostone), by S. Nilsson, et al. GYNECOLOGIC AND OBSTETRIC INVESTIGATION 12(4):203-210, 1981.

HLA alloimmunization as a cause of spontaneous abortion, by P. Kolevski, et al. BILTEN ZA HEMATOLOGIJU I TRANS-FUZIJU 7(2-3):131-135, 1979.

HSE confident it can cope. NATURE 277(5695):341, February 1, 1979.

Habitual abortion. Two factors of increasing frequency, by A. C. Weseley. DIAGNOSTIC GYNECOLOGY AND OBSTETRICS 3(2):119-121, Summer, 1981.

Habitual abortion and translocation (22q;22q): unexpected transmission from a mother to her phenotypically normal daughter, by V. G. Kirkels, et al. CLINICAL GENETICS 18 (6):456-461, December, 1980.

Habitual abortion of genetic origin, by J. Rosas Arceo, et al. GINECOLOGIA Y OBSTETRICIA DE MEXICO 47(284): 411-417, June, 1980.

Half an abortion in a case of twins [procedure at Mt. Sinai School of Medicine in New York] . SCIENCE NEWS 119:406, June 27, 1981.

Harris v. McRae (100 S Ct 2671), by M. C. Dunlap. WOMEN'S RIGHTS LAW REPORTER 6:166-168, Spring, 1980.

—: the Court retreats from Roe v. Wade. LOYOLA LAW RE-VIEW 26:749-760, Summer, 1980.

Harris v. McRae: the Hyde Amendment stands while rights of poor women fall [U.S. Supreme Court decision upholding the law prohibiting the use of federal funds for many thera-peutic abortions] , by C. C. Sewell, et al. KENTUCKY LAW JOURNAL 69(2):359-391, 1980-1981.

Harris v. McRae (100 S Ct 2671): indigent women must bear the consequences of the Hyde amendment. LOYOLA UNIVERSI-TY LAW JOURNAL 12:255-276, Winter, 1981.

—: whatever happened to the Roe v. Wade abortion right? PEP-PERDINE LAW REVIEW 8:861-897, March, 1981.

Health and family planning services in Bangladesh: a study in inequality, by O. Gish. INTERNATIONAL JOURNAL OF HEALTH SERVICES 11(2):263-281, 1981.

Health consequences of induced abortion in rural Northeast Thailand, by T. Narkavonnakit, et al. STUDIES IN FAMILY PLANNING 12(2):58-65, February, 1981.

The health implications of voluntary sterilization, presented at Association for Voluntary Sterlization 4th International Conference, Seoul, May 7-10, 1979. (4):54.

Health instructions concerning sexual activities and birth control, by H. Ogino, et al. JOSANPU ZASSHI 34(11):724-737, November, 1980.

Health needs of adolescent girls in the area of reproductive behavior, by M. Husar, et al. JUGOSLAVENSKA GINEKOLO-GIJAI OPSTETRICIJA 19(3-4):131-138, May-August, 1980.

Health systems and population control. In International Conference on the Unity of the Science [8th] November 22-25, 1979, Los Angeles, California. The responsibility of the academic community in the search for absolute values, by G. Samarawickrama. p669-678.

Hell's fury. ECONOMIST 279:32, May 30, 1981.

Hemorrhage and cardiac arrest during laparoscopic tubal ligation, by J. W. Chapin, et al. ANESTHESIOLOGY 53(4):342-343, October, 1980.

Hepatic angiosarcoma. Possible relationship to long-term oral contraceptive ingestion, by P. S. Monroe, et al. JAMA 246 (1):64-65, July, 1981.

Hepatocellular adenoma. Its transformation to carcinoma in a user of oral contraceptives, by H. Tesluk, et al. ARCHIVES OF PATHOLOGY AND LABORATORY MEDICINE 105(6): 296-299, June, 1981.

High rates of pregnancy and dissatisfaction mark first cervical cap trial. FAMILY PLANNING PERSPECTIVES 13:48, January-February, 1981.

Historic, cultural, legal, psychosocial and educational aspects of induced abortion, by F. Aguirre Zozaya, et al. GINECOLOGIA Y OBSTETRICIA DE MEXICO 48(286):111-135, August, 1980.

History and current status of legislation on abortion in the countries of the world, by V. K. Kuznetsov, et al. FEL'DSHER I AKUSHERKA 45(8):3-6, 1980.

Hong Kong. STUDIES IN FAMILY PLANNING 11(11):316, November, 1980.

The Hong Kong experience in promoting sterilization, by P. Lam, presented at Association for Voluntary Sterilization 4th International Conference, Seoul, May 7-10, 1979. p90.

Hong Kong married abortion applicants: a comparison with married women who elect to complete their pregnancies, by F. Lieh-Mak, et al. JOURNAL OF BIOSOCIAL SCIENCE 13 (1):71-80, January, 1981.

Hormonal contraception—side effects and surgical aspects, by G. Göretzlehner, et al. ZENTRALBLATT FUR CHIRURGIE 105(24):1601-1616, 1980.

Hormonal contraceptives cause depression? by J. M. Wenderlein. MEDIZINISCHE KLINIK 76(10):288-290, May 8, 1981.

Hormonal contraceptives of differentiated composition—effects on thrombocyte function, by M. Brandt, et al. ZENTRALBLATT FUR GYNAEKOLOGIE 103(11):631-643, 1981.

Hormonal profile in threatened abortion and its treatment with HCG, by G. Desanso, et al. MINERVA GINECOLOGIA 33 (5):421-428, May, 1981.

Hormonal protective therapy [letter], by S. Gardó. ORVOSI HETILAP 122(17):1043, April 26, 1981.

Hormonal supervision of threatened abortion. Diagnosis and therapy, by P. Knapstein. MMW 122(26):970-972, June 27, 1980.

Hospital requirement for abortions in second trimester is constitutional. THE CRIMINAL LAW REPORTER: COURT DECISIONS AND PROCEEDINGS 29(12):2248-2249, June 17, 1981.

Hospital support of legal abortion can overcome MD's negative attitudes. FAMILY PLANNING PERSPECTIVES 12:264-265, September-October, 1980.

Hospitals offer help in coping with stress—empathy classes. HOSPITALS 55(3):35-36, February 1, 1981.

House approves ban on federal abortion cover. BUSINESS INSURANCE 14:12, September 1, 1980.

How gossypol inhibits male fertility begins to emerge, by R. Rawls. CHEMICAL AND ENGINEERING NEWS 59:36-37, March 23, 1981.

How high is the real incidence of induced abortion? Facts and erroneous estimates, by W. Christian, et al. FORTSCHRITTE DER MEDIZIN 98(29):1123-1128, August 7, 1980.

How patients view mandatory waiting periods for abortion, by M. Lupfer, et al. FAMILY PLANNING PERSPECTIVES 13:75-79, March-April, 1981.

The "human" as a problem in bioethics, by P. D. Simmons. REVIEW AND EXPOSITOR 78:91-108, Winter, 1981.

Human chorionic gonadotropin, estradiol, progesterone, prolactin, and B-scan ultrasound minitoring of complications in early pregnancy, by B. H. Yuen, et al. OBSTETRICS AND GYNECOLOGY 57(2):207-214, February, 1981.

Human life amendment and the future of human life, by R. Eisler. HUMANIST 41:13-19+, September-October, 1981.

Human life amendment is bulls-eye on hit list target. OUR SUN-
DAY VISITOR 69:7, March 1, 1981.

The human life amendment . . . two views, by A. Neale, et al.
NATIONAL CATHOLIC REPORTER 17:10-11, April 24,
1981.

Human life and abortion [letter], by A. M. Bryson. MEDICAL
JOURNAL OF AUSTRALIA 1(2):94, January 24, 1981.

Human life and termination of pregnancy [letter], by A. Viliunas.
MEDICAL JOURNAL OF AUSTRALIA 1(12):656, June 13,
1981.

Human life bill arouses more opposition, by R. J. Smith. SCI-
ENCE 212:1372, June 19, 1981.

A human life statute [review of various Supreme Court decisions
which set precedents the Congress might cite in extending the
Fourteenth Amendment protection to include unborn children, by S. H. Galebach. HUMAN LIFE REVIEW 7:5-33,
Winter, 1981.

Human life testimony [letters]. SCIENCE 213:154+, July 10,
1981.

Humanae Vitae and the Catholic priest, by G. Stafford. HOMI-
LETIC AND PASTORAL REVIEW 81:30-32+, December,
1980.

Humanistic education for the EMT, by T. T. Luka. EMT JOUR-
NAL 4(3):45-46, September, 1980.

Hyde amendment: an analysis of its state progeny. UNIVERSI-
TY OF DAYTON LAW REVIEW 5:313-342, Summer, 1980.

Hyde amendment and Medicaid abortions, by S. Gunty. FORUM
16:825-840, Spring, 1981.

The Hyde Amendment in action. How did the restriction of
federal funds for abortion affect low-income women? by W.
Cates, Jr. JAMA 246(10):1109-1112, September 4, 1981.

Hyde amendment: new implications for equal protection claims. BAYLOR LAW REVIEW 33:295-306, Spring, 1981.

Hydrop degeneration. A histopathological investigation of 260 early abortions, by C. Ladefoged. ACTA OBSTETRICIA ET GYNECOLOGICA SCANDINAVICA 59(6):509-512, 1980.

Hyperplastic lesions and genign tumours associated with oral contraception. Report of ten cases, by A. Dumont, et al. ACTA GASTROENTEROLOGICA BELGICA 43(7-8):285-291, 1980.

Hypertension and hormonal contraceptives, by U. Retzke, et al. ZEITSCHRIFT FUR DIE GESAMTE INNERE MEDIZIN 35(21 Suppl):138-141, November 1, 1980.

Hypertension and oral contraceptive therapy, by M. Colliard, et al. SEMAINES DES HOPITAUX DE PARIS 56(33-36):1407-1411, September 18-25, 1980.

Hypertension in 45 females on oral contraceptives, by M. Salvador, et al. REVUE DE MEDECINE INTERNE 1(2):253-257, 1980.

The IBC as a means of implementing institutional oversight, by B. Talbot, et al. RECOMBINANT DNA TECHNICAL BULLETIN 4(1):19-20, April, 1981.

IUD advisory renews debate on health risk, by R. Alsop. WALL STREET JOURNAL p25, March 30, 1981.

IUD maker wants former insurer to pay for claims, by M. LeRoux. BUSINESS INSURANCE 14:9, July 7, 1980.

IUD update: is it the right contraceptive for you? by M. Newton. FAMILY HEALTH 13:56-57, May, 1981.

IUD users have fewer ectopic pregnancies than noncontraceptors. FAMILY PLANNING PERSPECTIVES 13:150, May-June, 1981.

Identifying biohazards in university research, by D. W. Dreesen.

AMERICAN JOURNAL OF PUBLIC HEALTH 70(10): 1108-1110, October, 1980.

Ideology and medical abortion, by W. Hollway. RADICAL SCIENCE JOURNAL 8:39-59, 1979.

The ideology and politics of birth control in inter-war England, by J. Lewis. WOMEN'S STUDIES INTERNATIONAL QUARTERLY 2(1):33-48, 1979.

If sterilization is oversold, or offered without careful counselling . . . it can blight a woman's life, by P. Toynbee. GUARDIAN p10, May 18, 1981.

Illegal abortion in Latin America, by F. Sanchez-Torres. DRAPER FUND REPORT p14-15, October, 1980.

Illinois abortion statute called 'unconstitutional straightjacket'. THE FAMILY LAW REPORTER: COURT OPINIONS 6(42): 2807-2808, September 2, 1980.

Immediate postabortion insertion of IUDs, by B. Backe, et al. TIDSSKRIFT FOR DEN NORSKE LAEGEFORENING 100 (25):1480-1482, September 10, 1980.

Immune reactivity of women on hormonal contraceptives. Phytohemagglutinin and concanavalin-A induced lymphocyte response, by G. Gerretsen, et al. CONTRACEPTION 22(1):25-29, 1980.

Immunological sterilization of male dogs by BCG, by R. K. Naz, et al. INTERNATIONAL JOURNAL OF ANDROLOGY 4 (1):111-128, February, 1981.

The impact of early use of prescription contraceptives on reducing premarital teenage pregnancies, by L. S. Zabin. FAMILY PLANNING PERSPECTIVES 13:72-74, March-April, 1981.

The impact of family planning clinic programs on adolescent pregnancy, by J. D. Forrest, et al. FAMILY PLANNING PERSPECTIVES 13(3):109-116, May-June, 1981.

The impact of the female marriage squeeze and the contraceptive revolution on sex roles and the women's liberation movement in the U. S., 1960-1975, by D. Heer. JOURNAL OF MARRIAGE AND THE FAMILY 43:49-66, February, 1981.

The impact of laparoscopy on tubal sterilization in United States hospitals, 1970 and 1975 to 1978, by H. B. Peterson, et al. AMERICAN JOURNAL OF OBSTETRICS AND GYNECOLOGY 140(7):811-814, August 1, 1981.

Impairment of antipyrine clearance with low-dose oral contraceptive steroid therapy, by D. R. Abernethy. CLINICAL RESEARCH 29(3):621A, 1980.

Impairment of antipyrine metabolism by low-dose oral contraceptive steroids, by D. R.Abernethy, et al. CLINICAL PHARMACOLOGY AND THERAPEUTICS 29(1):106-110, January, 1981.

Implantation in early abortions 18 previllous and 24 young villous oocytes, by E. Philippe. JOURNAL OF GYNECOLOGIE OBSTETRIQUE ET BIOLOGIE DE LA REPRODUCTION 9(5):513-521, 1980.

Implanted placental tissue simulating uterine fibroids ('inverted placental polyp'), by M. Waxman, et al. DIAGNOSTIC GYNECOLOGY AND OBSTETRICS 2(4):287-289, Winter, 1980.

The importance of clinical investigation in laparoscopy, by L. Keith. JOURNAL OF REPRODUCTIVE MEDICINE 24(6): 236-238, June, 1980.

Imposing mercy; abortion, the Church, and the unwanted, by J. Garvey. COMMONWEAL 108:485-486, September 11, 1981.

Improved results of vasovasostomy after sparing of nerves during vasectomy, by P. C. Esk, et al. FERTILITY AND STERILITY 35(3):363-364, March, 1981.

In defense of Humanae Vitae, by J. F. O'Connor. HOMILETIC AND PASTORAL REVIEW 82:51-54, October, 1981.

In the human life bill, by J. T. Noonan, Jr. CATHOLIC MIND 79:52-64, November, 1981.

In re Grady [(NJ) 405 A 2d 851] : the mentally retarded individual's right to choose sterilization. AMERICAN JOURNAL OF LAW AND MEDICINE 6:559-590, Winter, 1981.

In vitro studies of the characteristics of the release of prostaglandins from viscous solutions, by I. Z. MacKenzie, et al. BRITISH JOURNAL OF OBSTETRICS AND GYNAECOLOGY 87(4):292-295, April, 1980.

Incidence of cerebrovascular lesions in users of oral contraceptives, by D. Borovská, et al. CESKOSLOVENSKA NEUROLOGIE A NEUROCHIRURGIO 44(2):116-120, March, 1981.

The incidence of gonorrhea in an abortion population, by L. Querido, et al. CONTRACEPTION 22(4):441-444, October, 1980.

Incidence of miscarriage. BRIEFS 44:131-132, November, 1980.

Incidence of the 9qh+ variant in subjects with occupational exposure to radiation and in cases of reproductive pathology, by M. Milani-Comparetti, et al. BOLLETTINO DELLA SOCIETA ITALIANA DI BIOLOGIA SPERIMENTALE 57(4): 351-354, February 28, 1981.

Incidence of positive toxoplasmosis hemagglutination test in the nigerian (Ibo) women with recurrent abortions, by U. Megafu, et al. INTERNATIONAL JOURNAL OF FERTILITY 26(2): 132-134, 1981.

Incidence, prevalence and trends of acute pelvic inflammatory disease and its consequences in industrialized countries, by L. Westrom. AMERICAN JOURNAL OF OBSTETRICS AND GYNECOLOGY 138(7 Part 2):880-892, 1980.

Increased leukemia, lymphoma, and spontaneous abortion in Western New York following a flood disaster, by D. T. Janerich, et al. PUBLIC HEALTH REPORTS 96(4):350-

356, July-August, 1981.

Increased synthesis of aortic collagen and elastin in experimental atherosclerosis. Inhibition by contraceptive steroids, by G. M. Fischer, et al. ATHEROSCLEROSIS 39(4):463-467, July, 1981.

An incremental-dose combined oestrogen-progestogen oral contraceptive: cycle control and endometrial changes, by S. K. Khoo, et al. AUSTRALIAN AND NEW ZEALAND JOURNAL OF OBSTETRICS AND GYNAECOLOGY 20(3):168-171, August, 1980.

Indications for female sterilization in our surgical records, by D. Novaković, et al. JUGOSLAVENSKA GINEKOLOGIJA I OPSTETRICIJA 20(3-4):148-152, May-August, 1980.

Indonesia, by S. Surjaningrat, et al. STUDIES IN FAMILY PLANNING 11(11):320, November, 1980.

Indonesia plans ten years ahead. POPULI 8(1):14, 1981.

Induced abortion and health problems in developing countries [letter], by R. W. Rochat, et al. LANCET 2(8192):484, August 30, 1980.

Induced abortion and subsequent pregnancy loss [letter], by C. S. Chung. JAMA 245(11):1119, March 20, 1981.

Induced abortion by means of vaginal hysterectomy. Studies on the indications and risks of this method, by K. W. Schweppe, et al. ZENTRALBLATT FUR GYNAEKOLOGIE 102(24):1431-1436, 1980.

Induced abortion in developing countries [letter], by C. B. Goodhart. LANCET 2(8195 pt 1):645, September 20, 1980.

Induced abortion in the Netherlands: a decade of experience 1970-1980, by E. Ketting, et al. STUDIES IN FAMILY PLANNING 11:385-394, December, 1980.

Induced first-trimester abortion and fenestration of the uterine wall in a subsequent pregnancy, by G. Lindmark, et al. ACTA OBSTETRICIA ET GYNECOLOGICA SCANDINAVICA 60 (1):96, 1981.

Induction of abortion during the second and third trimester of pregnancy with sulprostone, by S. Heinzl, et al. GEBURT-SHILFE UND FRAUENHEILKUNDE 41(3):231-236, March, 1981.

Induction of abortion with sulprostone, a uteroselective prosta-glandin E2 derivative: intramuscular route of application, by K. Schmidt-Gollwitzer, et al. INTERNATIONAL JOURNAL OF FERTILITY 26(2):86-93, 1981.

Induction of labor with anencephalic fetus, by R. Osathanondh, et al. OBSTETRICS AND GYNECOLOGY 56(5):655-657, November, 1980.

Infant mortality and family planning, by S. Y. L. Arora. JOUR-NAL OF FAMILY WELFARE 26:73-78, June, 1980.

The influence of a combined oral contraceptive pill and menstru-al cycle phase on digital microvascular haemodynamics, by J. E. Tooke, et al. CLINICAL SCIENCE 61(1):91-95, July, 1981.

Influence of dietary fats and an oral contraceptive on plasma lipids, high density lipoproteins, gallstones, and atherosclero-sis in african green monkeys, by R. W. St. Clair, et al. ATHESCLEROSIS 37(1):103-121, September, 1980.

Influence of environmental chemicals on drug therapy in humans: studies with contraceptive steroids, by A. M. Breckenridge, et al. CIBA FOUNDATION SYMPOSIUM (76):289-306, 1980.

Influence of fatty acids and an oral contraceptive on the eyes of a nonhuman primate, by W. K. O'Steen, et al. EXPERI-MENTAL AND MOLECULAR PATHOLOGY 34(1):43-51, February, 1981.

The influence of memory factors on contraceptive information acquisition and choice, by W. D. Hoyer. DAI 42(3), 1981.

Influence of oral contraceptives of differing dosages on alpha-1-antitrypsin, gamma-glutamyltransferase and alkaline phosphatase, by B. Herbeth, et al. CLINICA CHIMICA ACTA 112(3):293-299, May, 1981.

Inhalation of gastric contents [letter] , by E. Mankowitz, et al. BRITISH JOURNAL OF ANAESTHESIA 53(7):778-779, 1981.

Initial action of synthetic sexual steroids on serum-haptoglobin concentration, by G. Klinger, et al. ZENTRALBLATT FUR GYNAEKOLOGIE 103(1):41-45, 1981.

Injectable contraception [letter] , by H. Ratner. MEDICAL JOURNAL OF AUSTRALIA 1(11):598-600, May 30, 1981.

Injectable and oral contraceptive steroids in relation to some neurotransmitters in the rat brain, by T. T. Daabees, et al. BIOCHEMICAL PHARMACOLOGY 30(12):1581-1585, June 15, 1981.

Injectable contraception [letter] , by J. R. Edwards. MEDICAL JOURNAL OF AUSTRALIA 1(12):651-652, June 13, 1981.

—, by H. Ratner. MEDICAL JOURNAL OF AUSTRALIA 1(11): 598-600, May 30, 1981.

Injury to retroperitoneal vessels; a serious complication of gynaecological laparoscopy, by M. Rust, et al. ANAESTHESIE—INTENSIVTHERAPIE—NOTFALLMEDEZIN 15(4):356-359, August, 1980.

Insulin receptors in circulating erythrocytes and monocytes from women on oral contraceptives or pregnant women near term, by J. C. Tsibris, et al. JOURNAL OF CLINICAL ENDOCRINOLOGY AND METABOLISM 51(4):711-717, October, 1980.

Interaction of ethinyloestradiol with ascorbic acid in man, by D. J. Back, et al. BRITISH MEDICAL JOURNAL 282(6275): 1516, May 9, 1981.

The interaction of phenobarbital and other anticonvulsants with oral contraceptive steroid therapy, by D. J. Back, et al. CONTRACEPTION 22(5):495-503, November, 1980.

Interindividual variation and drug interactions with hormonal steroid contraceptives, by D. J. Back, et al. DRUGS 21(1): 46-61, January, 1981.

Internal medicine problems regarding contraception. Part I, by M. Mall-Haefeli. SCHWEIZERISCHE MEDIZINISCHE WOCHENSCHRIFT 110(36):1314-1319, September 6, 1980.

The international politics of contraception [commenting on United States economic assistance programs], by J. Kasun. POLICY REPORT p135-152, Winter, 1981.

Interruption of pregnancy with the aspiration method. Technical suggestions, by E. Painvain, et al. MINERVA GINECOLOGIA 31(10):933-937, October, 1980.

Interstitial pregnancy after salpingectomy—not recognized in first trimester induced abortion, by W. Grunberger. GEBURTSHILFE UND FRAUENHEILKUNDE 40(8):722-724, August, 1980.

Interview of Bernard Nathanson; interview, by B. Nathanson. OUR SUNDAY VISITOR 70:3-5, September 20, 1981.

Intestinal infarction caused by mesenteric venous thrombosis during contraceptive treatment, by G. Melodia, et al. CHIRURGIA ITALIANA 31(6):1132-1137, December, 1979.

Intracervical application of prostaglandin F2 alpha gel as low risk method of cervical dilatation for therapeutic abortion, by H. Fritzsche, et al. GEBURTSHILFE UND FRAUENHEILKUNDE 41(3):237-238, March, 1981.

Intrauterine contraception with levonorgestrel: a comparative randomised clinical performance study, by C. G. Nilsson, et al. LANCET 1(8220 Pt 1):577-580, March 14, 1981.

Intrauterine haematoma. An ultrasonic study of threatened

abortion, by M. Mantoni, et al. BRITISH JOURNAL OF
OBSTETRICS AND GYNAECOLOGY 88(1):47-51, January, 1981.

Intrauterine infection with mumps virus, by A. G. Garcia, et al.
OBSTETRICS AND GYNECOLOGY 56(6):756-759, Decem-
ber, 1980.

Intravenous infusion of 10% ethanol as a method of inhibiting
uterine contraction in cases of threatened abortion and premature labor, by J. Czapla. GINEKOLOGIA POLSKA 52
(2):135-140, January, 1981.

Investigation of the prophylactic effect of tinidazole on the postoperative infection rate of patients undergoing vacuum aspiration, by K. Krohn. SCANDINAVIAN JOURNAL OF INFEC-
TIOUS DISEASES 26(Suppl):101-103, 1981.

Ireland's bishops decide, by M. Holland. NEW STATESMAN
101:6-8, April 3, 1981.

An Irish solution, by D. Fisher. COMMONWEAL 108:5-6, January 16, 1981.

Irish women's eyes aren't smiling, by M. Wilson. OFF OUR
BACKS January, 1981.

Irreversible contraception in women: a supplementary method
of family planning, by R. Sudik, et al. DAS DEUTSCHE
GESUNDHEITSWISSEN 35(45):1785-1794, 1980.

Is government paving abortion's way as shortcut cure? by F.
Franzonia. OUR SUNDAY VISITOR 69:6, April 5, 1981.

Is a hysterectomy justifiable to prevent post-tubal ligation
syndrome? by R. Maheux, et al. UNION MEDICALE DU
CANADA 109(12):1753-1756, December, 1980.

Is it right? 12,500 nurses speak out. How do your colleagues
view abortion, sterilization, and birth control? by R.
Sandroff. RN 43:24-30, October, 1980.

Is it worth dying for? by D. L. Breo. AMERICAN MEDICAL NEWS 24(19):16-18, May 15, 1981.

Is the pill dangerous? by H. Seiden. TODAY p21, December 13, 1980.

Is Swedish sex for us? by D. W. Ferm. COMMONWEAL 108:363-366, June 19, 1981.

Italian women give the world a victory, by H. Stavrou. MS MAGAZINE 10:21, August, 1981.

Italy's "third way" on abortion faces a test, by R. R. Ruether. CHRISTIAN CRISIS 41(130):141-143, May 11, 1981.

It's time to take male infertility seriously, by C. W. Cooke, et al. MS MAGAZINE 9:89-91, March, 1981.

Jaundice and hepatic hemangioma after ten years of oral contraception and recent administration of triacetyloleandomycin [letter], by D. Meyniel, et al. THERAPIE 35(6):754-755, November-December, 1980.

Jean-Paul II et l'avortement, by R. Bourgault. RELATIONS 40:295-296, November, 1980.

Joe Scheidler: pro-life's Green Beret, by D. Morris. OUR SUNDAY VISITOR 70:6+, September 6, 1981.

Judge O'Connor, continued. NATIONAL REVIEW 33:881-882, August 7, 1981.

Juli Loesch fights abortion and the nuclear arms race, by L. H. Pumphrey. OUR SUNDAY VISITOR 70:6, August 2, 1981.

Juridical considerations on the problem of sterilization, by E. Germano. MINERVA GINECOLOGIA 32(6):449-452, June, 1980.

Justice Harry A. Blackmun: the abortion decisions, by D. Fuqua. ARKANSAS LAW REVIEW 34:276-296, 1980.

Knowledge and use of contraceptive methods by university physicians and medical students, by G. C. Di Renzo, et al. ANNALI DI OSTETRICIA, GINECOLOGIA, MEDICINA PERINATALE 100(4):213-232, July-August, 1979.

Labor; fertility and the workplace, by J. W. Singer. ENVIRON-MENT 22:5+, December, 1980.

Laicismo e clericalismo nel Parlamento italiano tra la legge sul divorzio e quella sull'aborto, by A. Tempestini. POLITICA DEL DIRITTO 11(3):407-428, 1980.

Laparoscopic and minilaparotomy female sterilisation compared in 15,167 cases, by S. D. Mumford, et al. LANCET 2(8203): 1066-1070, November 15, 1980.

Laparoscopic sterilization in a community hospital with a two-year follow-up, by J. Tayloe. NORTH CAROLINA MEDI-CAL JOURNAL 41(9):581-582, September, 1980.

Laparoscopic sterilization—the Trinidad experience, by S. Roopnarinesingh. WEST INDIAN MEDICAL JOURNAL 30 (2):90-93, June, 1981.

Laparoscopic sterilization under local anesthesia, by O. H. Jensen, et al. TIDSSKRIFT FOR DEN NORSKE LAEGEFOREN-ING 100(34-36):2036-2037, December 10, 1980.

Laparoscopic sterilization using tubal rings and clips, by E. Borko, et al. JUGOSLAVENSKA GINEKOLOGIJA I OP-STETRICIJA 20(3-4):140-145, May-August, 1980.

Laparoscopic sterilization with Falope rings [letter], by H. J. Orford. SOUTH AFRICAN MEDICAL JOURNAL 59(11): 361, March 14, 1981.

Laparoscopic sterilization with the Falope ring: experience with 10,000 women in rural camps, by P. V. Mehta. OBSTETRICS AND GYNECOLOGY 57(3):345-350, March, 1981.

Laparoscopic sterilization with the Hulka-Clemens clip. Review of 215 cases, by C. Lecart, et al. JOURNAL DE GYNECOL-

OGIE OBSTETRIQUE ET BIOLOGIE DE LA REPRODUC-
TION 9(2):253-259, 1980.

Laparoscopic sterilization with room air insufflation: preliminary
report, by M. O. Diaz, et al. INTERNATIONAL JOURNAL
OF GYNAECOLOGY AND OBSTETRICS 18(2):119-122,
September-October, 1980.

Laparoscopic tubal electrocoagulation for sterilization: 5000
cases, by K. Limpaphayom, et al. INTERNATIONAL JOUR-
NAL OF GYNAECOLOGY AND OBSTETRICS 18(6):411-
413, 1980.

Laparoscopic tube sterilization. Methods and their safety, by H.
Frangenheim. GYNAEKOLOGISCHE RUNDSCHAU 20
(Suppl 1):142-143, June, 1980.

Late abortions linked to education, age and irregular periods.
FAMILY PLANNING PERSPECTIVES 13:86, March-April,
1981.

Late consequences of abortion [editorial]. BRITISH MEDICAL
JOURNAL 282(6276):1564-1565, May 16, 1981.

Late consequences of abortion [letter], by W. Savage. BRITISH
MEDICAL JOURNAL 283(6248):140-141, July 11, 1981.

Late tubal patency following tubal ligation, by G. M. Grunert.
FERTILITY AND STERILITY 35(4):406-408, April, 1981.

Law and the life sciences, by G. J. Annas. HASTINGS CENTER
REPORT 11:8-9, February, 1981.

Law and the life sciences—sterilization of the mentally retarded:
a decision for the courts, by G. Annas. HASTINGS CENTER
REPORT 11:23-24, April, 1981.

Law and the nurse. 5. From all points of view, by J. Finch.
NURSING MIRROR 153(1):29-30, July 1, 1981.

Law Lords split on prostglandin abortion, by J. Finch. NURS-
ING FOCUS 2:224-225, March, 1981.

Law of fertility regulation in the United States: a 1980 review, by S. L. Isaacs. JOURNAL OF FAMILY LAW 19:65-96, November, 1980.

Law 194 on voluntary abortion [letter], by M. M. Marzi, et al. ANNALI DI OSTETRICIA, GINECOLOGIA, MEDICINA PERINATALE 100(4):284-285, July-August, 1979.

Lectori Salutem, on the analysis of abortion letters in the Netherlands, by L. Brunt. THE NETHERLANDS JOURNAL OF SOCIOLOGY 15(2):141-153, December, 1979.

The left and the right to life; cond from The Progressive, by M. Meehan. CATHOLIC DIGEST 45:36-41, December, 1980.

Legal abortion, by C. Tietze. SCIENTIFIC AMERICAN 236:1, January 21-27, 1977.

Legal abortion, family planning services largest factors in reducing U. S. neonatal mortality rate. FAMILY PLANNING PERSPECTIVES 13:84-85, March-April, 1981.

Legal abortion. Preliminary evaluations at the S. Barbara di Rogliano Hospital, by C. Giannice, et al. MINERVA GINECOLOGIA 33(5):479-487, May, 1981.

Legal abortions among teenagers in Canada, 1974 through 1978, by A. Wadhera, et al. CANADIAN MEDICAL ASSOCIATION 122(12):1386-1390, June 21, 1980.

Legal abortions in Tennessee 1974-1978, by H. K. Atrash, et al. JOURNAL OF THE TENNESSEE MEDICAL ASSOCIATION 73(12):855-863, December, 1980.

The legal battle for reproductive rights in Europe, by A. D. Rollier. DRAPER FUND REPORT p16-18, October, 1980.

Legal crusade of the eternal children [mentally handicapped in Canada], by P. Jahn. MACLEANS 94:45-46, November 30, 1981.

Legal regulations as an instrument of family planning, by B.

Colaković, et al. JUGOSLAVENSKA GINEKOLOGIJA I OPSTETRICIJA 20(3-4):124-126, May-August, 1980.

The legal right to abortion: what's left? by A. H. Bernstein. HOSPITALS 55(9):41-42+, May 1, 1981.

Legal semantics. Nurses and non-surgical abortions, by K. Rae. NURSING TIMES 77(9):351, February 26, 1981.

The legal status of women in Israel, by S. E. Shanoff. CONGRESSIONAL MONITOR 48:9-12, June, 1981.

Legal statutes on sterilization, by K. Zupančič. JUGOSLAVENSKA GINEKOLOGIJA I OPSTETRICIJA 20(3-4):108-111, May-August, 1980.

Legal trends and issues in voluntary sterilization. POPULATION REPORTS 9(2):73, March-April, 1981.

Legislation and abortion: the fight continues. Pt. 4: the constitution under attack, by N. Z. Dershowitz. CONGRESSIONAL MONITOR 48:8, April, 1981.

Legislating life [strategy for reversing Roe v. Wade devised by S. Galebach]. NATION 232:355-356, March 28, 1981.

Legitimacy and limits of freedom of choice, by K. Cauthen. CHRISTIAN CENTURY 98:702-704, July 1-8, 1981.

Leon Rosenberg on the "human life" bill [excerpts from testimony, April 1981], by L. Rosenberg. SCIENCE 212:907, May 22, 1981.

Letter from Chiangmai, by H. Leong. FAR EASTERN ECONOMIC REVIEW 110:94-95, November 14-20, 1980.

Levonorgestrel, by S. J. Hopkins. DRUGS TODAY 16(6):186-190, 1980.

Life and the 14th amendment. AMERICA 144:397, May 16, 1981.

Limited usefulness of the breath test in evaluation of drug metabolism: a study in human oral contraceptive users treated with dimethylaminoantipyrine and diazepam, by A. Sonnenberg, et al. HEPATOGASTROENTEROLOGY 27 (2):104-108, April, 1980.

Limits of judicial intervention in abortion politics, by R. Tatalovich, et al. CHRISTIAN CENTURY 99:16-20, January 6-13, 1982.

Lincoln hospital: the sterile solution, by J. Conason. VILLAGE VOICE 26(2):1+, February 18, 1981.

Liver cell carcinoma in young women possibly induced by oral contraceptives, by F. Amtrup, et al. ACTA OBSTETRICIA ET GYNECOLOGICA SCANDINAVICA 59(6):567-569, 1980.

Liver function tests and low-dose estrogen oral contraceptives, by J. Dickerson, et al. CONTRACEPTION 22(6):597-603, December, 1980.

Liver rupture after prolonged use of contraceptive, by G. Böttger, et al. ZEITSCHRIFT FUR DIE GESAMTE INNERE MEDIZIN 36(3) Suppl):226-227, February 1, 1981.

La Logica Coerenza del Paradosso di una legge Senza Diritto: Un'interpretazione della legge sull'aborto, by S. Amato. RIVISTA INTERNAZIONALE DI FILOSOFIA DEL DIRITTO 57:197-1206, 1980.

Long-term follow-up of mothers who received high doses of stilboestrol and ethisterone in pregnancy [letter], by M. A. Vance, et al. BRITISH MEDICAL JOURNAL 281(6255): 1638, December 13, 1980.

The long term safety hormonal steroid contraceptives, by E. G. McQueen. DRUGS 21(6):460-463, June, 1981.

Long-term sequelae following legally induced abortion, by E. B. Obel. DANISH MEDICAL BULLETIN 27(2):61-74, April, 1980.

Looking at labels [use of terms pro-life and anti-abortion by the print media]. CHRISTIAN CENTURY 98:404, April 15, 1981.

Loss of blood in artificial abortion performed under paracervical anesthesia, by M. Oreščanin. JUGOSLAVENSKA GINEKOL-OGIJA I OPSTETRICIJA 19(3-4):167-169, May-August, 1980.

Low dose injectable contraceptive norethisterone enanthate 20mg monthly—I. Clinical trials, by K. Prema, et al. CON-TRACEPTION 23(1):11-22, January, 1981.

—. II. Metabolic side effects, by M. S. Bamji, et al. CONTRACEP-TION 23(1):23-36, January, 1981.

Low serum creatine kinase values in contraceptive steroid users [letter], by U. Gupta. CLINICAL CHEMISTRY 27(9): 1624, September, 1981.

Luteal function after tubal sterilization, by J. Donnez, et al. OB-STETRICS AND GYNECOLOGY 57(1):65-68, January, 1981.

Luteolytic activity of luteinizing hormone-releasing hormone and D-serine (*tert*-butyl)-6-deglysinamide luteinizing hor-mone-releasing hormone ethylamide: a new and physiological approach to contraception in women, by A. Leman, et al. INTERNATIONAL JOURNAL OF FERTILITY 25(3):203-212, 1980.

Maine abortion statutes of 1979: testing the constitutional limits. MAINE LAW REVIEW 32:315-353, 1980.

Malaysia. STUDIES IN FAMILY PLANNING 11(11):330, November, 1980.

Male "pill" blocks sperm enzyme [gossypol inhibition of lactate dehydrogenase X], by T. H. Maugh. SCIENCE 212:314, April 17, 1981.

Male pill [gossypol's inhibiting effect on lactate dehydrogenase

X. SCIQUEST 54:4, May-June, 1981.

Male "pill" seen as vaginal spermicide [gossypol] . MEDICAL WORLD NEWS 22:21-22, May 11, 1981.

Mandatory motherhood. PLAYBOY 27:66, November, 1980.

Manipulating the choice on CBS, by B. J. Uddo. AMERICA 144: 230-232, March 21, 1981.

Manipulation of duration of action of a synthetic prostaglandin analogue (TPT) assessed in the pregnant beagle bitch, by B. H. Vickery, et al. PROSTAGLANDINS AND MEDICINE 5(2):93-100, August, 1980.

Margaret Sanger: birth control's successful revolutionary, by D. Wardell. AMERICAN JOURNAL OF PUBLIC HEALTH 70: 736-742, July, 1980. Discussion. 71:91, January, 1981.

Marie Stopes; botany and birth control, by J. Timson. NEW SCIENTIST 88:177, October 16, 1980.

Marketing population control . . . Population Services International, by P. Drummond. HEALTH AND SOCIAL SERVICE JOURNAL 91:672, June 5, 1981.

Marketing strategies in health education, by G. Miaoulis, et al. JOURNAL OF HEALTH CARE MARKETING 1(1):35-44, Winter, 1980-1981.

Marymount Hospital, Garfield Heights, Ohio. Worry clinic teaches effective coping methods. HOSPITAL PROGRESS 62(7):12+, July, 1981.

Mass screening for neural tube defects, by G. B. Kolata. HAST-INGS CENTER REPORT 10:8-10, December, 1980.

Massachusetts abortion statute requiring waiting period upheld. THE FAMILY LAW REPORTER: COURT OPINIONS 6(47): 2900-2901, October 7, 1980.

Mater et Magistra revisited, by C. S. Mihanovich. SOCIAL JUS-

TICE 72:163-166, September-October, 1981.

Maternal employment and adolescent sexual behavior, by R. O. Hansson, et al. JOURNAL OF YOUTH AND ADOLESCENCE 10:55-60, February, 1981.

Matter of blood, sweat and the pill, by P. De Vries. MACLEAN'S 94:56-57, March 16, 1981.

Measuring potential fertility through null segments: an exploratory analysis, by R. G. Potter, et al. SOCIAL BIOLOGY 26: 314-329, Winter, 1979.

Measurement by isotope dilution mass spectrometry of 17 alpha-ethynyloestradiol-17 beta and norethisterone in serum of women taking oral contraceptives, by L. Siekmann, et al. BIOMEDICAL MASS SPECTROMETRY 7(11-12):511-514, November, 1980.

Mechanism of action of an orally active PGE1-analogue in pregnant guinea-pigs, by W. Elger, et al. PROSTAGLANDINS 21(2):259-266, February, 1981.

Medicaid not required to fund medically necessary abortions, by G. J. Annas. NURSING LAW AND ETHICS 1(8):3+, October, 1980.

Medical and social indications of sterilization, by L. Gagliardi, et al. MINERVA GINECOLOGIA 32(6):459-464, June, 1980.

Medical-behavioral 'explosion' affects hospital operation, policy, by C. V. Keeran, Jr., et al. HOSPITALS 55(9):56-59, May 1, 1981.

Medical news: are spermicides safe? by S. Katz. CHATELAINE 54:37, August, 1981.

—: the twice-a-year pellet, by S. Katz. CHATELAINE 54:37, August, 1981.

Medullary infarction—was it depo-provera? by C. J. Oon, et al. SINGAPORE MEDICAL JOURNAL 21(5):717-719, October, 1980.

Meeting of the Industrial Practices Subcommittee of the Federal Interagency Advisory Committee on Recombinant DNA Research [news]. RECOMBINANT DNA TECHNICAL BULLETIN 4(2):64-67, July, 1981.

Meeting of the Large-Scale Review Working Group of the Recombinant DNA Advisory Committee [news]. RECOMBINANT DNA TECHNICAL BULLETIN 4(2):68-70, July, 1981.

Men and the abortion experience: an exploration study on their self-reported educational interests, by K. L. Rotter, PhD. DAI 41(8)

Men and family planning, by B. Stokes. WORLDWATCH PAPER 41:50, December, 1980.

Menarche of young girls and tolerance of hormonal contraceptives-results of a field study of 33,000 cases, by J. M. Wenderlein. ZENTRALBLATT FUR GYNAEKOLOGIE 102(17): 974-980, 1980.

Menstrual blood loss with contraceptive subdermal levonorgestrel implants, by C. G. Nilsson, et al. FERTILITY AND STERILITY 35(3):304-306, March, 1981.

Menstrual pattern changes in laparoscopic sterilization patients whose last pregnancy was terminated by therapeutic abortion. A two-year follow-up study, by H. M. Kwak, et al. JOURNAL OF REPRODUCTIVE MEDICINE 25(2):67-71, August, 1980.

Messages with no meaning. POPULI 8(1):38, 1981.

Method of studying the sociomedical conditions of women with spontaneous abortions in the area of the Dr. Mara Maleeva-Zhivkova III Municipal Consolidated Hospital in the city of Sofia, by I. Vasileva. AKUSHERSTVO I GINEKOLOGIIA 20(1):13-17, 1981.

Methodological kit: monitoring statistics relating to the control of fertility and the provision of abortion, by J. R. Ashton. COMMUNITY MEDICINE 3(1):44-54, February, 1981.

Methods of contraception, with special reference to sterilization [letter], by L. Lampé. ORVOSI HETILAP 121(39):2422, September 28, 1980.

Methods of female sterilization, by A. Omaghen. JUGOSLA-VENSKA GINEKOLOGIJA I OPSTETRICIJA 20(3-4):135-139, May-August, 1980.

Methods of the sterilization of women in Norwegian hospitals, by P. E. Bordahl, et al. TIDSSKRIFT FOR DEN NORSKE LAEGEFORENING 100(34-36):2030-2032, December 10, 1980.

Metropolitan dominance and family planning in Barbados, by H. R. Jones. SOCIAL AND ECONOMIC STUDIES 26(3):327-338, September, 1977.

Microscoop method of doing two-layer vas anastomosis, by M. R. Sutton. JOURNAL OF UROLOGY 124(5):620-621, November, 1980.

Microscopic study of human fallopian tubes after laparoscopic sterilization, by J. Donnez, et al. JOURNAL DE GYNECOL-OGIE OBSTETRIQUE ET BIOLOGIE DE LA REPRODUC-TION 9(2):193-199, 1980.

Microsurgical anastomosis of vas deferens: technical aspects, by M. Srougi, et al. AMB; REVISTA DA ASSOCIACAO MEDI-CA BRASILEIRA 27(1):8-11, January, 1981.

Microsurgical reanastomosis of the fallopian tubes for reversal of sterilization, by G. M. Grunert, et al. OBSTETRICS AND GYNECOLOGY 58(2):148-151, August, 1981.

Microsurgical reversal of female sterilization [letter], by W. W. Hurd, et al. FERTILITY AND STERILITY 36(1):122-123, July, 1981.

Microsurgical reversal of vasectomy, by D. C. Martin. AMERI-CAN JOURNAL OF SURGERY 142(1):48-50, July, 1981.

Microsurgical tubal reanastomosis—the role of splints, by D. R. Meldrum. OBSTETRICS AND GYNECOLOGY 57(5):613-619, May, 1981.

Microsurgical two-layer vasovasostomy. Simplified technique using hinged, folding-approximating clamp, by A. M. Belker. UROLOGY 16(4):376-381, October, 1980.

Microsurgical vasovasostomy: immunologic consequences and subsequent fertility, by A. J. Thomas, Jr., et al. FERTILITY AND STERILITY 35(4):447-450, April, 1981.

Midtrimester abortion associated with septicaemia caused by Campylobacter jejuni, by G. L. Gilbert, et al. MEDICAL JOURNAL OF AUSTRALIA 1(11):585-586, May 30, 1981.

Mid-trimester abortion by vaginal administration of 9-deoxo-16, 16-dimethyl-9-methylene-PGE2, by M. Bygdeman, et al. CONTRACEPTION 22(2):153-164, August, 1980.

Midtrimester abortion induced by hyperosmolar urea and prosta-glandin F2 alpha in patients with previous cesarean section: clinical course and potential for uterine rupture, by M. F. Atienza, et al. AMERICAN JOURNAL OF OBSTETRICS AND GYNECOLOGY 138(1):55-59, September 1, 1980.

Miscarriage; excerpt from forthcoming book *When pregnancy fails, families coping with marriage, stillbirth, and infant death*, by S. O. Borg, et al. CHATELAINE 54:46+, May, 1981.

Miscarriage: putting the myths to rest, by L. A. Michel. LIFE AND HEALTH 96:16-18, February, 1981.

Missed abortion, hydatidiform mole and intra-uterine fetal death treated with 15-methyl-prostaglandin F 2-alpha, by E. G. Boes. SOUTH AFRICAN MEDICAL JOURNAL 58 (22):878-880, November 29, 1980.

Missed abortions and some organochlorine compounds: organo-
chlorine insecticides (OCI) and polychlorinated biphenyls
(PCBs), by B. Bercovici, et al. ACTA MEDICINAE LEGALIS
ET SOCIALIS 30(3):177-185, 1980.

Modern methods of regulating fertility, by S. I. Sleptsova.
AKUSHERSTVO I GINEKOLOGIIA (10):5-8, October,
1980.

Modified isthmography in the management of mid-trimester
abortion, by Y. A. Naguib, et al. JOURNAL OF THE EGYP-
TIAN MEDICAL ASSOCIATION 61(5-6):375-388, 1978.

Moral aspects of sterilization, by D. G. Arosio. MINERVA GINE-
COLOGIA 32(6):453, June, 1980.

The moral development of black adolescents and its relationship
to contraceptive use, by B. Fawcett. DAI 42(5), 1981.

Moral theology and family planning, by M. Reidy. FURROW 32:
343-361, June, 1981.

Morality, law, and politics: abortion [special issue; with editorial
comment]. COMMONWEAL 108:643-664, November 20,
1981.

The morality of birth control: unfinished business? by R. E.
Burns. US CATHOLIC 46:2-3, January, 1981.

More birth control blues [study by H. Jick linking use of spermicidal contraceptives to birth defects and miscarriages, by P.
DeVries. MACLEANS 94:47-48, May 11, 1981.

More children from the fit; less from the unfit, by M. C.
Schwartz. OUR SUNDAY VISITOR 70:5, June 14, 1981.

More contraindications to the pill [letter], by J. P. Realini.
PEDIATRICS 66(4):644-645, October, 1980.

Morning after pill—both synthetic, natural estrogens are effective. FAMILY PLANNING PERSPECTIVES 13:148, May-
June, 1981.

Morphologic effects of oral contraceptives (Norinyle) on the guinea pig liver, by C. S. Kim, et al. YONSEI MEDICAL JOURNAL 21(1):43-51, 1980.

Morphologic manifestations of immune responses in disrupted tubal pregnancy, by B. I. Glukhovets, et al. ARKHIV ANOTOMII, GISTOLOGII I EMBRIOLOGII 79(12):99-101, December, 1980.

Morphological alterations of rabbit oviducts after ligation of the isthmus or ampulla, by D. Bernhardt-Huth, et al. ARCHIVES OF GYNECOLOGY 229(3):167-176, 1980.

Morphological observations of placenta in 56 cases of mid-term abortion induced by Yuanhua preparations, by Y. G. Liang. CHUNG HUA FU CHAN KO TSA CHIH 14(4):290-292, 1979.

Morphology of Fallopian tubes removed from a patient after failure of clip sterilization, by K. A. Walz, et al. ARCHIVES OF GYNECOLOGY 230(2):123-135, 1980.

Morphology of rabbit oviduct after microsurgical techniques for reanastomosis of the isthmus or ampella, by D. Bernhardt-Huth, et al. ARCHIVES OF GYNECOLOGY 230(3):251-262, 1981.

Mortality associated with medical termination of pregnancy, by M. A. Deshmukh, et al. JOURNAL OF POSTGRADUATE MEDICINE 26(2):121-126, April, 1980.

Mortality in oral contraceptive users [letter], by M. P. Vessey, et al. LANCET 1(8219):549-550, March 7, 1981.

Mortality risk associated with female sterilization, by J. M. Aubert, et al. INTERNATIONAL JOURNAL OF GYNAE-COLOGY AND OBSTETRICS 18(6):406-410, 1980.

The most dangerous moment, by A. Cockburn. VILLAGE VOICE October 8, 1980.

Most dissent from church line on contraception [Irish students],

by J. Walshe. TIMES HIGHER EDUCATION SUPPLEMENT
413:5, October 3, 1980.

Most permanent birth control, by P. Span. GLAMOUR 79:236-
237+, March, 1981.

Motive and metaphor in Faulkner's That evening sun, by E. W.
Pitcher. STUDIES IN SHORT FICTION 18:131-135, Spring,
1981.

Multivariate relationships between modernity value orientations
and family planning indicators. Bishwa Nath Mukherjee,
Council for Social Development, New Delhi. POPULATION
AND ENVIRONMENT 4(1):24, Spring, 1981.

Musings on motherhood, Marshall, molecules: a passage through
the heart of maternal darkness from God's creation to man's,
by A. Wallach. BLACK LAW JOURNAL 6:88-141, 1978.

The myth of motherhood: a study of attitudes toward motherhood, by R. T. Hare-Mustin. PSYCHOLOGY OF WOMEN
QUARTERLY 4:114-128, Fall, 1979.

NAS enters human life bill debate [Helms-Hyde bill] . SCIENCE
NEWS 119:293, May 9, 1981.

NFP and ecological mothering, by G. G. Sweet. MARRIAGE 63:
21, September, 1981.

NFP: the facts, by J. Marshall. TABLET 234:1197-1198, December 6, 1980.

NFP programs provide consumer choice, benefit hospital, by K.
Daly, et al. HOSPITAL PROGRESS 61:56-58, October,
1980.

NIOSH perspective on commercial recombinant DNA/biotech-
nology development, by S. Pauker. RECOMBINANT DNA
TECHNICAL BULLETIN 4(2):61-64, July, 1981.

NJ Supreme Court drafts strict guidelines for sterilization of
mental incompetents: hospitals should require court authori-

zation, by R. L. Schwartz. HEALTH LAW VIGIL 4(10):6-7, May 15, 1981.

Nasal spray [LHRH] contraceptive, by J. Labreche. CHATE-LAINE 54:26, January, 1981.

Natural alternative [sympto-thermal]. TODAY p21, December 13, 1980.

Natural birth control, by A. Westmore. AUSTRALIAN NURSES JOURNAL 10:51-52, November, 1980.

Natural family planning III. Intermenstrual symptoms and estimated time of ovulation, by T. W. Hilgers, et al. OBSTETRICS AND GYNECOLOGY 58(2):152-153, August, 1981.

—. IV. The identification of postovulatory infertility, by T. W. Hilgers, et al. OBSTETRICS AND GYNECOLOGY 58(3): 345-350, September, 1981.

Natural family planning: periodic abstinence as a method of fertility control. SOCIAL JUSTICE REVIEW 72:185-187, September-October, 1981.

Natural family planning study validates treatment's success; St. Vincent Hospital, Green Bay, Wisconsin, by L. Dolack. HOSPITAL PROGRESS 62:58-61, October, 1981.

Natural family planning: women deserve the truth, by H. Hart. JOURNAL OF THE AMERICAN COLLEGE HEALTH ASSOCIATION 29(6):311, June, 1981.

Natural law, the teaching of the church, and the regulation of the rhythm of human fecundity, by J. T. Noonan, Jr. AMERICAN JOURNAL OF JURISPRUDENCE 25:16-37, 1980.

The natural way, by L. O'Connor. SIGN 61:30-33, September, 1981.

Navigating dangerous waters of public opinion polls, by F. Franzonia. OUR SUNDAY VISITOR 70:6, July 5, 1981.

Necrotic uterine myomatosis—a rare complication following vaginal termination of pregnancy by suction, by W. Gubisch, et al. ZENTRALBLATT FUR GYNAEKOLOGIE 103(8): 456-459, 1981.

A needs assessment of perceived life quality and life stressors among medical hospital employees, by D. L. Cresswell, et al. JOURNAL OF COMMUNITY PSYCHOLOGY 9(2):153-161, April, 1981.

Negativism, equivocation, and wobbly assent: public 'support' for the prochoice platform on abortion, by J. Blake, et al. DEMOGRAPHY 18(3):309-320, August, 1981.

Negligence in the treatment of a patient with interruption of pregnancy, by C. E. Lindahl. VARDFACKET 5(10:37-39, May 29, 1981.

Netherlands liberalizes abortion law after ten years of wide availability, low abortion rates. FAMILY PLANNING PERSPECTIVE 13:151, May-June, 1981.

Network repeats refusal to state abortion policy. NATIONAL CATHOLIC REPORTER 17:13, December 26, 1980.

Networks and resource sharing in family planning libraries and documentation centres, by S. C. Dhir. INTERNATIONAL LIBRARY REVIEW 12(3):259-261, July, 1980.

The neurological complications of the pill, by H. Damasio. MEDICAL TIMES 109(6):84-86+, June, 1981.

New abortion fight starts in Congress [proposed Hatch Amendment], by E. Doerr. HUMANIST 41:45-46, November-December, 1981.

A new abortion technique: intravaginal and intramuscular prostaglandin, by N. H. Lauersen, et al. OBSTETRICS AND GYNECOLOGY 58(1):96-100, July, 1981.

New antifertility agents active in the rabbit vaginal contraception (RVC) method, by W. L. Williams. CONTRACEPTION 22(6):

659-672, December, 1980.

A new balanced translocation in humans: t(3;8) (q21;124), by R. S. Verma, et al. JOURNAL OF REPRODUCTIVE MEDICINE 26(3):133-134, March, 1981.

New directions for contraception, by C. C. Korenbrot. TECHNOLOGY REVIEW 83:52-59+, November-December, 1980.

New form for termination of pregnancy [letter], by W. Savage. BRITISH MEDICAL JOURNAL 282(6262):478-479, February 7, 1981.

The new gene doctors, by M. Clark, et al. NEWSWEEK 96(20): 120+, May 18, 1981.

New laparoscopic sterilization with exteriorization of tubes (cauterization, legation): a preliminary report, by D. Muzsnai, et al. EUROPEAN JOURNAL OF OBSTETRICS, GYNECOLOGY AND REPRODUCTIVE BIOLOGY 11(4):281-289, February, 1981.

New light on Humanae Vitae. MONTH 13:293-294, September, 1980.

A new non-hormonal pregnancy-terminating agent, by G. Galliani, et al. CONTRACEPTION 23(2):163-180, February, 1981.

The new right: women's rights under attack, by J. Butterfield. RADICAL RELIGION 5(4):61-73, 1981.

New UK committee [news]. NATURE 287(5685):774, October 30, 1980.

News of pro-lifers' disarray is not really news at all, by J. Castelli. OUR SUNDAY VISITOR 70:8, October 11, 1981.

Nonclinical distribution of the pill in the developing world, by A. Rosenfield, et al. INTERNATIONAL FAMILY PLANNING PERSPECTIVES 6:130-136, December, 1980.

Nonprescription vaginal contraception, by D. A. Edelman. IN-

TERNATIONAL JOURNAL OF GYNAECOLOGY AND
OBSTETRICS 18(5):340-344, 1980.

Norethisterone enanthate as an injectable contraceptive in
puerperal and non-puerperal women, by G. B. Melis, et al.
CONTRACEPTION 23(1):77-88, January, 1981.

Normal fertility in women with post-pill amenorrhoea, by M. G.
Hull, et al. LANCET 1(8234):1329-1332, June 20, 1981.

Normative pressures in family planning, by E. Fried, et al. POP-
ULATION AND ENVIRONMENT 3(3-4):199, Fall-Winter,
1980.

Note sull'aborto e la contraccezione tra gli Nzema del Ghana, by
E. S. Tiberini. AFRICA 35(2):159-189, 1980.

Notes on the class character of the abortion problem, by K.
Winter, et al. ZEITSCHRIFT FUR AERZTLICHE FORT-
BILDUNG 74(5):193-195, March 1, 1980.

Notifying the parents. AMERICA 144:289-290, April 11, 1981.

The nurse practitioner in Planned Parenthood clinics, by M.
Manisoff. FAMILY PLANNING PERSPECTIVES 13(1):19-
21, January-February, 1981.

Nurses and the legality of abortion, by J. Finch. NURSING
FOCUS 2:159-161, January, 1981.

Nurses and the medical termination of pregnancy [letter].
BRITISH MEDICAL JOURNAL 281(6254):1564, December 6, 1980.

A nursing adventure: through a very small window, by J. Kulig.
RNABC NEWS 13(4):25, May-June, 1981.

Nursing protocol to improve the effectiveness of the contraceptive diaphragm, by E. Gara. AMERICAN JOURNAL OF
MATERNAL CHILD NURSING 6:41-45, January-February,
1981.

Nutrition, health, and population in strategies for rural development, by B. F. Johnston, et al. DISCUSSION 29:401-405+, January, 1981.

Nutritional deficiencies and the "pill". NURSES DRUG ALERT 5:42-43, May, 1981.

Nutritional effects of oral contraceptive use: a review, by J. L. Webb. JOURNAL OF REPRODUCTIVE MEDICINE 25(4): 150-156, October, 1980.

Nutritional effects of oral contraceptives, by B. H. Robinson, et al. ISSUES IN HEALTH CARE OF WOMEN 1(1):37-60, 1978.

Objections to tubal sterilization: what reversibility can and cannot overcome, by R. N. Shain. CONTRACEPTION 22(3): 213-225, September, 1980.

Observations on the antigenicity and clinical effects of a candidate antipregnancy vaccine: beta-subunit of human chorionic gonadotropin linked to tetanus toxoid, by H. Nash, et al. FERTILITY AND STERILITY 34(4):328-335, October, 1980.

O'Connor impact on abortion issues yet to be seen, by J. Castelli. OUR SUNDAY VISITOR 70:8, September 27, 1981.

Ocular side effects through oral contraceptives, by R. Rochels, et al. GEBURTSHILFE UND FRAUENHEILKUNDE 40(8): 713-715, August, 1980.

Oestrogen containing oral contraceptives decrease prostacyclin production [letter], by O. Ylikorkala, et al. LANCET 1 (8210):42, January 3, 1981.

Oestrogen containing oral contraceptives, decreased prostacyclin production, and haemolytic uraemic syndrome [letter], by D. Hauglustaine, et al. LANCET 1(8215):328-329, February 7, 1981.

Oestrus control and the incidence of mammary nodules in

bitches, a clinical study with two progestogens, by J. L. van Os, et al. TIJDSCHRIFT VOOR DIERGENEESKUNDE 106(2) Suppl 3):46-56, January 15, 1981.

Of many things [views of A. M. Schindler] , by J. A. O'Hare. AMERICA 144:inside cover, February 28, 1981.

Of marsupials and men: a thought experiment on abortion, by J. Morreall. DIALOGOS 16:7-8, April, 1981.

Office abortion: a humane approach to a traumatic experience, by P. S. Green. JOURNAL OF THE MEDICAL SOCIETY OF NEW JERSEY 77(12):809-811, November, 1980.

On control over fertility regulation, by M. Salo. SOCIAL PRAXIS 7:191-203, 1980.

On the dispersion capacity of an intro-vaginal contraceptive ovule. Results of an in-vivo study in sexually not stimulated women, by I. Schmid-Tannwald, et al. GEBURTSHILFE UND FRAUENHEILKUNDE 41(6):424-426, June, 1981.

On the mechanism of action of a new pregnancy-terminating agent. Part I: Effects of prostaglandin F2 alpha metabolism in the rat and the hamster, by F. Luzzani, et al. CONTRA-CEPTION 23(3):325-333, March, 1981.

On medical ethics [editorial] , by E. F. Payne, Jr. JOURNAL OF THE MEDICAL ASSOCIATION OF GEORGIA 69(9):780-781, September, 1980.

On the question of jursidiction [testimony of J. T. Noonan in defense of Helms-Hyde bill] , by W. F. Buckley, Jr. NA-TIONAL REVIEW 33:741, June 26, 1981.

Oncological aspects of hormonal contraception, by I. V. Bokh-man, et al. AKUSHERSTVO I GINEKOLOGIIA (4):3-5, April, 1981.

One baby for you, one baby for me, by T. Tung. AMERICAN SPECTATOR 14:15-17, January, 1981.

The one-hundredth anniversary of tubal sterilization, by A. M. Siegler, et al. FERTILITY AND STERILITY 34(6):610-613, December, 1980.

Only five minutes! Nurse-patient communications, by J. D. Hines. AMERICAN JOURNAL OF MATERNAL CHILD NURSING 5(4):271-274, July-August, 1980.

Opinions and beliefs regarding family size among a population of Nigerian undergraduate students, by O. Ikponmwosa. JOURNAL OF THE AMERICAN COLLEGE HEALTH ASSOCIATION 28(5):287-289, April, 1980.

Opinions of the Unites States Supreme Court: abortion. THE CRIMINAL LAW REPORTER: TEXT SECTION 28(25): 3105-3121, March 25, 1981.

Optimal terms for sterilization, by M. Ribic-Pucelj. JUGO-SLAVENSKA GINEKOLOGIJA I OPSTETRICIJA 20 (3-4):132-134, May-August, 1980.

Oral contraception and congenital abnormalities, by P. N. Kasan, et al. BRITISH JOURNAL OF OBSTETRICS AND GYNAE-COLOGY 87(7):545-551, July, 1980.

Oral contraception and myocardial infarction revisited: the effects of new preparations and prescribing patterns, by S. A. Adam, et al. BRITISH JOURNAL OF OBSTETRICS AND GYNAECOLOGY 88(8):838-845, August, 1981.

Oral contraception and thromboembolism: the role of progestogens [editorial]. NEW ZEALAND MEDICAL JOURNAL 92(665):98+, August 13, 1980.

Oral contraceptive and coronary thrombosis. Two clinicopathological cases, by R. Loire, et al. ARCHIVES DES MALADIES DU COEUR ET DES VAISSEAUX 73(4):432-437, April, 1980.

Oral contraceptive and physiological variables, by L. D. Ostrander. JAMA 244:677-679, August, 1980.

Oral contraceptive and trisomy 21. A retrospective study of 730 cases, by J. Lejeune, et al. SEMAINES DES HOPITAUX DE PARIS 55(43-44):1985-1990, December 18-25, 1979.

Oral contraceptive hazards—1981 [editorial], by J. W. Goldzieher. FERTILITY AND STERILITY 35(3):275-276, March, 1981.

Oral contraceptive history as a risk indicator in patients with pituitary tumors with hyperprolactinemia: a case comparison study of twenty patients, by L. Teperman, et al. NEUROSURGERY 7(6):571-573, December, 1980.

Oral contraceptive—induced chorea, by N. Kaplinsky, et al. AMERICAN JOURNAL OF OBSTETRICS AND GYNECOLOGY 138(2):237, September 15, 1980.

Oral contraceptive-induced hepatic adenoma and focal modular hyperplasia, by C. J. Bryant, et al. AUSTRALASIAN RADIOLOGY 24(3):289-292, November, 1980.

Oral contraceptive risk found negligible. CHEMICAL AND ENGINEERING NEWS 58:6, October 27, 1980.

Oral contraceptive steroid plasma concentrations in smokers and non-smokers, by F. E. Crawford, et al. BRITISH MEDICAL JOURNAL 282(6279):1829-1830, June 6, 1981.

Oral contraceptive steroids and atherosclerosis: lipogenesis in human arterial smooth muscle cells and dermal fibroblasts in presence of lipoprotein-deficient serum from oral contraceptive users, by P. V. Subbaiah, et al. ARTERY 6(6):437-457, 1980.

Oral contraceptive steroids as promoters of hepatocarcinogenesis in female Sprague-Dawley rats, by J. D. Yager, Jr., et al. CANCER RESEARCH 40(10):3680-3685, October, 1980.

Oral contraceptive use and blood pressure in a community-based cohort study, by C. H. Hennekens, et al. CIRCULATION 62(3):111-306, 1980.

Oral contraceptive use and diseases of the circulatory system in
Taiwan: an analysis of mortality statistics, by L. P. Chow, et
al. INTERNATIONAL JOURNAL OF GYNAECOLOGY
AND OBSTETRICS 18(6):420-432, 1980.

Oral contraceptive use and early abortion as risk factors for
breast cancer in young women, by M. C. Pike, et al. BRITISH
JOURNAL OF CANCER 43(1):72-76, January, 1981.

Oral contraceptive use and prevalence of infection with Chlamyd-
ia trachomatis in women, by G. R. Kinghorn, et al. BRITISH
JOURNAL OF VENEREAL DISEASES 57(3):187-190,
June, 1981.

Oral contraceptive use: its risks and benefits, by T. G. Skillman.
HOSPITAL FORMULARY 15:622-623+, August, 1980.

Oral contraceptive use, sexual activity, and cervical carcinoma,
by S. H. Swan, et al. AMERICAN JOURNAL OF OBSTET-
RICS AND GYNECOLOGY 139(1):52-57, January, 1981.

Oral contraceptives, by G. J. Petursson, et al. OPHTHALMOLO-
GY 88(4):368-371, April, 1981.

Oral contraceptives and benign tumorous conditions of the liver,
by R. Lesch, et al. RADIOLOGE 20(12):565-576, December,
1980.

Oral contraceptives and birth defects, by R. W. Smithells. DE-
VELOPMENTAL MEDICINE AND CHILD NEUROLOGY
23(3):369-372, June, 1981.

Oral contraceptives and breast cancer, by H. Jick, et al. AMERI-
CAN JOURNAL OF EPIDEMIOLOGY 112(5):577-585, November, 1980.

Oral contraceptives and cardiovascular disease, by J. E. Dalen, et
al. AMERICAN HEART JOURNAL 101(5):626-639, May,
1981.

Oral contraceptives and cardiovascular disease (second of two
parts), by B. V. Stadel. NEW ENGLAND JOURNAL OF

111

MEDICINE 305(12):672-677, September 17, 1981.

Oral contraceptives and cardiovascular diseases, by M. Aosaki, et al. NIPPON RINSHO 38(10):4187-4195, October, 1980.

Oral contraceptives and the decline in mortality from circulatory disease, by R. A. Wiseman, et al. FERTILITY AND STERILITY 35(3):277-283, March, 1981.

Oral contraceptives and depressive symptomatology: biologic mechanisms. COMPREHENSIVE PSYCHIATRY 20(4):347-358, July-August, 1979.

Oral contraceptives and family health in rural Bangladesh, by S. C. Huber, et al. INTERNATIONAL JOURNAL OF GYNAECOLOGY AND OBSTETRICS 18(4):268-274, 1980.

Oral contraceptives and liver disease, by D. Lockhat, et al. CANADIAN MEDICAL ASSOCIATION JOURNAL 124(8): 993-999, April 15, 1981.

Oral contraceptives and liver tumors, by R. Cavin, et al. SCHWEIZERISCHE MEDIZINISCHE WOCHENSCHRIFT 111(22):804-806, May 30, 1981.

Oral contraceptives and oral candidiasis, by G. Krekeler, et al. FORTSCHRITTE DER MEDIZIN 99(7):230-232, February 19, 1981.

Oral contraceptives and post-molar trophoblastic tumours [letters], by R. S. Berkowitz, et al. LANCET 2(8197):752, October 4, 1980.

Oral contraceptives and responsiveness of plasma renin activity and blood pressure in normotensive women, by F. H. Leenen, et al. CLINICAL AND EXPERIMENTAL HYPERTENSION 2(2):197-211, February, 1980.

Oral contraceptives and systematic lupus erythematosus, by M. Garovich, et al. ARTHRITIS AND RHEUMATISM 23(12): 1396-1398, 1980.

Oral contraceptives: effects on carbohydrate metabolism, insulin like activity and histology of the pancreas, by H. J. Kulkarni, et al. HORMONE AND METABOLIC RESEARCH 12(10): 497-504, October, 1980.

Oral contraceptives, lanosterol, and platelet hyperactivity in rat, by M. Ciavatti, et al. SCIENCE 210(4470):642-644, November 7, 1980.

Oral contraceptives. Liver diseases in 25 million women [news], by E. Roseau. NOUVELLE PRESSE MEDICALE 9(33):2296, September 20, 1980.

Oral contraceptives: misunderstood etiology of erythema nodosum, by G. Beaucaire, et al. SEMAINES DES HOPITAUX DE PARIS 56(33-36):1426-1428, September 18-25, 1980.

Oral contraceptives, side effects and drug interactions, by S. E. Thomas. EAST AFRICAN MEDICAL JOURNAL 57(12): 816-821, December, 1980.

Oral steroid contraception in hyperprolactinemia, by W. Völker, et al. GEBURTSHILFE UND FRAUENHEILKUNDE 41(3): 1990203, March, 1981.

Organochlorine pesticides in specimens from women undergoing spontaneous abortion, premature of full-term delivery, by M. C. Saxena, et al. JOURNAL OF ANALYTICAL TOXICOLOGY 5(1):6-9, January-February, 1981.

Orientations toward abortion: guilty or knowledge? by A. R. Allgeier, et al. ADOLESCENCE 16(62):273-280, Summer, 1981.

Out of the lockerroom and into the classroom: innovative approaches to the use of media and strategies in sex education for the deaf, by M. Kessler. AMERICAN ANNALS OF THE DEAF 125(6):822-825, September, 1980.

Outcome of pregnancies following the use of oral contraceptives, by E. Alberman, et al. INTERNATIONAL JOURNAL OF EPIDEMIOLOGY 9(3):207-213, September, 1980.

Outcome of pregnancy subsequent to induced abortion [letter],
by L. Iffy. AMERICAN JOURNAL OF OBSTETRICS AND
GYNECOLOGY 138(5):587-588, November 1, 1980.

Outpatient laparoscopic sterilisation: comparison between elec-
trocautery and clip application, by G. Hughes, et al. AUS-
TRALIAN AND NEW ZEALAND JOURNAL OF OBSTET-
RICS AND GYNAECOLOGY 20(2):119-121, May, 1980.

Ovulation method of family planning, by E. B. Martinez. AMER-
ICA 144:277-279, April 4, 1981.

Ovum pick-up following fimbriectomy and infundibular salpingostomy in rabbits, by S. A. Halbert, et al. JOURNAL OF
REPRODUCTIVE MEDICINE 26(6):299-304, June, 1981.

Oxytocin augmentation of intra-amniotic saline for termination
of pregnancy, by K. S. Karam, et al. JOURNAL OF MEDI-
CAL LIBANAIS 31(3):235-243, 1980.

Oxytocin augmentation of second-trimester abortion: safe or
hazardous? by W. Cates, Jr., et al. CONTRACEPTION 22
(5):513-525, November, 1980.

Oxytocin: oxytocic of choice in first trimester, by J. B. Lauritz,
et al. MEDICAL JOURNAL OF AUSTRALIA 2(6):319-320,
September 20, 1980.

Oxytocin potentiation with low dose intravenous prostaglandin
E2 in the management of therapeutic abortion, by J. M.
Beazley, et al. BRITISH JOURNAL OF CLINICAL PRAC-
TICE 34(11-12):329-333, November-December, 1980.

PID risk increased sharply among IUD users, British cohort,
U. S. case-control studies affirm. FAMILY PLANNING
PERSPECTIVES 13:182-184, July-August, 1981.

Papel de la conciencia en la calificación de los actos morales, by
M. S. J. Zalba. GREGORIANUM 62(1):135-157, 1981.

Parent and peer influence on sexual behavior, contraceptive use,
and pregnancy experience of young women, by F. Shah, et

114

al. JOURNAL OF MARRIAGE AND THE FAMILY 43: 339-348, May, 1981.

Parental support, locus orientation, and self esteem as they relate to contraceptive behavior of unmarried college students, by L. P. Weiser. DAI 42(2), 1981.

Parity, miscarriages and abortions in women with epilepsy, by J. J. Zieliński, et al. POLSKI TYGODNIK LEKARSKI 35 (18):655-657, May 5, 1980.

Participation of nurses in abortions [letter], by P. L. Neustatter. LANCET 2(8205):1199-1200, November 29, 1980.

Particularly small foetus papyraceus after full pregnancy period, by L. Nevermann, et al. ZEITSCHRIFT FUR GEBURT-SCHILFE UND PERINATOLOGIE 185(3):187-191, June, 1981.

A pastoral application of natural family planning, by T. G. Morrow. HOMILETIC AND PASTORAL REVIEW 81:54-63, June, 1981.

Paternal child-support tort parallels for the abortion on maternal demand era: the work of Regan, Levy and Duncan, by G. S. Swan. GLENDALE LAW REVIEW 3:249-284, 1978-1979.

Pathogenetic therapy of miscarriage in leukocytic imcompatibility, by V. V. Shcherbakova, et al. VOPROSY OKHRANY MATERINSTVA I DETSTVA 25(9):64-66, September, 1980.

Patient counseling model key to successful mini-lap [interview], by L. R. Levy. SAME DAY SURGERY 5(3):34-36, March, 1981.

Patient education—health promotion in Michigan's hospitals. Part I. MICHIGAN HOSPITALS 17(1):20-30, January, 1981.

Patients' rights—mental health—laetrile—abortion. ANNUAL SURVEY OF AMERICAN LAW 1980:321-367, 1980.

The pattern of abortion [editorial] . NEW ZEALAND MEDICAL
JOURNAL 92(668):237-238, September 24, 1980.

Pattern of acute pelvic inflammatory disease in abortion-related
admissions, by T. A. Sinnathuray, et al. AMERICAN JOUR-
NAL OF OBSTETRICS AND GYNCEOLOGY 138(7 Pt 2):
868-871, December 1, 1980.

Patterns of child-bearing: a report on the World Fertility Survey
[recent findings concerning developing countries; eight
articles] . PEOPLE 7(4):3-20, 1980.

'Pay-offs' and 'trade-offs': reflections of a nursing administrator
and a nursing educator on a collaborative study in the practice of nursing, by D. Walker, et al. JNE 19(6):54-57, June,
1980.

Peer-group orientation, sexual behavior, and attitudes of college
students toward abortion, by R. S. Tanas. DAI 41(9-10),
1981.

Pelvic infections following gynecologic procedures in Bangladesh,
by S. F. Begum. AMERICAN JOURNAL OF OBSTETRICS
AND GYNECOLOGY 138(7 Part 2):875-876, 1980.

Pelvic inflammatory disease and its consequences in the developing qorld, by D. G. Muir, et al. AMERICAN JOURNAL OF
OBSTETRICS AND GYNECOLOGY 138(7 Part 2):913-928,
1980.

Penetrating a biased press [press coverage of nomination of C. E.
Koop as Surgeon General] . CHRISTIANITY TODAY 25:30,
June 26, 1981.

Pennsylvania bans welfare abortions with new statute. THE
FAMILY LAW REPORTER: COURT OPINIONS 7(9):
2138-2139, January 6, 1981.

Perceived side effects of oral contraceptives among adolescent
girls, by E. S. Herold, et al. CANADIAN MEDICAL ASSOCI-
ATION JOURNAL 123(10):1022-1026, November 22, 1980.

Perception of methods of contraception: a semantic differential study, by P. K. Kee, et al. JOURNAL OF BIOSOCIAL SCIENCE 13:209-218, April, 1981.

Peripheral blood volume pulse associated with hot flashes following a hysterectomy—a preliminary case report, by F. S. Fehr, et al. JOURNAL OF SEX RESEARCH 17:152-156, May, 1981.

Periportal sinusoidal dilatation, inflammatory bowel disease, and the contraceptive pill, by M. Camilleri, et al. GASTROENTEROLOGY 80(4):810-815, April, 1981.

Persistence of progesterone secretion after foetal death induced by vasopressin in rabbits, by J. W. Wilks. ACTA ENDOCRINOLOGICA 97(4):569-572, August, 1981.

Persistent abnormalities of fibrinolytic activity and platelet function in patients with reversible oestrogen-associated hypertension, by A. A. Al-Khader, et al. BRITISH JOURNAL OF OBSTETRICS AND GYNAECOLOGY 87(8):672-677, August, 1980.

The personal dilemmas of sterilization, by S. Wernick. BOSTON 72:116+, December, 1980.

Personal experience with contraception in Algeria, by L. T. Almed. GYNECOLOGIE 31(2):131-133, 1980.

Personality correlates of the delayed abortion decision, by P. H. Crabtree, PhD. DAI 41(7), 1981.

Personality of women resorting to repeated voluntary abortions, by F. Lang, et al. ANNALES MEDICO-PSYCHOLOGIQUES 138(8):992-1002, 1980.

Perspectives on abortion law reform in Barbados, by W. C. Gilmore. ANGLO-AMERICAN LAW REVIEW 8:191-209, July-September, 1979.

Perspectives on birth control, by M. Vicars. ENVIRONMENT NEWS 3(5):18, December-January, 1980-1981.

The perils of a convenient society; interview, by C. E. Koop.
NEW COVENANT 10:8-11, March, 1981.

The pessimistic origins of the anti-life movement, by R. Dennehy.
STUDIES 70:5-16, Spring, 1981.

The Philippines. STUDIES IN FAMILY PLANNING 11(11):335,
November, 1980.

Physician knowledge and attitudes toward an emergency medical
services system, by T. K. Yolles, et al. ANNALS OF EMER-
GENCY MEDICINE 10(1):2-10, January, 1981.

Physician's liability for sequelae of failed sterilization, by H. J.
Rieger. DEUTSCHE MEDIZINISCHE WOCHENSCHRIFT
105(33):1141, August 15, 1980.

Physiological method and intrauterine devices for contraception,
by A. P. Kiriushchenkov. FEL'DSHER I AKUSHERKA 46
(1):55-57, 1981.

Pill and IUD [intrauterine device] discontinuation in the United
States, 1970-1075: the influence of the media. FAMILY
PLANNING PERSPECTIVES 12:293-300, November-Decem-
ber, 1980.

The pill at 20: an assessment, by H. W. Ory, et al. FAMILY
PLANNING PERSPECTIVES 12(6):278, November-December, 1980.

Pill revisited. SCIQUEST 54:26-27, September, 1981.

Pill use in 20 developing countries: a cross-country summary
from the World Fertility Survey, by D. Wulf. INTERNA-
TIONAL FAMILY PLANNING PERSPECTIVES 6:161-162,
December, 1980.

Pill's dangers don't go away, by J. Seligmann. NEWSWEEK 98:
54, August 31, 1981.

Pilot study into habitual abortion, by D. Gerl, et al. ZENTRAL-
BLATT FUR GYNAEKOLOGIE 102(2):93-98, 1980.

La pilule, c'est pour les males! by L. Vandelac. L'ACTUALITÉ 6:22, October, 1981.

Pituitary tumor made symptomatic during hormone therapy and induced pregnancy, by R. P. Mills, et al. ANNALS OF OPTHALMOLOGY 11(11):1672-1676, November, 1979.

The place of oral contraceptives and pregnancy in the aetiology of amenorrhoea, a study of 188 cases of secondary amenorrhoea lasting more than one year, by C. Le Pogamp, et al. JOURNAL DE GYNECOLOGIE OBSTETRIQUE ET BIOLOGIE DE LA REPRODUCTION 10(3):223-229, 1981.

Placental histological findings in women from the area polluted with TCDD, by M. Cattaneo, et al. ANNALI DI OSTETRICIA, GYNECOLOGIA, MEDICINA PERINATALE 102(3): 155-164, May-June, 1981.

Planification des naissances en Chine: quelle confiance accorder aux données locales, by L. Bianco. POPULATION 36(1):123-146, 1981.

Planned and unplanned births in the United States (1) Planning status of marital births, 1975-1976, by J. E. Anderson. FAMILY PLANNING PERSPECTIVES 13:62-69, March-April, 1981.

Planned birth in Tianjin, by K. C. Lyle. CHINA QUARTERLY (83):551-567, September, 1980.

Planned parenthood, by M. A. Walsh. OUR SUNDAY VISITOR 70:3-4, June 7, 1981; 70:8-9+, June 14, 1981.

Planned parenthood and active family planning, by W. Fijalkowski, et al. PIELEGNIARKA I POLOZNA (3):12-15, 1980.

Planning births in China: what confidence can be placed in local data, by L. Bianco. POPULATION 36:123-146, January-February, 1981.

Planning status of marital births, 1975-1976, by J. E. Anderson. FAMILY PLANNING PERSPECTIVES 13(2):62-63+, March-

April, 1981.

Plasma diamine oxidase levels in pregnancy complicated by threatened abortion, by M. Legge, et al. JOURNAL OF CLINICAL PATHOLOGY 34(2):187-188, February, 1981.

Plasma levels of levonorgestrel in women during longterm use of Norplants, by H. B. Croxatto, et al. CONTRACEPTION 22 (6):583-596, December, 1980.

Plasma lipids and lipoprotein lipase activating property in women on three different combinations of estrogens and progestrins, by S. G. Mendoza, et al. BIOCHEMICAL MEDICINE 25(3): 283-287, June, 1981.

Plasma pregnancy-associated alpha 2-glycoprotein concentrations in complications of pregnancy and foetal abnormality, by A. W. Thomson, et al. JOURNAL OF REPRODUCTIVE IM-MUNOLOGY 1(4):229-235, December, 1979.

Plasma progesterone, prostaglandin F2 alpha and 13,14-dihydro-15-ketoprostaglandin F2 alpha in the bovine before abortion or parturition, by A. L. Baetz, et al. CLINICAL CHEMIS-TRY 26(7):1045, 1980.

Plasma tocopherol and lipid levels in pregnancy and oral contra-ceptive users, by V. Jagadeesan, et al. BRITISH JOURNAL OF OBSTETRICS AND BYNAECOLOGY 87(10):903-907, October, 1980.

Political developments in the abortion area, by J. L. Robinson. CATHOLIC LAWYER 25:319-326, Autumn, 1980.

Political showdown over abortion coming, but when? by R. B. Shaw. OUR SUNDAY VISITOR 69:6, April 26, 1981.

The politics of fertility control, by M. Simms. NEW HUMANIST 96:73-75, January, 1981.

Poll reveals mixed feelings on abortion in U. S. OUR SUNDAY VISITOR 70:7, June 21, 1981.

Pope joins Italy abortion debate wholeheartedly, by P. Hebblethwaite. NATIONAL CATHOLIC REPORTER 17:1+, May
15, 1981.

Pope strongly refutes claim abortion is private matter. OUR
SUNDAY VISITOR 69:7, April 19, 1981.

Population and birth control in China, by J. A. Loraine. CON-
TEMPORARY REVIEW 239:126-130, September, 1981.

Population and migration problems in Mexico, by M. Alisky.
CURRENT HISTORY 80:365-369+, November, 1981.

Population control: free choice or coercion, by V. Ortiz.
CHURCH AND SOCIETY 71:78-80, March-April, 1981.

Population growth and global security [critical of the lack of
American leadership in this area and of the role of the
Roman Catholic Church], by S. Mumford. HUMANIST 41:
6-25+, January-February, 1981.

Population policy and public goods, by F. Miller, et al. PHILOS-
OPHY AND PUBLIC AFFAIRS 8:148-174, Winter, 1979.

Population policy in India: recent developments and current
prospects. POPULATION AND DEVELOPMENT REVIEW
6(2):299, June, 1980.

Population trends, population policy, and population studies
in China, by A. J. Coale. POPULATION AND DEVELOP-
MENT REVIEW 7:85-97, March, 1981.

The position of the Association of French Language Physicians
of Canada on the sterilization of the mentally-deficient, by
D. Robillard. CANADIAN MEDICAL ASSOCIATION JOUR-
NAL 124(9):1214, May 1, 1981.

Positive pregnancy tests at Stanford: a follow up study, 1978-
1980, by J. M. Dorman. JOURNAL OF THE AMERICAN
COLLEGE HEALTH ASSOCIATION 29(6):286-288, June,
1981.

Possible association of angiosarcoma with oral contraceptive agents, by E. C. Shi, et al. MEDICAL JOURNAL OF AUSTRALIA 1(9):473-474, May 2, 1981.

Postabortion depressive reactions in college women, by N. B. Gould. JOURNAL OF THE AMERICAN COLLEGE HEALTH ASSOCIATION 28:316-320, June, 1980.

Postabortion sepsis and antibiotic prophylaxis [letter]. BRITISH MEDICAL JOURNAL 282(6262):476-477, February 7, 1981.

Postcoital contraception, by J. Porter, et al. MEDICAL JOURNAL OF AUSTRALIA 1(2):68+, January 24, 1981.

Postpartum and postabortion psychotic reactions, by H. P. David, et al. FAMILY PLANNING PERSPECTIVES 13(2): 88-89+, March-April, 1981.

Postpartum family planning, by S. Walker. NURSING MIRROR 153:xxii-xxiv, September 9, 1981.

The potential impact of reversibility on selection of tubal sterilization, by R. N. Shain. CONTRACEPTION 22(3):227-240, September, 1980.

Potentiation of prostaglandin evoked contractions of isolated rat uterus by vasicine hydrochloride, by R. Lal, et al. INDIAN JOURNAL OF MEDICAL RESEARCH 73:641-648, April, 1981.

Power in families, communication, and fertility decision-making [based, in part, on data from Latin American fertility surveys and anthropological studies], by P. E. Hollerbach. POPULATION AND ENVIRONMENT 3:146-173, Summer, 1980.

Precursor stage of hepatocellular neoplasm following long exposure to orally administered contraceptives, by S. N. Thung, et al. HUMAN PATHOLOGY 12(5):472-474, May, 1981.

Predictors relating to implementation of family planning policy in the Philippines, by P. Klobus-Edwards, et al. JOURNAL OF SOUTHEAST ASIAN STUDIES 11:335-347, September, 1980.

Pregnancies after ineffective interruption of intrauterine procedure in early pregnancy, by W. Hardt, et al. GEBURTSHILFE UND FRAUENHEILKUNDE 40(7):654-657, July, 1980.

Pregnancy interruption and its complications, by H. Schmidt-Matthiesen. LEBENSVERSICHERUNGSMEDIZIN 32(3): 70-74, May, 1980.

Pregnancy risk following laparoscopic sterilization in nongravid and gravid women, by I. C. Chi, et al. JOURNAL OF REPRODUCTIVE MEDICINE 26(6):289-294, June, 1981.

Pregnancy risk-taking among young unmarried women: an analysis of its determinants and prevention, by S. B. Kar, et al. PATIENT COUNSELLING AND HEALTH EDUCATION 1:151-163, Summer-Fall, 1979.

Pregnancy terminating activity of a new non-hormonal anti-fertility agent, 2-(3-3thoxy-phenyl)-5,6-dihydro-s-triazole [5,1-a] isoquinoline (DL 204-IT) in the rat and the hamster. Studies on the factors affecting its activity, by G. Galliani, et al. ARZNEIMITTELFORSCH 30(6):972-977, 1980.

Pregnant low-income ttenagers: a social structural model of the determinants of abortion-seeking behavior, by R. Dworkin. YOUTH AND SOCIETY 11(3):295-309, March, 1980.

Preliminary results of experimental reanastomosis of uterine horns of laboratory rats after sterilization, by M. Bujas, et al. JUGOSLAVENSKA GINEKOLOGIJA I OPSTETRICIJA 20(3-4):157-162, May-August, 1980.

Preliminary testing of the contraceptive collagen sponge, by M. Chvapil, et al. OBSTETRICS AND GYNECOLOGY 56(4): 503-506, October, 1980.

Premarital sexual guilt and contraceptive attitudes and behavior, by E. S. Herold, et al. FAMILY RELATIONS 30:247-253, April, 1981.

Prenatal genetic diagnosis and elective abortion in women over 35: utilization and relative impact on the birth prevalence of Down syndrome in Washington State, by D. A. Luthy, et al. AMERICAN JOURNAL OF MEDICAL GENETICS 7(3): 375-381, 1980.

Preoperative administration of prostaglandin to avoid dilatation-induced damage in first-trimester pregnancy terminations, by S. Heinzl, et al. GYNECOLOGIE AND OBSTETRIC INVES-TIGATION 12(1):29-36, 1981.

Preparation of school-age children for surgery: a program in preventive pediatrics—Philippines, by P. D. Williams. INTER-NATIONAL JOURNAL OF NURSING STUDIES 17(2): 107-109, 1980.

Pre-pregnancy insertion of Mayer's pessary as therapy for infer-tility, by F. Drnek. CESKOSLOVENSKA GYNEKOLOGIE 46(6):465-466, July, 1981.

Present knowledge in the area of endocrine abortion. JOURNAL DE GYNECOLOGIE OBSTETRIQUE ET BIOLOGIE DE LA REPRODUCTION 9(1):59-98, 1980.

Present views on sterilization, by L. Andolsek-Jeras. JUGOSLA-VENSKA GINEKOLOGIJA I OPSTETRICIJA 20(3-4):103-107, May-August, 1980.

Presidential address at the 1980 NFCPG meeting, by E. F. Dia-mond. LINACRE 48:11-12, February, 1981.

President's remarks on abortion create some confusion. OUR SUNDAY VISITOR 69:7, March 22, 1981.

Prevalence and reporting of induced abortion in Turkey: two survey techniques, by S. Tezcan, et al. STUDIES IN FAMI-LY PLANNING 12:262-271, June-July, 1981.

Prevention of endocrine abortions by follicular stimulation, by

J. P. Dubecq, et al. JOURNAL DE GYNECOLOGIE OB-
STETRIQUE ET BIOLOGIE DE LA REPRODUCTION
9(1):95-98, 1980.

Prevention of infection after abortion with a supervised single
dose of oral doxycycline, by C. Brewer. BRITISH MEDICAL
JOURNAL 281(6243):780-781, September 20, 1980.

Prevention of recurrent abortion with leucocyte transfusions, by
C. Taylor, et al. LANCET 2(8237):68-70, July 11, 1981.

Prevention of recurrent menstrual psychosis by an oral contraceptive, by A. Felthouse. AMERICAN JOURNAL OF PSY-
CHIATRY 137(2):245-246, 1980.

Preventive hysterectomy versus paragraphs 224 and 225 of the
german penal code, by G. H. Schlund. GEBURTSHILFE
UND FRAUENHEILKUNDE 41(5):382-383, May, 1981.

Priest's pro-choice abortion ad draws strong reaction, by P. Kern.
OUR SUNDAY VISITOR 69:7, February 8, 1981.

Primary hepatocellular carcinoma developing in a female patient
on long term oral contraceptives—a case report, by C. J. Oon,
et al. ANNALS OF THE ACADEMY OF MEDICINE, SING-
APORE 9(3):402-404, July, 1980.

Primary malignant tumour of the liver associated with the ingestion of oral contraceptives, by J. Leclere, et al. NOUVELLE
PRESSE MEDICALE 8(5):346-349, January 27, 1979.

Prior abortions and neural tube defects, by T. J. David, et al.
CLINICAL GENETICS 18(3):201-202, September, 1980.

Privacy—includes right to obtain contraceptives; birth control—
may give contraceptive and not tell parent—United States.
JUVENILE LAW DIGEST 12(12):383-384, December, 1980.

Pro-abortion priest may be sued by Albany bishop, by L. H.
Phymphrey. OUR SUNDAY VISITOR 69:6, January 25,
1981.

Pro-abortionist ad campaigns escalating war on life, by W. Odel. OUR SUNDAY VISITOR 70:8, July 5, 1981.

Probable stenocardial effects of combined oral contraceptives, by G. Colucci, et al. MINERVA MEDICA 71(42):3123-3130, October 31, 1980.

The problem of public pretense, by R. Stith. INDIAN PHILO-SOPHICAL QUARTERLY 3:13-30, 1980.

The problem of sex chromosome aneuploidy in genetic counseling using amniocentesis, by E. Engel, et al. JOURNAL OF GENETICS 28(3):257-266, September, 1980.

The problem of sterilization, by E. Robecchi. MINERVA GINE-COLOGIA 32(6):445-446, June, 1980.

Problem patients and the 'pill', by F. M. Graham. DRUGS 21(2): 152-156, February, 1981.

Zur problematik der operativen sterilisation in katholischen krankenhausern, by J. Gründel. STIMMEN DER ZEIT 199: 671-677, October, 1981.

Problems of risk in genetic engineering research, by O. V. Shivt-sov. VESTNIK ACADEMII MEDITSINSKIKH NAUK SSSR (2):77-83, 1981.

Problems of sterilization in younger women—results of a questioning of patients wanting refertilization after sterilization within one year, by R. Grosspietzsch, et al. OEFFENTLICHE GESUNDHEITSWESEN 42(4):175-179, April, 1980.

Procedures for review of large-scale experiments. RECOMBI-NANT DNA TECHNICAL BULLETIN 4(2):81, July, 1981.

The process of problem pregnancy counseling, by J. Urman. JOURNAL OF THE AMERICAN COLLEGE HEALTH AS-SOCIATION 28(6):308-315, June, 1980.

Pro-choice is pro-life, by J. J. Christmas. ENCORE 10:14-16, December, 1981.

Pro-choice: United Presbyterians look at abortion in the '80s, by E. H. Verdesi, editor. CHURCH AND SOCIETY 71:3-103, March-April, 1981.

Progestagens in threatened abortion [letter], by G. Tognoni, et al. LANCET 2(8206):1242-1243, December 6, 1980.

Prognosis and treatment of threatened abortion. A. Prognostic value of maternal serum determination of choriogonadotropin and its free alpha and beta subunits in threatened abortion of the first trimester: correlation with ultrasonographic examination, by U. Gaspard, et al. JOURNAL OF GYNECOLOGIE OBSTETRIQUE ET BIOLOGIE DE LA REPRODUCTION 9(1):62-66, 1980.

—. B. Plasma hormone determinations in the prognostic evaluation of hemorrhage in the first trimester of pregnancy, by G. Crépin, et al. JOURNAL OF GYNECOLOGIE OBSTETRIQUE ET BIOLOGIE DE LA REPRODUCTION 9(1):67-72, 1980.

—. C. Longitudinal study of normal and pathologic pregnancy using plasma hormone determinations, by G. Crépin, et al. JOURNAL OF GYNECOLOGIE OBSTETRIQUE ET BIOLOGIE DE LA REPRODUCTION 9(1):73-78, 1980.

—. E. Management of the danger of abortion, by J. J. Leng. JOURNAL OF GYNECOLOGIE OBSTETRIQUE ET BIOLOGIE DE LA REPRODUCTION 9(1):90-94, 1980.

Prognosis of pregnancy after threatened abortion, by B. Adelusi, et al. INTERNATIONAL JOURNAL OF GYNAECOLOGY AND OBSTETRICS 18(6):444-447, 1980.

Prognosis of threatened early pregnancy, by P. Jouppila. JOURNAL OF PERINATAL MEDICINE 9(Suppl 1):72-74, 1981.

Program applications. POPULATION REPORTS 9(3):M-183, May-June, 1981.

Prolactin changes in maternal plasma following termination by vacuum curettage and the effect of bromocriptine treatment

on these changes, by O. Ylikorkala, et al. BRITISH JOUR-
NAL OF OBSTETRICS AND GYNAECOLOGY 87(10):911-
915, October, 1980.

Prolactin producing pituitary adenomas, by M. McInerney.
JOURNAL OF NEUROSURGICAL NURSING 13:15-17,
February, 1981.

Pro-life doesn't stop at birth, by M. Schwartz. LIGUORIAN 69:
7-11, January, 1981.

Pro-life education: a practical parish plan, by J. W. Anderson.
LIGUORIAN 69:34-35, July, 1981.

Pro-life forces riled by tone of Reagan letter. OUR SUNDAY
VISITOR 70:7, August 30, 1981.

"Pro-life" interest groups try a new tactic in effort to crack down
on abortion; abandoning the amendment? by N. Cohodas.
CONGRESSIONAL QUARTERLY WEEKLY REPORT 39:
383+, February 28, 1981.

Pro-life is a very pregnant issue [with reader's comments], by M.
A. Walsh. U.S. CATHOLIC 46:13-17, December, 1981.

Prolife leaders hurdle O'Connor nomination: decide to back
Reagan for the long race [news], by T. Minnery. CHRIS-
TIANITY TODAY 25:55+, October 2, 1981.

Pro-life: pro-peace, by J. Loesch. SIGN 61:11-14, September,
1981.

Pro-life rift develops over human life bill, by R. B. Shaw. OUR
SUNDAY VISITOR 70:6, May 17, 1981.

Pro-lifers demand action [constituional amendment issue].
CHRISTIAN CENTURY 98:159-161, February 18, 1981.

Prolonged pill use, many sex partners may lead to cervical cancer
to precursors, studies find. FAMILY PLANNING PERSPEC-
TIVES 13:45-46, January-February, 1981.

'Prolonged pregnancy' after oral contraceptive therapy, by G. J. Ratten. MEDICAL JOURNAL OF AUSTRALIA 1(12):641-642, June 13, 1981.

Prophylactic antibiotics in first-trimester abortions: a clinical, controlled trial, by S. Sonne-Holm, et al. AMERICAN JOURNAL OF OBSTETRICS AND GYNECOLOGY 139(6):693-696, March 15, 1981.

Proposed human life statute: abortion as murder? by C. E. M. Kolb. AMERICAN BAR ASSOCIATION JOURNAL 67: 1123-1126, September, 1981.

Pros and cons. ECONOMIST 279:76, May 30, 1981.

Prospective carbohydrate metabolism studies in women using a low-estrogen oral contraceptive for one year, by W. N. Spellacy, et al. JOURNAL OF REPRODUCTIVE MEDICINE 26(6):295-298, June, 1981.

A prospective multicentre trial of the ovulation method of natural family planning. I. The teaching phase. FERTILITY AND STERILITY 36(2):152-158, August, 1981.

Prospective studies into pregnancies of primiparae with record of therapeutic termination of previous pregnancies or of spontaneous abortion and assessment of fertility. Second communication, by G. Schott, et al. ZENTRALBLATT FUR GYNAEKOLOGIE 102(16):939-944, 1980.

A prospective study of the effects of the progestagen content of oral contraceptives on measures of affect, automatization, and perceptual restructuring ability, by A. Worsley. PSYCHO-PHARMACOLOGY 67(3):289-296, 1980.

Prostaglandin abortions: nurses' actions legitimate. BRITISH MEDICAL JOURNAL 282:1164-1165, April 4, 1981.

Prostaglandin termination of pregnancy [letter], by B. Eton. BRITISH MEDICAL JOURNAL 282(6257):72-73, January 3, 1981.

Prostaglandins and thromboxanes in amniotic fluid during rivanol-induced abortion and labour, by A. Olund, et al. PROSTAGLANDINS 19(5):791-803, May, 1980.

Prostaglandins for the management of anencephalic pregnancy, by M. Thiery, et al. PROSTAGLANDINS 21(2):207-215, February, 1981.

Prostaglandins in gel for abortion [letter], by O. Djahanbakhch, et al. BRITISH MEDICAL JOURNAL 283(6291):614, August 29, 1981.

Prostaglandins in gel for mid-trimester abortion: a method to minimise nursing involvement, by D. H. Smith, et al. BRITISH MEDICAL JOURNAL 282(6281):2012, June 20, 1981.

Prostaglandins in obstetrics [editorial]. BRITISH MEDICAL JOURNAL 282(6262):418-419, February 7, 1981.

Protect the innocents, by L. McArthur. CANADA AND THE WORLD 46:19, January, 1981.

Prototype for a new class of antifertility agents, 3,5-Bis (dimethylamino)-1,2,4,-dithiazolium chloride, by D. W. Hahn, et al. CONTRACEPTION 21(5):529-535, May, 1980.

Provision of induced abortion in Wessex Health Region: unmet need and feasibility of compensatory day care, by J. R. Ashton. JOURNAL OF THE ROYAL SOCIETY OF MEDICINE 73(3):191-196, March, 1980.

The psychiatrist in a family planning center, by G. Maruani, et al. ANNALES MÉDICO-PSYCHOLOGIQUES 136:6-8, June-October, 1978.

Psychic disturbances in women during oral contraception, by P. Petersen. MMW. MUNCHENER MEDIZINISCHE WOCHENSCHRIFT 123(27):1109-1112, July 3, 1981.

Psychological affects of oral contraceptives, by A. R. Dabbs, et al. EGYPTIAN JOURNAL OF PSYCHIATRY 2(1):98-111, April, 1979.

Psychological aftermath of female voluntary sterilization: a comparison of client and agency perceptions, by E. Bisconti, PhD. DAI 41(9), 1981.

Psychological alterations following induced abortion, by P. Petersen. MMW 123(27):1105-1108, July 3, 1981.

Psychological aspects in contraception counseling, by H. Sjöström. KATILOLEHTI 86(2):60-64, February, 1981.

Psychological aspects of sterilization, by N. Kapor-Stanulović. JUGOSLAVENSKA GINEKOLOGIJA I OPSTETRICIJA 20(3-4):172-175, May-August, 1980.

Psychological factors that predict reaction to abortion, by D. T. Moseley, et al. JOURNAL OF CLINICAL PSYCHOLOGY 37 (2):276-279, April, 1981.

The psychological implications of spontaneous abortions, by M. Seibel, et al. JOURNAL OF REPRODUCTIVE MEDICINE 25(4):161-165, October, 1980.

Psychological viewpoints in counseling on contraceptives. KA— TILOLEHTI 86(3):106+, March, 1981.

Psychosis associated with oral contraceptive-induced chorea, by I. Sale, et al. MEDICAL JOURNAL OF AUSTRALIA 1(2): 79-80, January 24, 1981.

The psychosocial outcome of induced abortion, by J. R. Ashton. BRITISH JOURNAL OF OBSTETRICS AND GYNAECOLOGY 87(12):1115-1122, December, 1980.

Psychosocial situation of women after termination of pregnancy, by M. Simon. MEDIZINISCHE KLINIK 75(16):592-595, August 1, 1980.

Psychosocial support of residents in family practice programs, by J. K. Berg, et al. JOURNAL OF FAMILY PRACTICE 11(6): 915-920, November, 1980.

Psycho-somatic considerations in surgical contraception, by F.

Berger, et al. GEBURTSHILFE UND FRAUENHEILKUNDE 40(5):448-455, May, 1980.

Public funding of medically necessary abortions is not required under the Medicaid act. TEXAS TECHNICAL LAW REVIEW 12:483-499, 1981.

Putting a lid on the cap [FDA restrictions on distribution of cervical caps]. PROGRESSIVE 45:13, March, 1981.

Q fever in the etiology of spontaneous abortion, by A. Michev, et al. AKUSHERSTVO I GINEKOLOGIIA 20(1):34-36, 1981.

Qualitative changes in reproductive policy and induced abortion, by J. Rothe. ZEITSCHRIFT FUR AERZTLICHE FORT-BILDUNG 74(9):437-440, May 1, 1980.

Quantitative analysis of some decision, rules for family planning in an oriental society, by T. N. Goh. INTERFACES 11:31-37, April, 1981.

Quantitative morphological-investigations in livers and liver tumors after taking contraceptives, by D. Kranz, et al. ZEN-TRALBLATT FUR ALLGEMEINE PATHOLOGIE 124(5): 441-447, 1980.

A question of balance, by A. Martin. NURSING MIRROR 151 (12):9, September 18, 1980.

Quinacrine hydrochloride pellets: preliminary date on a non-surgical method of female sterilization, by J. Zipper, et al. INTERNATIONAL JOURNAL OF GYNAECOLOGY AND OBSTETRICS 18(4):275-279, 1980.

Religion and abortion [Harris vs. McRae and the constitutionality of the Hyde Amendment], by J. R. Nelson. CENTER MAGAZINE 14:51-55, July-August, 1981.

The R.C.G.P. oral contraception study [letter], by E. C. Grant, et al. LANCET 1(8231):1206-1207, May 30, 1981.

A randomized, double-blind study of two combined oral contraceptives containing the same progestogen, but different estrogens. World Health Organization Task Force on Oral Contraception. CONTRACEPTION 21(5):445-459, May, 1980.

Rapid fibrinolysis, augmented Hageman factor (factor XII) fiters, and decreased C1 esterase inhibitor titers in women taking oral contraceptives, by E. M. Gordon, et al. JOURNAL OF LABORATORY AND CLINICAL MEDICINE 96 (5):762-769, November, 1980.

Rare form of uterine infection connected with interruptio, by B. Stubert, et al. ZENTRALBLATT FUR GYNAEKOLOGIE 102(13):734-737, 1980.

Rawls and children, by W. Evers. JOURNAL OF LIBERTARIAN STUDIES 2:109-114, Summer, 1978.

Reagan may soon have to back claimed prolife stance, by R. B. Shaw. OUR SUNDAY VISITOR 70:8, August 16, 1981.

The reality of abortion, by L. D. Kozaryn. SOLDIERS 36:20-25, March, 1981.

The rebirth of the cervical cap, by J. D. Capiello, et al. JOURNAL OF NURSE-MIDWIFERY 26:13-18, September-October, 1981.

Recanalization and fistulization of the fallopian tubes are thought to be the causes of pregnancies following female sterilization [letter], by A. M. McCausland. AMERICAN JOURNAL OF OBSTETRICS AND GYNECOLOGY 139(1): 114-115, January, 1981.

Recent advances in contraception [editorial], by R. P. Shearman. MEDICAL JOURNAL OF AUSTRALIA 1(2):55-57, January 24, 1981.

The recent demographic history of sterilization in Korea. INTERNATIONAL FAMILY PLANNING PERSPECTIVES 6:136-145, December, 1980.

Recent developments in China's population planning, by J. M. Maloney. PACIFIC AFFAIRS 54:100-115, Spring, 1981.

Recent developments in the health care area, by T. D. Harper, et al. JOURNAL OF THE MEDICAL ASSOCIATION OF GEORGIA 69(9):785-787, September, 1980.

Recent trends in deaths declared as due to abortion, by G. F. Dumont, et al. POPULATION 36:410-413, March-April, 1981.

Recent trends in sterilization, by M. Bone. POPULATION TRENDS 13:13-16, Autumn, 1978.

Reciprocal translocation with special reference to reproductive failure, by I. Subrt. HUMAN GENETICS 55(3):303-307, 1980.

Recombinant DNA experiments to remain under safety guidelines [news], by D. Dickson. NATURE 282(5739):545, December 6, 1979.

Recombinant DNA guidelines wear thin [news], by D. Dickson. NATURE 291(5810):3, May 7, 1981.

Recombinant DNA technology: the biochemical manipulation of genes, by R. H. Burdon. SCOTTISH MEDICAL JOURNAL 26(1):4-5, January, 1981.

Reconciliation: missing piece in abortion picture, by E. M. Bryce. ORIGINS 11:181-184, September 3, 1981.

Reducing stress in patients having cardiac catheterization, by C. Finesilver. AMERICAN JOURNAL OF NURSING 80(10): 1805-1807, October, 1980.

Refertilisation by implantation of both tubes, by T. Bobscheff. ZENTRALBLATT FUR GYNAEKOLOGIE 102(19):1100-1104, 1980.

Reflections on Canadian abortion law: evacuation and destruction—two separate issues, by M. A. Somerville. UNIVERSITY

134

OF TORONTO LAW JOURNAL 31:1-26, Winter, 1981.

Refusal to fund constitutionally protected right held valid. WASHINGTON UNIVERSITY LAW QUARTERLY 59:247-260, 1981.

The refusal to sterilize. PROGRESS IN CLINICAL AND BIO-LOGICAL RESEARCH 50:133-154, 1981.

Regeneration processes in human oviducts following sterilization procedures, by E. Philipp. MEDIZINISCHE KLINIK 76(1): 15-19, January 2, 1981.

Regulation of implantation as a contraceptive method, by J. J. Hicks-Gomez. GACETA MEDICA DE MEXICO 116(7):318-323, July, 1980.

Relation between semen quality and fate of pregnancy: retrospective study on 534 pregnancies, by Z. T. Homonnai, et al. INTERNATIONAL JOURNAL OF ANDROLOGY 3(5): 574-584, October, 1980.

Relationship between condom strength and failure during use, by M. J. Free, et al. CONTRACEPTION 22(1):31-37, July, 1980.

The relationship between contraceptive sex role stereotyping and attitudes toward male contraception among males, by S. Weinstein, et al. JOURNAL OF SEX RESEARCH 15(3):235-242, August, 1979.

Relationship-centered family planning services: role of the family counselor, by C. Figley. AMERICAN JOURNAL OF FAMILY THERAPY 7(2):64-68, Summer, 1979.

Relationships between interruption abortion, and premature birth and low birth weight, by C. Zwahr, et al. ZENTRALBLATT FUR GYNAEKOLOGIE 102(13):738-747, 1980.

Religiosity and abortion attitudes among couples in the early stage of the family formation process, by B. Granger, PhD. DAI 41(7-8), 1981.

Religious involvement, asceticism and abortion among low income black women, by J. M. Robbins. SOCIOLOGICAL ANALYSIS 41:365-374, Winter, 1980.

Renin substrate, active and acid-activatable renin concentrations in human plasma and endometrium during menstrual cycles controlled by oral contraceptive preparations, by I. R. Johnson. BRITISH JOURNAL OF OBSTETRICS AND GYNAECOLOGY 87(10):883-888, October, 1980.

Report on the ibc chairperson's meeting, by E. Milewski. RECOMBINANT DNA TECHNICAL BULLETIN 4(1):26-27, April, 1981.

Representative Ballentine: 'Government failed by giving everybody everything', by W. Weddon. MICHIGAN MEDICINE 80(11):172, April, 1981.

Reproductive health curbs ahead: birth control imperiled, by J. Wells-Schooley. NEW DIRECTIONS FOR WOMEN 10:1+, March-April, 1981.

Reproductive pharmacology of LHRH and agonists in females and males, by A. Corbin, et al. ACTA EUROPAEA FERTILITATIS 11(2):113-130, June, 1980.

Reproductive rights national network: a rough road ahead. OFF OUR BACKS 11:10+, August-September, 1981.

Republic of Korea. STUDIES IN FAMILY PLANNING 11(11): 324, November, 1980.

Request for sterilization reversal, by K. G. Metz, et al. NEDERLANDS TIJDSCHRIFT VOOR GENEESKUNDE 125(11): 409-412, March 14, 1981.

Research on repeated abortion: state of the field—1973-1979, by G. D. Gibb, et al. PSYCHOLOGICAL REPORTS 48:415-424, April, 1981.

Researchers give evidence of safety for low-dose OCs. DRUG TOPICS 124:27-28, October 17, 1980.

Responsible parenthood and social justice [intervention, Synod of Bishops, 1980] , by P. Iteka. AFER 23:65-66, February-April, 1981.

Results of refertilization with end-to-end anastomosis following microsurgical sterilization, by H. Hepp, et al. THERAPEU-TISCHE UMSCHAU 37(6):473-478, June, 1980.

Retrospective self-insight on factors considered in product evaluation, by B. Weitz, et al. JOURNAL OF CONSUMER RE-SEARCH 6:280-294, December, 1979.

A retrospective survey of female sterilisation for the years 1968 to 1973. Analysis of morbidity and post-sterilisation complications for five years, by J. R. Newton, et al. CONTRACEP-TION 22(3):295-312, September, 1980.

Return of ovulation after abortion and after discontinuation of oral contraceptives, by P. Lähteenmäki, et al. FERTILITY AND STERILITY 34(3):246-249, September, 1980.

Return of the sheath, by I. Felstein. MIDWIFE, HEALTH VISI-TOR AND COMMUNITY NURSE 16(10):422-424, October, 1980.

Return to realism: a profile agenda, by J. Krastel. AMERICA 144: 101-102, February 7, 1981.

Reversal of female sterilization, by C. F. Pill, et al. BRITISH JOURNAL OF OBSTETRICS AND GYNAECOLOGY 88 (3):314-316, March, 1981.

—: comparison of microsurgical and gross surgical techniques for tubal anastomosis, by S. R. Henderson. AMERICAN JOUR-NAL OF OBSTETRICS AND GYNECOLOGY 139(1):73-79, January, 1981.

Reversal of long-standing renal insufficiency by captopril in a patient with relapsing hemolytic uremic syndrome due to an oral contraceptive, by S. J. Hoorntje, et al. ANNALS OF INTERNAL MEDICINE 94(3):355-357, March, 1981.

Reversal of tubal sterilization, by R. M. Winston. CLINICAL OBSTETRICS AND GYNECOLOGY 23(4):1261-1268, December, 1980.

Reversal of vasectomy and the treatment of male infertility. Role of microsurgery, vasoepididymostomy, and pressure-induced changes of vasectomy, by S. J. Silber. UROLOGIC CLINICS OF NORTH AMERICA 8(1):53-62, February, 1981.

Reversal of vasectomy. A simple procedure, by G. D. Burfield, et al. AUSTRALIAN FAMILY PHYSICIAN 10(2):94-95, February, 1981.

Reversing female sterilization. POPULATION REPORTS 8(5):97, September, 1980.

A Review of women requesting reversal of tubal sterilization, by J; Murray. AUSTRALIAN AND NEW ZEALAND JOURNAL OF OBSTETRICS AND GYNAECOLOGY 20(4):211-213, November, 1980.

Rhesus monkey study links vasectomy and atherosclerosis. FAMILY PLANNING PERSPECTIVES 12:311-313, November-December, 1980.

Richly vascularized liver tumors, by H. M. Zonderland, et al. NEDERLANDS TIJDSCHRIFT VOOR GENEESKUNDE 124(33):1372-1376, August 16, 1980.

Rift Valley fever as a possible cause of human abortions [letter], by A. A. Abdel-Aziz, et al. TRANSACTIONS OF THE ROYAL SOCIETY OF TROPICAL MEDICINE AND HYGIENE 74(5):685-686, 1980.

The right to do wrong: Reform Judaism and abortion, by R. A. Block. JOURNAL OF REFORM JUDAISIM 28:3-15, September, 1981.

Right-to-life activists split on federal tactics [editorial], by J. M. Wall. CHRISTIANITY CENTURY 98:1332-1333, December 23, 1981.

Right to life breakthrough [views of S. Galebach], by W. F. Buckley, Jr. NATIONAL REVIEW 33:313, March 20, 1981.

Right-to-life split, by T. Noah. NEW REPUBLIC 184:7-9, March 21, 1981.

Right to lifers find a key friend. US NEWS AND WORLD RE-PORT 90:8, February 2, 1981.

Right to lifers learn facts of life [in applying for abortions], by A. J. Fugh-Berman. OFF OUR BACKS 11:4, June, 1981.

The right to live and the right to die: some considerations of law and society in America, by G. Z. F. Bereday. VALUES, ETHICS AND HEALTH CARE 4:233-256, 1979.

Right to strife. NEW REPUBLIC 184:5-6, June 6, 1981.

Rights of the born, by B. J. Leonard. CHRISTIAN CENTURY 99:7-8, January 6-13, 1982.

The rights of child before birth, by G. López Garcia. REVISTA CHILENA DE PEDIATRIA 51(1):39-47, January-February, 1980.

The rights of personhood: the Dred Scott case and the question of abortion [Roe vs Wade], by M. C. Sernett. RELIGION IN LIFE 49:461-476, Winter, 1980.

Rise in female-initiated sexual activity at ovulation and its suppression by oral contraceptives, by D. Adams. THE NEW ENGLAND JOURNAL OF MEDICINE November 23, 1978.

Risk factors for benign breast disease, by L. A. Brinton, et al. AMERICAN JOURNAL OF EPIDEMIOLOGY 113(3):203-214, March, 1981.

Risk of carcinogenesis among pill users, by N. N. Chowdhury. JOURNAL OF THE INDIAN MEDICAL ASSOCIATION 74 (5):98-99, March 1, 1980.

Risk of myocardial infarction in relation to current and discon-

tinued use of oral contraceptives, by D. Slone, et al. NEW
ENGLAND JOURNAL OF MEDICINE 305(8):420-424,
August 20, 1981.

Risk of pelvic inflammatory disease among users of intrauterine
devices, irrespective of previous pregnancy, by S. Osser, et al.
AMERICAN JOURNAL OF OBSTETRICS AND GYNECOL-
OGY 138(7 Part 2):864-867, 1980.

Risks in legal, induced abortion. Review of the literature, by H. E.
Stamm. GYNAEKOLOGISCHE RUNDSCHAU 20(2):65-
84, 1980.

The risks of teenage abortion, by W. Cates, et al. AMERICAN
JOURNAL OF EPIDEMIOLOGY 112(3):434, 1980.

Role of angiotensin II in oral contraceptive hypertension in
anesthetized rats, by D. H. Stubbs, et al. LIFE SCIENCES
27(5):435-440, August 4, 1980.

Role of chlorinated hydrocarbon pesticides in abortions and premature labour, by M. C. Saxena, et al. TOXICOLOGY 17(3):
323-331, 1980.

Role of detection of alphafoetoprotein in serum of pregnant
women with risk of abortion, by P. Skalba, et al. ZENTRAL-
BLATT FUR GYNAEKOLOGIE 102(18):1025-1030, 1980.

Role of induced abortion in secondary infertility, by J. R. Daling,
et al. OBSTETRICS AND GYNECOLOGY 57(1):59-61,
January, 1981.

The role of nurse practitioners as family planning clinicians in
Tennessee, by H. K. Atrash, et al. JOURNAL OF THE
TENNESSEE MEDICAL ASSOCIATION 74(1):15-20, 1981.

Role of the pharmacist in the delivery of family planning services
to college students, by M. C. Smith, et al. JOURNAL OF
THE AMERICAN COLLEGE HEALTH ASSOCIATION 29:
292-294, June, 1981.

Role of physical trauma and overexertion in the etiology of spon-

taneous abortion, by T. V. Zhukova. ZDRAVOOKHRA-
NENIYE BELORUSSII 0(6):65-66, 1979.

Ruled out . . . special report, by C. Hicks. NURSING TIMES 76:
2041, November 20, 1980.

Rupture of the uterus after midtrimester prostaglandin abortion,
by L. L. Cederqvist, et al. JOURNAL OF REPRODUCTIVE
MEDICINE 25(3):136-138, September, 1980.

Ruptured benign hepatic tumors. Influence of oral contraception (apropos of two cases), by G. Grall, et al. LILLE MEDI-
CAL 25(10):569-573, December, 1980.

Rural development and family planning behaviour in Bangladesh
villages [based on conference paper], by M. Alauddin. BANG
BANGLADESH DEVELOPMENT STUDIES 7:25-58, Winter,
1979.

St. Louis law regulating sale of contraceptives, sexual devices OK.
THE CRIMINAL LAW REPORTER: COURT DECISIONS
AND PROCEEDINGS 28(10):2228-2229, December 13,
1980.

St. Rita says no, by P. B. Donham. ATLANTIC INSIGHT 3:18-
19, April, 1981.

Salmonella septic abortion, by B. S. Sengupta, et al. INTERNA-
TIONAL SURGERY 65(2):183-186, March-April, 1980.

Salpingitis: overview of etiology and epidemiology, by K. K.
Holmes, et al. AMERICAN JOURNAL OF OBSTETRICS
AND GYNECOLOGY 138(7 Part 2):893-900, 1980.

The sanctity of human life, by M. Burke. IRISH NURSING
NEWSLETTER pp4-6, May, 1981.

Saving one, dooming another [abortion of mongoloid fraternal
twin at Manhattan's Mount Sinai Medical Center]. TIME
117:59, June 29, 1981.

Scheinberg v. Smith, 482 F. Supp 529. JOURNAL OF FAMILY

LAW 19:149-153, November, 1980.

Schwangerschaftsabbruch—jetzt foderalistisch [Switzerland], by
  C. Blocher. REFORMATIO: EVANGELISCHE ZEIT-
  SCHRIFT FUR KULTUR AND POLITIK 30:513-515,
  September, 1981.

Science and the 'human life bill', by H. S. Meyer. JAMA 246(8):
  837-839, August 21, 1981.

Science challenges Humanae Vitae, by W. P. Messenger. NATION-
  AL CATHOLIC REPORTER 17:7+, October 16, 1981.

Sciuriaga v. Powell, Queen's Bench Div. May 18, 1979, Transcript
  No. 1978/NJ/262; (1979) 76 L S Gaz 567. MODERN LAW
  REVIEW 44:215-219, March, 1981.

The search for an alternative, by P. Steinfels. COMMONWEAL
  108:660-664, November 20, 1981.

Seasonal variation in spontaneous abortions, by C. W. Warren, et
  al. AMERICAN JOURNAL OF PUBLIC HEALTH 70(12):
  1297-1299, December, 1980.

Second-trimester amniocentesis [letter], by J. J. Delaney. OB-
  STETRICS AND GYNECOLOGY 57(6):768, June, 1981.

Secret synod proposition's rule on sex, by P. Hebblethwaite.
  NATIONAL CATHOLIC REPORTER 17:19, November 7,
  1980.

Secretary Schweiker and that Schwenkfelder power, by W. F.
  Willoughby. OUR SUNDAY VISITOR 69:5, March 1, 1981.

Secular infallibility, by F. Zepezauer. NATIONAL REVIEW 33:
  1484-1485, December 11, 1981.

Selective abortion saves normal fetus. NEW SCIENTIST 90:820,
  June 25, 1981.

Selective birth in twin pregnancy with disordancy for Down's
  syndrome, by T. D. Kerenyi, et al. NEW ENGLAND JOUR-

NAL OF MEDICINE 304(25):1525-1527, June 18, 1981.

Selective pregnancy termination in thalassaemia [letter], by P. Denton. MEDICAL JOURNAL OF AUSTRALIA 1(12):654+- June 13, 1981.

Self-concept and contraception: pre-conception decision-making. POPULATION AND ENVIRONMENT 4(1):11, Spring, 1981.

Self esteem, locus of control, and adolescent contraception, by E. Herold. THE JOURNAL OF PSYCHOLOGY 101(1):83-88, January, 1979.

Seminar stresses pharmacist's role as advisor in use of contraceptives. AMERICAN DRUGGIST 182:63-70, July, 1980.

Senate commences hearings on 'human life' [news], by C. Holden. SCIENCE 212(4495):648-649, May 8, 1981.

Senate hearing on abortion amendments, by O. Hatch, et al. ORIGINS 11:293+, October 22, 1981.

A sensitive enzyme immunoassay for norethisterone in plasma and saliva, by A. Turkes, et al. JOURNAL OF ENDO-CRINOLOGY 85(2):19-20, 1980.

A seperate mechanism of gonadotropin recovery after pregnancy termination, by R. P. Marrs, et al. JOURNAL OF CLINICAL ENDOCRINOLOGY AND METABOLISM 52(3):545-548, March, 1981.

Serum hCG, hPL and progesterone levels in threatened abortions, by N. Sugita, et al. NIPPON SANKA FUJINKA GAKKAI ZASSHI 32(7):851-858, July, 1980.

Serum high density lipoprotein cholesterol levels in women using a contraceptive injection of depot-medroxyprogesterone acetate, by J. Kremer, et al. CONTRACEPTION 22(4):359-367, October, 1980.

Serum leucine aminopeptidase activity in threatened abortion, prolonged pregnancy and pregnancy toxemias, by W. Nikodem. POLSKI TYGODNIK LEKARSKI 36(14):497-499, April 6, 1981.

Serum levels of ethinylestradiol following its ingestion alone or in oral contraceptive formulations, by P. F. Brenner, et al. CONTRACEPTION 22(1):85-95, July, 1980.

Serum progesterone, 17 alpha-hydroxyprogestrone, human chorionic gonadotropin, and prolactin in early pregnancy and a case of spontaneous abortion, by P. D. Manganiello, et al. FERTILITY AND STERILITY 36(1):55-60, July, 1981.

Serum prolactin levels in women before and after the use of copper IUD, by R. S. Raikar. INDIAN JOURNAL OF MEDICAL RESEARCH 69:436-439, March, 1979.

Seventeen's answers to your questions about birth control [teenagers], by E. R. Dobell. SEVENTEEN 40:142-143+, October, 1981.

Several provisions of North Dakota's abortion law held unconstitutional. THE CRIMINAL LAW REPORTER: COURT DECISIONS AND PROCEEDINGS 28(7):2158-2159, November 12, 1980.

Sex, abortion and the Supreme Court [teen-age abortion]. NEWSWEEK 97:83, April 6, 1981.

Sex differences in correlates of abortion attitudes among college students, by B. A. Finlay. JOURNAL OF MARRIAGE AND THE FAMILY 43:571-582, August, 1981.

Sex on the dole, by C. Doyle. OBSERVER p33, July 26, 1981.

Sex problems in practice. Training and referral. Institute of Psychosexual Medicine, Margaret Pyke Centre, and Brook Advisory Centres, by P. Tunnadine, et al. BRITISH MEDICAL JOURNAL 282(6277):1669-1672, May 23, 1981.

Sex selection abortion: a constitutional analysis of the abortion liberty and a person's right to know, by J. R. Schaibley. INDIANA LAW JOURNAL 56:281-320, Winter, 1981.

Sexual behaviour and contraceptive use among socioeconomic groups of young women in the United States, by K. Ford, et al. JOURNAL OF BIOSOCIAL SCIENCE 13(1):31-45, January, 1981.

Sexual experience, birth control usage, and sex education of unmarried Canadian university students: changes between 1968 and 1978, by F. M. Barrett. ARCHIVES OF SEXUAL BEHAVIOR 9(5):367-390, October, 1980.

Sexual experience and responses to a birth control film, by E. Herold. JOURNAL OF SCHOOL HEALTH 50(2):66-68, February, 1980.

Sexuality and contraception, by J. F. Porter. AUSTRALASIAN NURSES JOURNAL 10:10-12+, May, 1981.

Sexuality and contraception. Studies of 420 university students concerning correlation between menarche, beginning of sexual activity and contraception, by M. Conti. ANNALI DI OSTETRICIA, GINECOLOGIA, MEDICINA PERINATALE 100(4):233-238, July-August, 1979.

Sexuality and contraception. A study of 548 female university students, by M. Conti. MINERVA GINECOLOGIA 32(11): 1013-1018, November, 1980.

Shifts in abortion. Attitudes: 1972-1978, by C. A. Haney, et al. JOURNAL OF MARRIAGE AND THE FAMILY 42(3):491-499, August, 1980.

Shortcut to outlaw abortion [Helms-Hyde bill], by L. Sager. NEW YORK REVIEW OF BOOKS 28:39-42, June 25, 1981.

Should abortions be outlawed? [proposed Helms-Hyde bill, interviews], by H. J. Hyde, et al. US NEWS AND WORLD REPORT 90:31-32, May 4, 1981.

Should the community subsidize conventional contraceptives? by B. Grünfeld. NORDISK MEDICIN 95(8-9):218, September, 1980.

145

Should the media advertise contraceptives? by D. E. Greydanus. AMERICAN JOURNAL OF DISEASES OF CHILDREN 135 (8):687-688, August, 1981.

Side effects of extra-amniotic PGF2 alpha in the induction of labor in retained abortion and in the intrauterine death of the fetus, by A. Paladini, et al. MINERVA GINECOLOGIA 32(9):781-786, September, 1980.

Side effects of oral contraceptives, by O. Blaskova, et al. BRA-TISLAVSKE LEKARSKE LISTY 75(2):167-172, February, 1981.

Side effects of using modern contraceptive methods for a period of 9192 cycles, by B. Nalbanski. AKUSHERSTVO I GINE-KOLOGIIA 19(5-6):553-556, 1980.

Sielkundige implikasies van gesinsbe—planning, by H. Viljoen. DIE SUID-AFRIKAANSE TYDSKRIF VIV SOSIOLOGIE p53-65, September 18, 1978.

Signing the pledge, by J. Kettle. EXECUTIVE 23:16, February, 1981.

Simultaneous-equation model of labor supply, fertility and earnings of married women: the case of registered nurses, by C. R. Link, et al. SOUTHERN ECONOMIC JOURNAL 47: 977-989, April, 1981.

Singapore, by D. Sivakami, et al. STUDIES IN FAMILY PLAN-NING 11(11):341, November, 1980.

Single dose extra-amniotic prostaglandin gel for midtrimester termination of pregnancy, by M. A. Quinn, et al. AUSTRALI-AN AND NEW ZEALAND JOURNAL OF OBSTETRICS AND GYNAECOLOGY 20(2):77-79, May, 1980.

Six cases of listeriosis during pregnancy, by R. Guillermin, et al. GYNAEKOLOGISCHE RUNDSCHAU 20(Suppl 1):103-105, June, 1980.

Skin changes from taking hormonal contraceptives, by H. Zaun.

MEDIZINISCHE MONATSSCHRIFT FUR PHARMA-
ZEUTEN 4(6):161-165, June, 1981.

The sluggish gallbladder of pregnancy [editorial] , by S. Cohen.
NEW ENGLAND JOURNAL OF MEDICINE 302:397-399,
February 14, 1980.

Sociaal-psychologische aspecten van abortus provacatus, by F.
Deven. TIJDSCHRIFT VOOR SOCIALE WETENSCHAPPEN
21(3):241-264, July-September, 1976.

Social and emotional aspects of voluntary childlessness in vasectomized childless men, by R. H. Magarick, et al. JOURNAL
OF BIOSOCIAL SCIENCE 13:157-168, April, 1981.

Social commentary: values and legal personhood, by J. A. Parness. WEST VIRGINIA LAW REVIEW 83:487-503, Spring,
1981.

Social security and public welfare—abortion—the Hyde amendment substantively altered state funding obligations under
title XIX of the social security act of 1965, requiring states
to fund only the abortions specified in the amendment.
UNIVERSITY OF DETROIT JOURNAL OF URBAN LAW
58:95-117, Fall, 1980.

Social structure in cases of induced abortion (results of a one-
year study conducted by the Indication Bureau of the City
of Nuremberg, by K. G. Friedrich. OEFFENTLICHE GE-
SUNDHEITSWESEN 42(9):600-611, 1980.

Social work as an integral part of family planning service for
low-income families: an example of U.S. experience, by K.-
T. Sung. INTERNATIONAL SOCIAL WORK 21(2):23-32,
1978.

Socialization for childbearing, by S. G. Philliber. JOURNAL OF
SOCIAL ISSUES 36(1):30-44, 1980.

Society: look, little guy, you just don't measure up. OUR SUN-
DAY VISITOR 70:7, July 5, 1981.

Society today. Moral battlegrounds. NEW SOCIETY 55:957, 1981.

The sociopolitics of contraception [news] . JAMA 244(13):1415, September 26, 1980.

Socio-sanitary analysis of the first 300 voluntary interruptions of pregnancy carried out in the obstetrical-gynecological division of the Bassini Hospital of Milan, by M. M. Marzi, et al. MINERVA GINECOLOGIA 32(10):939-944, October, 1980.

Somatic complications in abortion, by R. Wille, et al. BEITRAEGE ZUR GERICHTLICHEN MEDIZIN 38:17-19, 1980.

Some characteristics of intentionally childless wives in Britain, by F. Baum, et al. JOURNAL OF BIOSOCIAL SCIENCE 12(3):287-299, July, 1980.

Some fault anti-abortion statute as ambiguous. NATIONAL CATHOLIC REPORTER 17:3-4, February 6, 1981.

Some psychological correlates of family planning among women, by P. Kumar, et al. INDIAN JOURNAL OF SOCIAL WORK 42:81-86, April, 1981.

Soul and the person: defining life, by R. Gist. CHRISTIAN CENTURY 98:1022-1024, October 14, 1981.

Spasmogenic effects of the anti-fertility agent, zoapatanol, by J. B. Smith, et al. LIFE SCIENCES 28(24):2743-2746, June 15, 1981.

Sperm hazard, by B. Dixon. OMNI 3:18, November, 1980.

Spermicidal saponins from Pittosporum nilghrense, by G. K. Jouri, et al. INDIAN JOURNAL OF PHARMACEUTICAL SCIENCES 42(1):12-13, 1980.

Split within anti-abortion movement hits myths, by M. Meehan. NATIONAL CATHOLIC REPORTER 18:3, November 6,

1981.

Spontaneous abortion after hand-foot-and-mouth disease caused by Coxsackie virus A16, by M. M. Ogilvie, et al. BRITISH MEDICAL JOURNAL 281(6254):1527-1528, December 6, 1980.

Spontaneous abortion and environmental monitering: electrophoretic study, by D. Serman, et al. MUTATION RE-SEARCH 74(3):197-198, 1980.

Spontaneous abortion over time: comparing occurrence in two cohorts of women a generation apart, by A. Wilcox. AMER-ICAN JOURNAL OF EPIDEMIOLOGY 112(3):453-454, 1980.

Spontaneous abortion rate in patients with endometriosis, by J. D. Naples, et al. OBSTETRICS AND GYNECOLOGY 57(4): 509-512, April, 1981.

Spontaneous abortions among women employed in the metal industry in Finland, by K. Hemminki, et al. INTERNA-TIONAL ARCHIVES OF OCCUPATIONAL AND ENVI-RONMENTAL HEALTH 47(1):53-60, 1980.

Spontaneous abortions by occupation and social class in Finland, by K. Hemminki, et al. INTERNATIONAL JOURNAL OF EPIDEMIOLOGY 9(2):149-153, June, 1980.

Spontaneous foetal losses in women using different contraceptives around the time of conception, by S. Harlap, et al. INTERNATIONAL JOURNAL OF EPIDEMIOLOGY 9(1): 49-56, March, 1980.

Spontaneous recanalization of tubes after surgical sterilization, by S. Bojovic. JUGOSLAVENSKA GINEKOLOGIJA I OP-STETRICIJA 20(3-4):153-156, May-August, 1980.

Spontaneous resolution of oral-contraceptive-associated liver tumor, by R. R. Penkava, et al. JOURNAL OF COMPUTER ASSISTED TOMOGRAPHY 5(1):102-103, February, 1981.

Spontaneous rupture of the pregnant uterus following voluntary interruption of pregnancy, by P. E. Fehr. MINNESOTA MEDICINE 64(4):203-204, April, 1981.

Starting family life and sex education programs: a health agency's perspective, by E. Wagman, et al. JOURNAL OF SCHOOL HEALTH 51(4):247-252, April, 1981.

Statewide family planning programs in Tennessee—a 1980 update, by B. Campbell, et al. JOURNAL OF THE TENNESSEE MEDICAL ASSOCIATION 73(9):629-634, September, 1980.

Status of family planning in the Philippines, by A. Sugiyama. JOSANPU ZASSHI 34(8):568, August, 1980.

The status of sterilization in proposed legislation in Serbia, by M. Husar. JUGOSLAVENSKA GINEKOLOGIJA I OPSTET-RICIJA 20(3-4):112-116, May-August, 1980.

Statutes and ordinances—abortion. THE CRIMINAL LAW REPORTER: COURT DECISIONS AND PROCEEDINGS 28(5): 2120, October 29, 1980.

"The steady-state economy" in economics, ecology, ethics, by H. Daly. SAN FRANSISCO FREEMAN p324-356, 1980.

Stepping out of Down's syndrome [moral questions of aborting genetically defective children], by J. R. Nelson. CHRISTIAN CENTURY 98:789-790, August 12-19, 1981.

Sterilization and mental deficiency: survey among obstetricians and gynecologists in Québec, by A. Dupras. UNION MEDICALE DU CANADA 110(6):538-544+, June, 1981.

Sterilization and the retarded female: another perspective [letter], by L. S. Crain. PEDIATRICS 66(4):650-651, October, 1980.

Sterilization and the welfare of the retarded [letter], by R. Sherlock. HASTINGS CENTER REPORT 10(3):4+, June, 1980.

Sterilization as part of a family planning service [editorial].
LANCET 2(8239):186, July 25, 1981.

Sterilization by minilaparotomy, by M. Beckmann. MEDI-
ZINISCHE WELT 31(17):633-635, April 25, 1980.

Sterilization of men and women according to present regula-
tions with particular emphasis on the Vojvodina region, by
Berić, et al. JUGOSLAVENSKA GINEKOLOGIJA I OP-
STETRICIJA 20(3-4):117-120, May-August, 1980.

Sterilization of the mentally retarded: a decision for the courts,
by G. J. Annas. JASTINGS CENTER REPORT 11:18-19,
August, 1981.

Sterilization of mentally retarded minors [letter]. BRITISH
MEDICAL JOURNAL 281(6250):1281-1282, November 8,
1980.

Sterilization of the mentally retarded: position of the Committee
of Deontology of the Association of the French Speaking
Physicians of Canada [editorial]. UNION MEDICALE DU
CANADA 110(3):280-281, March, 1981.

Sterilization of the retarded [editorial], by L. E. Karp. AMERI-
CAN JOURNAL OF MEDICAL GENETICS 9(1):1-3, 1981.

Sterilization of women in Chile. Results of two samples of
Valdivia and Santiago, by D. Menanteau Horta. REVISTA
CHILENA DE OBSTETRICIA Y GINECOLOGIA 44(1):
27-33, 1979.

Sterilization operations in Australia, by T. Selwood, et al. MED-
ICAL JOURNAL OF AUSTRALIA 2(9):499-501, Novem-
ber 1, 1980.

Sterilization. A preventive method for both men and women.
LAKARTIDNINGEN 77(48):4499-4526, November 26,
1980.

Sterilization under discussion, by G. Tassinari. MINERVA
GINECOLOGIA 32(6):473, June, 1980.

Sterilization with Hulka clips, by E. Qvigstad, et al. TIDSS-KRIFT FOR DEN NORSKE LAEGEFORENING 100(34-36):2033-2035, December 10, 1980.

Steroid contraception and hyperprolactinemia, by W. Voelker, et al. ACTA ENDOCRINOLOGICA 94(234):8, 1980.

Steroid releasing vaginal rings, by I. D. Nuttal, et al. ACTA EUROPAEA FERTILITATIS 11(3):225-230, September, 1980.

Still looser UK guidelines [news]. NATURE 287(5780):265-266, September 25, 1980.

Strafrechtlicher Bevölkerungsschutz und Bevölkerungsplanung in der Türkischen Republik [based on conference paper], by O. Oehring. ORIENT 21(3):345-370, 1980.

Straight talk on abortion; reprint from S. Louis Review, August 29, September 5 and September 12, 1980. CATHOLIC MIND 79:42-49, March, 1981.

Stressful life events and marital dysfunction, by H. W. Bird, et al. HOSPITAL AND COMMUNITY PSYCHIATRY 32(7):486-490, July, 1981.

Stromal and epithelial changes in the fallopian tube following hormonal therapy, by S. E. Mills, et al. HUMAN PATHOLO-GY 11(5 Suppl):583-585, September, 1980.

Structure and activity relationships of alpha-chlorohydrin-bis-nitro benzoates as antifertility agents in male rats, by F. R. Rooney, et al. IRCS MEDICAL SCIENCE: LIBRARY COMPENDIUM 8(11):817-818, 1980.

Studies on non-steroidal antifertility agents—synthesis and antifertility effects of 1,1-diphenyl-2-naphthyl ethylenes, by Y. L. Hu, et al. YAO HSUEH HSUEH PAO 14(12):715-719, December, 1979.

Studies on the viability of trophoblast after termination of various kinds of pregnancies, by K. Kanda. NIPPON SANKA

FUJINKA GAKKAI ZASSHI 32(10):1575-1582, October, 1980.

Study finds sharp rise in teen sexual activity. YOUTH ALTERNATIVES 9(4):14, April, 1981.

A study of adolescent attitudes toward sexuality, contraception and pregnancy, by J. J. O'Leary. DAI 41(9-10), 1981.

Study of blood pressure in women taking oral contraceptives, by K. A. Bano, et al. JPMA 30(7):157-159, July, 1980.

A study of interaction of low-dose combination oral contraceptive with Ampicillin and Metronidazole, by J. V. Joshi, et al. CONTRACEPTION 22(6):643-652, December, 1980.

A study of interaction of a low-dose combination oral contraceptive with anti-tubercular drugs, by J. V. Joshi, et al. CONTRACEPTION 21(6):617-629, June, 1980.

A study of the mechanism of weight gain in medroxyprogesterone acetate users, by K. Amatayakul, et al. CONTRACEPTION 22(6):605-622, December, 1980.

A study of menstrual patterns following laparoscopic sterilization with silastic rings, by T. H. Goh, et al. INTERNATIONAL JOURNAL OF FERTILITY 26(2):116-119, 1981.

A study of postpill amenorrhea, by R. Chatterjee, et al. INTERNATIONAL JOURNAL OF GYNAECOLOGY AND OBSTETRICS 18(2):113-114, September-October, 1980.

Study of registered ayurvedic practitioners in five M.O.H. divisions and the Kandy district,—on their role in maternal and child care and family planning, by C. Sivagnanasundram, et al. CEYLON MEDICAL JOURNAL 24(1-2):21-28, March-June, 1979.

A study of twenty-three cases of postvasectomy sterility operated for recanalization, by D. K. Paliwal, et al. INTERNATIONAL SURGERY 65(2):165-169, March-April, 1980.

Study of the use of contraceptives by a town and a country population of northern Italy, by G. G. Novelli, et al. ACTA EUROPAEA FERTILITATIS 11(2):167-179, June, 1980.

Study of women seeking abortion, by K. Sidenius. SOCIAL SCIENCE AND MEDICINE 12(5A):423-424, September, 1978.

A study on the effects of induced abortion on subsequent pregnancy outcome, by C. Madore, et al. AMERICAN JOURNAL OF OBSTETRICS AND GYNECOLOGY 139(5):516-521, March 1, 1981.

A study on motivational factors influencing sterilization (vasectomy) in a mass family planning camp, by S.T.D. Gopala Krishnan. JOURNAL OF FAMILY WELFARE 27:16-24, March, 1981.

Study on re-establishment of ovulation after termination of sexsteroidal treatment—compared with re-appearance of ovulation after abortion and premature delivery, by K. Hayashi, et al. KEIO JOURNAL OF MEDICINE 28(4):173-193, December, 1979.

Subsidized abortion: moral rights and moral compromise, by G. Sher. PHILOSOPHY AND PUBLIC AFFAIRS 10:361-372, Fall, 1981.

Successful pregnancy soon after oral contraceptive-associated malignant hypertension, by J. H. Silas, et al. POSTGRADUATE MEDICAL JOURNAL 56(661):790-791, November, 1980.

Sul Dritto Alla E Sul Paradosso della Posizione Antiaborista: Una Republica, by M. Mori. REVISTA INTERNAZIONALE DI FILOSOFIA DEL DIRITTO 58:178-183, January-March, 1981.

The Supreme Court, abortion and state response, by J. Nicholson. PUBLIUS 8(1):159-178, 1978.

The Supreme Court and abortion: the irrelevance of medical

judgment, by G. J. Annas. HASTINGS CENTER REPORT 10(5):23-24, October, 1980.

The Supreme Court and Abortion: 1. Upholding constitutional principles, by J. T. Noonan, Jr. HASTINGS CENTER REPORT 10(6):14-16, December, 1980.

—: 2. Sidestepping social realities, by D. Mechanic. HASTINGS CENTER REPORT 10(6):17-19, December, 1980.

Supreme court backs parental notification on abortion. OUR SUNDAY VISITOR 69:7, April 5, 1981.

The Supreme Court decided: social security—abortion. THE FAMILY LAW REPORTER 6(34):3055-3074, July 1, 1980.

Supreme Court report: abortion . . . federal funds, by R. L. Young. AMERICAN BAR ASSOCIATION JOURNAL 66: 994-996, August, 1980.

Surgery during pregnancy and fetal outcome, by J. B. Brodsky, ed al. AMERICAN JOURNAL OF OBSTETRICS AND GYNECOLOGY 138(8):1165-1167, December 15, 1980.

Surgical fertility regulation among women on the Navajo Indian reservation. 1972-1978. AMERICAN JOURNAL OF PUBLIC HEALTH 71(4):403, April, 1981.

Surgical procedure problems in the treatment of septic abortion complicated by acute kidney failure, by S. Dotseva, et al. AKUSHERSTVO I GINEKOLOGIIA 19(5-6):522-525, 1980.

Surgical procedures for the sterilization of females (vaginal approach), by F. Rio. MINERVA GINECOLOGIA 32(6): 469-472, June, 1980.

Surgical procedures for tubal sterilization (by addominal approach), by G. Ferraris. MINERVA GINECOLOGIA 32(6): 465-468, June, 1980.

Surgical sterilization in women, by V. Lehmann. MEDI-
ZINISCHE KLINIK 75(21):747-750, October 10, 1980.

Surgical sterilization: now more popular than the pill. FUTUR-
IST 15:75, December, 1981.

Surgical treatment of post abortum endometriosis of the blad-
der and postoperative bladder function, by S. Fianu, et al.
SCANDINAVIAN JOURNAL OF UROLOGY AND
NEPHROLOGY 14(2):151-155, 1980.

A survey of attitudes towards permanent contraceptive methods,
by A. E. Reading, et al. JOURNAL OF BIOLOGICAL
SCIENCE 12(4):383, October, 1980.

Survey of family planning services provided to teenagers in five
public health projects, by H. G. Green. PUBLIC HEALTH
REPORTS 96:279-285, May-June, 1981.

Susceptibility of abortion patients to infection: correlation to
cervical flora, by J. Paavonen, et al. INTERNATIONAL
JOURNAL OF GYNAECOLOGY AND OBSTETRICS
18(1):44-47, July-August, 1980.

Switzerland to consider revised guidelines [news], by A. Hay.
NATURE 277(5695):341-342, February 1, 1979.

Synergism between testosterone and a superactive gonadotropin-
releasing hormone analog in suppressing gonadotropin secretion, by D. Heber, et al. CLINICAL RESEARCH 28(1):
24A, 1980.

The synthesis of A-nor-19-nordiethynyl steroids, by L. Y. Zhu, et
al. YAO HSUEH HSUEH PAO 16(3):211-217, March, 1981.

Synthesis of some flavonoid compounds with 3'- or 4'-substi-
tuted methyl group, by J. M. Yang. YAO HSUEH HSUEH
PAO 15(11):684-687, November, 1980.

Synthetic estro-progestational (contraceptive) agents and cerebral ischemic complications: cerebral pseudo-tumours,
thrombosis of intracranial venous sinuses. Apropos of 60

cases, by G. Rancurel, et al. SEMAINES DES HOPITAUX
DE PARIS 56(39-40):1583-1587, October 18-25, 1980.

Synthetic studies of contraceptive drugs. II. The synthesis of
16 alpha, 17 alpha-dihydroxyprogesterone acetophenide, by
D. G. Han, et al. YAO HSUEH HSUEH PAO 15(12):725-
729, December, 1980.

Systemic lupus erythematosus and habitual abortion. Case re-
port, by A. L. Hartikainen-Sorri, et al. BRITISH JOURNAL
OF OBSTETRICS AND GYNAECOLOGY 87(8):729-731,
August, 1980.

Systems of transportation of hospital-specific waste, by A. Kern.
OEFFENTLICHE GESUNDHEITSWESEN 42(6):351-354,
June, 1980.

Tailoring contraception to patients. MEDICAL WORLD NEWS
22:47-48+, February 16, 1981.

Taiwan, Republic of China, by C. M. Wang, et al. STUDIES IN
FAMILY PLANNING 11(11):343, November, 1980.

Teaching family planning management and evaluation skills, by
M. E. Gorosh, et al. INTERNATIONAL JOURNAL OF
HEALTH EDUCATION 23(2):107-115, 1980.

Technical failures in tubal ring sterilization: incidence perceived
reasons, outcome, and risk factors, by I. Chi, et al. AMERI-
CAN JOURNAL OF OBSTETRICS AND GYNECOLOGY
138(3):307-312, October 1, 1980.

Teenage childbearing and abortion patterns—United States, 1977.
CLINICAL PEDIATRICS 19(12):831-832, December, 1980.

Teen-agers and abortion. ORIGINS 10:657+, April 2, 1981.

Telling parents: clinic policies and adolescents' use of family
planning and abortion services, by A. Torres, et al. FAMILY
PLANNING PERSPECTIVES 12(6):284-292, November-
December, 1980.

Teratogenic hazards of oral contraceptives analyzed in a national malformation register, by E. Savolainen, et al. AMERICAN JOURNAL OF OBSTETRICS AND GYNECOLOGY 140(5): 521-524, July 1, 1981.

Termination of early gestation with a single vaginal suppository of (15S)-15-methyl-prostaglandin F2alpha methyl ester, by S. Roy, et al. CONTRACEPTION 22(2):137-152, August, 1980.

Termination of early pregnancy in ewes by use of a prostaglandin analogue and subsequent fertility, by R. N. Tyrrell, et al. AUSTRALIAN VETERINARY JOURNAL 57(2):76-78, February, 1981.

Termination of pregnancy by menstrual extraction, by W. M. Rodney, et al. JOURNAL OF FAMILY PRACTITIONERS 11(6):955-958, November, 1980.

Termination of pregnancy during or after treatment of carcinoma of the breast. A review, by K. W. Schweppe, et al. ZEIT-SCHRIFT FUR GEBURTSCHILFE UND PERINATOLOGIE 184(1):1-10, February, 1980.

Termination of pregnancy in patients with missed abortion and intrauterine dead fetuses by a single intracervical application of prostaglandin E2 in viscous gel, by G. Ekman, et al. ZENTRALBLATT FUR GYNAEKOLOGIE 102(4):219-222, 1980.

Termination of pregnancy in a woman with hereditary anti-thrombin deficiency under antithrombotic protection with subcutaneous heparin and infusion of plasma, by J. Jespersen. GYNECOLOGIC AND OBSTETRIC INVESTIGATION 12 (5):267-271, 1981.

Tetracycline and oral contraceptives [letter], by R. J. Coskey. JOURNAL OF THE AMERICAN ACADEMY OF DERMA-TOLOGY 5(2):222, August, 1981.

Texas abortion law: consent requirements and special statutes, by T. O. Tottenham, et al. HOUSTON LAW REVIEW 18:

819-848, May, 1981.

Text of US Supreme Court decision: Harris v McRae. JOURNAL OF CHURCH AND STATE 22:575-595, Autumn, 1980.

Thailand, by S. Varakamin, et al. STUDIES IN FAMILY PLANNING 11(11):374, November, 1980.

Thailand's Mr. Contraception [M. Viravaidya; director of Family Planning Services]. TIME 117:67, March 23, 1981.

That all may have life. NATIONAL CATHOLIC REPORTER 16:12, October 17, 1980.

Theology and politics [Helms-Hyde bill], by E. Doerr. HUMANIST 41:47-48, May-June, 1981.

Theology of pro-choice: a feminist perspective [two parts], by B. W. Harrison. WITNESS 64:14-18; 64:18-21, September, 1981.

Therapeutic abortion during the second trimester of pregnancy, using intracervical injection of PgF2 alpha, by B. Maria, et al. NOUVEAU PRESSE MEDICALE 10(22):1825-1827, May 16, 1981.

There is a frustrating logical gap between the assertion that recombinant DNA poses potential risks . . . and the containment levels imposed by current guidelines' [news], by F. Rolleston. NATURE 281(5733):626-627, October 25, 1979.

Third report on oral contraceptives. THESA JOURNAL 20(5): 49-52, June, 1980.

Thirty million illegal abortions, 10 million complications [in countries without legal abortion], by A. Henry. OFF OUR BACKS 11:5, June, 1981.

A thirty-four year-old woman with pelvic pain not relieved by hysterectomy and salpingo-oophorectomy for endometriosis, by F. Ingersoll. NEW ENGLAND JOURNAL OF MEDI-

CINE June 12, 1980.

This is not a last resort treatment but a valid method of birth control, by P. Toynbee. GUARDIAN p8, March 9, 1981.

Threatened abortion, hormone therapy, and malformed embryos: a comment [letter], by D. M. Sheehan, et al. TERATOLOGY 22(3):351-352, December, 1980.

Thrombin inhibitors in women on oral contraceptives, by E. Guagnellini, et al. ACTA HAEMATOLOGICA 65(3):205-210, 1981.

Thrombosis and oral contraception, by K. D. MacRae. BRITISH JOURNAL OF HOSPITAL MEDICINE 24(5):438-440+, November, 1980.

Thrombosis and sex hormones: a perplexing liaison, by S. Wessler. JOURNAL OF LABORATORY AND CLINICAL MEDICINE 96(5):757-761, November, 1980.

The titanium/silicone rubber clip for female sterilization, by G. M. Filshie, et al. BRITISH JOURNAL OF OBSTETRICS AND GYNAECOLOGY 88(6):655-662, June, 1981.

To deal with the right to life forces, by A. Neier. CURRENT 229:29-30, January, 1981.

Too bad for you, Humpty Dumpty, by W. J. Morton. JOURNAL OF THE MEDICAL ASSOCIATION OF GEORGIA 69(11): 901-902, November, 1980.

Toward efficient allocation of fertility reduction expenditures, by B. Berelson, et al. EVALUATION REVIEW 5:147-166, April, 1981.

Towards an understanding of the american abortion rate, by C. Francorne. JOURNAL OF BIOSOCIAL SCIENCE 11(3): 303-313, July, 1979.

Toxic-shock syndrome and the diaphragm [letter], by E. E. Hymowitz. NEW ENGLAND JOURNAL OF MEDICINE

305(14):834, October 1, 1981.

Transient postoperative hypertension: role of obesity and oral contraceptives [letter], by L. H. Honoré JOURNAL OF THE ROYAL SOCIETY OF MEDICINE 72(7):543, July, 1979.

Transitory ischemic attacks, migraine and progestogen drugs. Etiopathogenetic correlations, by G. Moretti, et al. MINERVA MEDICA 71(30:2125-2129, August 25, 1980.

Transplacental carcinogens and mutagens: childhood cancer, malformations, and abortions as risk indicators, by K. Hemminki, et al. JOURNAL OF TOXICOLOGY AND ENVIRONMENTAL HEALTH 6(5-6):1115-1126, September-November, 1980.

The trauma of abortion politics, by R. Tatalovich, et al. COMMONWEAL 108:644-649, November 20, 1981.

Treatment of Asherman's syndrome (intra-uterine synechia), by I. Smid, et al. ZENTRALBLATT FUR GYNAEKOLOGIE 102(7):386-392, 1980.

Trends in cesarean section rates for the United States, 1970-1978, by P. J. Placek, et al. PUBLIC HEALTH REPORTS 95(6):540-548, November-December, 1980.

Trends in contraceptive method of use by California family planning clinic clients aged 10-55, 1976-1979, by B. M. Aved. AMERICAN JOURNAL OF PUBLIC HEALTH 71 (10):1162-1164, October, 1981.

Trends in contraceptive use at one university: 1974-1978, by S. M. Harvey. FAMILY PLANNING PERSPECTIVES 12: 301-304, November-December, 1980.

Trends in fertility, family size preferences and family planning practice—Taiwan, 1961-1980, by M. C. Chang, et al. STUDIES IN FAMILY PLANNING 12:211-228, May, 1981.

Triage in the womb [abortion performed on mongoloid fetus while preserving life of the healthy twin. COMMONWEAL

108:421, July 31, 1981.

Trials of the new right: from abortion to Island Park, by M. Kramer. NEW YORK 14:20-21, February 16, 1981.

Triploidy in 40 human spontaneous abortuses: assessment of phenotype in embryos, by M. J. Harris, et al. OBSTETRICS AND GYNECOLOGY 57(5):600-606, May, 1981.

Tubal anastomosis after tubectomy, by R. Chandra. JOURNAL OF THE INDIAN MEDICAL ASSOCIATION 76(3):41-43, February 1, 1981.

Tubal factors as possible causes of sterility or infertility of primi-gravidae, following therapeutic abortion, by G. Schott, et al. ZENTRALBLATT FUR GYNAEKOLOGIE 103(6):355-362, 1981.

Tubal lesions subsequent to sterilization and their relation to fertility after attempts at reversal, by G. Vasquez, et al. AMERICAN JOURNAL OF OBSTETRICS AND GYNECOL-OGY 138(1):86-92, September 1, 1980.

Tubal ligation: good medicine? Good morality? by J. R. Connery. LINACRE 48:112-114, May, 1981.

Tubal ligation via laparoscopy: report of 84 cases, by G. Y. Fan. CHUNG HUA FU CHAN KO TSA CHIH 15(2):110-111, 1980.

Tubal occlusion by laparoscopy with unipolar current, by J. D. Ortiz Mariscal, et al. GINECOLOGIA Y OBSTETRICIA DE MEXICO 48(287):191-197, September, 1980.

Tubal patency following 'uchida' tubal ligation, by R. J. Stock. OBSTETRICS AND GYNECOLOGY 56(4):521-525, October, 1980.

Tubal ring sterilization: experience with 10,086 cases, by S. D. Mumford, et al. OBSTETRICS AND GYNECOLOGY 57(2): 150-157, February, 1981.

Tubal sterilization and later hospitalizations, by P. A. Poma. JOURNAL OF REPRODUCTIVE MEDICINE 25(5):272-278, November, 1980.

Tubal sterilization by bipolar laparoscopy: report of 232 cases, by J. S. Seiler, et al. OBSTETRICS AND GYNECOLOGY 58(1):92-95, July, 1981.

Tubal torsion, a late complication of sterilization? by R. E. Bernardus, et al. NEDERLANDS TIJDSCHRIFT VOOR GENEESKUNDE 125(18):707-710, May 2, 1981.

Twin pregnancy, one fetus with Down syndrome removed by sectio parva, the other delivered mature and healthy, by L. Beck, et al. GEBURTSCHILFE UND FRAUENHEILKUNDE 40(5):397-400, May, 1980.

Two abortions may endanger later pregnancy, by N. Mallovy. HOMEMAKER'S MAGAZINE 16:78, March, 1981.

Two cases of benign liver tumour in women on oral contraceptives, by J. Dauplat, et al. JOURNAL DE CHIRURGIE 116 (11):651-657, November, 1979.

UCSD gene splicing incident ends unresolved [news], by N. Wade. SCIENCE 209(4464):1494-1495, September 26, 1980.

U.S. bishops cite dissent: ask contraception review, by P. Hebblethwaite. NATIONAL CATHOLIC REPORTER 16:1, October 10, 1980.

U.S. theologians' hopes dashed by synod results, by J. W. Michaels. NATIONAL CATHOLIC REPORTER November 7, 1980.

Ultrasonic evaluation of ovular viability in threatened abortion, by F. Santi, et al. RIVISTA ITALIANA DI GINECOLOGIA 58(5):401-408, September-October, 1977.

Ultrastructure of human spermatozoa in the presence of the spermicide nonoxinol-9 and a vaginal contraceptive containing nonoxinol-9, by W. B. Schill, et al. ANDROLOGIA 13(1):

163

42-49, January-February, 1981.

Ultrasonic sonography in the management of incomplete abortion, by W. G. Jeong, et al. JOURNAL OF REPRODUCTIVE MEDICINE 26(2):90-92, February, 1981.

Ultrasonography before abortion? [letter], by J. J. Crittenden. JAMA 246(10):1088-1089, September 4, 1981.

The ultrastructural features of progestagen-induced decidual cells in the rhesus monkey (Macaca mulatta), by P. F. Wadsworth, et al. CONTRACEPTION 22(2):189-198, August, 1980.

The United States Supreme Court legalizes abortion, by W. C. Ellis. CASE STUDIES IN HEALTH ADMINISTRATION 2: 29-32, 1980.

Unmet demand [legal abortion]. SCIENTIFIC AMERICAN 244: 88, June, 1981.

Unplanned pregnancy—liability of the gynecologist, by G. H. Schlund. GEBURTSHILFE UND FRAUENHEILKUNDE 40 (10):893-895, October, 1980.

Unusual complication of laparoscopy [letter], by D. D. McCormack. MEDICAL JOURNAL OF AUSTRALIA 1(13):667-668, June 28, 1980.

Unwanted pregnancy—the role of the general practitioner, by S. Furman. SOUTH AFRICAN MEDICAL JOURNAL 58(23): 941-942, December 6, 1980.

Up against the 97th Congress: round one, by G. Christgau. VILLAGE VOICE 26(2):22, February 11, 1981.

Up to 16 weeks of gestation, abortions performed as safely in nonhospital facilities as in hospitals. FAMILY PLANNING PERSPECTIVES 13:181-182, July-August, 1981.

Urban-rural differentials in contraceptive use, by R. E. Lightbourne. INTERNATIONAL STATISTICAL INSTITUTE REVIEW May, 1980.

Urinary bile acids in women treated with contraceptive steroids. A study using computerized gas chromatography-mass spectrometry, by P. A. Thomassen. ACTA OBSTETRICIA ET GYNECOLOGICA SCANDINAVICA 60(2):173-176, 1981.

Urinary excretion of chorionic gonadotropins in threatened and habitual abortion, by W. Szymański, et al. GINEKOLOGIA POLSKA 51(12):1129-1134, December, 1980.

Use-effectiveness of standard-dose and low-dose oral contraceptives in Dacca, by A. R. Measham, et al. INTERNATIONAL JOURNAL OF GYNAECOLOGY AND OBSTETRICS 18(5): 354-356, 1980.

Use of cervical caps at the University of California/Berkeley, by G. G. Smith. JOURNAL OF THE AMERICAN COLLEGIATE HEALTH ASSOCIATION 29:93-94, October, 1980.

The use of condoms by VD clinic patients. A survey, by Y. M. Felman, et al. CUTIS 27(3):330-336, March, 1981.

Use of contraception among married women in New South Wales, Australia, by F. Yusuf. JOURNAL OF BIOSOCIAL SCIENCE 12(1):41-49, 1980.

Use of exteriorized stents in vasovasostomy, by F. S. Shessel, et al. UROLOGY 17(2):163-165, February, 1981.

Use of intramuscular prostaglandin for failure of mid-trimester abortion by another method, by P. C. Schwallie, et al. CONTRACEPTION 22(6):623-642, December, 1980.

Use of heparin in cases of septic abortion, by P. Wille. ZENTRALBLATT FUR GYNAEKOLOGIE 102(5):298-302, 1980.

The use of intrauterine device inserted during the immediate postabortion time, by R. L. Reynoso, et al. GINECOLOGIA Y OBSTETRICIA DE MEXICO 47(283):311-320, May, 1980.

The use of the laparoscope in rural Thailand, by K. Chatura-

165

chinda. INTERNATIONAL JOURNAL OF GYNAECOLO-
GY AND OBSTETRICS 18(6):414-419, 1980.

Use of modern contraceptives in Indonesia: a challenge to the
conventional eisdom, by R. Freedman, et al. INTERNATION-
AL FAMILY PLANNING PERSPECTIVES 7:3-15, March,
1981.

Use of nutrition surveys for family planning program evaluation.
The case of the Arab Republic of Egypt nutrition status, by
H. E. Aly, et al. JOURNAL OF THE EGYPTIAN PUBLIC
HEALTH ASSOCIATION 54(5-6):290-312, 1979.

Use of PGF2 alpha to induce abortion in patients with risk factors in first and second thirds of gravidity, by K. Rudolf, et
al. ZENTRALBLATT FUR GYNAEKOLOGIE 102(10):
575-583, 1980.

Use of preventive measures and level of information among abor-
tion seekers at Haukeland Hospital, Gynecologic Clinic, by R.
Ekanger. TIDSSKRIFT FOR DEN NORSKE LAEGEFOREN-
ING 101(11):615-618, April 20, 1981.

The use of prostaglandin E1 analogue pessaries in patients having
first trimester induced abortions, by R. Nakano, et al. BRIT-
ISH JOURNAL OF OBSTETRICS AND GYNAECOLOGY
87(4):287-291, April, 1980.

The use of 16-16 dimethyl trans delta 2 PGE1 methyl ester
(ONO 802) vaginal suppositories for the termination of early
pregnancy. A comparative study, by S. K. Smith, et al.
BRITISH JOURNAL OF OBSTETRICS AND GYNAECOL-
OGY 87(8):712-717, August, 1980.

The use of socio-economic and accessibility information for im-
proving MCH/FP services—the Nigerian case, by A. A. Udo.
JOURNAL OF TROPICAL PEDIATRICS AND ENVIRON-
MENTAL CHILD HEALTH 26(5):203-208, October, 1980.

The use of sulprostone, a prostaglandin E2 derivative, in intrauterine fetal death and therapeutic abortion, by T. H. Lippert, et
al. PROSTAGLANDINS AND MEDICINE 5(4):259-265,

October, 1980.

Use, nonuse, and risk of pregnancy. POPULATION REPORTS 9(3):M-171, May-June, 1981.

The user perspective: an evolutionary step in contraceptive service programs, by G. Zeidenstein. STUDIES IN FAMILY PLANNING 11(1):24-29, January, 1980.

Utah. THE STATE CAPITALS: JUVENILE DELINQUENCY AND FAMILY RELATIONS 5:3-4, May 1, 1981.

Uterine and sigmoid perforations following voluntary interruption of pregnancy by aspiration. A case report, by G. Aulagnier, et al. JOURNAL FDE CHIRURGIE 118(5):339-341, May, 1981.

Uterine perforation during sterilization by laparoscopy and mini-laparotomy, by I. Chi, et al. AMERICAN JOURNAL OF OBSTETRICS AND GYNECOLOGY 139(6):735-736, March 15, 1981.

Utilizing male partners of adolescent abortion patients as change agents: results of an experimental intervention, by K. D. Brosseau. DAI 42(1), 1981.

Vaccine terminates pregnancy. SCIENCE DIGEST 89:102, March, 1981.

Vacuum aspiration method of terminating pregnancy and its early complications, by T. Despodova, et al. AKUSHERST-VO I GINEKOLOGIIA 19(4):281-285, 1980.

Vaginal administration of 15-methyl-PGF2 alpha methyl ester for preoperative cervical dilatation. Task force on prostaglandins for fertility regulation. The World Health Organization. CONTRACEPTION 23(3):251-259, March, 1981.

Vaginal application of a chemotherapeutic agent before legal abortion. A way of reducing infectious complication? by O. Meirik, et al. ACTA OBSTETRICIA ET GYNECOLOGICA SCANDINAVICA 60(3):233-235, 1981.

Vaginal bleeding in early pregnancy [editorial] . BRITISH MEDI-CAL JOURNAL 281(6238):470, August 16, 1980.

Vaginal chemophylaxis in gonorrhea reinfection, by C. H. Cole. SALUD PUBLICA DE MEXICO 22(5):537-546, September-October, 1980.

Vaginal chemoprophylaxis in the reduction of reinfection in women with gonorrhoea. Clinical evaluation of the effectiveness of a vaginal contraceptive, by C. H. Cole, et al. BRITISH JOURNAL OF VENEREAL DISEASES 56(5):314-318, October, 1980.

Vaginal tubal ligation, by D. B. Stephens. SOUTHERN MEDICAL JOURNAL 73(12):1578-1580, December, 1980.

Value conflicts and the uses of research: the example of abortion, by S. Budner. VALUES, ETHICS AND HEALTH CARE 1 (19):14, Fall, 1975.

Value orientation family planning, by A. Bhowmik. SOCIETY AND CULTURE July, 1975.

Variance and reliability in estimates of OC use [letter] , by G. E. Hendershot, et al. AMERICAN JOURNAL OF PUBLIC HEALTH 71(3):316-317, March, 1981.

Various aspects of individual attitudes to irreversible contraception. Results of a survey, by G. Klinger, et al. ZENTRAL-BLATT FUR GYNAEKOLOGIE 103(2):121-123, 1981.

Vas micro-anastomosis. Fundamentals and modifications, by M. R. Sutton. JOURNAL OF UROLOGY 126(2):185-186, August, 1981.

Vascular thrombosis and oral contraceptives—a risk correlated study, by V. Beaumont, et al. JOURNAL OF MEDICINE 12(1):51-61, 1981.

Vascular thrombosis in synthetic estrogen-progestogen users: an immune mechanism, by V. Beaumont, et al. NOUVELLE PRESSE MEDICALE 10(7):503-507, February 21, 1981.

Vasectomy [letter], by H. Klosterhalfen. DEUTSCHE MEDI-
ZINISCHE WOCHENSCHRIFT 105(22):786, May 30, 1980.

Vasectomy counseling and clinical social work, by H. Y. Smith.
HEALTH AND SOCIAL WORK 6:64-70, August, 1981.

Vasectomy reversal [letter], by E. LeBeck, et al. JOURNAL OF
UROLOGY 125(4):604, April, 1981.

—, by L. Taylor, et al. MEDICAL JOURNAL OF AUSTRALIA
1(2):94, January 24, 1981.

Vasectomy reversal [editorial]. LANCET 2(8195 pt 1):625-626,
September 20, 1980.

Vasovasostomy: four year experience at Ochsner Medical Institu-
tions, by H. A. Fuselier, Jr., et al. JOURNAL OF THE
LOUISIANA STATE MEDICAL SOCIETY 132(12):195-196,
December, 1980.

Vasovasostomy—is the microscope necessary? by H. Fenster, et
al. UROLOGY 18(1):60-64, July, 1981.

Venous thrombosis of the upper extremity after hormonal contraception, by M. Kohoutek, et al. CESKOSLOVENSKA
GYNEKOLOGIE 46(4):302-306, May, 1981.

Verbal judgments of Taiwanese family planning field workers
about induced abortion, by G. P. Cernada, et al. AMERICAN
JOURNAL OF PUBLIC HEALTH 71:420-422, April, 1981.

Very troubling search, by R. Dolphin, et al. ALBERTA REPORT
8:22-23, April 24, 1981.

Viability and fetal life in state criminal abortion laws, by E.
Griffin. JOURNAL OF CRIMINAL LAW AND CRIMINOL-
OGY 72:324-344, Spring, 1981.

Viability and the morality of abortion, by A. Zaitchik. PHILOS-
OPHY AND PUBLIC AFFAIRS 10:18-26, Winter, 1981.

Victims of the medical lobby, by R. Whymant. GUARDIAN 24:

12, March, 1981.

Views on sterilization of the Stage I Commission on Abortion in Ljubljana, by M. Macek. JUGOSLAVENSKA GINEKOLO-GIJA I OPSTETRICIJA 20(3-4):127-131, May-August, 1980.

Violence against women: some considerations regarding its causes and elimination, by D. Klein. CRIME AND DELINQUENCY 27(1):64-80, January, 1981.

The vitamin E concentration in the trophoblast and blood serum of women in the course of an abortion, by J. Kotarski. ANNALES UNIVERSITATIS MARIAE CURIE–SKLO-DOWSKA 34:403-413, 1979.

Voluntary childlessness and the nurse's role, by T. Rosenthal. AMERICAN JOURNAL OF MATERNAL CHILD NURSING 5:398-402, November-December, 1980.

Voluntary interruption of pregnancy in an area hospital on the outskirst of Turin, by M. Tanferna, et al. MINERVA MED-ICA 72(16):1021-1026, April 21, 1981.

Voluntary sterilization. HUMANIST 41:57, January-February, 1981.

Voluntary sterilization in Flanders, by R. L. Cliquet, et al. JOUR-NAL OF BIOSOCIAL SCIENCE 13:47-62, January, 1981.

Voluntary sterilization. Medico-legal considerations, by M. Portigliatti-Barbos. MINERVA GINECOLOGIA 32(6):454-458, June, 1980.

Voluntary sterilization, non-injury, justified injury or offense, by M. Del Re. GIUSTIZIA PENAL 85(1):50-63, 1980.

Voluntary sterilization of women and men in Croatia, by P. Drobnjak. JUGOSLAVENSKA GINEKOLOGIJA I OPSTET-RICIJA 20(3-4):121-123, May-August, 1980.

Voluntary termination of pregnancy, by R. Merger. BULLETIN DE L'ACADEMIE NATIONALE DE MEDICINE 163(8):

869-876, November 6-27, 1979.

Voluntary termination of pregnancy. Role of the anesthesiologist [letter] , by C. Buttigieg. ANESTHESIA AND ANALGESIA 37(7-8):451, 1980.

La vraie nature de la vasectomie, by P. Sormany. L'ACTUALITÉ 6:60, January, 1981.

The Walnut Creek Contraceptive Drug Study. A prospective study of the side effects of oral contraceptives. Volume III, an interim report: a comparison of disease occurrence leading to hospitalization or death in users and nonusers of oral contraceptives, by S. Ramcharan, et al. JOURNAL OF REPRODUCTIVE MEDICINE 25(6 Suppl):345-372, December, 1980.

Wan, xi, shao [later, longer, fewer] : how China meets its population problem [based on address] , by H. Tien. INTERNATIONAL FAMILY PLANNING PERSPECTIVES 6:65-73, June, 1980.

The war against choice [1980 National Right to Life Committee meeting, Anaheim, California] , by D. English. MOTHER JONES 6:16+, February-March, 1981.

Warning on spermicides [risk of birth defects] , by J. Seligmann. NEWSWEEK 97:84, April 13, 1981.

Was Serpico a sperm bank? [accusation by F. Serpico that woman tricked him into fathering a child] , by M. Starr, et al. NEWSWEEK 98:42, November 16, 1981.

Watch on the right—abortion rights: taking the offensive, by N. Weisstein. MS MAGAZINE 10:36+, September, 1981.

— backstage with the antiabortion forces, by L. C. Wohl. MS MAGAZINE 9:48+, Fall, 1981.

— beware the "research shows . . ." ploy (attempt to link child abuse and abortion), by J. Gelles, et al. MS MAGAZINE 9: 100, June, 1981.

Watch on the right: danger—a Human Life Amendment is on the way, by R. Copelon. MS MAGAZINE 9:46+, February, 1981.

—ultimate invasion of privacy, by G. Steinem. MS MAGAZINE 9:43-44, February, 1981.

The way to the back-street abortionist is still open. Abortion in France, by J. Hermann. THERAPIE DER GEGENWART 119 (7):810-815, July, 1980.

We walk the line: the struggle at preterm. RADICAL AMERI-CAN 13(2):8-24, 1979.

Weighing the facts about oral contraceptives, by S. R. Cavanaugh. LIFE AND HEALTH 96:14-15, May, 1981.

What bioethics should be, by T. F. Ackerman. JOURNAL OF MEDICAL PHILOSOPHY 5(3):260-275, September, 1980.

What do lovers whisper when the sexometer's on? 'I'll check my chip, dear: [computerized thermometer that signals if sex without fear of pregnancy is possible] . PEOPLE 15:129, April 6, 1981.

What do teens know about the facts of life? by R. G. Amonker. JOURNAL OF SCHOOL HEALTH 50(9):527-530, November, 1980.

What happens now? by A. Martin. NURSING MIRROR 151(22): 8, November 27, 1980.

What progeny for pro-life bedfellows? by J. McKinley. NATION-AL CATHOLIC REPORTER 17:21, July 17, 1981.

Whatever happened to the human race? could come to television in your area, by M. E. Lorentzen. CHRISTIANITY TODAY 25:26-27, January 23, 1981.

Whatever happened to new methods of birth control? ECONO-MIST 279:25-27, May 30, 1981.

When does human life begin? by E. Switzer. VOGUE 171:546-

547+, September, 1981.

When does life begin? An expert says the debate is shedding more heat than light [implications of Helms-Hyde bill; interview by N. Faber], by C. Grobstein. PEOPLE 15:79-80+, June 8, 1981.

When does the life of a human being start? [editorial], by J. Lejeune. PAEDIATRIE UND PAEDOLOGIE 16(2):101-110, 1981.

When something goes wrong: an estimated 15 to 20 percent of all pregnancies end in miscarriage, by A. Pappert. HOME-MAKER'S MAGAZINE 16:54-58+, May, 1981.

When Uncle Sam stops paying, by D. French. FORBES 127:32, June 22, 1981.

Where angels fear, by K. Ashton. NURSING TIMES 77(4):143, January 22, 1981.

Who says oral contraceptives are safe? [misleading claims of safety in drug industry press releases], by B. O'Malley. NATION 232:170-172, February 14, 1981.

Who will control your body? by B. Rose. VOGUE 171:547+, September, 1981.

Why does a woman decide on a abortion? by E. Rautanen, et al. DUODECIM 96(20):1328-1336, 1980.

Why Pro-Life; symposium: Why I am pro-life, by Bp. H. Gracida. Why I am pro-life: a feminist approach, by A. O'Donnell. The 12 most common questions about abortion. Why I am pro-life: a social justice perspective, by T. Hesburgh. Why I am pro-life: a dontor's perspective; interview of J. Willke, by C. Anthony. Why I am pro-life: because there are alternatives, by R. Hanley. OUR SUNDAY VISITOR 69:3-9+, January 18, 1981.

Why the Supreme Court was plainly wrong in the Hyde amendment case: a brief comment on Harris v. McRae (100 S Ct

2671), by M. J. Perry. STANFORD LAW REVIEW 32:1113-1128, July, 1980.

Why women take a chance with birth control, by F. Maynard. WOMAN'S DAY p41-44, November 25, 1980.

Women's rights action group. St. Louis and the right: the anti-abortion front] demonstration against abortion rights] . OFF OUR BACKS 11:10, January, 1981.

Wrongful death, wrongful birth, wrongful life: the evolution of prenatal tort law, by M. W. Kronisch. TRIAL 16:34-36+, December, 1980.

Yes, for you, by N. Giovanni. ENCORE 10:18-19, March-April, 1981.

You and contraceptives, by D. Edmondson. PARENTS 56:67-74, July, 1981.

Your tax dollars at work promoting abortion, by M. A. Walsh. OUR SUNDAY VISITOR 70:4-5, June 7, 1981.

A year ago this week . . . a case for more counselling about sterilization. NURSING MIRROR 152:26, March 26, 1981.

The zaps on judgment day, by F. Moira. OFF OUR BACKS 11:4, November, 1981.

Zinc and copper nutriture of women taking oral contraceptive agents, by S. C. Vir, et al. AMERICAN JOURNAL OF CLINICAL NUTRITION 34(8):1479-1483, August, 1981.

Zoning control of abortion clinics, by J. R. Novak. CLEVELAND STATE LAW REVIEW 28(3):507-527, 1979.

PERIODICAL LITERATURE

SUBJECT INDEX

ABORTION (GENERAL)
Abortion, 1954, by S. Matulis. PROGRESSIVE 45:66, August, 1981.

Abortion and the casual theory of names, by J. A. Nelson, PhD. DAI 41(7-8), 1981.

Abortion and civil disobedience, by D. Morris. OUR SUNDAY VISITOR 70:6-7, September 6, 1981.

Abortion and the "right-to-life": facts, fallacies, and frauds, by J. Prescott. THE HUMANIST 38(4):18-24, July-August, 1978.

—. II, by J. Prescott. THE HUMANIST 38(6):36-42, November-December, 1978.

Abortion as holocaust: a colloquy. pt. 1: A crippling analogy, by E. J. Fisher; pt. 2: The victims of rhetoric, by B. Brick Brickner. CONGRESSIONAL MONTHLY 48:13-15, January, 1981.

Abortion chic, by L. Savan. VILLAGE VOICE 26:32, February 4, 1981.

Abortion: 1. Definitions and implications [editorial], by B. M. Dickens. CANADIAN MEDICAL ASSOCIATION JOURNAL 124(2):113-114, January 15, 1981.

Abortion: an important decision. TABLET 234:1115-1116, November 15, 1980.

Abortion in proportion, by M. G. Gregory. JOURNAL OF THE TENNESSEE MEDICAL ASSOCIATION 73(7): 518-519, July, 1980.

Abortion: the modern temptation, by B. B. Morton. ST. ANTHONY MESSENGER 88:24-27, May, 1981.

Abortion: the new facts of life, by B. M. Campbell. ES- SENCE 12:86-87+, September, 1981.

Abortion 1981: the search for perspective [editorial] , by J. M. Healey. CONNECTICUT MEDICINE 45(7):467, July, 1981.

Abortion, or the way to a social technique, by W. Becker. CONCEPTE 16(9):6-13, 1980.

Abortion rights: taking the offensive, by N. Weisstein. MS MAGAZINE 10:36+, September, 1981.

Abortion weights [letter] , by C. B. Goodhart. LANCET 1(8235):1429, June 27, 1981.

Abortive activity of mimosine and its prevention, by J. Perea- Sasiain, et al. REPRODUCTION 5(2):113-118, April- June, 1981.

Aspects of abortion: clarity can be confusing, by W. S. Coffin. CHRISTIANITY AND CRISIS 41:274+, October 19, 1981.

Assessment of an intervention program for partners of abor- tion patients, by A. J. Lubman. DAI 41(8), 1981.

Attack on abortion, by D. M. Alpern, et al. NEWSWEEK 97: 38+, April 6, 1981.

ABORTION

The attack on women's rights, by L. Cooper. CRIME AND
SOCIAL JUSTICE 15:39-41, 1981.

Characteristics of special groups of abortion patients from
one health district, by J. R. Ashton. JOURNAL OF BIO-
SOCIAL SCIENCE 13(1):63-69, January, 1981.

Complete abortion of early ectopic pregnancy, by G. Ohel, et
al. INTERNATIONAL JOURNAL OF GYNAECOLOGY
AND OBSTETRICS 17(6):596-597, May-June, 1980.

Conception and misconception. TIMES LITERARY SUP-
PLIMENT p1253, October 30, 1981.

Contraceptive risk-taking in a population with limited access
to abortion, by D. R. Horowitz, et al. JOURNAL OF
BIOLOGICAL SCIENCE 12(4):373, October, 1980.

The crossing of swords on abortion, by C. Gerster. PHEONIX
p15-18, November, 1980.

La demande d'interruption volontaire de grossesse, by E.
Zucker-Rouvillois. POPULATION ET FAMILLE 3(45):
47-75, 1978.

Destructive operations, by G. P. Dutta, et al. JOURNAL OF
INDIAN MEDICAL ASSOCIATION 74(1):1-5, January,
1980.

Dutch get tough [news], by J. Becker. NATURE 290(5806):
436, April 9, 1981.

Early reproductive loss and the factors that may influence its
occurrence, by P. S. Weathersbee. JOURNAL OF REPRO-
DUCTIVE MEDICINE 25(6):315-318, December, 1980.

Effect of halothane vapors on the course of pregnancy, by F.
Kolasa, et al. GINEKOLOGIA POLSKA 51(10):931-933,
October, 1980.

Examination of abortuses [letter], by A. J. Barson. BRITISH MEDICAL JOURNAL 280(6220):1055, April 12, 1980.

Human life testimony [letters]. SCIENCE 213:154+, July 10, 1981.

The IBC as a means of implementing institutional oversight, by B. Talbot, et al. RECOMBINANT DNA TECHNICAL BULLETIN 4(1):19-20, April, 1981.

Ideology and medical abortion, by W. Hollway. RADICAL SCIENCE JOURNAL 8:39-59, 1979.

Late abortions linked to education, age and irregular periods. FAMILY PLANNING PERSPECTIVES 13:86, March-April, 1981.

Late consequences of abortion [editorial]. BRITISH MEDICAL JOURNAL 282(6276):1564-1565, May 16, 1981.

Late consequences of abortion [letter], by W. Savage. BRITISH MEDICAL JOURNAL 283(6248):140-141, July 11, 1981.

Legal abortion, by C. Tietze. SCIENTIFIC AMERICAN 236: 1, January 21-27, 1977.

The legal right to abortion: what's left? by A. H. Bernstein. HOSPITALS 55(9):41-42+, May 1, 1981.

Legitimacy and limits of freedom of choice, by K. Cauthen. CHRISTIAN CENTURY 98:702-704, July 1-8, 1981.

La Logica Coerenza del Paradosso di una legge Senza Diritto: Un' interpretazione della legge sull' aborto, by S. Arnato. RIVISTA INTERNAZIONALE DI FIOLOSFIA DEL DIRITTO 57:197-1206, 1980.

Mater et Magistra revisited, by C. S. Mihanovich. SOCIAL

ABORTION

JUSTICE REVIEW 72:163-166, September-October, 1981.

Messages with no meaning. POPULI 8(1):28, 1981.

The most dangerous moment, by A. Cockburn. VILLAGE VOICE October 8, 1980.

A new balanced translocation in humans: t(3;8) (q21;124), by R. S. Verma, et al. JOURNAL OF REPRODUCTIVE MEDICINE 26(3):133-134, March, 1981.

New light on Humanae Vitae. MONTH 13:293-294, September, 1980.

Notes on the class character of the abortion problem, by K. Winter, et al. ZEITSCHRIFT FUR AERZTLICHE FORT-BILDUNG 74(5):193-195, March 1, 1980.

O'Connor impact on abortion issues yet to be seen, by J. Castelli. OUR SUNDAY VISITOR 70:8, September 27, 1981.

One baby for you, one baby for me, by T. Tung. AMERI-CAN SPECTATOR 14:15-17, January, 1981.

Particularly small foetus papyraceus after full pregnancy period, by L. Nevermann, et al. ZEITSCHRIFT FUR GEBURTSHILFE UND PERINATOLOGIE 185(3):187-191, June, 1981.

Patient's rights—mental health—laetrile—abortion. ANNUAL SURVEY OF AMERICAN LAW 1980:321-367, 1980.

The pattern of abortion [editorial]. NEW ZEALAND MEDI-CAL JOURNAL 92(668):237-238, September 24, 1980.

The perils of a convenient society; interview, by C. E. Koop. NEW COVENANT 10:8-11, March, 1981.

179

Personality correlates of the delayed abortion decision, by P. H. Crabtree, PhD. DAI 41(7), 1981.

The pessimistic origins of the anti-life movement, by R. Dennehy. STUDIES 70:5-16, Spring, 1981.

Placental histological findings in women from the area polluted with TCDD, by M. Cattaneo, et al. ANNALI DI OSTETRICIA, GINECOLOGIA, MEDICINA PERINATALE 102(3):155-164, May-June, 1981.

Plasma pregnancy-associated alpha 2-glycoprotein concentration in complications of pregnancy and foetal abnormality, by A. W. Thomson, et al. JOURNAL OF REPRODUCTIVE IMMUNOLOGY 1(4):229-235, December, 1979.

Prenatal genetic diagnosis and elective abortion in women over 35:utilization and relative impact on the birth prevalence of Down syndrome in Washington State, by D. A. Luthy, et al. AMERICAN JOURNAL OF MEDICAL GENETICS 7(3):375-381, 1980.

Present knowledge in the area of endocrine abortion. JOURNAL DE GYNECOLOGIE OBSTETRIQUE ET BIOLOGIE DE LA REPRODUCTION 9(1):59-98, 1980.

Prior abortions and neural tube defects, by T. J. David, et al. CLINICAL GENETICS 18(3):201-202, September, 1980.

The problem of sex chromosome aneuploidy in genetic counseling using amniocentesis, by E. Engel, et al. JOURNAL OF GENETICS 28(3):257-266, September, 1980.

Problems of risk in genetic engineering research, by O. V. Shivtsov. VESTNIK ACADEMII MEDITSINSKIKH NAUK SSSR (2):77-83, 1981.

Prolactin producing pituitary adenomas, by M. McInerney. JOURNAL OF NEUROSURGICAL NURSING 13:15-17,

February, 1981.

Pro-life is a very pregnant issue [with readers' comments], by M. A. Walsh. U.S. CATHOLIC 46:13-17, December,

Pro-life; pro-peace, by J. Loesch. SIGN 61:11-14, September, 1981.

Rawls and children, by W. Evers. JOURNAL OF LIBERTAR-IAN STUDIES 2:109-114, Summer, 1978.

Reconciliation: missing piece in abortion picture, by E. M. Bryce. ORIGINS 11:181-184, September 3, 1981.

Relationships between interruption abortion, and premature birth and low birth weight, by C. Zwahr, et al. ZEN-TRALBLATT FUR GYNAEKOLOGIE 102(13):738-747, 1980.

Report on the ibc chairperson's meeting, by E. Milewski. RECOMBINANT DNA TECHNICAL BULLETIN 4(1): 26-27, April, 1981.

Reproductive pharmacology of LHRH and agonists in fe-males and males, by A. Corbin, et al. ACTA EUROPAEA FERTILITATIS 11(2):113-130, June, 1980.

Reproductive rights national network: a rough road ahead. OFF OUR BACKS 11:10+, August-September, 1981.

Return of ovulation after abortion and after discontinuation of oral contraceptives, by P. Lähteenmäki, et al. FERTIL-ITY AND STERILITY 34(3):246-249, September, 1980.

Return of sheath, by I. Felstein. MIDWIFE, HEALTH VISI-TOR AND COMMUNITY NURSE 16(10):422-424, Oc-tober, 1980.

Return to realism: a profile agenda, by J. Krastel. AMERICA

144:101-102, February 7, 1981.

Rift Valley fever as a possible cause of human abortions [letter], by A. A. Abdel-Aziz, et al. TRANSACTIONS OF THE ROYAL SOCIETY OF TROPICAL MEDICINE AND HYGIENE 74(5):685-686, 1980.

Role of detection of alphafoetoprotein in serum of pregnant women with risk of abortion, by P. Skalba, et al. ZENTRALBLATT FUR GYNAEKOLOGIE 102(18):1025-1030, 1980.

Ruled out . . . special report, by C. Hicks. NURSING TIMES 76:2041, November 20, 1980.

Salpingitis: overview of etiology and epidemiology, by K. K. Holmes, et al. AMERICAN JOURNAL OF OBSTETRICS AND GYNECOLOGY 138(7 Part 2):893-900, 1980.

Schwangerschaftsabbruch—jetzt foderalistisch [Switzerland], by C. Blocher. REFORMATIO: EVANGELISCHE ZEITSCHRIFT FUR KULTUR AND POLITIK 30:513-515, September, 1981.

The search for an alternative, by P. Steinfels. COMMONWEAL 108:660-664, November 20, 1981.

Second-trimester amniocentesis [letter], by J. J. Delaney. OBSTETRICS AND GYNECOLOGY 57(6):768, June, 1981.

Selective birth in twin pregnancy with discordancy for Down's syndrome, by T. D. Kerenyi, et al. NEW ENGLAND JOURNAL OF MEDICINE 304(25):1525-1527, June 18, 1981.

A separate mechanism of gonadotropin recovery after pregnancy termination, by R. P. Marrs, et al. JOURNAL OF CLINICAL ENDOCRINOLOGY AND METABOLISM

52(3):545-548, March, 1981.

Spontaneous rupture of the pregnant uterus following voluntary interruption of pregnancy, by P. E. Fehr. MINNE-
SOTA MEDICINE 64(4):203-204, April, 1981.

Straight talk on abortion; reprint from St. Louis Review, by
J. L. May. CATHOLIC MIND 79:42-49, March, 1981.

Stressful life events and marital dysfunction, by H. W. Bird,
et al. HOSPITAL AND COMMUNITY PSYCHIATRY 32
(7):486-490, July, 1981.

Study of women seeking abortion, by K. Sidenius. SOCIAL
SCIENCE AND MEDICINE 12(5A):423-424, September,
1978.

Sul dritto alla e sul paradosso della posizione antiaborista:
una republica, by M. Mori. RIVISTA INTERNAZION-
ALE DI FILOSOFIA DEL DIRITTO 58:178-183, January-March, 1981.

Surgery during pregnancy and fetal outcome, by J. B. Brodsky, et al. AMERICAN JOURNAL OF OBSTETRICS
AND GYNECOLOGY 138(8):1165-1167, December 15,
1980.

Surgical treatment of post abortum endometriosis of the
bladder and postoperative bladder function, by S. Fianu,
et al. SCANDINAVIAN JOURNAL OF UROLOGY AND
NEPHROLOGY 14(2):151-155, 1980.

Systems of transportation of hospital-specific waste, by A.
Kern. OEFFENTLICHE GESUNDHEITSWESEN 42(6):
351-354, June, 1980.

'There is a frustrating logical gap between the assertion that
recombinant DNA poses potential risks . . . and the containment levels imposed by current guidelines' [news],

by F. Rolleston. NATURE 281(5733):626-627, October 25, 1979.

To deal with the right to life forces, by A. Neiser. CURRENT 229:29-30, January, 1981.

Too bad for you, Humpty Dumpty, by W. J. Morton. JOURNAL OF THE MEDICAL ASSOCIATION OF GEORGIA 69(11):901-902, November, 1980.

Treatment of Asherman's syndrome (intra-uterine synechia), by I. Smid, et al. ZENTRALBLATT FUR GYNAEKOLOGIE 102(7):386-392, 1980.

Trends in cesarean section rates for the United States, 1970-1978, by P. J. Placek, et al. PUBLIC HEALTH REPORTS 95(6):540-548, November-December, 1980.

Trials of the new right:from abortion to Island Park, by M. Kramer. NEW YORK 14:20-21, February 16, 1981.

Ultrasonography before abortion? [letter], by J. J. Crittenden. JAMA 246(10):1088-1089, September 4, 1981.

Unmet demand [legal abortion]. SCIENTIFIC AMERICAN 244:88, June, 1981.

Viability and the morality of abortion, by A. Zaitchik. PHILOSOPHY AND PUBLIC AFFAIRS 10:18-26, Winter, 1981.

Violence against women: some considerations regarding its causes and elimination, by D. Klein. CRIME AND DELINQUENCY 27(1):64-80, January, 1981.

The vitamin E concentration in the trophoblast and blood serum of women in the course of an abortion, by J. Kotarski. ANNALES UNIVERSITATIS MARIAE CURIE-SKLODOWSKA 34:403-413, 1979.

Voluntary termination of pregnancy, by R. Merger. BULLE-
TIN DE L'ACADEMIE NATIONALE DE MEDICINE
163(8):869-876, November 6-27, 1979.

—. Role of the anesthesiologist [letter] , by C. Buttigieg.
ANESTHESIA AND ANALGESIA 37(7-8):451, 1980.

Was Serpico a sperm bank? [accusation by F. Serpico that
woman tricked him into fathering a child] , by M. Starr,
et al. NEWSWEEK 98:42, November 16, 1981.

Watch on the right: ultimate invation of privacy, by G.
Steinem. MS MAGAZINE 9:43-44, February, 1981.

What happens now? by A. Martin. NURSING MIRROR 151
(22):8, November 27, 1980.

What progeny for pro-life bedfellows? by J. McKinley. NA-
TIONAL CATHOLIC REPORTER 17:21, July 17, 1981.

When does human life begin? by E. Switzer. VOGUE 171:
546-547+, September, 1981.

When does the life of a human being start? [editorial] by J.
Lejeune. PAEDIATRIE UND PAEDOLOGIE 16(2):101-
110, 1981.

Who will control your body? by B. Rose. VOGUE 171:547+,
September, 1981.

Why does a woman decide on a abortion? by E. Rautanen, et
al. DUODECIM 96(20):1328-1336, 1980.

Yes, for you, by N. Giovanni. ENCORE 10:18-19, March-
April, 1981.

The zaps on judgment day, by F. Moira. OFF OUR BACKS
11:4, November, 1981.

ABORTION

AFRICA
Demographic transition in the Middle East and North Africa, by J. Allman. INTERNATIONAL JOURNAL OF MIDDLE EASTERN STUDIES 12:277-301, November, 1980.

Note sull'aborto e la contraccezione tra gli Nzema del Ghana, by E. S. Tiberini. AFRICA 35(2):159-189, 1980.

BANGLADESH
Complications from induced abortion in Bangladesh related to types of practitioner and methods, and impact on mortality, by A. R. Measham, et al. LANCET 1(8213):199-202, January 24, 1981.

Pelvic infections following gynecologic procedures in Bangladesh, by S. F. Begum. AMERICAN JOURNAL OF OBSTETRICS AND GYNECOLOGY 138(7 Part 2):875-876, 1980.

BARBADOS
Perspectives on abortion law reform in Barbados, by W. C. Gilmore. ANGLO-AMERICAN LAW REVIEW 8: 191-209, July-September, 1979.

CANADA
Canadian Catholics: at odds on abortion, by T. Sinclair-Faulkner. CHRISTIAN CENTURY 98:870-871, September 9, 1981.

Changes in attitudes toward abortion in a large population of Canadian university students between 1968 and 1978, by F. M. Barrett. CANADIAN JOURNAL OF PUBLIC HEALTH 71(3):195-200, May-June, 1980.

Legal abortions among teenagers in Canada, 1974 through 1978, by A. Wadhera, et al. CANADIAN MEDICAL

ABORTION

CANADA
ASSOCIATION JOURNAL 122(12):1386-1390,
June 21, 1980.

Legal crusade of the eternal children [mentally handicapped in Canada] , by P. Jahn. MACLEANS 94:45-
46, November 30, 1981.

CHINA
China cracks down. WORLD PRESS REVIEW 28:58,
February, 1981.

China's people at bay, by P. G. Andrews. TABLET 235:
360-361, April 11, 1981.

Planification des naissances en Chine: quelle confiance
accorder aux données locales, by L. Bianco. POPULA-
TION 36(1):123-146, 1981.

COSTA RICA
The age at first birth and timing of the second in Costa
Rica and Guatemala, by A. R. Pebley. POPULATION
STUDIES 35:387-397, November, 1981.

CZECHOSLAVACHIA
Czech women, burdened by their dual roles, rely on con-
traception, abortion to keep families small. FAMILY
PLANNING PERSPECTIVES 13:189-190, July-
August, 1981.

DENMARK
Drop in pill sales may have lead to increase in Denmark's
abortion rate. FAMILY PLANNING PERSPECTIVES
12:313-314, November-December, 1980.

DEVELOPING COUNTRIES
Attitudes towards legislation of abortion among a cross-
section of women in metropolitan, by R. H. Chaudhury. JOURNAL OF BIOSOCIAL SCIENCE 12(4):

ABORTION

DEVELOPING COUNTRIES
417-428, October, 1980.

Induced abortion and health problems in developing
countries [letter] , by R. W. Rochat, et al. LANCET
2(8192):484, August 30, 1980.

Induced abortion in developing countries [letter] , by C.
B. Goodhart. LANCET 2(8195 pt 1):645, September
20, 1980.

FINLAND
Spontaneous abortions among women employed in the
metal industry in Finland, by K. Hemminki, et al.
INTERNATIONAL ARCHIVES OF OCCUPATION-
AL AND ENVIRONMENTAL HEALTH 47(1);53-
60, 1980.

Spontaneous abortions by occupation and social class in
Finland, by K. Hemminki, et al. INTERNATIONAL
JOURNAL OF EPIDEMIOLOGY 9(2):149-153,
June, 1980.

FRANCE
The way to the back-street abortionist is still open. Abor-
tion in France, by J. Hermann. THERAPIE DER
GEGENWART 119(7):810-815, July, 1980.

GREAT BRITAIN
Attitudes of women in Britain to abortion: trends and
changes, by C. M. Langford. POPULATION TRENDS
p11-13, Winter, 1980.

Prostaglandin abortions: nurses' actions legitimate. BRIT-
ISH MEDICAL JOURNAL 282:1164-1165, April 4,
1981.

GUATEMALA
The age at first birth and timing of the second in Costa

188

GUATEMALA
and Guatemala, by A. R. Pebley. POPULATION
STUDIES 35:387-397, November, 1981.

HONG KONG
Hong Kong married abortion applicants: a comparison
with married women who elect to complete their
pregnancies, by F. Lieh-Mak, et al. JOURNAL OF
BIOSOCIAL SCIENCE 13(1):71-80, January, 1981.

INDIA
Abortion practices in the rural areas around Najafgarh, by
T. Verghese, et al. NURSING JOURNAL OF INDIA
71(6):153-154, June, 1980.

IRELAND
Abortion: torchlight marchers condemn abortions [Dub-
lin, Ireland] ; Spain; Mexico; Soviet Union. OFF OUR
BACKS 11:4, April, 1981.

Campaign for pro-life amendment to the constitution . . .
Ireland. WORLD OF IRISH NURSING 10:2, July-
August, 1981.

An Irish solution, by D. Fisher. COMMONWEAL 108:5-
6, January 16, 1981.

ISRAEL
Abortion committees in Israel—a reflection of a social
dilemma—from the viewpoint of social workers
(Hebrew), by N. Laron, et al. SOCIETY AND WEL-
FARE 3(3):334-347, 1980.

Abortion in Israel: social demand and political responses,
by Y. Yisai. THE POLICY STUDIES JOURNAL
Winter, 1978.

ITALY
Abortion in Italy, by J. Emanuel. TABLET 235:547-548,

ITALY
June 6, 1981.

Abortion lives. ECONOMIST 279:60, May 23, 1981.

Abortion politics: Italian-style, by M. Bosworth. RE-
FRACTORY GIRL (22):25-26, May, 1981.

Abortion voting reveals deep change in Italy, by E. Grace.
CHRISTIANITY AND CRISIS 41:212-213, July 20,
1981.

Crusader under attack [effect of Pope John Paul II's
proclamations on referendum to tighten abortion
laws in Italy. TIME 117:54, May 18, 1981.

Epidemiology of voluntary abortion in the region of
Emilia Romagna and in Italy, by M. Filicori, et al.
ACTA EUROPAEA FERTILITATIS 11(2):157-165,
June, 1980.

Italian women give the world a victory, by H. Stavrou.
MS MAGAZINE 10:21, August, 1981.

Italy's "third way" on abortion faces a test, by R. R.
Ruether. CHRISTIAN CRISIS 41(130):141-143,
May 11, 1981.

Socio-sanitary analysis of the first 300 voluntary interruptions of pregnancy carried out in the obstetrical-
gynecological division of the Bassini Hospital of Milan,
by M. M. Marzi, et al. MINERVA GINECOLOGIA 32
(10):939-944, October, 1980.

KOREA
Cytogenic analysis of conceptus material of Korean wo-
men at first trimester, by K. Y. Kim, et al. YONSEI
MEDICAL JOURNAL 20(2):113-126, 1979.

ABORTION

LATIN AMERICA
Illegal abortion in Latin America, by F. Sanchez-Torres.
DRAPER FUND REPORT p14-15, October, 1980.

MEXICO
The abortion struggle in Mexico, by E. Haley. HECATE 7
(1):78-87, 1981.

Abortion: torchlight marchers condemn abortions [Dub-
lin, Ireland] ; Spain; Mexico; Soviet Union. OFF OUR
BACKS 11:4, April, 1981.

MIDDLE EAST
Demographic transition in the Middle East and North
Africa, by J. Allman. INTERNATIONAL JOURNAL
OF MIDDLE EASTERN STUDIES 12:277-301, No-
vember, 1980.

THE NETHERLANDS
Induced abortion in the Netherlands: a decade of experi-
ence, 1970-1980, by E. Ketting, et al. STUDIES IN
FAMILY PLANNING 11:385-394, December, 1980.

Lectori Salutem, on the analysis of abortion letters in the
Netherlands, by L. Brunt. THE NETHERLANDS
JOURNAL OF SOCIOLOGY 15(2):141-153, Decem-
ber, 1979.

Netherlands liberalizes abortion law after ten years of
wide availability, low abortion rates. FAMILY PLAN-
NING PERSPECTIVE 13:151, May-June, 1981.

POLAND
Contraception and abortion in Poland, by D. P. Mazur.
FAMILY PLANNING PERSPECTIVES 13:195-198,
July-August, 1981.

SPAIN
Abortion: torchlight marchers condemn abortions [Dub-

SPAIN
lin, Ireland] ; Spain; Mexico; Soviet Union. OFF OUR
BACKS 11:4, April, 1981.

SWEDEN
Is Swedish sex for us? by D. W. Ferm. COMMONWEAL
108:363-366, June 19, 1981.

SWITZERLAND
Switzerland to consider revised guidelines [news] , by A.
Hay. NATURE 277(5695):341-342, February 1,
1979.

THAILAND
Abortion: an epidemiologic study at Ramathibodi Hospital, Bangkok, by K. Chaturachinda, et al. STUDIES
IN FAMILY PLANNING 12(6-7):257, June-July,
1981.

Health consequences of induced abortion in rural Northeast Thailand, by T. Narkavonnakit, et al. STUDIES
IN FAMILY PLANNING 12(2):58-65, February,
1981.

Letter from Chiangmai, by H. Leong. FAR EASTERN
ECONOMIC REVIEW 110:94-95, November 14-20,
1980.

TURKEY
Prevalence and reporting of induced abortion in Turkey:
two survey techniques, by S. Tezcan, et al. STUDIES
IN FAMILY PLANNING 12:262-271, June-July,
1981.

UNITED KINGDOM
New UK committee [news] . NATURE 287(5785):774,
October 30, 1980.

Still looser UK guidelines [news] . NATURE 287(5780):

UNITED KINGDOM
265-266, September 25, 1980.

UNITED STATES
Abortion alternatives leader up for U.S. job, by M. B. Papa. NATIONAL CATHOLIC REPORTER 17:6, February 27, 1981.

Abortion in American teenagers, 1972-1978, does race matter? by D. Kramer. AMERICAN JOURNAL OF EPIDEMIOLOGY 112(3):433, 1980.

Abortion in Odessa is trashy business, Texans learn, by M. Mawyer. OUR SUNDAY VISITOR 69:7, January 18, 1981.

Abortion in the United States, 1978-1979, by S. Henshaw, et al. FAMILY PLANNING PERSPECTIVES 13:6-18, January-February, 1981.

Abortion surveillance—United States, 1978. MMWR 30 (19):222-225, May 22, 1981.

Illinois abortion statute called 'unconstitutional straight-jacket'. THE FAMILY LAW REPORTER: COURT OPINIONS 6(42):2807-2808, September 2, 1980.

Increased leukemia, lymphoma, and spontaneous abortion in Western New York following a flood disaster, by D. T. Janerich, et al. PUBLIC HEALTH REPORTS 96:350-356, July-August, 1981.

Legal abortion, family planning services largest factors in reducing United States neonatal mortality rate. FAMILY PLANNING PERSPECTIVES 13:84-85, March-April, 1981.

Legal abortions in Tennessee 1974-1978, by H. K. Atrash, et al. JOURNAL OF THE TENNESSEE MEDICAL

ABORTION

UNITED STATES
ASSOCIATION 73(12):855-863, December, 1980.

Teenage childbearing and abortion patterns—United
States, 1977. CLINICAL PEDIATRICS 19(12):831-
832, December, 1980.

USSR
Abortion: torchlight marchers condemn abortions [Dub-
lin, Ireland] ; Spain; Mexico; Soviet Union. OFF OUR
BACKS 11:4, April, 1981.

ABORTION: ATTITUDES
Abortion as fatherhood lost: problems and reforms, by A.
Shostak. THE FAMILY COORDINATOR 28(4):569-
574, 1979.

Abortion from the ethical point of view, by W. Vossenkuhl.
MMW 123(6):198-200, February 6, 1981.

Aggregate mortality, socio-demographic factors and attitudes
toward abortion and euthanasia, by S. Steele, PhD. DAI
41(11-12, 1981.

Anti-abortion, anti-birth control, anti-woman, by S. Dawson.
OFF OUR BACKS 11:17, March, 1981.

Antiabortion, antifeminism, and the rise of the New Right,
by R. P. Petchesky. FEMINIST STUDIES 7:206-246,
Summer, 1981.

Anti-choice forces gain, by B. Hurwitz. NEW DIRECTIONS
FOR WOMEN 10:3+, May-June, 1981.

Aspects of abortion: what happens at conception? by G. H.
Ball. CHRISTIANITY AND CRISIS 41:274+, October
19, 1981.

Attitudes of medical practitioners towards abortion: a

Queensland study, by M. C. Sheehan, et al. AUSTRALI-
AN FAMILY PHYSICIAN 9(8):565-570, August, 1980.

Attitudes of patients after 'genetic' termination of pregnancy,
by P. Donnai, et al. BRITISH MEDICAL JOURNAL 282
(6264):621-622, February 21, 1981.

Attitudes of women in Britain to abortion: trends and
changes, by C. M. Langford. POPULATION TRENDS 22:
11-13, Winter, 1980.

The battle over abortion. TIME 117(14):20, April 6, 1981.

But is it a person? [human life bill] , by J. Adler, et al. NEWS-
WEEK 99:44, January 11, 1982.

'But that's no longer necessary nowadays?!', by H. Doppenberg. TIJDSCHRIFT VOR ZIEKENVERPLEGING 34
(13):575-580, June 23, 1981.

Can a fetus be murdered? [case of R. L. Hollis indicted for
murder in successful effort to abort his wife's fetus] .
NEWSWEEK 98:72, August 24, 1981.

Case of the unborn patient, by G. F. Will. NEWSWEEK 97:
92, June 22, 1981.

The childless marriage: a moral observation, by J. A. Selling.
BIJDRAGEN 42:158-173, 1981.

Children born to women denied abortion: an update, by H.
P. David, et al. FAMILY PLANNING PERSPECTIVES
13(1):32-34, January-February, 1981.

The concept of a person in the context of abortion, by S.
Sherwin. BIOETHICS QUARTERLY 3:21-24, Spring,
1981.

Concerning abortion: an attempt at a rational view, by C.

Hartshorne. CHRISTIAN CENTURY 98:42-45, January 21, 1981.

Contraception—abortion lifeline, by G. E. Richardson. HEALTH EDUCATION 12(2):37, March-April, 1981.

A critique of the pro-choice argument, by W. J. Voegeli, Jr. REVIEW OF POLITICS 43:560-571, October, 1981.

The dead baby joke cycle, by A. Dundes. WESTERN FOLK-LORE 38(3):145-157, 1979.

Decision making by single women seeking abortion, by M. Quinn. NEW ZEALAND NURSING FORUM 8(2):4-7, 1980.

Every child a wanted child, by C. Sevitt. CANADA AND THE WORLD 46:18, January, 1981.

Factors influencing morbidity in termination of pregnancy, by C. R. Harman, et al. AMERICAN JOURNAL OF OB-STETRICS AND GYNECOLOGY 139(3):333-337, February 1, 1981.

Fertility and abortion inside and outside marriage, by J. Thompson. POPULATION TRENDS 5:5-8, Autumn, 1976.

For life—against abortion, by M. F. Jefferson. ENCORE 10: 18-19, October, 1981.

The growing queue for the ultimate alternative, by I. Allen. GUARDIAN p12, October 28, 1981.

The "human" as a problem in bioethics, by P. D. Simmons. REVIEW AND EXPOSITOR 78:91-108, Winter, 1981.

Interview of Bernard Nathanson; interview, by B. Nathanson. OUR SUNDAY VISITOR 70:3-5, September 20, 1981.

Joe Scheidler: pro-life's Green Beret, by D. Morris. OUR SUNDAY VISITOR 70:6+, September 6, 1981.

The left and the right to life; condensed from The Progressive, September, 1980. CATHOLIC DIGEST 45:36-41, December, 1980.

Mandatory motherhood. PLAYBOY 27:66, November, 1980.

Musings on motherhood, Marshall, molecules: a passage through the heart of maternal darkness from God's creation to man's, by A. Wallach. BLACK LAW JOURNAL 6:88-141, 1978.

The myth of motherhood: a study of attitudes toward motherhood, by R. T. Hare-Mustin. PSYCHOLOGY OF WOMEN QUARTERLY 4:114-128, Fall, 1979.

Navigating dangerous waters of public opinion polls, by F. Franzonia. OUR SUNDAY VISITOR 70:6, July 5, 1981.

News of pro-lifers' disarray is not really news at all, by J. Castelli. OUR SUNDAY VISITOR 70:8, October 11, 1981.

Of many things [views of A. M. Schindler], by J. A. O'Hare. AMERICA 144:inside cover, February 28, 1981.

Pro-choice is pro-life, by J. J. Christmas. ENCORE 10:14-16, December, 1981.

Protect the innocents, by L. McArthur. CANADA AND THE WORLD 46:19, January, 1981.

The sanctity of human life, by M. Burke. IRISH NURSING NEWSLETTER :4-6, May, 1981.

Shifts in abortion. Attitudes: 1972-1978, by C. A. Haney, et al. JOURNAL OF MARRIAGE AND THE FAMILY 42

ABORTION: ATTITUDES

(3):491-499, August, 1980.

Sociaal-psychologische aspecter van abortus provacatus, by F. Deven. TIJDSCHRIFT VOOR SOCIALE WETENSCHAP-PEN 21(3):241-264, July-September, 1976.

Society: look, little guy, you just don't measure up. OUR SUNDAY VISITOR 70:7, July 5, 1981.

Society today. Moral battlegrounds. NEW SOCIETY 55:957, 1981.

Soul and the person: defining life, by R. Gist. CHRISTIAN CENTURY 98:1022-1024, October 14, 1981.

Stepping out of Down's syndrome [moral questions of abort-ing genetically defective children], by J. R. Nelson. CHRISTIAN CENTURY 98:789-790, August 12-19, 1981.

Theology of pro-choice: a feminist perspective [two parts], by V. Wildung. WITNESS 64:14-18, July; :18-21, September, 1981.

ABORTION: COMPLICATIONS
Abortion facilities and the risk of death, by D. A. Grimes, et al. FAMILY PLANNING PERSPECTIVES 13:30-31, January-February, 1981.

Abortion incidence following fallopian tube repair, by R. P. Jansen. OBSTETRICS AND GYNECOLOGY 56(4):499-502, October, 1980.

Abortion rate and chromosomal abnormality [letter], by R. J. Gardner. LANCET 2(8244):474-475, August 29, 1981.

Analgesia with buprenorphin (Temgesic) in abortions with sulproston (PGE2 derivative), by S. Heinzl, et al. GYNAE--KOLOGISCHE RUNDSCHAW 20(Suppl 1):69-71, June,

198

1980.

Anesthesiological problems and choice in operations for the termination of pregnancy. A study of 1500 cases, by G. B. Paolella, et al. MINERVA ANESTESIOLOGICA 47(1-2): 37-40, January-February, 1981.

Artificial interruption of pregnancy after a course of treatment for gonorrhea, by V. P. Zherebtsov. AKUSHERST-VO I GINEKOLOGIIA (3):57-58, March, 1981.

Choriocarcinoma presenting as a complication of elective first trimester abortion, by F. A. Lyon, et al. MINNESOTA MEDICINE 63(10):733-735, October, 1980.

Clinical and ultrasonic aspects in the diagnosis and follow-up of patients with early pregnancy failure, by P. Jouppila. ACTA OBSTETRICIA ET GYNECOLOGICA SCANDI-NAVICA 59(5):405-409, 1980.

Colo-uterine fistula. An unusual case report and a literature review, by F. R. Kaban, et al. AMERICAN JOURNAL OF PROCTOLOGY, GASTROENTEROLOGY AND COLON AND RECTAL SURGERY 32(7):36-37+, July, 1981.

Comparative risks of rhesus autoimmunisation in two different methods of mid-trimester abortion, by C. Brewer, et al. BRITISH MEDICAL JOURNAL 282(6280):1929-1930, June 13, 1981.

Complications of abortion in developing countries. POPULA-TION REPORTS Series F(7):F105-155, July, 1980.

—. POPULATION REPORTS 8(4):1, July, 1980.

Cytologic findings in postpartum and postabortal smears, by T. K. Kobayashi, et al. ACTA CYTOLOGICA 24(4):328-334, July-August, 1980.

Distributions of amenorrhoea and anovulation, by R. G. Potter, et al. POPULATION STUDIES 35:85-99, March, 1981.

Down's syndrome, amniocentesis, and abortion: prevention or elimination? by J. D. Smith. MENTAL RETARDA- TION 19(1):8-11, February, 1981.

Fetal loss after implantation. A prospective study, by J. F. Miller, et al. LANCET 2(8194):554-556, September 13, 1980.

Implanted placental tissue simulating uterine fibroids ('in- verted placental polyp'), by M. Waxman, et al. DIAGNOS- TIC GYNECOLOGY AND OBSTETRICS 2(4):287-289, Winter, 1980.

The incidence of gonorrhea in an abortion population, by L. Querido, et al. CONTRACEPTION 22(4):441-444, Octo- ber, 1980.

Incidence of the 9qh+ variant in subjects with occupational exposure to radiation and in cases of reproductive pathol- ogy, by M. Milani-Comparetti, et al. BOLLETTINO DELLA SOCIETA ITALIANA DI BIOLOGIA SPERI- MENTALE 57(4):351-354, February 28, 1981.

Inhalation of gastric contents [letter], by E. Mankowitz, et al. BRITISH JOURNAL OF ANAESTHESIA 53(7):778- 779, July, 1981.

Is it worth dying for? by D. L. Breo. AMERICAN MEDICAL NEWS 24(19):16-18, May 15, 1981.

Loss of blood in artificial abortion performed under para- cervical anesthesia, by M. Orescanin. JUGOSLAVENSKA GINEKOLOGIJA I OPSTETRICIJA 19(3-4):167-169, May-August, 1980.

Midtrimester abortion associated with septicaemia caused by Campylobacter jejuni, by G. L. Gilbert, et al. MEDICAL JOURNAL OF AUSTRALIA 1(11):585-586, May 30, 1981.

Morphologic manifestations of immune responses in disrupted tubal pregnancy, by B. I. Glukhovets, et al. ARKHIV ANOTOMII, GISTOLOGII I EMBRIOLOGII 79(12):99-101, December, 1980.

Necrotic uterine myomatosis—a rare complication following vaginal termination of pregnancy by suction, by W. Gubisch, et al. ZENTRALBLATT FUR GYNAEKOLOGIE 103(8):456-459, 1981.

Negligence in the treatment of a patient with interruption of pregnancy, by C. E. Lindahl. VARDFACKET 5(10):37-39, May 29, 1981.

Postabortion sepsis and antibiotic prophylaxis [letter]. BRITISH MEDICAL JOURNAL 282(6262):476-477, February 7, 1981.

Postpartum and postabortion psychotic reactions, by H. P. David, et al. FAMILY PLANNING PERSPECTIVES 13 (2):88-89+, March-April, 1981.

Pregnancy interruption and its complications, by H. Schmidt-Matthiesen. LEBENSVERSICHERUNGSMEDIZIN 32(3): 70-74, May, 1980.

Prevention of endocrine abortions by follicular stimulation, by J. P. Dubecq, et al. JOURNAL DE GYNECOLOGIE OBSTETRIQUE ET BIOLOGIE DE LA REPRODUCTION 9(1):95-98, 1980.

Prevention of infection after abortion with a supervised single dose of oral doxycycline, by C. Brewer. BRITISH MEDICAL JOURNAL 281(6243):780-781, September,

1980.

Rare form of uterine infection connected with interruptio, by B. Stubert, et al. ZENTRALBLATT FUR GYNAE-KOLOGIE 102(13):734-737, 1980.

Recent trends in deaths declared as due to abortion, by G. F. Dumont, et al. POPULATION 36:410-413, March-April, 1981.

Role of chlorinated hydrocarbon pesticides in abortions and premature labour, by M. C. Saxena, et al. TOXICOLOGY 17(3):323-331, 1980.

Selective pregnancy termination in thalassaemia [letter], by P. Denton. MEDICAL JOURNAL OF AUSTRALIA 1 (12):654+, June 13, 1981.

Side effects of extra-amniotic PGF2 alpha in the induction of labor in retained abortion and in the intrauterine death of the fetus, by A. Paladini, et al. MINERVA GINECOLO-GIA 32(9):781-786, September, 1980.

Six cases of listeriosis during pregnancy, by R. Guillermin, et al. GYNAEKOLOGISCHE RUNDSCHAU 20(Suppl 1): 103-105, June, 1980.

Somatic complications in abortion, by R. Wille, et al. BEITRAEGE ZUE GERICHTLICHEN MEDIZIN 38:17-19, 1980.

Study on re-establishment of ovulation after termination of sex-steroidal treatment—compared with re-appearance of ovulation after abortion and premature delivery, by K. Hayashi, et al. KEIO JOURNAL OF MEDICINE 28(4): 173-193, December, 1979.

Susceptibility of abortion patients to infection: Correlation to cervical flora, by J. Paavonen, et al. INTERNATION-

AL JOURNAL OF GYNAECOLOGY AND OBSTE-
TRICS 18(1):44-47, July-August, 1980.

Termination of pregnancy during or after treatment of carci-
noma of the breast. A review, by K. W. Schweppe, et al.
ZEITSCHRIFT FUR GEBURTSCHILFE UND PERINA-
TOLOGIE 184(1):1-10, February, 1980.

Termination of pregnancy in a woman with hereditary anti-
thrombin deficiency under antithrombotic protection
with subcutaneous heparin and infusion of plasma, by J.
Jespersen. GYNECOLOGIC AND OBSTETRIC INVESTI-
GATION 12(5):267-271, 1981.

Transplacental carcinogens and mutagens: childhood cancer,
malformations, and abortions as risk indicators, by K.
Hemminki, et al. JOURNAL OF TOXICOLOGY AND
ENVIRONMENTAL HEALTH 6(5-6):1115-1126, September-November, 1980.

Two abortions may endanger later pregnancy, by N. Mallovy.
HOMEMAKER'S MAGAZINE 16:78, March, 1981.

Uterine and sigmoid perforations following voluntary interruption of pregnancy by aspiration. A case report, by G.
Aulagnier, et al. JOURNAL DE CHIRURGIE 118(5):339-
341, May, 1981.

Vaginal application of a chemotherapeutic agent before legal
abortion. A way of reducing infectious complication? by
O. Meirik, et al. ACTA OBSTETRICIA ET GYNECOLO-
GICA SCANDINAVICA 60(3):233-235, 1981.

Vaginal bleeding in early pregnancy [editorial]. BRITISH
MEDICAL JOURNAL 281(6238):470, August 16, 1980.

Vaginal chemophylaxis in gonorrhea reinfection, by C. H.
Cole. SALUD PUBLICA DE MEXICO 22(5):537-546,
September-October, 1980.

ABORTION: COMPLICATIONS: PSYCHOLOGICAL

Aftermath of abortion: Anniversary depression and abdominal pain, by J. Cavenar, et al. BULLETIN OF THE MINNINGER CLINIC 42(5):433-438, September, 1978.

Psychological factors that predict reaction to abortion, by D. T. Moseley, et al. JOURNAL OF CLINICAL PSYCHOLOGY 37(2):276-279, April, 1981.

Psychosocial situation of women after termination of pregnancy, by M. Simon. MEDIZINISCHE KLINIK 75(16): 592-595, August 1, 1980.

ABORTION: ECONOMICS
Abortion and judicial review: of burdens and benefits, hard cases and some bad law [commenting on two 1980 Supreme Court decisions holding that neither federal nor state governments are constitutionally required to fund medically necessary abortions in otherwise general programs of medical assistance for the poor], by R. W. Bennett. NORTHWESTERN UNIVERSITY LAW REVIEW 75:978-1017, February, 1981.

Abortion-funding issue: a study in mixed constitutional cues, by T. E. Yarbrough. NORTH CAROLINA LAW REVIEW 59:611-627, March, 1981.

Abortion funding ruling: the controversy rages, by M. Middleton. AMERICAN BAR ASSOCIATION JOURNAL 66: 945, August, 1980.

Abortions for the poor. AMERICA 145:134, September 19, 1981.

All freedoms are not free: the tab for abortions should be picked up by those who want them, by B. Amiel. MACLEAN'S 94:11, July 27, 1981.

Common outpatient procedures represent malpractice 'gold mine', by R. Lucas. SAME DAY SURGERY 4(12):126-

127, December, 1980.

Constitutional law—abortion funding and the demise of maternal health consideration. SUFFOLK UNIVERSITY LAW REVIEW 15:285-305, April, 1981.

Critique of the abortion funding decisions: on private rights in the public sector, by L. F. Goldstein. HASTINGS CONSTITUTIONAL LAW QUARTERLY 8:313-342, Winter, 1981.

Effects of restricted public funding for legal abortions: a second look, by R. M. Selik, et al. AMERICAN JOURNAL OF PUBLIC HEALTH 71(1):77-81, January, 1981.

Funding of abortions under the Medicaid program—constitutionality of the Hyde amendment. AMERICAN JOURNAL OF TRIAL ADVOCACY 4:708-717, Spring, 1981.

Government funding for elective abortions. PROGRESS IN CLINICAL AND BIOLOGICAL RESEARCH 50:213-243, 1981.

Harris v. McRae: the Hyde Amendment stands while rights of poor women fall, by C. C. Sewell, et al. KENTUCKY LAW JOURNAL 69(2):359-391, 1980-1981.

The Hyde Amendment in action. How did the restriction of federal funds for abortion affect low-income women? by W. Cates, Jr. JAMA 246(10):1109-1112, September 4, 1981.

Hyde amendment: new implications for equal protection claims. BAYLOR LAW REVIEW 33:295-306, Spring, 1981.

Medicaid not required to fund medically necessary abortions, by G. J. Annas. NURSING LAW AND ETHICS 1(8):3+, October, 1980.

Public funding of medically necessary abortions is not required under the Medicaid act. TEXAS TECHNICAL LAW REVIEW 12:483-499, 1981.

Religious involvement, asceticism and abortion among low income Black women, by J. M. Robbins. SOCIOLOGICAL ANALYSIS 41:365-374, Winter, 1980.

Social security and public welfare—abortion—the Hyde amendment substantively altered state funding obligations under title XIX of the social security act of 1965, requiring states to fund only the abortions specified in the amendment. UNIVERSITY OF DETROIT JOURNAL OF URBAN LAW 58:95-117, Fall, 1980.

"The steady-State economy" in economics, ecology, ethics, by H. Daly. SAN FRANSISCO FREEMAN pp324-356, 1980.

Subsidized abortion: moral rights and moral compromise, by G. Sher. PHILOSOPHY AND PUBLIC AFFAIRS 10:361-372, Fall, 1981.

Supreme Court report: abortion . . . federal funds, by R. L. Young. AMERICAN BAR ASSOCIATION JOURNAL 66: 994-996, August, 1980.

When Uncle Sam stops paying [aftermath of Hyde amendment], by D. French. FORBES 127:32, June 22, 1981.

Why the Supreme Court was plainly wrong in the Hyde Amendment case: a brief comment on Harris v. McRae [1980 decision upholding the law which prohibits federal funding of abortion under the Medicaid program except under certain specified circumstances], by M. J. Perry. STANFORD LAW REVIEW 32:1113-1128, July, 1980.

Your tax dollars at work promoting abortion, by M. A. Walsh. OUR SUNDAY VISITOR 70:4-5, June 7, 1981.

ABORTION: FAILED

Use of intramuscular prostaglandin for failure of mid-trimester abortion by another method, by P. C. Schwallie, et al. CONTRACEPTION 22(6):623-642, December, 1980.

ABORTION: HABITUAL

Autosomal translocation in an apparently normospermic male as a cuse of habitual abortion, by M. Granat, et al. JOURNAL OF REPRODUCTIVE MEDICINE 26(1):52-55, January, 1981.

Balneological treatment of spontaneous habitual abortion caused by the uterine factor or hormonal deficiency, by K. Marzinek, et al. GINEKOLOGIA POLSKA 51(6):545-549, June, 1980.

Blood groups and histocaompatibility antigens in habitual abortion, by E. Carapella-de Luca, et al. HAEMATOLOGIA 13(1-4):105-111, 1980.

Cytogenetic findings in habitual abortion. Chromosomal analysis in 123 couples, by P. Husslein, et al. WIENER KLINISCHE WOCHENSCHRIFT 92(16):575-578, August 29, 1980.

The etiology, physiopathology and clinical aspects of habitual abortion, by G. B. Candiani, et al. ANNALI DI OSTETRICIA, GINECOLOGIA, MEDICINA PERINATALE 101(5):295-318, September-October, 1980.

Habitual abortion. Two factors of increasing frequency, by A. C. Weseley. DIAGNOSTIC GYNECOLOGY AND OBSTETRICS 3(2):119-121, Summer, 1981.

Habitual abortion and translocation (22q;22q): unexpected transmission from a mother to her phenotypically normal daughter, by V. G. Kirkels, et al. CLINICAL GENETICS 18(6):456-461, December, 1980.

Habitual abortion of genetic origin, by J. Rosas Arceo, et al.

ABORTION: HABITUAL

GINECOLOGIA Y OBSTETRICIA DE MEXICO 47(284): 411-417, June, 1980.

Pilot study into habitual abortion, by D. Gerl, et al. ZEN-TRALBLATT FUR GYNAEKOLOGIE 102(2):93-9, 1980.

Systemic lupus erythematosus and habitual abortion. Case report, by A. L. Hartikainen-Sorri, et al. BRITISH JOURNAL OF OBSTETRICS AND GYNAECOLOGY 87(8): 729-731, August, 1980.

Urinary excretion of chorionic gonadotropins in threatened and habitual abortion, by W. Szymański, et al. GINE-KOLOGIA POLSKA 51(12):1129-1134, December, 1980.

ABORTION: HISTORY
Abortion in the nineteenth century Maori: a historical and ethnopsychiatric review, by L. K. Gluckman. NEW ZEALAND MEDICAL JOURNAL 93(685):384-386, June 10, 1981.

History and current status of legislation on abortion in the countries of the world, by V. K. Kuznetsov, et al. FEL' DSHER I AKUSHERKA 45(8):3-6, 1980.

ABORTION: ILLEGAL
A cluster of septic complications associated with illegal induced abortions, by J. Gold, et al. OBSTETRICS AND GYNECOLOGY 56(3):311-315, September, 1980.

Illegal abortion in Latin America, by F. Sanchez-Torres. DRAPER FUND REPORT pp14-15, October, 1980.

Thirty million illegal abortions, ten million complications [in countries without legal abortion], by A. Henry. OFF OUR BACKS 11:5, June, 1981.

Continuous monitoring of uterine contractions to control intra-amniotic administration of prostaglandin F2 alpha for therapeutic and missed abortion, by C. J. Roux, et al. SOUTH AFRICAN INCOMPLETE 59(23):819-821, May 30, 1981.

Ultrasonic sonography in the management of incomplete abortion, by W. G. Jeong, et al. JOURNAL OF REPRODUCTIVE MEDICINE 26(2):90-92, February, 1981.

ABORTION: INDUCED

Alternatives in midtrimester abortion induction, by J. Robins. OBSTETRICS AND GYNECOLOGY 56(6):716-722, December, 1980.

Anesthetic gases and occupational hazard [letter], by C. J. Göthe, et al. SCANDINAVIAN JOURNAL OF WORK, ENVIRONMENT AND HEALTH 6(4):316, December, 1980.

A cluster of septic complications associated with illegal induced abortions, by J. Gold, et al. OBSTETRICS AND GYNECOLOGY 56(3):311-315, September, 1980.

The coagulation system in Rivanol-induced abortion, by A. Olund, et al. ZENTRALBLATT FUR GYNAEKOLOGIE 102(9):507-512, 1980.

Commentary on Rosner's "Induced abortion and Jewish morality", by R. B. Reeves, Jr. VALUES, ETHICS AND HEALTH CARE 1:225-226, Spring, 1976.

Comparative blood coagulation studies in PGF2a- and 15-methyl-PGF2a-induced therapeutic abortion, by R. During, et al. FOLIA HAEMATOLOGICA 107(3):502-507, 1980.

Comparison of two intramuscular prostaglandin analogs for inducing abortion in the first pregnancy trimester, by B.

Schüssler, et al. GYNAEKOLOGISCHE RUNDSCHAU 20(2):102-109, 1980.

Complications from induced abortion in Bangladesh related to types of practitioner and methods, and impact on mortality, by A. R. Measham, et al. LANCET 1(8213): 199-202, January 24, 1981.

Embryo-maternal transfusions in 100 therapeutic induced abortions, by P. Spelina, et al. GYNAEKOLOGISCHE RUNDSCHAU 20(Suppl 1):113-116, June, 1980.

Epidural morphine analgesia in second-trimester induced abortion, by F. Magora, et al. AMERICAN JOURNAL OF OBSTETRICS AND GYNECOLOGY 138(3):260-262, October 1, 1980.

Fatal ectopic pregnancy after attempted legally induced abortion, by G. L. Rubin, et al. JAMA 244(15):1705-1708, October 10, 1980.

Follow-up study of mid-term abortion induced by five different methods, by X. X. Zhong. CHUNG HUA FU CHAN KO TSA CHIH 15(4):216-218, October, 1980.

Gynaecological sequelae of induced abortion, by M. Brudenell. PRACTITIONER 224(1347):893-898, September, 1980.

Historic, cultural, legal, psychosocial and educational aspects of induced abortion, by F. Aguirre Zozaya, et al. GINECOLOGIA Y OBSTETRICIA DE MEXICO 48(286):111-135, August, 1980.

How high is the real incidence of induced abortion? Facts and erroneous estimates, by W. Christian, et al. FORTSCHRITTE DER MEDIZIN 98(29):1123-1128, August 7, 1980.

How patients view mandatory waiting periods for abortion, by M. Lupfer, et al. FAMILY PLANNING PERSPECTIVES 13:75-79, March-April, 1981.

Induced abortion and health problems in developing countries [letter], by R. W. Rochat, et al. LANCET 2(8192): 484, August 30, 1980.

Induced abortion and subsequent pregnancy loss [letter], by C. S. Chung. JAMA 245(11):1119, March 20, 1981.

Induced abortion by means of vaginal hysterectomy. Studies on the indications and risks of this method, by K. W. Schweppe, et al. ZENTRALBLATT FUR GYNAEKOLOGIE 102(24):1431-1436, 1980.

Induced abortion in developing countries [letter], by C. B. Goodhart. LANCET 2(8195 pt 1):645, September 20, 1980.

Induced abortion in the Netherlands: a decade of experience, 1970-1980, by E. Ketting, et al. STUDIES IN FAMILY PLANNING 11:385-394, December, 1980.

Induction of abortion during the second and third trimester of pregnancy with sulprostone, by S. Heinzl, et al. GEBURTSHILFE UND FRAUENHEILKUNDE 41(3): 231-236, March, 1981.

Induction of abortion with sulprostone, a uteroselective prostaglandin E2 derivative: intramuscular route of application, by K. Schmidt-Gollwitzer, et al. INTERNATIONAL JOURNAL OF FERTILITY 26(2):86-93, 1981.

Induction of labor with anencephalic fetus, by R. Osathanondh, et al. OBSTETRICS AND GYNECOLOGY 56(5): 655-657, November, 1980.

Interstitial pregnancy after salpingectomy—not recognized in

first trimester induced abortion, by W. Grünberger. GE-
BURTSHILFE UND FRAUENHEILKUNDE 40(8):722-
724, August, 1980.

Long-term sequelae following legally induced abortion, by E.
B. Obel. DANISH MEDICAL BULLETIN 27(2):61-74,
April, 1980.

Morphological observations of placenta in 56 cases of mid-
term abortion induced by Yuanhua preparations, by Y.
G. Liang. CHUNG HUA FU CHAN KO TSA CHIH 14(4):
290-292, 1979.

Outcome of pregnancy subsequent to induced abortion [let-
ter], by L. Iffy. AMERICAN JOURNAL OF OBSTE-
TRICS AND GYNECOLOGY 138(5):587-588, November 1, 1980.

Persistence of progesterone secretion after foetal death induced by vasopressin in rabbits, by J. W. Wilks. ACTA
ENDOCRINOLOGICA 97(4):569-572, August, 1981.

Prostaglandins and thromboxanes in amniotic fluid during
rivanol-induced abortion and labour, by A. Olund, et al.
PROSTAGLANDINS 19(5):791-803, May, 1980.

Provision of induced abortion in Wessex Health Region: un-
met need and feasibility of compensatory day care, by J.
R. Ashton. JOURNAL OF THE ROYAL SOCIETY OF
MEDICINE 73(3):191-196, March, 1980.

Psychological alterations following induced abortion, by P.
Petersen. MMW 123(27):1105-1108, July 3, 1981.

The psychosocial outcome of induced abortion, by J. R.
Ashton. BRITISH JOURNAL OF OBSTETRICS AND
GYNAECOLOGY 87(12):1115-1122, December, 1980.

Qualitative changes in reproductive policy and induced abortion, by J. Rothe. ZEITSCHRIFT FUR AERZTLICHE FORTBILDUNG 74(9):437-440, May 1, 1980.

Risks in legal, induced abortion. Review of the literature, by H. E. Stamm. GYNAEKOLOGISCHE RUNDSCHAU 20 (2):65-84, 1980.

Role of induced abortion in secondary infertility, by J. R. Daling, et al. OBSTETRICS AND GYNECOLOGY 57 (1):59-61, January, 1981.

Social structure in cases of induced abortion (results of a one-year study conducted by the Indication Bureau of the City of Nuremberg—, by K. G. Friedrich. OEFFENT-LICHE GESUNDHEITSWESEN 42(9):600-611, 1980.

A study on the effects of induced abortion on subsequent pregnancy outcome, by C. Madore, et al. AMERICAN JOURNAL OF OBSTETRICS AND GYNECOLOGY 139 (5):516-521, March 1, 1981.

Use of PGF2 alpha to induce abortion in patients with risk factors in first and second thirds of gravidity, by K. Rudolf, et al. ZENTRALBLATT FUR GYNAEKOLO-GIE 102(10):575-583, 1980.

The use of prostaglandin E1 analogue pessaries in patients having first trimester induced abortions, by R. Nakano, et al. BRITISH JOURNAL OF OBSTETRICS AND GY-NAECOLOGY 87(4):287-291, April, 1980.

ABORTION: INDUCED: COMPLICATIONS
Early and late complications in induced abortions of primi-gravidae (including suggested measures), by H. Kreibich, et al. ZEITSCHRIFT ZUR AERZTLICHE FORTBILD-UNG 74(7):311-316, April 1, 1980.

Early inflammatory complications in induction of abortion by means of intrauterine extra-amnial administration of prostaglandin F 2 alpha in primigravidae, by G. Koinzer, et al. ZEITSCHRIFT ZUR AERZTLICHE FORTBILD-UNG 73(21):1007-1009, November 1, 1979.

Induced first-trimester abortion and fenestration of the uterine wall in a subsequent pregnancy, by G. Lindmark, et al. ACTA OBSTETRICIA ET GYNECOLOGICA SCANDINAVICA 60(1):96, 1981.

Pattern of acute pelvic inflammatory disease in abortion-related admissions, by T. A. Sinnathuray, et al. AMERI-CAN JOURNAL OF OBSTETRICS AND GYNECOLO-GY 138(7 pt 2):868-871, December 1, 1980.

Preoperative administration of prostaglandin to avoid dilata-tion-induced damage in first-trimester pregnancy termina-tions, by S. Heinzl, et al. GYNECOLOGIE AND OBSTE-TRIC INVESTIGATION 12(1):29-36, 1981.

ABORTION: JOURNALISM
Looking at labels [use of terms pro-life and anti-abortion by the print media]. CHRISTIAN CENTURY 98:404, April 15, 1981.

Motive and metaphor in Faulkner's That evening sun, by E. W. Pitcher. STUDIES IN SHORT FICTION 18:131-135, Spring, 1981.

Penetrating a biased press [press coverage of nomination of C. E. Koop as Surgeon General]. CHRISTIANITY TO-DAY 25:30, June 26, 1981.

ABORTION: LAWS AND LEGISLATION
Abortion [Helms-Hyde bill], by E. Switzer. WORKING WO-MAN 6:32+, July, 1981.

Abortion and criminal law, by H. R. S. Ryan. QUEEN'S LAW JOURNAL 6:362-371, Spring, 1981.

Abortion and judicial review: of burdens and benefits, hard cases and some bad law, by R. W. Bennett. NORTH-WESTERN UNIVERSITY LAW REVIEW 75:978-1017, February, 1981.

Abortion—attorney's fees. THE FAMILY LAW REPORTER: COURT OPINIONS 6(46):2889, September 30, 1980.

Abortion: can the constitution rule it out? by M. Patterson. NATIONAL CATHOLIC REPORTER 17:9-10, April 24, 1981.

Abortion, the Constitution, and the human life statute, by F. J. Flaherty. COMMONWEAL 108:586-593, October 23, 1981.

Abortion—constitutional rights—religion—due process. THE FAMILY LAW REPORTER: COURT OPINIONS 7(9): 2136, January 6, 1981.

The abortion controversy: an overview, by D. Granberg. HU-MANIST 41:28-38, July-August, 1981.

Abortion: 2. Fetal status and legal representation [editorial], by B. M. Dickens. CANADIAN MEDICAL ASSOCIA-TION JOURNAL 124*3):253-254, February 1, 1981.

Abortion on demand: policy and implementation, by M. Cohen, et al. HEALTH AND SOCIAL WORK 6:65-72, February, 1981.

An abortion perspective: legal considerations, by F. A. Lyon. MINNESOTA MEDICINE 63(9):659-661, September, 1980.

Abortion: religious differences and public policy, by H. Sieg-man. CONGRESSIONAL MONTHLY 48:3-4, June, 1981.

Abortion: will we lose our right to choose? by J. Coburn.
MADEMOISELLE 87:32, July, 1981.

Abortions—appeals. THE FAMILY LAW REPORTER:
COURT OPINIONS 7(8):2119, December 23, 1980.

Attitudes towards legislation of abortion among a cross-
section of women in metropolitan Dacca, by R. H. Chaudhury. JOURNAL OF BIOSOCIAL SCIENCE 12(4):417-
428, October, 1980.

Bill would give legal person status to unborn babies. OUR
SUNDAY VISITOR 69:6, February 22, 1981.

Bill would make abortion illegal, by T. Dejanikus. OFF OUR
BACKS 11:11, August-September, 1981.

Bishops and the abortion amendment. AMERICA 145:312,
November 21, 1981.

Brigade zaps Senate hearings: Protest leads to arrest, 1;
Activist set cornerstone for abortion rights [interview
with Julie Huff, who in 1971 as Mary Doe was plaintiff
in abortion case in Washington, D.C.], by E. Soldinger.
NEW DIRECTIONS FOR WOMEN 10:4+, July-August,
1981.

But is it a person? [human life bill], by J. Adler, et al. NEWS-
WEEK 99:44, January 11, 1982.

Doe v. Irwin. AMERICAN JOURNAL OF TRIAL ADVO-
CACY 4:470-473, Fall, 1980.

Harris v. McRae (100 S Ct 2671): the Court retreats from
Roe v. Wade. LOYOLA LAW REVIEW 26:749-760,
Summer, 1980.

Human life and abortion [letter], by A. M. Bryson. MEDI-
CAL JOURNAL OF AUSTRALIA 1(2):94, January 24,

1981.

Human life and termination of pregnancy [letter], by A. Viliunas. MEDICAL JOURNAL OF AUSTRALIA 1(12): 656, June 13, 1981.

Judge O'Connor. NATIONAL REVIEW 33:881-882, August 7, 1981.

Law 194 on voluntary abortion [letter], by M. M. Marzi, et al. ANNALI DI OSTETRICIA, GINECOLOGIA, MEDI-CINA PERINATALE 100(4):284-285, July-August, 1979.

The legal battle for reproductive rights in Europe, by A. D. Rollier. DRAPER FUND REPORT p16-18, October, 1980.

Network repeats refusal to state abortion policy. NATIONAL CATHOLIC REPORTER 17:13, December 26, 1980.

Perspectives on abortion law reform in Barbados, by W. C. Gilmore. ANGLO-AMERICAN LAW REVIEW 8:191-209, July-September, 1979.

Refusal to fund constitutionally protected right held valid. WASHINGTON UNIVERSITY LAW QUARTERLY 59: 247-260, 1981.

The rights of child before birth, by G. López Garcia. REVIS-TA CHILENA DE PEDIATRIA 51(1):39-47, January-February, 1980.

Science and the 'Human life bill', by H. S. Meyer. JAMA 246 (8):837-839, August 21, 1981.

Sciuriaga v. Powell, Queen's Bench Division May 18, 1979. Transcript No. 1978/NJ/262; (1979) 76 L S Gaz 567. MODERN LAW REVIEW 44:215-219, March, 1981.

Some fault anti-abortion statute as ambiguous. NATIONAL CATHOLIC REPORTER 17:3-4, February 6, 1981.

Split within anti-abortion movement hits myths, by M. Meehan. NATIONAL CATHOLIC REPORTER 18:3, November 6, 1981.

Watch on the right—abortion rights: taking the offensive, by N. Weisstein. MS MAGAZINE 10:36+, September, 1981.

— danger—a Human Life Amendment is on the way, by R. Copelon. MS MAGAZINE 9:46+, February, 1981.

Wrongful death, wrongful birth, wrongful life: the evolution of prenatal tort law, by M. W. Kronisch. TRIAL 16:34-36+, December, 1980.

When does life begin? An expert says the debate is shedding more heat than light [implications of Helms-Hyde bill; interview by N. Faber], by C. Grobstein. PEOPLE 15: 79-80+, June 8, 1981.

When Uncle Sam stops paying, by D. French. FORBES 127: 32, June 22, 1981.

CANADA
   Reflections on Canadian abortion law: evacuation and destruction—two separate issues, by M. A. Somerville. UNIVERSITY OF TORONTO LAW JOURNAL 31: 1-26, Winter, 1981.

GREAT BRITAIN
   Doctor's dilemma over abortion, by A. Veitch. GUARDI-AN p8, July 13, 1981.

ISRAEL
   The legal status of women in Israel, by S. E. Shanoff. CONGRESSIONAL MONITOR 48:9-12, June, 1981.

ABORTION: LAWS AND LEGISLATION

ITALY
Abortion 1, Pope 1 [John Paul II's support of unsuccessful referendum to tighten abortion laws in Italy], by T. Sheehan. COMMONWEAL 108:357-359, June 19, 1981.

Laicismo e clericalismo nel Parlamento italiano tra la legge sul divorzio e quella sull'aborto, by A. Tempestini. POLITICA DEL DIRITTO 11(3):407-428, 1980.

TURKEY
Strafrechtlicher Bevölkerungsschutz und Bevölkerungsplanung in der Türkischen Republik [based on conference paper], by O. Oehring. ORIENT 21(3):345-370, 1980.

UNITED STATES
Abortion and infant mortality before and after the 1973 U.S. Supreme Court decision on abortion, by L. S. Robertson. JOURNAL OF BIOSOCIAL SCIENCE 13: 275-280, July, 1981.

Abortions for minors after Bellotti II (Bellotti v. Baird, 99 S Ct 3035): an analysis of state law and a proposal. ST. MARY LAW JOURNAL 11:946-997, 1980.

Abortion: hell's fury. ECONOMIST 279:22, May 30, 1981.

Abortion—in an action seeking declaratory and injunctive relief, several provisions of the 1979 Missouri statute regulating abortions were found unconstitutional. JOURNAL OF FAMILY LAW 19:342-350, March, 1981.

The abortion law that could divide America, by P. Levi. DAILY TELEGRAPH p15, March 18, 1981.

Abortion laws, religious beliefs and the First Amendment,

ABORTION: LAWS AND LEGISLATION

UNITED STATES
by S. L. Skahn. VALPARAISO UNIVERSITY LAW
REVIEW 14:487-526, Spring, 1980.

Abortion policy in 1978: a follow-up analysis, by D.
Stewart. PUBLIUS 9(1):161-168, 1979.

Abortion regulation: the circumscription of state intervention by the doctrine of informed consent. GEOR-
GIA LAW REVIEW 15:681-713, Spring, 1981.

Abortion: a severe testing. COMMONWEAL 108:643,
November 20, 1981.

Abortion—state statutes—informed consent—waiting
period. THE CRIMINAL LAW REPORTER: COURT
DECISIONS AND PROCEEDINGS 27(22):2492,
September 3, 1980.

Abortion—strict limitations on federal Medicaid reimbursements for abortions imposed by the Hyde a-
mendment held permissible. Participating states held
not obligated to fund medically necessary abortions
not federally funded. JOURNAL OF FAMILY LAW
19:335-341, March, 1981.

Another violation of N1H guidelines [news], by D. Dickson. NATURE 286(5774):649, August 14, 1980.

Anti-abortion groups spar over amendment tactic [news].
CHRISTIANITY TODAY 25:84, February 6, 1981.

Appeals Courts decision reverses former minors' contraceptive position, by A. S. Kerr. MICHIGAN MEDI-
CINE 79(17):331, June, 1980.

As annual march nears, pro-lifers focus on amendment,
by F. Franzonia. OUR SUNDAY VISITOR 69:3,
January 18, 1981.

UNITED STATES
Barnstorming on feminist Air Force One [organizing Project 13 to override an antiabortion amendment], by G. Steinem. MS MAGAZINE 10:79-80+, December, 1981.

Bill to ban abortions [views of S. Galebach]. CHRISTIANITY TODAY 25:14-15, May 8, 1981.

Bishops' aide: Congress lacks human life bill authority. OUR SUNDAY VISITOR 69:7, April 26, 1981.

Bishops support Hatch amendment; Capitol Hill testimony, by J. R. Roach. ORIGINS 11:359+, November 19, 1981.

Case and comment: abortion, by R. Williams, et al. THE CRIMINAL LAW REVIEW p169-170, March, 1981.

The case for a human life amendment. ORIGINS 11:360-372, November 19, 1981.

Compliance and the state legislature: an empirical analysis of abortion and aid to non-public schools in Illinois and Minnesota, by C. Neal, PhD. DAI 41(11-12): 38, 1981.

Conference examines proposed human life amendment; report of the human life amendment conference, St. Louis. HOSPITAL PROGRESS 62:22-23, October, 1981.

Congress and the zygote [Helms-Hyde Human Life bill], by H. Kohn. ROLLING STONE p13, June 11, 1981.

Congress to reexamine antiabortion amendment [news], by C. Holden. SCIENCE 213(4506):421, July 24, 1981.

UNITED STATES
Congress turns a serious eye toward Human Life bill, by R. B. Shaw. OUR SUNDAY VISITOR 69:8, March 29, 1981.

Congressional confusion over "conception" [Helms-Hyde bill], by J. L. Marx. SCIENCE 212:423, April 24, 1981.

Conservatives, liberals back Denton's chastity bill. OUR SUNDAY VISITOR 70:7, October 11, 1981.

Constitutional law—abortion funding and the demise of maternal health consideration. SUFFOLK UNIVERSITY LAW REVIEW 15:285-305, April, 1981.

Constitutional law—health law—constitutionality of the Hyde amendment—medically necessary abortions need not be funded by the state or federal government under Medicaid. WHITTIER LAW REVIEW 3: 381-408, 1981.

Constitutional law—Supreme Court upholds validity of Hyde amendment—states need not fund all abortions under Medicaid. CREIGHTON LAW REVIEW 14: 607-628, 1981.

Controversy destined to dog Supreme Court's heels, by R. B. Shaw. OUR SUNDAY VISITOR 70:5, July 26, 1981.

Court case: should your conscience by your guide? NURSINGLIFE 1(1):15, July-August, 1981.

Court ruling suggests justices seeking pro-family label, by R. B. Shaw. OUR SUNDAY VISITOR 69:6, April 12, 1981.

Court upholds Utah law requiring preabortion notice of

UNITED STATES
minors' parents, by P. Geary. HOSPITAL PRO-
GRESS 62:22-23, May, 1981.

Disagreement over proposed human life bill. ORIGINS
11:100-105, July 2, 1981.

Dr. Koop and Mr. Hyde. ECONOMIST 278:25+, March
28-April 3, 1981.

Effect of legalized abortion on wrongful life actions.
FLORIDA STATE UNIVERSITY LAW REVIEW 9:
137-156, Winter, 1981.

Experience with and remarks one year's application of
the abortion law 194, by A. Benedetti, et al. MI-
NERVA GINECOLOGIA 33(4):377-379, April, 1981.

Federal abortion. AMERICA 145:232-233, October 24,
1981.

Fetal personhood treat [Helms-Hyde bill] . MS MAGA-
ZINE 9:19, June, 1981.

Fetal viability and individual autonomy: resolving medical and legal standards for abortion. UCLA LAW RE-
VIEW 27:1340-1364, August, 1980.

First FDA medical device regulations will affect development of many experimental contraceptives. FAMILY
PLANNING PERSPECTIVES 12:212-213, July-August, 1980.

Funding of abortions under the Medicaid program—con-
stitutionality of the Hyde amendment. AMERICAN
JOURNAL OF TRIAL ADVOCACY 4:708-717,
Spring, 1981.

Gap between law and moral order: an examination of the

UNITED STATES
legitimacy of the Supreme Court abortion decisions, by L. D. Wardle. BRIGHAM YOUNG UNIVERSITY LAW REVIEW 1980:811-835, 1980.

Gooley v. Moss (Ind) 398 N E 2d 1314. NEW ENGLAND JOURNAL OF PRISON LAW 6:321-323, Summer, 1980.

Grady, In re (NJ) 405 A 2d 851. SETON HALL LAW REVIEW 10:756-758, 1980.

HSE confident it can cope. NATURE 277(5695):341, February, 1979.

Harris v. McRae (100 s Ct 2671), by M. C. Dunlap. WOMEN'S RIGHTS LAW REPORTER 6:166-168, Spring, 1980.

Harris v. McRae: the Hyde Amendment stands while rights of poor women fall [U.S. Supreme Court decision upholding the law prohibiting the use of federal funds for many therapeutic abortions], by C. C. Sewell, et al. KENTUCKY LAW JOURNAL 69(2): 359-391, 1980-1981.

Harris v. McRae (100 S Ct 2671): indigent women must bear the consequences of the Hyde amendment. LOYOLA UNIVERSITY LAW JOURNAL 12:255-276, Winter, 1981.

—: whatever happened to the Roe v. Wade abortion right?. PEPPERDINE LAW REVIEW 8:861-897, March, 1981.

Hell's fury. ECONOMIST 279:32, May 30, 1981.

House approves ban on federal abortion cover. BUSINESS INSURANCE 14:12, September 1, 1980.

UNITED STATES
Human life amendment and the future of human life, by
R. Eisler. HUMANIST 41:13-19+, September-October, 1981.

Human life amendment is bulls-eye on hit list target.
OUR SUNDAY VISITOR 69:7, March 1, 1981.

The human life amendment . . . two views, by A. Neale,
et al. NATIONAL CATHOLIC REPORTER 17:10-
11, April 24, 1981.

Human life bill arouses more opposition, by R. J. Smith.
SCIENCE 212:1372, June 19, 1981.

A human life statute [review of various Supreme Court
decisions which set precedents the Congress might
cite in extending the Fourteenth Amendment protection to include unborn children, by S. H. Galebach.
HUMAN LIFE REVIEW 7:5-33, Winter, 1981.

Hyde amendment: an analysis of its state progeny. UNI-
VERSITY OF DAYTON LAW REVIEW 5:313-342,
Summer, 1980.

Hyde amendment and Medicaid abortions, by S. Gunty.
FORUM 16:825-840, Spring, 1981.

The Hyde Amendment in action. How did the restriction
of federal funds for abortion affect low-income women? by W. Cates, Jr. JAMA 246(10):1109-1112,
September 4, 1981.

Hyde amendment: new implications for equal protection
claims. BAYLOR LAW REVIEW 33:295-306, Spring,
1981.

Illinois abortion statute called 'unconstitutional straight-
jacket'. THE FAMILY LAW REPORTER: COURT

UNITED STATES
    OPINIONS 6(42):2807-2808, September 2, 1980.

In the human life bill, by J. T. Noonan, Jr. CATHOLIC
    MIND 79:52-64, November, 1981.

The international politics of contraception [commenting
    on United States economic assistance programs], by
    J. Kasun. POLICY REPORT p135-152, Winter, 1981.

Is government paving abortion's way as shortcut cure? by
    F. Franzonia. OUR SUNDAY VISITOR 69:6, April
    5, 1981.

Justice Harry A. Blackmun: the abortion decisions, by D.
    Fuqua. ARKANSAS LAW REVIEW 34:276-296,
    1980.

Law and the life sciences, by G. J. Annas. HASTINGS
    CENTER REPORT 11:8-9, February, 1981.

Legislation and abortion: the fight continues. pt. 4: The
    constitution under attack, by N. A. Dershowitz. CON-
    GRESSIONAL MONITOR 48:8, April, 1981.

Legislating life [strategy for reversing Roe v. Wade de-
    vised by S. Galebach]. NATION 232:355-356, March
    28, 1981.

Leon Rosenberg on the "human life" bill [excerpts from
    testimony, April 1981], by L. Rosenberg. SCIENCE
    212:907, May 22, 1981.

Life and the 14th amendment. AMERICA 144:397, May
    16, 1981.

Maine abortion statutes of 1979: testing the constitu-
    tional limits. MAINE LAW REVIEW 32:315-353,
    1980.

ABORTION: LAWS AND LEGISLATION

UNITED STATES
Massachusetts abortion statute requiring waiting period
upheld. THE FAMILY LAW REPORTER: COURT
OPINIONS 6(47):2900-2901, October 7, 1980.

NAS enters human life bill debate [Helms-Hyde bill].
SCIENCE NEWS 119:293, May 9, 1981.

New abortion fight starts in Congress [proposed Hatch
Amendment], by E. Doerr. HUMANIST 41:45-46,
November-December, 1981.

The new right: women's rights under attack, by J. Butterfield. RADICAL RELIGION 5(4):61-73, 1981.

Notifying the parents [Utah law requiring parental per-
mission before an abortion could be perfomed on a
minor upheld]. AMERICA 144:289-290, April 11,
1981.

On the question of jurisdiction [testimony of J. T.
Noonan in defense of Helms-Hyde bill], by W. F.
Buckley, Jr. NATIONAL REVIEW 33:741, June 26,
1981.

Opinions of the United States Supreme Court: abortion.
THE CRIMINAL LAW REPORTER: TEXT SEC-
TION 28(25):3105-3121, March 25, 1981.

Orientations toward abortion: guilty or knowledge? by
A. R. Allgeier, et al. ADOLESCENCE 16(62):273-
280, Summer, 1980.

Paternal child-support tort parallels for the abortion on
maternal demand era: the work of Regan, Levy and
Duncan, by G. S. Swan. GLENDALE LAW REVIEW
3:249-284, 1978-1979.

Pennsylvania bans welfare abortions with new statute.

227

ABORTION: LAWS AND LEGISLATION

UNITED STATES
THE FAMILY LAW REPORTER: COURT OPIN-
IONS 7(9):2138-2139, January 6, 1981.

President's remarks on abortion create some confusion.
OUR SUNDAY VISITOR 69:7, March 22, 1981.

Privacy—includes right to obtain contraceptives; birth
control—may give contraceptive and not tell parent—
United States. JUVENILE LAW DIGEST 12(12):383-
384, December, 1980.

Pro-life doesn't stop at birth, by M. Schwartz. LIGUORI-
AN 69:7-11, January, 1981.

Pro-life forces riled by tone of Reagan letter. OUR SUN-
DAY VISITOR 70:7, August 30, 1981.

"Pro-life" interest groups try a new tactic in effort to
crack down on abortion; abandoning the amendment? CONGRESSIONAL QUARTERLY WEEKLY
REPORT 39:383+, February 28, 1981.

Pro-life rift develops over human life bill, by R. B. Shaw.
OUR SUNDAY VISITOR 70:6, May 17, 1981.

Pro-lifers demand action [constitutional amendment is-
sue]. CHRISTIAN CENTURY 98:159-161, February
18, 1981.

Proposed human life statute: abortion as murder? by C.
E. M. Kolb. AMERICAN BAR ASSOCIATION JOUR-
NAL 67:1123-1126, September, 1981.

Public funding of medically necessary abortions is not required under the Medicaid act. TEXAS TECHNICAL
LAW REVIEW 12:483-499, 1981.

Religion and abortion [Harris vs. McRae and the constitu-

UNITED STATES
tionality of the Hyde Amendment], by J. R. Nelson.
CENTER MAGAZINE 14:51-55, July-August, 1981.

Right-to-life activists split on federal tactics [editorial],
by J. M. Wall. CHRISTIAN CENTURY 98:1332-
1333, December 23, 1981.

Right to life breakthrough [views of S. Galebach], by W.
F. Buckley, Jr. NATIONAL REVIEW 33:313, March
20, 1981.

Right-to-life split, by T. Noah. NEW REPUBLIC 184:7-9,
March 21, 1981.

Right to lifers find a key friend. US NEWS AND WORLD
REPORT 90:8, February 2, 1981.

Right to lifers learn facts of life [in applying for abor-
tions], by A. J. Fugh-Berman. OFF OUR BACKS 11:
4, June, 1981.

The right to live and the right to die: some considerations
of law and society in America, by G. Z. F. Bereday.
VALUES, ETHICS AND HEALTH CARE 4:233-256,
1979.

Right to strife. NEW REPUBLIC 184:5-6, June 6, 1981.

Rights of the born, by B. J. Leonard. CHRISTIAN CEN-
TURY 99:7-8, January 6-13, 1982.

The rights of personhood: the Dred SCott case and the
question of abortion [Roe vs Wade], by M. C. Sernett.
RELIGION IN LIFE 49:461-476, Winter, 1980.

Scheinberg v. Smith. JOURNAL OF FAMILY LAW 19:
149-153, November, 1980.

UNITED STATES
Science challenges Humanae Vitae, by W. P. Messenger.
NATIONAL CATHOLIC REPORTER 17:7+, October 16, 1981.

Senate commences hearings on 'human life' [news], by C.
Holden. SCIENCE 212(4495):648-649, May 8, 1981.

Senate hearing on abortion amendments, by O. Hatch, et
al. ORIGINS 11:293+, October 22, 1981.

Senator Hatch offers amendment to regulate abortion.
OUR SUNDAY VISITOR 70:7, October 4, 1981.

Several provisions of North Dakota's abortion law held
unconstitutional. THE CRIMINAL LAW REPORTER:
COURT DECISIONS AND PROCEEDINGS 28(7):
2158-2159, November 12, 1980.

Sex, abortion and the Supreme Court [teen-age abortion].
NEWSWEEK 97:83, April 6, 1981.

Sex selection abortion: a constitutional analysis of the
abortion liberty and a person's right to know, by J.
R. Schaibley. INDIANA LAW JOURNAL 56:281-
320, Winter, 1981.

Shortcut to outlaw abortion [Helms-Hyde bill], by L.
Sager. NEW YORK REVIEW OF BOOKS 28:39-42,
June 25, 1981.

Should abortions be outlawed? [proposed Helms-Hyde
bill; interviews], by H. J. Hyde, et al. US NEWS AND
WORLD REPORT 90:31-32, May 4, 1981.

Social commentary: values and legal personhood, by J. A.
Parness. WEST VIRGINIA LAW REVIEW 83:487-
503, Spring, 1981.

UNITED STATES
Social security and public welfare—abortion—the Hyde amendment substantively altered state funding obligations under title XIX of the social security act of 1965, requiring states to fund only the abortions specified in the amendment. UNIVERSITY OF DETROIT JOURNAL OF URBAN LAW 58:95-117, Fall, 1980.

Statutes and ordinances—abortion. THE CRIMINAL LAW REPORTER: COURT DECISIONS AND PROCEEDINGS 28(5):2120, October 29, 1980.

The Supreme Court, abortion and state response, by J. Nicholson. PUBLIUS 8(1):159-178, 1978.

The Supreme Court and abortion: the irrelevance of medical judgment, by G. J. Annas. HASTINGS CENTER REPORT 10(5):23-24, October, 1980.

—: 1. Upholding constitutional principles, by J. T. Noonan, Jr. HASTINGS CENTER REPORT 10(6): 14-16, December, 1980.

—: 2. Sidestepping social realities, by D. Mechanic. HASTINGS CENTER REPORT 10(6):17-19, December, 1980.

Supreme court backs parental notification on abortion. OUR SUNDAY VISITOR 69:7, April 5, 1981.

The Supreme Court decided: social security—abortion. THE FAMILY LAW REPORTER: TEXT SECTION NO. 11 6(34):3055-3074, July 1, 1980.

Supreme Court report: abortion . . . federal funds. AMERICAN BAR ASSOCIATION JOURNAL 66:994-996, August, 1980.

ABORTION: LAWS AND LEGISLATION

UNITED STATES
Texas abortion law: consent requirements and special
statutes, by T. O. Tottenham, et al. HOUSTON
LAW REVIEW 18:819-848, May, 1981.

Text of US Supreme Court decision: Harris v McRae.
JOURNAL OF CHURCH AND STATE 22:575-595,
Autumn, 1980.

The United States Supreme Court legalizes abortion, by
W. C. Ellis. CASE STUDIES IN HEALTH ADMINIS-
TRATION 2:29-32, 1980.

Utah. FROM THE STATE CAPITALS: JUVENILE DE-
LINQUENCY AND FAMILY RELATIONS 5:3-4,
May 1, 1981.

Viability and fetal life in state criminal abortion laws, by
E. Griffin. JOURNAL OF CRIMINAL LAW AND
CRIMINOLOGY 72:324-344, Spring, 1981.

The war against choice [1980 National Right to Life
Committee meeting, Anaheim, California], by D.
English. MOTHER JONES 6:16+, February-March,
1981.

Why the Supreme Court was plainly wrong in the Hyde
amendment case: a brief comment on Harris v. Mc-
Rae (100 S Ct 2671), by M. J. Perry. STANFORD
LAW REVIEW 32:1113-1128, July, 1980.

Women's Rights Action Group—St. Louis and the right:
the anti-abortion front [demonstration against abortion rights]. OFF OUR BACKS 11:10, January, 1981.

ABORTION: MISSED
Extra-amniotic instillation of rivanol in the management of
patients with missed abortion and fetal death, by A.
Olund. ACTA OBSTETRICIA ET GYNECOLOGICA

ABORTION: MISSED

SCANDINAVICA 60(3):313-315, 1981.

Foetus compressus, by B. Prasad, et al. JOURNAL OF THE INDIAN MEDICAL ASSOCIATION 74(8):154-155, April 16, 1980.

Missed abortion, hydatidiform mole and intra-uterine fetal death treated with 15-methyl-prostaglandin F 2-alpha, by E. G. Boes. SOUTH AFRICAN MEDICAL JOURNAL 58 (22):878-880, November 29, 1980.

Missed abortions and some organochlorine compounds: organochlorine insecticides (OCI) and polychlorinated biphenyls (PCBs), by B. Bercovici, et al. ACTA MEDICINAE LEGALIS ET SOCIALIS 30(3):177-185, 1980.

Termination of pregnancy in patients with missed abortion and intrauterine dead fetuses by a single intracervical application of prostaglandin E2 in viscous gel, by G. Ekman, et al. ZENTRALBLATT FUR GYNAEKOLOGIE 102(4); 219-222, 1980.

ABORTION: MORTALITY AND MORTALITY STATISTICS
Abortion and infant mortality before and after the 1973 U. S. Supreme Court decision on abortion, by L. S. Robertson. JOURNAL OF BIOSOCIAL SCIENCE 13:275-280, July, 1981.

Abortion-related mortality—United States, 1977. THE FORENSIC SCIENCE GAZETTE 10(3):5-6, July-September, 1979.

Black genocide [view that abortion is a means of genocide against blacks], by D. L. Cuddy. AMERICA 145:181, October 3, 1981.

Effects of child mortality on fertility in Thailand, by M. Hashimoto, et al. ECONOMIC DEVELOPMENT AND CULTURAL CHANGE 29:781-794, July, 1981.

ABORTION: MORTALITY AND MORTALITY STATISTICS

Morality, law, and politics: abortion [special issue; with editorial comment] . COMMONWEAL 108:643-664, November 20, 1981.

Mortality associated with medical termination of pregnancy, by M. A. Deshmukh, et al. JOURNAL OF POSTGRADUATE MEDICINE 26(2):121-126, April, 1980.

ABORTION: PSYCHOLOGY AND PSYCHIATRY
Abortion, euthanasia and the pluralist society, by D. J. Ryan. OR 672(8):18, February 23, 1981.

ABORTION: REPEATED
A balanced translocation t(4;9) (q35;q12) with a breakpoint within the heterochromatic region of chromosome 9 in a woman with recurrent abortion, by G. Neri, et al. CLINICAL GENETICS 18(4):239-243, October, 1980.

Chromosomal analysis of couples with repeated spontaneous abortions, by L. J. Sant-Cassia, et al. BRITISH JOURNAL OF OBSTETRICS AND GYNAECOLOGY 88(1): 52-58, January, 1981.

Cytogenetic findings in 122 couples with recurrent abortions, by C. Stoll. HUMAN GENETICS 57(1):101-103, 1981.

A cytogenetic study of repeated spontaneous abortions, by T. J. Hassold. AMERICAN JOURNAL OF HUMAN GENETICS 32(5):723-730, September, 1980.

A familial t(9;13) balanced translocation associated with recurrent abortion. Repository identification No. GM2492, by A. Serra, et al. CYTOGENETICS AND CELL GENETICS 27(4):269, 1980.

Genetic compatibility may explain recurrent spontaneous abortions [news], by C. Yarbrough. JAMA 246(4):315-316, July 24-31, 1981.

Incidence of positive toxoplasmosis hemagglutination test in the nigerian (Ibo) women with recurrent abortions, by U. Megafu, et al. INTERNATIONAL JOURNAL OF FERTILITY 26(2):132-134, 1981.

Personality of women resorting to repeated voluntary abortions, by F. Lang, et al. ANNALES MEDICO-PSYCHOLOGIQUES 138(8):992-1002, 1980.

Prevention of recurrent abortion with leucocyte transfusions, by C. Taylor, et al. LANCET 2(8237):68-70, July 11, 1981.

Research on repeated abortion: state of the field—1973-1979, by G. D. Gibb, et al. PSYCHOLOGICAL REPORTS 48: 415-424, April, 1981.

ABORTION: RESEARCH
Abortion and the limitations of science, by B. G. Zack. SCIENCE 213:291, July 17, 1981.

Analysis of serum-mediated immunosuppression in normal pregnancy, abortion and contraception, by B. Masset, et al. ALLERGOLOGIA ET IMMUNOPATHOLOGIA 8(5): 569-578, September-October, 1980.

Behavior of maternal serum immunoglobulins in abortion, by A. Tolino, et al. ARCHIVIO DI OSTETRICIA E GINECOLOGIA 85(1-2):45-51, January-April, 1980.

Content of blood group A and B factors in sera of placental and abortive blood, their fractions at different stages of alcoholic fractionation and in immunoglobulin preparations, by E. V. Volevach, et al. ZHURNAL MIKROBIOLOGII, EPIDEMIOLOGII I IMMUNOGIOLOGII (10): 63-67, October, 1980.

Diagnosis of septic abortion in dairy cows, by R. Higgins, et al. CANADIAN JOURNAL OF COMPARATIVE MEDI-

CINE 45(2):159-166, April, 1981.

Effect of silver nitrate on pregnancy termination in cynomolgus monkeys, by N. H. Dubin, et al. FERTILITY AND
STERILITY 36(1):106-109, July, 1981.

Effects of D-tryptophan-6-proline-9-N-ethyl luteinizing hormone-releasing hormone on reproductive functions in the
male rat, by C. Rivier, et al. INTERNATIONAL JOUR-
NAL OF FERTILITY 25(3):145-150, 1980.

Effects of prostaglandin—F2 alpha and a plant protein
'Trichosanthin', on 10-day pregnant rabbits, by S. K.
Saksena, et al. PROSTAGLANDINS AND MEDICINE 5
(5):383-390, November, 1980.

Excerpts from a National Conference on Recombinant DNA
and the Federal Government. Department of Health and
Human Services perspective [news], by L. T. Harmison.
RECOMBINANT DNA TECHNICAL BULLETIN 4(2):
49-51, July, 1981.

Hydrop degeneration. A histopathological investigation of
260 early abortions, by C. Ladefoged. ACTA OB-
STETRICIA ET GYNECOLOGICA SCANDINAVICA 59
(6):509-512, 1980.

Identifying biohazards in university research, by D. W.
Dreesen. AMERICAN JOURNAL OF PUBLIC HEALTH
70(10):1108-1110, October, 1980.

Meeting of the Industrial Practices Subcommittee of the
Federal Interagency Advisory Committee on Recombi-
nant DNA Research [news]. RECOMBINANT DNA
TECHNICAL BULLETIN 4(2):64-67, July, 1981.

Meeting of the Large-Scale Review Working Group of the Recombinant DNA Advisory Committee [news]. RECOMBI-
NANT DNA TECHNICAL BULLETIN 4(2):68-70, July,

1981.

NIOSH perspective on commercial recombinant DNA/bio-technology development, by S. Pauker. RECOMBINANT DNA TECHNICAL BULLETIN 4(2):61-64, July, 1981.

Plasma progesterone, prostaglandin F2alpha and 13,14-dihydro-15-ketoprostaglandin F2alpha in the bovine before abortion or parturition, by A. L. Baetz, et al. CLINICAL CHEMISTRY 26(7):1045, 1980.

Procedures for review of large-scale experiments. RECOMBINANT DNA TECHNICAL BULLETIN 4(2):81, July, 1981.

UCSD gene splicing incident ends unresolved [news], by N. Wade. SCIENCE 209(4464):1494-1495, September 26, 1980.

Value conflicts and the uses of research: the example of abortion, by S. Budner. VALUES, ETHICS AND HEALTH CARE 1(19):14, Fall, 1975.

Watch on the right: beware the "research shows . . ." ploy [attempt to link child abuse and abortion], by J. Gelles, et al. MS MAGAZINE 9:100, June, 1981.

ABORTION: SEPTIC
Delay, limited access found key factors in septic abortion deaths. FAMILY PLANNING PERSPECTIVES 13:46-47, January-February, 1981.

Fatal septic abortion in the United States, 1975-1977, by D. A. Grimes, et al. OBSTETRICS AND GYNECOLOGY 57 (6):739-744, June, 1981.

Salmonella septic abortion, by B. S. Sengupta, et al. INTERNATIONAL SURGERY 65(2):183-186, March-April, 1980.

ABORTION: SEPTIC

Surgical procedure problems in the treatment of septic abortion complicated by acute kidney failure, by S. Dotseva, et al. AKUSHERSTVO I GINEKOLOGIIA 19(506):522-525, 1980.

Use of heparin in cases of septic abortion, by P. Wille. ZENTRALBLATT FUR GYNAEKOLOGIE 102(5):298-302, 1980.

ABORTION: SEPTIC: COMPLICATIONS
Acute kidney insufficiency after septic abortion according to data from the Pirogov RNPISMP, by P. Petrov, et al. AKUSHERSTVO I KINEKOLOGIIA 19(4):304-309, 1980.

ABORTION: SPONTANEOUS
Alcohol and spontaneous abortion [letter], by R. J. Sokol. LANCET 2(8203):1079, November 15, 1980.

Anatomic and chromosal anomalies in 639 spontaneous abortuses, by T. Kajii, et al. HUMAN GENETICS 55(1): 87-98, 1980.

Antibiotic peritoneal lavage in acute peritonitis resulting from spetic abortion or a ruptured pyosalpinx, by H. Nel. SOUTH AFRICAN MEDICAL JOURNAL 57(4):114-116, January 26, 1980.

Balanced translocations in the karyotype as the cause of spontaneous abortion and reproductive disorders, by S. Adzic, et al. SRPSKI ARHIV ZA CELOKUPNO LEKARSTVO 108(1-10), January, 1980.

Balneological treatment of spontaneous habitual abortion caused by the uterine factor or hormonal deficiency, by K. Marzinek, et al. GINEKOLOGIA POLSKA 51(6):545-549, June, 1980.

Chromosomal analysis of couples with repeated spontaneous

abortions, by L. J. Sant-Cassia, et al. BRITISH JOUR-
NAL OF OBSTETRICS AND GYNAECOLOGY 88(1):
52-58, January, 1981.

Circulating antiprothrombinase anticoagulant, thrombosis
and spontaneous abortions; a new syndrome [letter] , by
L. Gabriel, et al. NOUVELLE PRESSE MEDICALE 9
(31):2159, August 30-September 6, 1980.

A cytogenetic study of repeated spontaneous abortions, by
T. J. Hassold. AMERICAN JOURNAL OF HUMAN
GENETICS 32(5):723-730, September, 1980.

Discontinued intrauterine device use and spontaenous abortion, by D. W. Kaufman, et al. AMERICAN JOURNAL
OF PEIDEMIOLOGY 112(3):434, 1980.

The effect of artificial and spontaneous abortions on the
secondary human sex ratio, by G. D. Golovachev, et al.
HUMAN BIOLOGY 52(4):721-729, December, 1980.

Genetic compatibility may explain recurrent spontaneous
abortions [news] , by C. Yarbrough. JAMA 246(4):315-
316, July 24-31, 1981.

HLA alloimmunization as a cause of spontaneous abortion,
by P. Kolevski, et al. BILTEN ZA HEMATOLOGIJU I
TRANSFUZIJU 7(2-3):131-135, 1979.

Method of studying the sociomedical conditions of women
with spontaneous abortions in the area of the Dr. Mara
Maleeva-Zhivkova III Municipal Consolidated Hospital in
the city of Sofia, by I. Vasileva. AKUSHERSTVO I
GINEKOLOGIIA 20(1):13-17, 1981.

Organochlorine pesticides in specimens from women undergoing spontaneous abortion, premature of full-term
delivery, by M. C. Saxena, et al. JOURNAL OF
ANALYTICAL TOXICOLOGY 5(1):6-9, January-

February, 1981.

Prospective studies into pregnancies of primiparae with record of therapeutic termination of previous pregnancies or of spontaneous abortion and assessment of fertility. Second communication, by G. Schott, et al. ZENTRALBLATT FUR GYNAEKOLOGIE 102(16):939-944, 1980.

The psychological implications of spontaneous abortions, by M. Seibel, et al. JOURNAL OF REPRODUCTIVE MEDICINE 25(4):161-165, October, 1980.

Q fever in the etiology of spontaneous abortion, by A. Michev, et al. AKUSHERSTVO I GINEKOLOGIIA 20 (1):34-36, 1981.

Role of physical trauma and overexertion in the etiology of spontaneous abortion, by T. V. Zhukova. ZDRAVOOKHRANENIYE BELORUSSII 0(6):65-66, 1979.

Seasonal variation in spontaneous abortions, by C. W. Warren, et al. AMERICAN JOURNAL OF PUBLIC HEALTH 70 (12):1297-1299, December, 1980.

Serum progesterone, 17 alpha-hydroxyprogesterone, human chorionic gonadotropin, and prolactin in early pregnancy and a case of spontaneous abortion, by P. D. Manganiello, et al. FERTILITY AND STERILITY 36(1):55-60, July, 1981.

Spontaneous abortion after hand-foot-and-mouth disease caused by Coxsackie virus A16, by M. M. Ogilvie, et al. BRITISH MEDICAL JOURNAL 281(6254):1527-1528, December 6, 1980.

Spontaneous abortion and environmental monitering: electrophoretic study, by D. Serman, et al. MUTATION RESEARCH 74(3):197-198, 1980.

ABORTION: SPONTANEOUS

Spontaneous abortion over time: comparing occurrence in 2 cohorts of women a generation apart, by A. Wilcox. AMERICAN JOURNAL OF EPIDEMIOLOGY 112(3): 453-454, 1980.

Spontaneous abortion rate in patients with endometriosis, by J. D. Naples, et al. OBSTETRICS AND GYNECOLOGY 57(4):509-512, April, 1981.

Spontaneous foetal losses in women using different contraceptives around the time of conception, by S. Harlap, et al. INTERNATIONAL JOURNAL OF EPIDEMIOLOGY 9(1):49-56, March, 1980.

Triploidy in 40 human spontaneous abortuses: assessment of phenotype in embryos, by M. J. Harris, et al. OBSTETRICS AND GYNECOLOGY 57(5):600-606, May, 1981.

ABORTION: SPONTANEOUS: COMPLICATIONS
Birth weight before and after a spontaneous abortion, by E. Alberman, et al. JOURNAL OF OBSTETRICS AND GYNAECOLOGY 87(4):275-280, April, 1980.

Complications after the premature termination of an unwanted pregnancy as an etiological factor in spontaneous abortions and the motives for abortions on demand, by I. Vasileva. AKUSHERSTVO I GINEKOLOGIIA 19(4): 300-303, 1980.

Increased leukemia, lymphoma, and spontaneous abortion in Western New York following a flood disaster, by D. T. Janerich, et al. PUBLIC HEALTH REPORTS 96(4):350-356, July-August, 1981.

ABORTION: STATISTICS
Clinical observations on 201 cases of mid-term abortion induced by Yuanhuacine. CHUNG HUA FU CHAN KO TSA CHIH 14(4):287-289, 1979.

Coercive and noncoercive abortion deterrence policies: a comparative state analysis, by C. A. Johnson, et al. LAW AND POLICY QUARTERLY 2:106-108, January, 1980.

Implantation in early abortions 18 previllous and 24 young villous oocytes, by E. Philippe. JOURNAL OF GYNE-COLOGIE OBSTETRIQUE ET BIOLOGIE DE LA RE-PRODUCTION 9(5):513-521, 1980.

Methodological kit: monitoring statistics relating to the control of fertility and the provision of abortion, by J. R. Ashton. COMMUNITY MEDICINE 3(1):44-54, February, 1981.

Relation between semen quality and fate of pregnancy: retrospective study on 534 pregnancies, by Z. T. Homonnai, et al. INTERNATIONAL JOURNAL OF ANDROLOGY 3 (5):574-584, October, 1980.

Towards an understanding of the american abortion rate, by C. Francome. JOURNAL OF BIOSOCIAL SCIENCE 11 (3):303-313, July, 1979.

ABORTION: TECHNIQUES
Abortion in the 2d trimester by extra-amniotic infusion. Description of 149 cases, by M. Blum. MINERVA GINE-COLOGICA 33(2-3):253-256, February-March, 1981.

Anaesthesia for termination of pregnancy, by I. S. Grant. BRITISH JOURNAL OF ANAESTHESIOLOGY 52(8): 711-713, August, 1980.

Anesthesiological problems and choice in operations for the termination of pregnancy. A study of 1500 cases, by G. B. Paolella, et al. MINERVA ANESTESIOLOGICA 47 (1-2):37-40, January-February, 1981.

Biological action and half life in plasma or intramuscular sulprostone for termination of second trimester pregnancy, by R. C. Briel, et al. PROSTAGLANDINS AND MEDI-CINE 6(1):1-8, January, 1981.

A clinical double-blind study on the effect of prophylactical-ly administered single dose tinidazole on the occurrence of endometritis after first trimester legal abortion, by L. Weström, et al. SCANDINAVIAN JOURNAL OF INFEC-TIOUS DISEASES SUPPLEMENT 26:104-109, 1981.

Clinical experience from transcervical intra-amnionic hyper-tonic saline instillation for termination of pregnancy in second trimester, by E. Ehrig, et al. ZENTRALBLATT FUR GYNAEKOLOGIE 102(22):1288-1293, 1980.

Dilatation of the cervix prior to vacuum aspiration by single vaginal administration of 15-methyl-PGF2 alpha methyl ester, by O. Frankman, et al. CONTRACEPTION 21(6): 571-576, June, 1980.

Dilation and evacuation: a preferred method of midtrimester abortion, by K. I. Cadesky, et al. AMERICAN JOURNAL OF OBSTETRICS AND GYNECOLOGY 139(3):329-332, February 1, 1981.

The effect of abortion method on the outcome of subsequent pregnancy, by P. E. Slater, et al. JOURNAL OF REPRO-DUCTIVE MEDICINE 26(3):123-128, March, 1981.

Electrocardiographic changes induced by suction curettage for elective termination of pregnancy, by L. M. Mabee, Jr., et al. AMERICAN JOURNAL OF OBSTETRICS AND GYNECOLOGY 138(2):181-184, September 15, 1980.

Experimental studies of intra-amniotic pargyline and/or re-serpine for termination of midterm pregnancy, by M. Q. Zheng. CHUNG HUA FU CHAN KO TSA CHIH 15(2): 105-107, 1980.

Extraovular instillations of normal saline for termination of midtrimester pregnancy, by A. Rofé, et al. INTERNATIONAL JOURNAL OF GYNAECOLOGY AND OBSTETRICS 18(5):351-353, 1980.

Fertility following abortion, using Boero's method, by S. Lembrych, et al. ZENTRALBLATT FUR GYNAEKOLOGIE 103(3):154-156, 1981.

Feto-placentopathies in practice, by E. Philippe. ARCHIVES D'ANATOMIE ET DE CYTOLOGIE PATHOLOGIQUE 28(5):286-293, 1980.

Follow-up study of mid-term abortion induced by five different methods, by X. X. Zhong. CHUNG HUA FU CHAN KO TSA CHIH 15(4):216-218, October, 1980.

Half an abortion in a case of twins [procedure at Mt. Sinai School of Medicine in New York]. SCIENCE NEWS 119: 406, June 27, 1981.

Interruption of pregnancy with the aspiration method. Technical suggestions, by E. Painvain, et al. MINERVA GINECOLOGIA 32(10):933-937, October, 1980.

Investigation of the prophylactic effect of tinidazole on the postoperative infection rate of patients undergoing vacuum aspiration, by K. Krohn. SCANDINAVIAN JOURNAL OF INFECTIOUS DISEASES 26:101-103, 1981.

Prolactin changes in maternal plasma following termination by vacuum curettage and the effect of bromocriptine treatment on these changes, by O. Ylikorkala, et al. BRITISH JOURNAL OF OBSTETRICS AND GYNAECOLOGY 87(10):911-915, October, 1980.

Prophylactic antibiotics in first-trimester abortions: a clinical, controlled trial, by S. Sonne-Holm, et al. AMERICAN

JOURNAL OF OBSTETRICS AND GYNECOLOGY 139 (6):693-696, March 15, 1981.

Modified isthmography in the management of mid-trimester abortion, by Y. A. Naguib, et al. JOURNAL OF THE EGYPTIAN MEDICAL ASSOCIATION 61(5-6):375-388, 1978.

A new abortion technique: intravaginal and intramuscular prostaglandin, by N. H. Lauersen, et al. OBSTETRICS AND GYNECOLOGY 58(1):96-100, July, 1981.

New form for termination of pregnancy [letter], by W. Savage. BRITISH MEDICAL JOURNAL 282(6262):478-479, February 7, 1981.

Oxytocin augmentation of intra-amniotic saline for termination of pregnancy, by K. S. Karam, et al. JOURNAL OF MEDICAL LIBANAIS 31(3):235-243, 1980.

Oxytocin augmentation of second-trimester abortion: safe or hazardous? by W. Cates, Jr., et al. CONTRACEPTION 22 (5):513-525, November, 1980.

Oxytocin: oxytocic of choice in first trimester, by J. B. Lauritz, et al. MEDICAL JOURNAL OF AUSTRALIA 2(6):319-320, September 20, 1980.

Saving one, dooming another [abortion of mongoloid fraternal twin at Manhattan's Mount Sinai Medical Center]. TIME 117:59, June 29, 1981.

Selective abortion saves normal fetus. NEW SCIENTIST 90: 820, June 25, 1981.

Socio-sanitary analysis of the first 300 voluntary interruptions of pregnancy carried out in the obstetrical-gynecological division of the Bassini Hospital of Milan], by M. M. Marzi, et al. MINERVA GINECOLOGIA 32(10):939-

ABORTION: TECHNIQUES

944, October, 1980.

Studies on the viability of trophoblast after termination of various kinds of pregnancies, by K. Kanda. NIPPON SANKA FUJINKA GAKKAI ZASSHI 32(10):1575-1582, October, 1980.

Termination of pregnancy by menstrual extraction, by W. M. Rodney, et al. JOURNAL OF FAMILY PRACTITION-ERS 11(6):955-598, November, 1980.

Triage in the womb [abortion performed on mongoloid fetus while preserving life of the healthy twin]. COMMON-WEAL 108:421, July 31, 1981.

Twin pregnancy, one fetus with Down syndrome removed by sectio parva, the other delivered mature and healthy, by L. Beck, et al. GEBURTSHILFE UND FRAUENHEIL-KUNDE 40(5):397-400, May, 1980.

Vaccine terminates pregnancy. SCIENCE DIGEST 89:102, March, 1981.

Vacuum aspiration method of terminating pregnancy and its early complications, by T. Despodova, et al. AKU-SHERSTVO I GINEKOLOGIIA 19(4):281-285, 1980.

ABORTION: THERAPEUTIC
Abortion, by H. Jung. ZEITSCHRIFT FUR GEBURT-SHILFE UND PERINATOLOGIE 184(2):83-93, April, 1980.

—. 3. Therapeutic abortion committees and third parties [editorial], by B. M. Dickens. CANADIAN MEDICAL ASSOCIATION JOURNAL 124(4):362-363+, February, 1981.

Catecholamines and dopamine-beta-hydroxylase activity during therapeutic abortion induced by sulprostone, by S.

Saarikoski, et al. PROSTAGLANDINS 20(3):487-492, September, 1980.

Comparative blood coagulation studies in PGF2a- and 15-methyl-PGF2a-induced therapeutic abortion, by R. During, et al. FOLIA HAEMATOLOGICA 107(3):502-507, 1980.

A comparison of the efficacy and acceptability of the Copper-7 intrauterine device following immediate or delayed insertion after first-trimester therapeutic abortion, by P. G. Gillett, et al. FERTILITY AND STERILITY 34(2): 121-124, August, 1980.

Continuous monitoring of uterine contractions to control intra-amniotic administration of prostaglandin F2 alpha for therapeutic and missed abortion, by C. J. Roux, et al. SOUTH AFRICAN MEDICAL JOURNAL 59(23):819-821, May 30, 1981.

Embryo-maternal transfusions in 100 therapeutic induced abortions, by P. Spelina, et al. GYNAEKOLOGISCHE RUNDSCHAU 20(Suppl 1):113-116, June, 1980.

Evaluation of therapeutic results of gestagen preparations in imminent abortion and preterm deliveries, by J. Vierik, et al. BRATISLAVSKE LEKARSKE LISTY 74(3):347-353, September, 1980.

Menstrual pattern changes in laparoscopic sterilization patients whose last pregnancy was terminated by therapeutic abortion. A two-year follow-up study, by H. M. Kwak, et al. JOURNAL OF REPRODUCTIVE MEDICINE 25(2):67-71, August, 1980.

Oxytocin potentiation with low dose intravenous prostaglandin E2 in the management of therapeutic abortion, by J. M. Beazley, et al. BRITISH JOURNAL OF CLINICAL PRACTICE 34(11-12):329-333, November-

ABORTION: THERAPEUTIC

December, 1980.

Therapeutic abortion during the second trimester of pregnancy, using intracervical injection of PGF2 alpha, by B. Maria, et al. NOUVEAU PRESSE MEDICALE 10(22): 1825-1827, May 16, 1981.

Tubal factors as possible causes of sterility or infertility of primigravidae, following therapeutic abortion, by G. Schott, et al. ZENTRALBLATT FUR GYNAEKOLOGIE 103(6):355-362, 1981.

The use of sulprostone, a prostaglandin E2 derivative, in intrauterine fetal death and therapeutic abortion, by T. H. Lippert, et al. PROSTAGLANDINS AND MEDICINE 5(4):259-265, October, 1980.

ABORTION: THREATENED

Allylestrenol: three years of experience with Gestanon in threatened abortion and premature labor, by J. Cortés-Prieto, et al. CLINICAL THERAPEUTICS 3(3):200-208, 1980.

Comparative studies of the human chorionic gonadotropin levels in threatened abortion by the passive hemagglutination inhibition and Gravindex tests in the first and second trimesters of pregnancy, by B. Berliński, et al. WIADOMOSCI LEKARSKI 33(23):1887-1889, December 1, 1980.

Comparative value of biophysical and biochemical parameters in threatened abortion, by A. Tolino, et al. ARCHIVIO DI OSTETRICIA E GINECOLOGIA 85(1-2):13-20, January-April, 1980.

Cytochemical studies of the vaginal squamous epithelial cells in pregnancy and threatened abortion, by V. S. Tolmachev. LABORATORNOE DELO (2):72-74, 1981.

Degree of perinatal pathology risk in a history of threatened abortion, by L. V. Moissenko. SKUSHERSTVO I GINE-KOLOGIIA (7):20-21, July, 1980.

Diagnostic ultrasound in threatened abortion and suspected ectopic pregnancy, by C. Jörgensen, et al. ACTA OB-STETRICIA ET GYNECOLOGIA SCANDINAVICA 59 (3):233-235, 1980.

The diagnostic value of maternal pregnancy-specific beta 1-glycoprotein in threatened abortion, by N. J. Karg, et al. ZEITSCHRIFT FUR GEBURTSHILFE UND PERINA-TOLOGIE 185(1):38-40, February, 1981.

A double blind study of the treatment of threatened abortion with fenoterol hydrobromide, by E. Ruppin, et al. GE-BURTSHILFE UND FRAUENHEILKUNDE 41(3):218-221, March, 1981.

Evaluation of hormonal treatment of threatened abortion, by Z. Skolicki. FOLIA MEDICA CRACOVIENSIA 22(1): 137-149, 1980.

Evaluation of the prognosis of threatened abortion by the determination of HCG in serum and urine, by O. Reiert-sen, et al. TIDSSKRIFT FOR DEN NORSKE LAEGE-FORENING 100(34-36):2038-2040, December 10, 1980.

Evaluation of threatened abortion by human chorionic gona-dotropin levels and ultrasonography, by H. A. Sande, et al. INTERNATIONAL JOURNAL OF GYNAECOLOGY AND OBSTETRICS 18(2):123-127, September-October, 1980.

Hormonal profile in threatened abortion and its treatment with HCG, by G. Desanso, et al. MINERVA GINECOLO-GIA 33(5):421-428, May, 1981.

Intrauterine haaematoma. An ultrasonic study of threatened

abortion, by M. Mantoni, et al. BRITISH JOURNAL OF
OBSTETRICS AND GYNAECOLOGY 88(1):47-51,
January, 1981.

Intravenous infusion of 10% ethanol as a method of inhibiting uterine contraction in cases of threatened abortion
and premature labor, by J. Czapla. GINEKOLOGIA
POLSKA 52(2):135-140, January, 1981.

Plasma diamine oxidase levels in pregnancy complicated by
threatened abortion, by M. Legge, et al. JOURNAL OF
CLINICAL PATHOLOGY 34(2):187-188, February,
1981.

Progestagens in threatened abortion [letter], by G. Tognoni,
et al. LANCET 2(8206):1242-1243, December 6, 1980.

Prognosis and treatment of threatened abortion. A. Prognostic value of maternal serum determination of choriogonadotropin and its free alpha and beta subunits in threatened abortion of the first trimester: correlation with
ultrasonographic examination, by U. Gaspard, et al.
JOURNAL OF GYNECOLOGIE OBSTETRIQUE ET BI-
OLOGIE DE LA REPRODUCTION 9(1):62-66, 1980.

—. B. Plasma hormone determinations in the prognostic evaluation of hemorrhage in the first trimester of pregnancy,
by J. Crépin, et al. JOURNAL OF GYNECOLOGIE,
OBSTETRIQUE ET BIOLOGIE DE LA REPRODUC-
TION 9(1):67-72, 1980.

—. C. Longitudinal study of normal and pathologic pregnancy
using plasma hormone determinations, by G. Crépin, et
al. JOURNAL OF GYNECOLOGIE OBSTETRIQUE ET
BIOLOGIE DE LA REPRODUCTION 9(1):73-78, 1980.

—. E. Management of the danger of abortion, by J. J. Leng.
JOURNAL OF GYNECOLOGIE OBSTETRIQUE ET
BIOLOGIE DE LA REPRODUCTION 9(1):90-94, 1980.

ABORTION: THREATENED

Prognosis of pregnancy after threatened abortion, by B.
Adelusi, et al. INTERNATIONAL JOURNAL OF GY-
NAECOLOGY AND OBSTETRICS 18(6):444-447, 1980.

Prognosis of threatened early pregnancy, by P. Jouppila.
JOURNAL OF PERINATAL MEDICINE 9(Suppl 1):72-
74, 1981.

Serum hCG, hPL and progesterone levels in threatened abortions, by N. Sugita, et al. NIPPON SANKA FUJINKA
GAKKAI ZASSHI 32(7):851-858, July, 1980.

Serum leucine aminopeptidase activity in threatened abortion,
prolonged pregnancy and pregnancy toxemias, by W.
Nikodem. POLSKI TYGODNIK LEKARSKI 36(14):497-
499, April 6, 1981.

Threatened abortion, hormone therapy, and malformed
embryos: a comment [letter], by D. M. Sheehan, et al.
TERATOLOGY 22(3):351-352, December, 1980.

Ultrasonic evaluation of ovular viability in threatened abortion, by F. Santi, et al. RIVISTA ITALIANA DI GINE-
COLOGIA 58(5):401-408, September-October, 1977.

Urinary excretion of chorionic gonadotropins in threatened
and habitual abortion, by W. Szymański, et al. GINE-
KOLOGIA POLSKA 51(12):1129-1134, December,
1980.

ABORTION AND ADOLESCENTS
Abortion in American teenagers, 1972-1978, does race
matter? by D. Kramer. AMERICAN JOURNAL OF
EPIDEMIOLOGY 112(3):433, 1980.

Court upholds Utah law requiring preabortion notice of
minors' parents, by P. Geary. HOSPITAL PROGRESS
62:22-23, May, 1981.

251

ABORTION AND ADOLESCENTS

Legal abortions among teenagers in Canada, 1974 through
1978, by A. Wadhera, et al. CANADIAN MEDICAL
ASSOCIATION 122(12):1386-1390, June 21, 1980.

Sex, abortion and the Supreme Court [teenage abortion].
NEWSWEEK 97:83, April 6, 1981.

ABORTION AND COLLEGE STUDENTS
Changes in attitude toward abortion in a large population
of Canadian university students between 1968 and 1978,
by F. Barrett. CANADIAN JOURNAL OF PUBLIC
HEALTH 71:195-200, May-June, 1980.

Postabortion depressive reactions in college women, by N. B.
Gould. JOURNAL OF THE AMERICAN COLLEGE
HEALTH ASSOCIATION 28:316-320, June, 1980.

Sex differences in correlates of abortion attitudes among college students, by B. A. Finlay. JOURNAL OF MAR-
RIAGE AND THE FAMILY 43:571-582, August, 1981.

ABORTION AND CRIMINALS
Criminal abortion. Fact or fiction? by D. A. Bowen. AMER-
ICAN JOURNAL OF FORENSIC MEDICINE AND
PATHOLOGY 1(3):219-221, September, 1980.

Criminal liability of physicians: an encroachment on the
abortion right? AMERICAN CRIMINAL LAW REVIEW
18:591-615, Spring, 1981.

Viability and fetal life in state criminal abortion laws, by E.
Griffin. JOURNAL OF CRIMINAL LAW AND CRIMI-
NOLOGY 72(1):324-344, 1981.

ABORTION AND HORMONES
Antifertility effects of luteinizing hormone-releasing hormone analog in male rats and dogs, by J. Sandow, et al.
INTERNATIONAL JOURNAL OF FERTILITY 25(3):
213-221, 1980.

ABORTION AND HORMONES

Balneological treatment of spontaneous habitual abortion
caused by the uterine factor or hormonal deficiency, by
K. Marzinek, et al. GINEKOLOGIA POLSKA 51(6):545-
549, June, 1980.

Clinical experiences with a new gel for intracervical application of prostaglandin E2 before therapeutic abortion or
induction of term labor, by U. Ulmsten, et al. PROSTA-
GLANDINS 20(3):533-546, September, 1980.

Comparison of two intramuscular prostaglandin analogs for
inducing abortion in the first pregnancy trimester, by B.
Schüssler, et al. GYNAEKOLOGISCHE RUNDSCHAU
20(2):102-109, 1980.

A comparison of two stable prostaglandin E analogues for
termination of early pregnancy and for cervical dilatation, by M. Bygdeman, et al. CONTRACEPTION 22(5):
471-483, November, 1980.

Diploidy in second trimester prostaglandin E2 induced abortuses, by K. H. Sit, et al. AUSTRALIAN PAEDIATRICS
JOURNAL 16(3):201-204, September, 1980.

The effect of a 15(S)-15-methyl prostaglandin F2 alpha
(methyl ester) suppository upon termination of early
pregnancy, by J. F. Roux, et al. CONTRACEPTION 22
(1):57-61, July, 1980.

Effect of selected progestational hormones used for the protection of high-risk pregnancy on the clinical course,
morphological changes and proliferative activity of the
trophoblast, by Z. Papierowski. GINEKOLOGIA
POLSKA 52(3):298-303, 1981.

Effectiveness and side-effects of intracervical application of
prostaglandin F2-alpha-gel in the early weeks of pregnancy, by U. Neeb. GEBURTSHILFE UND FRAUEN-
HEILKUNDE 40(10):901-903, October, 1980.

253

Evaluation of hormonal treatment of threatened abortion, by Z. Skolicki. FOLIA MEDICA CRACOVIENSIA 22(1): 137-149, 1980.

First trimester termination of pregnancy. The value of treating the cervix pre-operatively in the primigravid patient by extra-amniotic administration of a single dose of F2-alpha prostaglandin gel, by P. De Grandi, et al. JOURNAL DE GYNECOLOGIE OBSTETRIQUE ET BIOLOGIE DE LA REPRODUCTION 9(5):587-594, 1980.

HCG, progesterone and 17-beta-estradiol levels during extra-amniotically induced early abortion by a new prostaglandin derivative (Sulprostone), by S. Nilsson, et al. GYNECOLOGIC AND OBSTETRIC INVESTIGATION 12(4):203-210, 1981.

Hormonal protective therapy [letter], by S. Gardó. ORVOSI HETILAP 122(17):1043, April 26, 1981.

Hormonal supervision of threatened abortion. Diagnosis and therapy, by P. Knapstein. MMW 122(26):970-972, June 27, 1980.

Human chorionic gonadotropin, estradiol, progesterone, prolactin, and B-scan ultrasound monitoring of complications in early pregnancy, by B. H. Yuen, et al. OBSTETRICS AND GYNECOLOGY 57(2):207-214, February, 1981.

In vitro studies of the characteristics of the release of prostaglandins from viscous solutions, by I. Z. MacKenzie, et al. BRITISH JOURNAL OF OBSTETRICS AND GYNAECOLOGY 87(4):292-295, April, 1980.

Induction of abortion during the second and third trimester of pregnancy with sulprostone, by S. Heinzl, et al. GEBURTSHILFE UND FRAUENHEILKUNDE 41(3): 231-236, March, 1981.

Induction of abortion with sulprostone, a uteroselective prostaglandin E2 derivative: intramuscular route of application, by K. Schmidt-Gollwitzer, et al. INTERNATIONAL
JOURNAL OF FERTILITY 26(2):86-93, 1981.

Intracervical application of prostaglandin F2 alpha gel as low
risk method of cervical dilatation for therapeutic abortion, by H. Fritzsche, et al. GEBURTSHILFE UND
FRAUENHEILKUNDE 41(3):237-238, March, 1981.

Law Lords split on prostaglandin abortion, by J. Finch.
NURSING FOCUS 2:224-225, March, 1981.

Long-term follow-up of mothers who received high doses of
stilboestrol and ethisterone in pregnancy [letter], by M.
A. Vance, et al. BRITISH MEDICAL JOURNAL 281
(6255):1638, December 13, 1980.

The long term safety of hormonal steroid contraceptives, by
E. G. McQueen. DRUGS 21(6):460-463, June, 1981.

Mid-trimester abortion by vaginal administration of 9-deoxo-
16, 16-dimethyl-9-methylene-PGE2, by M. Bygdeman, et
al. CONTRACEPTION 22(2):153-164, August, 1980.

Midtrimester abortion induced by hyperosmolar urea and
prostaglandin F2 alpha in patients with previous cesarean
section: clinical course and potential for uterine rupture,
by M. F. Atienza, et al. AMERICAN JOURNAL OF OB-
STETRICS AND GYNECOLOGY 138(1):55-59, September 1, 1980.

A new non-hormonal pregnancy-terminating agent, by G.
Galliani, et al. CONTRACEPTION 23(2):163-180, February, 1981.

On the mechanism of action of a new pregnancy-terminating
agent. Part I: Effects of prostaglandin F2 alpha metabolism in the rat and the hamster, by F. Luzzani, et al.

CONTRACEPTION 23(3):325-333, March, 1981.

Pituitary tumor made symptomatic during hormone therapy and induced pregnancy, by R. P. Mills, et al. ANNALS OF OPHTHALMOLOGY 11(11):1672-1676, November, 1979.

Potentiation of prostaglandin evoked contractions of isolated rat uterus by vasicine hydrochloride, by R. Lal, et al. INDIAN JOURNAL OF MEDICAL RESEARCH 73:641-648, April, 1981.

Pregnancy terminating activity of a new non-hormonal anti-fertility agent, 2-(3-ethoxy-phenyl)-5,6-dihydro-s-triazole [5,1-a] isoquinoline (DL 204-IT) in the rat and the hamster. Studies on the factors affecting its activity, by G. Galliani, et al. ARZNEIMITTELFORSCH 30(6):972-977, 1980.

Prostaglandin termination of pregnancy [letter], by B. Eton. BRITISH MEDICAL JOURNAL 282(6257):72-73, January 3, 1981.

Prostaglandins for the management of anencephalic pregnancy, by M. Thiery, et al. PROSTAGLANDINS 21(2): 207-215, February, 1981.

Prostaglandins in gel for abortion [letter], by O. Djahan-bakhch, et al. BRITISH MEDICAL JOURNAL 283 (6291):614, August 29, 1981.

Prostaglandins in gel for mid-trimester abortion: a method to minimise nursing involvement, by D. H. Smith, et al. BRITISH MEDICAL JOURNAL 282(6281):2012, June 20, 1981.

Prostaglandins in obstetrics [editorial]. BRITISH MEDICAL JOURNAL 282(6262):418-419, February 7, 1981.

Rupture of the uterus after midtrimester prostaglandin abortion, by L. L. Cederqvist, et al. JOURNAL OF REPRODUCTIVE MEDICINE 25(3):136-138, September, 1980.

A sensitive enzyme immunoassay for norethisterone in plasma and saliva, by A. Turkes, et al. JOURNAL OF ENDOCRINOLOGY 85(2):19-20, 1980.

Single dose extra-amniotic prostaglandin gel for midtrimester termination of pregnancy, by M. A. Quinn, et al. AUSTRALIAN AND NEW ZEALAND JOURNAL OF OBSTETRICS AND GYNAECOLOGY 20(2):77-79, May, 1980.

Synergism between testosterone and a superactive gonadotropin-releasing hormone analog in suppresssing gonadotropin secretion, by D. Heber, et al. CLINICAL RESEARCH 28(1):24A, 1980.

Termination of early gestation with a single vaginal suppository of (15S)-15-methyl-prostaglandin F2alpha methyl ester, by S. Roy, et al. CONTRACEPTION 22(2):137-152, August, 1980.

Termination of early pregnancy in ewes by use of a prostaglandin analogue and subsequent fertility, by R. N. Tyrrell, et al. AUSTRALIAN VETERINARY JOURNAL 57(2):76-78, February, 1981.

The use of 16-16 dimethyl trans delta 2 PGE1 methyl ester (ONO 802) vaginal suppositories for the termination of early pregnancy. A comparative study, by S. K. Smith, et al. BRITISH JOURNAL OF OBSTETRICS AND GYNAECOLOGY 87(8):712-717, August, 1980.

Vascular thrombosis in synthetic estrogen-progestogen users: an immune mechanism, by V. Beaumont, et al. NOUVELLE PRESSE MEDICALE 10(7):503-507, February 21, 1981.

Abortion: an epidemiologic study at Ramathibody Hospital, Bangkok, by K. Chaturachinda, et al. STUDIES IN FAMILY PLANNING 12:257-261, June-July, 1981.

Hospital requirement for abortions in second trimester is constitutional. THE CRIMINAL LAW REPORTER: COURT DECISIONS AND PROCEEDINGS 29(12):2248-2249, June 17, 1981.

Hospital support of legal abortion can overcome MD's negative attitudes. FAMILY PLANNING PERSPECTIVES 12:264-265, September-October, 1980.

Hospitals offer help in coping with stress—empathy classes. HOSPITALS 55(3):35-36, February 1, 1981.

Humanistic education for the EMT, by T. T. Luka. EMT JOURNAL 4(3):45-46, September, 1980.

Legal abortion. Preliminary evaluations at the S. Barbara di Rogliano Hospital, by C. Giannice, et al. MINERVA GINECOLOGIA 33(5):479-487, May, 1981.

Marymount Hospital, Garfield Heights, Ohio. Worry clinic teaches effective coping methods. HOSPITAL PROGRESS 62(7):12+, July, 1981.

Medical-behavioral 'explosion' affects hospital operation, policy, by C. V. Keeran, Jr., et al. HOSPITALS 55(9):56-59, May 1, 1981.

A needs assessment of perceived life quality and life stressors among medical hospital employees, by D. L. Cresswell, e et al. JOURNAL OF COMMUNITY PSYCHOLOGY 9 (2):153-161, April, 1981.

Patient education—health promotion in Michigan's hospitals. Part I. MICHIGAN HOSPITALS 17(1):20-30, January, 1981.

ABORTION AND HOSPITALS

Up to 16 weeks of gestation, abortions performed as safely
in nonhospital facilities as in hospitals. FAMILY PLAN-
NING PERSPECTIVES 13:181-182, July-August, 1981.

Voluntary interruption of pregnancy in an area hospital on
the outskirts of Turin, by M. Tanferna, et al. MINERVA
MEDICA 72(16):1021-1026, April 21, 1981.

ABORTION AND MALES
Abortion: are men there when women need them most? by
C. L. Mithers. MADEMOISELLE 87:230-231+, April,
1981.

Of marsupials and men: a thought experiment on abortion,
by J. Morreall. DIALOGOS 16:7-18, April, 1981.

ABORTION AND THE MENTALLY RETARDED
Legal crusade of the eternal children [mentally handicapped
in Canada], by P. Jahn. MACLEANS 94:45-46, November 30, 1981.

ABORTION AND THE MILITARY
Barnstorming on feminist Air Force One [organizing Project
13 to override an antiabortion amendment], by G.
Steinem. MS MAGAZINE 10:79-80+, December, 1981.

The reality of abortion, by L. D. Kozaryn. SOLDIERS 36:
20-25, March, 1981.

ABORTION AND NURSES
The design of a stress management program for Stanford in-
tensive care nurses, by J. T. Bailey, et al. JOURNAL OF
NURSING EDUCATION 19(6):26-29, June, 1980.

Is it right? 12,500 nurses speak out. How do your colleagues
view abortion, sterilization, and birth control? by R.
Sandroff. RN 43:24-30, October, 1980.

Law and the nurse. 5. From all points of view, by J. Finch.

259

ABORTION AND NURSES

NURSING MIRROR 153(1):29-30, July 1, 1981.

Legal semantics. Nurses and non-surgical abortions, by K.
Rae. NURSING TIMES 77(9):351, February 26, 1981.

Men and the abortion experience: an exploration study on
their self-reported educational interests, by K. L. Potter,
PhD. DAI 41(8), 1981.

Nurses and the legality of abortion, by J. Finch. NURSING
FOCUS 2:159-161, January, 1981.

Nurses and the medical termination of pregnancy [letter].
BRITISH MEDICAL JOURNAL 281(6254):1564, December 6, 1980.

A nursing adventure: through a very small window, by J.
Kulig. RNABC NEWS 13(4):25, May-June, 1981.

Only five minutes! Nurse-patient communications, by J. D.
Hines. AMERICAN JOURNAL OF MATERNAL CHILD
NURSING 5(4):271-274, July-August, 1980.

Participation of nurses in abortions [letter], by P. L. Neustatter. LANCET 2(8205):1199-1200, November 29, 1980.

'Pay-offs' and 'trade-offs': reflections of a nursing administrator and a nursing educator on a collaborative study in the
practice of nursing, by D. Walker, et al. JOURNAL OF
NURSING EDUCATION 19(6):54-57, June, 1980.

Peer-group orientation, sexual behavior, and attitudes of college students toward abortion, by R. S. Tanas. DAI 41
(9-10), 1981.

Prostaglandin abortions: nurses' action legitimate. BRITISH
MEDICAL JOURNAL 282(6270):1164-1165, April 4,
1981.

A question of balance, by A. Martin. NURSING MIRROR

ABORTION AND NURSES

151(12):9, September 18, 1980.

Where angels fear, by K. Ashton. NURSING TIMES 77(4):
143, January 22, 1981.

ABORTION AND PARENTAL CONSENT
Abortion—parental notification. THE CRIMINAL LAW RE-
PORTER: SUPREME COURT PROCEEDINGS 28(4):
4049-4050, October 22, 1980.

Responsible parenthood and social justice [intervention,
Synod of Bishops, 1980], by P. Iteka. AFER 23:65-66,
February-April, 1981.

ABORTION AND PHYSICIANS
Abortion: Dr. Koop and Mr. Hyde. ECONOMIST 278:25+,
March 28, 1981.

The abortion problem from the ophthalmologist's point of
view, by L. Mewe. KLINISCHE MONATSBLAETTER
FUR AUGENHEILKUNDE 178(3):219-223, March,
1981.

As the abortion furor flares again in Washington, two doctors
lead an emotional debate [views of J. Willke and G.
Ryan], by G. Breu. PEOPLE 16:47-48+, September 21,
1981.

Attitudes of medical practitioners towards abortion: a
Queensland study, by M. C. Sheehan, et al. AUSTRALI-
AN FAMILY PHYSICIAN 9(8):565-570, August, 1980.

Barriers to acceptance of genetic counseling among primary
care physicians, by R. Weitz. SOCIAL BIOLOGY 26:189-
197, Fall, 1979.

Consultant gynaecologists and attitudes towards abortion, by
A. Chamberlain. JOURNAL OF BIOSOCIAL SCIENCE
12(4):407-415, October, 1980.

Criminal liability of physicians: an encroachment on the abortion right? AMERICAN CRIMINAL LAW REVIEW 18:591-615, Spring, 1981.

Doctor ordered to disclose copies of public aid patients' ID cards. THE CRIMINAL LAW REPORTER: COURT DECISIONS AND PROCEEDINGS 29(7):2140-2141, May 13, 1981.

Doctor's dilemma over abortion, by A. Veitch. GUARDIAN p8, July 13, 1981.

The new gene doctors, by M. Clark, et al. NEWSWEEK 97 (20):120+, May 18, 1981.

Office abortion: a humane approach to a traumatic experience, by P. S. Green. JOURNAL OF THE MEDICAL SOCIETY OF NEW JERSEY 77(12):809-811, November, 1980.

On medical ethics [editorial], by E. F. Payne, Jr. JOURNAL OF THE MEDICAL ASSOCIATION OF GEORGIA 69 (9):780-781, September, 1980.

Physician knowledge and attitudes toward an emergency medical services system, by T. K. Yolles, et al. ANNALS OF EMERGENCY MEDICINE 10(1):2-10, January, 1981.

Unplanned pregnancy—liability of the gynecologist, by G. H. Schlund. GEBURTSHILFE UND FRAUENHEILKUNDE 40(10):893-895, October, 1980.

Unwanted pregnancy—the role of the general practitioner, by S. Furman. SOUTH AFRICAN MEDICAL JOURNAL 58(23):941-942, December 6, 1980.

ABORTION AND POLITICS
"Abhorrent and offensive": from the witness chair, Sandra

O'Connor said that about abortion [news; photos], by B. Spring. CHRISTIANITY TODAY 25:52-53, October 23, 1981.

The abortion activists . . . the National Abortion Rights Action League and the National Right to Life Committee, by D. Granberg. FAMILY PLANNING PERSPECTIVES 13:157-163, July-August, 1981.

Abortion and American population politics, by J. M. Ostheimer. THE POLICY STUDIES JOURNAL 6(2): 216-223, Winter, 1977.

Abortion and coalition politics: whose survival? [Failure of Mobilization for Survival, anti-nuclear and pro-disarmament coalition, to take a stand on abortion, by T. Dejanikus. OFF OUR BACKS 11:2+, April, 1981.

Abortion and the elections: a statement, by H. S. Medeiros. CATHOLIC MIND 79:8-9, January, 1981.

Abortion bill praised, hit by Catholics. NATIONAL CATHOLIC REPORTER 18:18, November 13, 1981.

Abortion: Dr. Koop and Mr. Hyde. ECONOMIST 278:25+, March 28, 1981.

Abortion—due process. THE FAMILY LAW REPORTER: COURT OPINIONS 6(49):2939, October 21, 1980.

Abortion foe tags move an ouster. NATIONAL CATHOLIC REPORTER 17:3, January 9, 1981.

Abortion-funding issue: a study in mixed constitutional cues, by T. E. Yarbrough. NORTH CAROLINA LAW REVIEW 59:611-627, March, 1981.

Abortion 1980' the debate continues, by J. M. Healey. CONNECTICUT MEDICINE 44(9):605, September, 1980.

Abortion policy: ideology, political cleavage and the policy process, by H. A. Palley. THE POLICY STUDIES JOURNAL 7(2):224-233, Winter, 1978.

Abortion politics and family life: an intepretation, by P. T. Lynch, PhD. DAI 41(3-4), 1981.

Abortion politics: Italian-style, by M. Bosworth. REFRAC-TORY GIRL (22):25-26, May, 1981.

Abortion prompts emotional lobbying, by N. Cohodas. CON-GRESSIONAL QUARTERLY WEEKLY REPORT 39: 384-387, February 28, 1981.

Abortion—strict limitations on federal Medicaid reimbursements for abortions imposed by the Hyde amendment held permissible. Participating states held not obligated to fund medically necessary abortions not federally funded. JOURNAL OF FAMILY LAW 19:335-341, March, 1981.

Abortion threatens political parties, by R. Gustaitus. OKLA-HOMA OBSERVER 13:15, January 25, 1981.

Anti-abortion Congress members blast hit list, by C. P. Winner. NATIONAL CATHOLIC REPORTER 17:6+, June 19, 1981.

Anti-abortion groups spar over amendment tactics. CHRIS-TIANITY TODAY 25:84, February 6, 1981.

Anti-abortionists: the right takes aim. ECONOMIST 277: 27+, October 4, 1980.

As the abortion furor flares again in Washington, two doctors lead an emotional debate [views of J. Willke and G. Ryan], by G. Breu. PEOPLE 16:47-48+, September 21, 1981.

Bill Baird's holy war [member of pro-choice movement], by A. Merton. ESQUIRE 95:25-31, February, 1981.

Brigade zaps Senate hearings: protest leads to arrest, 1; Activist set cornerstone for abortion rights [interview with Julie Huff, who in 1971 as Mary Doe was plaintiff in abortion case in Washington, D. C.], by E. Soldinger. NEW DIRECTIONS FOR WOMEN 10:4+, July-August, 1981.

Changing tactics in the war on abortion [Helms-Hyde bill redefining the beginning of life], by M. Kramer. NEW YORK 14:28+, April 27, 1981.

Conservatives and Liberals on prolife issues, by C. DeCelles. AMERICA 144:365-368, May 2, 1981.

Dire warnings by pro-abortionists found in error. OUR SUNDAY VISITOR 70:7, August 23, 1981.

Enigma of when personhood begins generates lively legislative fight, by E. E. Plowman. CHRISTIANITY TODAY 25:30, May 29, 1981.

Feminists disrupt anti-abortion hearings in U.S. Senate, by T. Dejanibus, et al. OFF OUR BACKS 11:2-3+, June, 1981.

For the pro-life movement, it's a matter of time, by R. McMunn. OUR SUNDAY VISITOR 69:5, April 19, 1981.

The great abortion battle of 1981, by R. Kramer. VILLAGE VOICE 26:1, March 11, 1981.

Group prods pro-life, peace work; interview by T. C. Fox, by J. Loesch. NATIONAL CATHOLIC REPORTER 18:2, December 4, 1981.

In defense of Humanae Vitae, by J. F. O'Connor. HOMILETIC AND PASTORAL REVIEW 82:51-54, October,

1981.

Juli Loesch fights abortion and the nuclear arms race, by L. H. Pumphrey. OUR SUNDAY VISITOR 70:6, August 2, 1981.

Limits of judicial intervention in abortion politics, by R. Tatalovich, et al. CHRISTIAN CENTURY 99:16-20, January 6-13, 1982.

Negativism, equivocation, and wobbly assent: public 'support' for the prochoice platform on abortion, by J. Blake, et al. DEMOGRAPHY 18(3):309-320, August, 1981.

Political developments in the abortion area, by J. L. Robinson. CATHOLIC LAWYER 25:319-326, Autumn, 1980.

Political showdown over abortion coming, but when? by R. B. Shaw. OUR SUNDAY VISITOR 69:6, April 26, 1981.

Presidential address at the 1980 NFCPG meeting, by E. F. Diamond. LINACRE 48:11-12, February, 1981.

Prolife leaders hurdle O'Connor nomination: decide to back Reagan for the long race [news], by T. Minnery. CHRISTIANITY TODAY 25:55+, October 2, 1981.

Reagan may soon have to back claimed prolife stance, by R. B. Shaw. OUR SUNDAY VISITOR 70:8, August 16, 1981.

'Government failed by giving everybody everything', by W. Weddon. MICHIGAN MEDICINE 80(11):172, April, 1981.

Secretary Schweiker and that Schwenkfelder power, by W. F. Willoughby. OUR SUNDAY VISITOR 69:5, March 1, 1981.

Should abortions be outlawed? Yes: interview with Representative Henry J. Hyde, Republican of Illinois; No: interview with Karen Mulhauser, executive director, National Abortion Rights Action League. US NEWS AND WORLD REPORT 90:31-32, May 4, 1981.

Theology and politics [Helms-Hyde bill] , by E. Doerr. HUMANIST 41:47-48, May-June, 1981.

The trauma of abortion politics, by R. Tatalovich, et al. COMMONWEAL 108:644-649, November 20, 1981.

Up against the 97th Congress: round one, by G. Christgau. VILLAGE VOICE 26(2):22, February 11, 1981.

Why Pro-Life; symposium: Why I am pro-life, by H. Gracida. Why I am pro-life: a feminist approach, by A. O'Donnell. The 12 most common questions about abortion. Why I am pro-life: a social justice perspective, by T. Hesburgh. Why I am pro-life: a doctor's perspective; interview of J. Willke, by C. Anthony. Why I am pro-life: because there are alternatives, by R. Hanley. OUR SUNDAY VISITOR 69:3-9+, January 18, 1981.

Watch on the right: backstage with the antiabortion forces, by L. C. Wohl. MS MAGAZINE 9:48+, February, 1981.

ABORTION AND RELIGION
Abortion laws, religious beliefs and the First Amendment, by S. L. Skahn. VALPARAISO UNIVERSITY LAW REVIEW 14:487-526, Spring, 1980.

Abortion 1, Pope 0 [John Paul II's support of unsuccessful referendum to tighten abortion laws] , by T. Sheehan. COMMONWEAL 108:357-359, June 19, 1981.

Abortion: religious differences and public policy, by H. Siegman. CONGRESSIONAL MONTHLY 48:3-4, June, 1981.

Abortion rights group to sue three dioceses. NATIONAL
CATHOLIC REPORTER 16:3+, October 3, 1980.

Abortion rights group sues nation's Catholic bishops. OUR
SUNDAY VISITOR 69:7, March 1, 1981.

Abortion: toward developing a policy in a Catholic social
service agency, by D. C. Dendinger, et al. SOCIAL
THOUGHT 6:33-46, Fall, 1980.

Activist pro-life priest ousted: board defends actions, by F.
Franzonia. OUR SUNDAY VISITOR 69:8, December
28, 1980.

After a decade, Respect Life program is still growing, by J.
Castelli. OUR SUNDAY VISITOR 70:6, October 4, 1981.

Attitudes of Catholic and Protestant clergy on euthanasia and
abortion, by M. H. Nagi, et al. PASTORAL PSYCHOLO-
GY 29:178-190, Spring, 1981.

Bill Baird abortion survey misleading, anti-Catholic. OUR
SUNDAY VISITOR 69:7, January 25, 1981.

Bishops' aide: Congress lacks human life bill authority. OUR
SUNDAY VISITOR 69:7, April 26, 1981.

The bishops and the abortion amendment. AMERICA 145:
312-313, November 21, 1981.

Canadian Catholics: at odds on abortion, by T. Sinclair-
Faulkner. CHRISTIAN CENTURY 98:870-871, September 9, 1981.

Cardinal's view on abortion fails to defeat liberals, by J. W.
Michaels. NATIONAL CATHOLIC REPORTER 16:1,
September 26, 1980.

Catholic liberals and abortion, by M. Meehan. COMMON-

WEAL 108:650-654, November 20, 1981.

Challenge of pluralism [Humanae vitae], by C. E. Curran.
COMMONWEAL 108:45-46, January 30, 1981.

Crusader under attack [effect of Popy John Paul II's proclamations on referendum to tighten abortion laws]. TIME
117:54, May 18, 1981.

Free choice [Catholics for a Free Choice]. HUMANIST 41:
57-58, January-February, 1981.

Humanae Vitae and the Catholic priest, by G. Stafford.
HOMILETIC AND PASTORAL REVIEW 81:30-32+,
December, 1980.

Imposing mercy; abortion, the Church, and the unwanted, by
J. Garvey. COMMONWEAL 108:485-486, September 11,
1981.

Jean Paul II et l'avortement, by R. Bourgault. RELATIONS
40:295-296, November, 1980.

Papel de la conciencia en la calificación de los actos morales,
by S. J. Zalba. GREGORIANUM 62(1):135-157, 1981.

Pope joins Italy abortion debate wholeheartedly, by P.
Hebblethwaite. NATIONAL CATHOLIC REPORTER
17:1+, May 15, 1981.

Pope strongly refutes claim abortion is private matter. OUR
SUNDAY VISITOR 69:7, April 19, 1981.

Priest's pro-choice abortion ad draws strong reaction, by P.
Kern. OUR SUNDAY VISITOR 69:7, February 8, 1981.

Pro-abortion priest may be sued by Albany bishop, by L. H.
Pumphrey. OUR SUNDAY VISITOR 69:6, January 25,
1981.

Pro-abortionist ad campaigns escalating war on life, by W. Odel. OUR SUNDAY VISITOR 70:8, July 5, 1981.

Pro-choice: United Presbyterians look at abortion in the '80s, by E. H. Verdesi. CHURCH AND SOCIETY 71:3-103, March-April, 1981.

Pro-life education: a practical parish plan, by J. W. Anderson. LIGUORIAN 69:34-35, July, 1981.

Religion and abortion [Harris vs. McRae and the constitutionality of the Hyde Amendment], by J. R. Nelson. CENTER MAGAZINE 14:51-55, July-August, 1981.

Religiosity and abortion attitudes among couples in the early stage of the family formation process, by B. Granger, PhD. DAI 41(7-8), 1981.

Religious involvement, asceticism and abortion among low income black women, by J. M. Robbins. SOCIOLOGICAL ANALYSIS 41:365-374, Winter, 1980.

The right to do wrong: Reform Judaism and abortion, by R. A. Block. JOURNAL OF REFORM JUDAISM 28:3-15, September, 1981.

Secular infallibility, by F. Zepezauer. NATIONAL REVIEW 33:1484-1485, December 11, 1981.

That all may have life. NATIONAL CATHOLIC REPORTER 16:12, October 17, 1980.

Theology and politics [Helms-Hyde bill], by E. Doerr. HUMANIST 41:47-48, May-June, 1981.

U.S. theologians' hopes dashed by synod results, by J. W. Michaels. NATIONAL CATHOLIC REPORTER November 7, 1980.

ABORTION AND RELIGION

Vatican: aborting the deformed is pseudo-humanism. OUR
SUNDAY VISITOR 69:7, March 29, 1981.

ABORTION AND YOUTH
Abortions for minors after Bellotti II (Bellotti v. Baird, 99
S Ct 3035); an analysis of state law and a proposal. ST.
MARY LAW JOURNAL 11:946-997, 1980.

Analysis of attitudes of Oklahomans of voting age toward sex
education, teen contraception and abortion, by N. L.
Turner. DAI 42(5), 1981.

Can parents of a dughter under legal age oppose pregnancy
interruption? by G. H. Schlund. GEBURTSHILFE UND
FRAUENHEILKUNDE 40(9):834-835, September, 1980.

Notifying the parents. AMERICA 144:289-290, April 11,
1981.

Oral contraceptive use and early abortion as risk factors for
breast cancer in young women, by M. D. Pike, et al.
BRITISH JOURNAL OF CANCER 43(1):72-76, January,
1981.

Pregnancy risk-taking among young unmarried women: an
analysis of its determinants and prevention, by S. B. Kar,
et al. PATIENT COUNSELLING AND HEALTH EDU-
CATION 1:151-163, Summer-Fall, 1979.

Pregnant low-income teenagers: a social structural model of
the determinants of abortion-seeking behavior, by R.
Dworkin. YOUGH AND SOCIETY 11(3):295-309,
March, 1980.

The risks of teenage abortion, by W. Cates, et al. AMERICAN
JOURNAL OF EPIDEMIOLOGY 112*3):434, 1980.

Teen-agers and abortion. ORIGINS 10:657+, April 2, 1981.

ABORTION AND YOUTH

Telling parents: clinic policies and adolescents' use of family
planning and abortion services, by A. Torres, et al.
FAMILY PLANNING PERSPECTIVES 12(6):284-292,
November-December, 1980.

Utilizing male partners of adolescent abortion patients as
change agents: results of an experimental intervention, by
K. D. Brosseau. DAI 42(1), 1981.

ABORTION CLINICS
Use of preventive measures and level of information among
abortion seekers at Haukeland Hospital, Gynecologic
Clinic, by R. Ekanger. TIDSSKRIFT FOR DEN
NORSKE LAEGEFORENING 101(11):615-618, April
20, 1981.

We walk the line: the struggle of preterm. RADICAL AMER-
ICAN 13(2):8-24, 1979.

Zoning control of abortion clinics, by J. R. Novak. CLEVE-
LAND STATE LAW REVIEW 28(3):507-527, 1979.

ABORTION COUNSELING
The abortion decision—perspective: counseling, by C. Dornblaser. MINNESOTA MEDICINE 64(1):45-47, January,
1981.

Counselling needs of women seeking abortions, by M. J.
Hare, et al. JOURNAL OF BIOSOCIAL SCIENCE 13:
269-274, July, 1981.

BIRTH CONTROL
The availability of birth control: Victoria 1971-1975, by K.
Betts. AUSTRALIAN JOURNAL OF SOCIAL ISSUES
15(1):17-29, February, 1980.

Beyond proof and disproof, by J. Garvey. COMMONWEAL
108:360-361, June 19, 1981.

BIRTH CONTROL

Beyond the stereotypes, by J. R. Kelly. COMMONWEAL
108:654-656+, November 20, 1981.

Birth control, by J. Selby. JOURNAL OF NURSING 1(16):
701-703, August, 1980.

Factors influencing birth control habits in Victoria, by T.
Selwood, et al. AUSTRALIAN FAMILY PHYSICIAN 10
(2):96-101, February, 1981.

Margaret Sanger: birth control's successful revolutionary, by
D. Wardell. AMERICAN JOURNAL OF PUBLIC
HEALTH 70:736-742, July, 1980; Discussion 71:91,
January, 1981.

Marie Stopes; botany and birth control, by J. Timson. NEW
SCIENTIST 88:177, October 16, 1980.

Mechanism of action of an orally active PGE1-analogue in
pregnant guinea-pigs, by W. Elger, et al. PROSTAGLAN-
DINS 21(2):259-266, February, 1981.

The morality of birth control: unfinished business? by R. E.
Burns. US CATHOLIC 46:2-3, January, 1981.

Observations on the antigenicity and clinical effects of a
candidate antipregnancy vaccine: beta-subunit of human
chorionic gonadotropin linked to tetanus toxoid, by H.
Nash, et al. FERTILITY AND STERILITY 34(4):328-
335, October, 1980.

Persistent abnormalities of fibrinolytic activity and platelet
function in patients with reversible oestrogen-associated
hypertension, by A. A. Al-Khader, et al. BRITISH
JOURNAL OF OBSTETRICS AND GYNAECOLOGY
87(8):672-677, August, 1980.

Perspectives on birth control, by M. Vicars. ENVIRONMENT
NEWS 3(5):18, December 1980-January 1981.

The problem of public pretense, by R. Stith. INDIAN PHILO-
SOPHICAL QUARTERLY 3:13-30, 1980.

Recent developments in the health care area, by T. D. Harper,
et al. JOURNAL OF THE MEDICAL ASSOCIATION OF
GEORGIA 69(9):785-787, September, 1980.

Reproductive health curbs ahead: birth control imperiled, by
J. Wells-Schooley. NEW DIRECTIONS FOR WOMEN 10:
1+, March-April, 1981.

Retrospective self-insight on factors considered in product
evaluation, by B. Weitz, et al. JOURNAL OF CON-
SUMER RESEARCH 6:280-294, December, 1979.

Vas micro-anastomosis. Fundamentals and modifications,
by M. R. Sutton. JOURNAL OF UROLOGY 126(2):185-
186, August, 1981.

Why women take a chance with birth control, by F. Maynard.
WOMAN'S DAY p41-44, November 25, 1980.

Whatever happened to the human race? could come to television in your area, by M. E. Lorentzen. CHRISTIANITY
TODAY 25:26-27, January 23, 1981.

CANADA
Sexual experience, birth control usage, and sex education
of unmarried Canadian university students: changes
between 1968 and 1978, by F. M. Barrett. AR-
CHIVES OF SEXUAL BEHAVIOR 9:367-390, October, 1980.

CHINA
Birth control in China: local data and their reliability, by
L. Bianco. CHINA QUARTERLY 85:119-137, March,
1981.

Population and birth control in China, by J. A. Loraine.

BIRTH CONTROL

CHINA
　　　CONTEMPORARY REVIEW 239:126-130, September, 1981.

　　　Signing the pledge, by J. Kettle. EXECUTIVE 23:16, February, 1981.

　　　Wan, xi, shao [later, longer, fewer] : how China meets its population problem [based on address] , by H. Y. Tien. INTERNATIONAL FAMILY PLANNING PERSPECTIVES 6:65-73, June, 1980.

CUBA
　　　Birth planning in Cuba: a basic human right, by J. M. Swanson. INTERNATIONAL JOURNAL OF NURSING STUDIES 18(2):81-88, 1981.

EGYPT
　　　The circus come to town, by A. Soueif. OBSERVER p38, June 28, 1981.

GREAT BRITAIN
　　　The coil and the law, by C. Brewer. GUARDIAN p11, February 18, 1981.

　　　The ideology and politics of birth control in inter-war England, by J. Lewis. WOMEN'S STUDIES INTERNATIONAL QUARTERLY 2(1):33-48, 1979.

　　　Some characteristics of intentionally childless wives in Britain, by F. Baum, et al. JOURNAL OF BIOSOCIAL SCIENCE 12(3):287-299, July, 1980.

GUATEMALA
　　　Birth control—Guatemala [letters] . NATIONAL CATHOLIC REPORTER 17:11, November 14, 1980.

INDIA
　　　Death loses its race with birth. ECONOMIST 278:69,

BIRTH CONTROL

INDIA
Death loses its race with birth. ECONOMIST 278:69, March 28, 1981.

Etiology of pelvic infections treated by the gynecologic service of the Kasturba Hospital, Delhi, India, by M. Kochar. AMERICAN JOURNAL OF OBSTETRICS AND GYNECOLOGY 138(7 Part 2):872-874, 1980.

IRELAND
The coil and the law, by C. Brewer. GUARDIAN p11, February 18, 1981.

Dublin students defy birth control curbs, by J. Walshe. TIMES HIGHER EDUCATION SUPPLEMENT 419: 6, November 14, 1980.

Ireland's bishops decide, by M. Holland. NEW STATES-MAN 101:6-8, April 3, 1981.

JAPAN
Victims of the medical lobby, by R. Whymant. GUARDI-AN p12, March 24, 1981.

MEXICO
Developing print materials in Mexico for people who do not read, by A. Leonard. EDUCATIONAL BROAD-CASTING INTERNATIONAL 13(4):168-173, December, 1980.

THAILAND
Facts of life in Thailand, by M. Ho. TECHNOLOGY RE-VIEW 83:60-61, November-December, 1980.

UNITED STATES
Birth control and the fertility of the U.S. black population, 1880-1980, by J. A. McFalls, et al. JOURNAL OF FAMILY HISTORY 6:104-106, Spring, 1981.

BIRTH CONTROL: ADVERTISING

Billboards censored. MARKETING 86:1, March 2, 1981.

Manipulating the choice on CBS, by F. J. Uddo. AMERICA 144:230-232, March 21, 1981.

Marketing population control . . . Population Services International, by P. Drummond. HEALTH AND SOCIAL SERVICE JOURNAL 91:672, June 5, 1981.

Marketing strategies in health education, by G. Miaoulis, et al. JOURNAL OF HEALTH CARE MARKETING 1(1): 35-44, Winter, 1980-1981.

BIRTH CONTROL: ATTITUDES
Anti-abortion, anti-birth control, anti-woman, by S. Dawson. OFF OUR BACKS 11:17, March, 1981.

Barriers to birth control, by M. Potts. NEW SCIENTIST 88 (1224):221, October 23, 1980.

Changing attitudes to birth control, by I. Allen. NEW SOCIETY p15-16, April 2, 1981.

Socialization for childbearing, by S. G. Philliber. JOURNAL OF SOCIAL ISSUES 36(1):30-44, 1980.

BIRTH CONTROL: COMPLICATIONS
Estrogen regimen of women with endometrial carcinoma. A retrospective case-control study at Radiumhemmet, by A. Obrink, et al. ACTA OBSTETRICIA ET GYNECOLOGICA SCANDINAVICA 60(2):191-197, 1981.

Incidence, prevalence and trends of acute pelvic inflammatory disease and its consequences in industrialized countries, by L. Westrom. AMERICAN JOURNAL OF OBSTETRICS AND GYNECOLOGY 138(7 Part 2):880-892, 1980.

Injury to retroperitoneal vessels; a serious complication of

gynaecological laparoscopy, by M. Rust, et al. ANES-
THESIE—INTENSIVTHERAPIE—NOTFALLMEDEZIN
15(4):356-359, August, 1980.

Interaction of ethinyloestradio with ascorbic acid in man, by
D. J. Back, et al. BRITISH MEDICAL JOURNAL 282
(6275):1516, May 9, 1981.

Intrauterine infection with mumps virus, by A. G. Garcia, et
al. OBSTETRICS AND GYNECOLOGY 56(6):756-759,
December, 1980.

Mass screening for neural tube defects, by G. B. Kolata.
HASTINGS CENTER REPORT 10:8-10, December,
1980.

Plasma levels of levonorgestrel in women during longterm use
of Norplants, by H. B. Croxatto, et al. CONTRACEP-
TION 22(6):583-596, December, 1980.

Reducing stress in patients having cardiac catheterization, by
C. Finesilver. AMERICAN JOURNAL OF NURSING 80
(10):1805-1807, October, 1980.

Richly vascularized liver tumors, by H. M. Zonderland, et al.
NEDERLANDS TIJDSCHRIFT VOOR GENEESKUNDE
124(33):1372-1376, August 16, 1980.

BIRTH CONTROL: EDUCATION
The effects of school sex education programs: a review of
the literature, by D. Kirby. JOURNAL OF SCHOOL
HEALTH 50(10):559-563, December, 1980.

The experts rate important features and outcomes of sex
education programs, by D. Kirby. JOURNAL OF
SCHOOL HEALTH 50(9):497-502, November, 1980.

Out of the lockerroom and into the classroom: innovative
approaches to the use of media and strategies in sex edu-

cation for the deaf, by M. Kressler. AMERICAN AN-
NALS OF THE DEAF 125(6):822-825, September,
1980.

Sexual experience and responses to a birth control film, by E.
Herold. JOURNAL OF SCHOOL HEALTH 50(2):66-
68, February, 1980.

BIRTH CONTROL: LAWS AND LEGISLATION
Constitutional rights—birth control. THE FAMILY LAW
REPORTER: COURT OPINIONS 7(1):2010, Novem-
ber 4, 1980.

BIRTH CONTROL: METHODS
Another barrier to pregnancy. TIME 117:57, January 26,
1981.

BIRTH CONTROL: PSYCHOLOGY OF
Birth control effects on ethanol pharmacokinetics, acetaldehyde, and cardiovascular measures in Caucasian females,
by P. S. Keg, et al. PSYCHOPHYSIOLOGY 17(3):294,
1980.

Diet supplements lead to more mouths to feed [diet, breast
feeding, and natural birth control]. NEW SCIENTIST
86:193, April 24, 1980.

Health instructions concerning sexual activities and birth
control, by H. Ogino, et al. JOSANPU ZASSHI 34(11):
724-737, November, 1980.

Microscoop method of doing 2-layer vas anastomosis, by M.
R. Sutton. JOURNAL OF UROLOGY 124(5):620-621,
November, 1980.

Microsurgical anastomosis of vas deferens: technical aspects,
by M. Srougi, et al. AMB; REVISTA DA ASSOCIACAO
MEDICA BRASILEIRA 27(1):8-11, January, 1981.

More birth control blues [study by H. Jick linking use of spermicidal contraceptives to birth defects and miscarriages] , by P. De Vries. MACLEANS 94:47-48, May 11, 1981.

Most permanent birth control, by P. Span. GLAMOUR 79: 236-237+, March, 1981.

The natural way, by L. O'Conner. SIGN 61:30-33, September, 1981.

La pilule, c'est pour les males! by L. Vandelac. L'ACTUALITÉ 6:22 aout, 1981.

Preparation of school-age children for surgery: a program in preventive pediatrics—Philippines, by P. D. Williams. INTERNATIONAL JOURNAL OF NURSING STUDIES 17(2):107-109, 1980.

Pre-pregnancy insertion of Mayer's pessary as therapy for infertility, by F. Drnek. CESKOSLOVENSKA GYNEKOLOGIE 46(6):465-466, July, 1981.

Steroid releasing vaginal rings, by I. D. Nuttal, et al. ACTA EUROPAEA FERTILITATIS 11(3):225-230, September, 1980.

This is not a last resort treatment but a valid method of birth control, by P. Toynbee. GUARDIAN p8, March 9, 1981.

Whatever happened to new methods of birth control? ECONOMIST 279:25-27, May 30, 1981.

BIRTH CONTROL: RESEARCH
Birth control in the year 2001, by C. Djerassi. BULLETIN OF THE ATOMIC SCIENTISTS 37(2):24, March, 1981.

Birth control: the new findings, by S. Dillon. MCCALLS 108:57-58, April, 1981.

Birth control: the safety story now, by M. L. Schildkraut. GOOD HOUSEKEEPING 193:215-216, August, 1981.

Changes in the N1H Guidelines for Recombinant DNA Research (Appendix 3: September 1979-April 1980), by W. Szybalski. GENE 10(4):375-377, September, 1980.

DNA guidelines: bowing out [news], by D. Dickson. NATURE 288(5791):529-530, December 11, 1980.

DNA guidelines for further attenuation [news], by D. Dickson. NATURE 290(5804):281, March 26, 1981.

DNA guidelines. More relaxation [news], by D. Dickson. NATURE 287(5781):380-381, October 2, 1980.

DNA recombination forces resignation [news], by D. Dickson. NATURE 287(5779):179-180, September 18, 1980.

Endocrinology of sexual function, by J. Bancroft. CLINICAL OBSTETRICS AND GYNAECOLOGY 7(2):253-282, 1980.

Estrogen and lipid regulation in normal rats, by J. N. Wilson, et al. CLINICAL RESEARCH 28(1):27A, 1980.

Oestrus control and the incidence of mammary nodules in bitches, a clinical study with two progestogens, by J. L. van Os, et al. TIJDSCHRIFT VOOR DIERGENEES-KUNDE 106(2 Suppl 3):46-56, January 15, 1981.

Ovum pick-up following fimbriectomy and infundibular salpingostomy in rabbits, by S. A. Halbert, et al. JOURNAL OF REPRODUCTIVE MEDICINE 26(6):299-304, June, 1981.

Reciprocal translocation with special reference to reproductive failure, by I. Subrt. HUMAN GENETICS 55(3):303-307, 1980.

BIRTH CONTROL: RESEARCH

Recombinant DNA experiments to remain under safety
guidelines [news], by D. Dickson. NATURE 282(5739):
545, December 6, 1979.

Recombinant DNA guidelines wear thin [news], by D. Dickson. NATURE 291(5810):3, May 7, 1981.

Recombinant DNA technology: the biochemical manipulation of genes, by R. H. Burdon. SCOTTISH MEDICAL
JOURNAL 26(1):4-5, January, 1981.

BIRTH CONTROL: STATISTICS
Birth control in China: local data and their reliability, by L.
Bianco. CHINA QUARTERLY 85:119-137, March,
1981.

Boost for birth control and fertility studies, by L. Cohen.
TIMES HIGHER EDUCATIONAL SUPPLEMENT 427:
5, January 9, 1981.

Health systems and population control. In International
Conference on the Unity of the Science [8th] November
22-25, 1979, Los Angeles, California. The responsibility
of the academic community in the search for absolute
values, by G. Samarawickrama. pp669-678.

BIRTH CONTROL: TECHNIQUES
An applicator for the Hulka fallopian tube clip, by P. Renou.
AMERICAN JOURNAL OF OBSTETRICS AND GYNE-
COLOGY 139(6):665-668, March 15, 1981.

Birth control—medical practices—torts—wrongful birth. THE
FAMILY LAW REPORTER: COURT OPINIONS 7(12):
2184, January 27, 1981.

Breast is best; for birth control. NEW SCIENTIST 88:416,
November 13, 1980.

Natural alternative [sympto-thermal]. TODAY p21, December 13, 1980.

Natural birth control, by A. Westmore. AUSTRALIAN
NURSES JOURNAL 10:51-52, November, 1980.

BIRTH CONTROL AND HORMONES
Distribution of lipoproteins triglyceride and lipoprotein
cholesterol in an adult population by age, sex, and
hormone use—the Pacific Northwest Bell Telephone
Company health survey, by P. W. Wahl, et al. ATHERO-
SCLEROSIS 39(1):111-124, April, 1981.

Manipulation of duration of action of a synthetic prostaglandin analogue (TPT) assessed in the pregnant beagle
bitch, by B. H. Vickery, et al. PROSTAGLANDINS AND
MEDICINE 5(2):93-100, August, 1980.

Plasma lipids and lipoprotein lipase activating property in
women on three different combinations of estrogens and
progestins, by S. G. Mendoza, et al. BIOCHEMICAL
MEDICINE 25(3):283-287, June, 1981.

The synthesis of A-nor-19-nordiethynyl steroids, by L. Y.
Zhu, et al. YAO HSUEH HSUEH PAO 16(3):211-217,
March, 1981.

BIRTH CONTROL AND MALES
Fathers and birth control, by D. Spangler. AMERICAN
BABY 43:20+, September, 1981.

BIRTH CONTROL AND NURSES
Changing the system to meet the needs of patient and nurse,
by V. L. Derby, et al. AMERICAN JOURNAL OF MA-
TERNAL CHILD NURSING 6:225-226+, July-August,
1981.

Is it right? 12,500 nurses speak out. How do your colleagues
view abortion, sterilization, and birth control? by R.
Sandroff. RN 43:24-30, October, 1980.

BIRTH CONTROL AND NURSES

Voluntary childlessness and the nurse's role, by T. Rosenthal. AMERICAN JOURNAL OF MATERNAL CHILD NURS-ING 5:398-402, November-December, 1980.

BIRTH CONTROL AND PHYSICIANS
Ask a doctor, by C. Carver. CHATELAINE 54:33, September, 1981.

Aussie doctor Evelyn Billings promotes a new birth control device—a woman's own body, by J. Dunn. PEOPLE 16: 83-84, October 12, 1981.

BIRTH CONTROL AND POLITICS
Concise report on the monitoring of population policies [prepared by the U.N. Secretariat for the World Population Plan of Action]. POPULATION BULLETIN (12):20-40, 1979.

An end to birth control controversy? by J. H. Wright. AMER-ICA 144:175-178, March 7, 1981.

BIRTH CONTROL AND RELIGION
Birth control ban [Pope John Paul II, December 15, 1981; news]. CHRISTIAN CENTURY 98:1361-1362, December 30, 1981.

Birth control controversy, continued [Catholic Church]. AMERICA 145:66-68, August 15-22, 1981.

Birth control, personalism, and the Pope, by R. Modras. CURRENTS IN THEOLOGY AND MISSION 8:283-290, October, 1981.

Desacralization of Venus [Catholic Church], by C. Derrick. AMERICA 145:106-109, September 12, 1981.

Ireland's bishops decide, by M. Holland. NEW STATES-MAN p6-8, April 3, 1981.

Comparison of minors' and adults' pregnancy decisions, by C. C. Lewis. AMERICAN JOURNAL OF ORTHOPSY-CHOLOGY 50:446-453, July, 1980.

Health needs of adolescent girls in the area of reproductive behavior, by M. Husar, et al. JUGOSLAVENSKA GINE-KOLOGIJAI OPSTETRICIJA 19(3-4):131-138, May-August, 1980.

Maternal employment and adolescent sexual behavior, by R. O. Hansson, et al. JOURNAL OF YOUTH AND ADO-LESCENCE 10:55-60, February, 1981.

Seventeen's answers to your questions about birth control [teenagers], by E. R. Dobell. SEVENTEEN 40:142-143, October, 1981.

Sexual experience, birth control usage, and sex education of unmarried Canadian university students: changes between 1968 and 1978, by F. M. Barrett. ARCHIVES OF SEX-UAL BEHAVIOR 9(5):367-390, October, 1980.

CONTRACEPTION AND CONTRACEPTIVES
Accidental pregnancy: why do some women play sexual roulette? by F. Maynard. CHATELAINE 57(37):61-64, March, 1981.

Biodegradable drug delivery systems based on aliphatic poly-esters: application to contraceptives and narcotic antago-nists, by C. G. Pitt, et al. NATIONAL INSTITUTE ON DRUG ABUSE RESEARCH MONOGRAPH SERIES 28: 232-253, 1981.

A comprehensive review of injectable contraception with special emphasis on depot medroxyprogesterone acetate, by I. S. Fraser, et al. MEDICAL JOURNAL OF AUS-TRALIA 1(1 Suppl):3-19, January 24, 1981.

Contraception, by C. Lane, et al. PRIMARY CARE 8(1):45-

53, March, 1981.

Contraception after the act. NURSES DRUG ALERT 5:23, March, 1981.

Contraception: burdens impossible, by J. P. Breen. NATIONAL CATHOLIC REPORTER 17:38, February 13, 1981.

Contraception in the eighties, by J. Klein. WORKING WOMEN 6:32+, February, 1981.

Contraception: a proposal for the Synod, by J. R. Quinn. CATHOLIC MIND 79:25-34, February, 1981.

Contraceptive availability. POPULATION REPORTS 9(3):M-176, May-June, 1981.

Contraceptive efficacy among married women aged 15-44 years, by B. Vaughan, et al. VITAL HEALTH STATISTICS 23(5):1-62, May, 1980.

Contraceptive use. POPULATION REPORTS 9(3):M-167, May-June, 1981.

Contraceptives. DRUG TOPICS 124:50, June, 1980.

—. DRUG TOPICS 125:82, July 3, 1981.

—: the latest news on how to choose, by S. Connelly. LADIES HOME JOURNAL 98:56+, March, 1981.

Influence of dietary fats and an oral contraceptive on plasma lipids, high density lipoproteins, gallstones, and atherosclerosis in african green monkeys, by R. W. St. Clair, et al. ATHEROSCLEROSIS 37(1):103-121, September, 1980.

Nasal spray [LHRH] contraceptive, by J. Labreche. CHATE-

LAINE 54:26, January, 1981.

New directions for contraception, by C. C. Korenbrot. TECHNOLOGY REVIEW 83:52-59+, November-December, 1980.

Pros and cons. ECONOMIST 279:76, May 30, 1981.

Psychological aspects in contraception counseling, by H. Sjöström. KATILOLEHTI 86(2):60-64, February, 1981.

Psychological viewpoints in counseling on contraceptives. KATILOLEHTI 86(3):106+, March, 1981.

Self-concept and contraception: pre-conception decision-making. POPULATION AND ENVIRONMENT 4(1):11, Spring, 1981.

Seminar stresses pharmacist's role as advisor in use of contraceptives. AMERICAN DIGEST 182:68+, July, 1980.

Sexuality and contraception, by J. F. Porter. AUSTRALA-SIAN NURSES JOURNAL 10:10-12+, May, 1981.

Should the community subsidize conventional contraceptives? by B. Grünfeld. NORDISK MEDICIN 95(8-9):218, September, 1980.

Tailoring contraception to patients. MEDICAL WORLD NEWS 22:47-48+, February 16, 1981.

Variance and reliability in estimates of OC use [letter], by G. E. Hendershot, et al. AMERICAN JOURNAL OF PUBLIC HEALTH 71(3):316-317, March, 1981.

The user perspective: an evolutionary step in contraceptive service programs, by G. Zeidenstein. STUDIES IN FAMILY PLANNING 11:1, January 24-29, 1980.

CONTRACEPTION AND CONTRACEPTIVES: LAWS AND
LEGISLATION

Establishing regulatory control over contraception, by C.
Djerassi. USA TODAY 109:7-8, April, 1981.

St. Louis law regulating sale of contraceptives, sexual devices
OK. THE CRIMINAL LAW REPORTER: COURT DE-
CISIONS AND PROCEEDINGS 28(10):2228-2229,
December 3, 1980.

CONTRACEPTION AND CONTRACEPTIVES: RESEARCH
Advances in the research of the contraceptive action of LH-
RH analogs, by Y. Pardo, et al. HAREFUAH 99(8):229-
231, October 15, 1980.

Analysis of serum-mediated immunosuppression in normal
pregnancy, abortion and contraception, by B. Masset, et
al. ALLERGOLOGIA ET IMMUNOPATHOLOGIA 8(5):
569-578, September-October, 1980.

Brief note on rubber technology and contraception: the diaphragm and the condom, by V. L. Bullough. TECH-
NOLOGY AND CULTURE 22:104-111, January, 1981.

A clinical trial of Neo Sampoon vaginal contraceptive tablets,
by S. F. Begum, et al. CONTRACEPTION 22(6):573-
582, December, 1980.

Contraception breakthroughs. HARPER'S BAZAAR 114:
90+, September, 1981.

Contraception in the light of immunological studies, by A.
Bromboszcz, et al. WIADOMOSCI LEKARSKIE 33(14):
1141-1143, July 15, 1980.

Contraceptive research [letter]. FAMILY PLANNING PER-
SPECTIVES 13(1):5+, January-February, 1981.

Contraceptive vaccine research: still an art [news], by E. R.
González. JAMA 244(13):1414-1415+, September 26,
1980.

Effects of d-norgestrel-releasing intracervical devices in the nonhuman primate, Erythrocebus patas, by G. E. Dagle, et al. CONTRACEPTION 22(4):409-423, October, 1980.

Effects of an intra-epididymal and intra-scrotal copper device on rat spermatozoa, by N. J. Chinoy, et al. INTERNATIONAL JOURNAL OF ANDROLOGY 3(6):719-737, December, 1980.

Further studies of an intravasal copper device in rats, by R. K. Ahsan, et al. JOURNAL OF REPRODUCTIVE FERTILITY 59(2):341-345, July, 1980.

Injectable and oral contraceptive steroids in relation to some neurotransmitters in the rat brain, by T. T. Daabees, et al. BIOCHEMICAL PHARMACOLOGY 30(12):1581-1585, June 15, 1981.

Low dose injectable contraceptive norethisterone enanthate 20 mg monthly—I. Clinical trials, by K. Prema, et al. CONTRACEPTION 23(1):11-22, January, 1981.

—. II. Metabolic side effects, by M. S. Bamji, et al. CONTRACEPTION 23(1):23-36, January, 1981.

New antifertility agents active in the rabbit vaginal contraception (RVC) method, by W. L. Williams. CONTRACEPTION 22(6):659-672, December, 1980.

Oral contraceptives, lanosterol, and platelet hyperactivity in rat, by M. Ciavatti, et al. SCIENCE 210(4470):642-644, November 7, 1980.

Preliminary testing of the contraceptive collagen sponge, by M. Chvapil, et al. OBSTETRICS AND GYNECOLOGY 56(4):503-506, October, 1980.

Prototype for a new class of antifertility agents, 3,5-Bis (dimethylamino)-1,2,4-dithiazolium chloride, by D. W.

Hahn, et al. CONTRACEPTION 21(5):529-535, May, 1980.

Recent advances in contraception [editorial], by R. P. Shearman. MEDICAL JOURNAL OF AUSTRALIA 1 (2):55-57, January 24, 1981.

Synthesis of some flavonoid compounds with 3'- or 4'-substituted methyl group, by J. M. Yang. YAO HSUEH HSUEH PAO 15(11):684-687, November, 1980.

Synthetic estro-progestational (contraceptive) agents and cerebral ischemic complications: cerebral pseudo-tumours, thrombosis of intracranial venous sinuses. Apropos of 60 cases, by G. Rancurel, et al. SEMAINES DES HOPITAUX DE PARIS 56(39-40):1583-1587, October 18-25, 1980.

Synthetic studies of contraceptive drugs. II. The synthesis of 16 alpha, 17 alpha-dihydroxyprogesterone acetophenide, by D. G. Han, et al. YAO HSUEH HSUEH PAO 15(12): 725-729, December, 1980.

The ultrastructural features of progestagen-induced decidual cells in the rhesus monkey (Macaca mulatta), by P. F. Wadsworth, et al. CONTRACEPTION 22(2):189-198, August, 1980.

CONTRACEPTIVE AGENTS: COMPLICATIONS
Effects of contraceptive agents on the biochemical and protein composition of human endometrium, by K. Umapathysivam, et al. CONTRACEPTION 22(4):425-440, October, 1980.

CONTRACEPTIVE AGENTS: FEMALE: ORAL: COMPLICATIONS
Adverse effects of oral contraceptives, by H. J. Engel. MEDIZINISCHE MONATSSCHRIFT FUR PHARMAZEUTEN 2(7):199-204, July, 1979.

CONTRACEPTIVES

AFRICA
Personal experience with contraception in Algeria, by
L. T. Ahmed. GYNECOLOGIE 31(2):131-133, 1980.

ASIA
Oral contraceptive use and diseases of the circulatory sys-
tem in Taiwan: an analysis of mortality statistics, by
L. P. Chow, et al. INTERNATIONAL JOURNAL OF
GYNAECOLOGY AND OBSTETRICS 18(6):420-
432, 1980.

AUSTRALIA
Use of contraception among married women in New
South Wales, Australia, by F. Yusuf. JOURNAL OF
BIOSOCIAL SCIENCE 12(1):41-49, January, 1980.

BANGLADESH
A comparative study of standard-dose and low-dose oral
contraceptives in rural Bangladesh, by R. Bairagi, et
al. INTERNATIONAL JOURNAL OF GYNAECOL-
OGY AND OBSTETRICS 18(4):264-267, 1980.

Contraceptive distribution in Bangladesh: some lessons
learned, by M. Rahman, et al. STUDIES IN FAMILY
PLANNING 11(6):191-201, June, 1980.

Dizziness associated with discontinuation of oral contra-
ceptives in Bangladesh, by A. R. Measham, et al.
INTERNATIONAL JOURNAL OF GYNAECOLOGY
AND OBSTETRICS 18(2):109-112, September-
October, 1980.

BRAZIL
Oral contraceptives and family health in rural Bangladesh,
by S. C. Huber, et al. INTERNATIONAL JOURNAL
OF GYNAECOLOGY AND OBSTETRICS 18(4):
268-274, 1980.

291

CONTRACEPTIVES

CANADA

Differences between women who begin pill use before and after first intercourse: Ontario, Canada, by E. S. Herold, et al. FAMILY PLANNING PERSPECTIVES 12:304-305, November-December, 1980.

Premarital sexual guilt and contraceptive attitudes and behavior, by E. S. Herold, et al. FAMILY RELATIONS 30:247-253, April, 1981.

CHINA

China progresses with male contraceptive. CHEMISTRY AND INDUSTRY p630, August 16, 1980.

Contraception in China, by G. Perkin. POPULI 7(4):16-25, 1980.

COLUMBIA

Conocimiento y uso de métodos anticonceptivos: un análisis comparativo con datos de los informes de países en América Latina [Colombia, Costa Rica, the Dominican Republic, Panama and Peru], by E. Taucher. NOTAS DE POBLACION 8:9-43, December, 1980.

COSTA RICA

Conocimiento y uso de métodos anticonceptivos: un análisis comparativo con datos de los informes de páises en América Latina [Colombia, Costa Rica, the Dominican Republic, Panama and Peru], by E. Taucher. NOTAS DE POBLACION 8:9-43, December, 1980.

CZECHOSLOVACHIA

Czech women, burdened by their dual roles, rely on contraception, abortion to keep families small. FAMILY PLANNING PERSPECTIVES 13:189-190, July-August, 1981.

CONTRACEPTIVES

DEVELOPING COUNTRIES
Attitudes towards and practice of contraception in
Indore and surrounding villages, by S. Deshpande, et
al. JOURNAL OF FAMILY WELFARE 27:25-30,
December, 1980.

Fertility and contraception in 12 developed countries.
FAMILY PLANNING PERSPECTIVES 13(2):93,
March-April, 1981.

Nonclinical distribution of the pill in the developing
world, by A. Rosenfield, et al. INTERNATIONAL
FAMILY PLANNING PERSPECTIVES 6:130-136,
December, 1980.

Pill use in 20 developing countries: a cross-country sum-
mary from the World Fertility Survey, by D. Wulf.
INTERNATIONAL FAMILY PLANNING PERSPEC-
TIVES 6:161-162, December, 1980.

Urban-rural differentials in contraceptive use, by R. E.
Lightbourne. INTERNATIONAL STATISTICAL
INSTITUTE REVIEW (10), May, 1980.

DOMINICAN REPUBLIC
Conocimiento y uso de métodos anticonceptives: un
análisis comparativo con datos de los informes de
países en América Latina [Colombia, Costa Rica,
the Dominican Republic, Panama and Peru], by E.
Taucher. NOTAS DE POBLACION 8:9-43, December, 1980.

GREAT BRITAIN
British pill studies stress importance of relation between
progestogen content and vascular disease. FAMILY
PLANNING PERSPECTIVES 12:262-264, September-October, 1980.

Contraceptive behaviour and fertility patterns in an inner

293

CONTRACEPTIVES

GREAT BRITAIN
London group practice, by P. C. Stott. JOURNAL OF THE ROYAL COLLEGE OF GENERAL PRACTITIONERS 30(215):340-346, June, 1980.

L'Église anglicane et la contraception. SUPPLÉMENT 138: 434-455, September, 1981.

INDONESIA
Use of modern contraceptives in Indonesia: a challenge to the conventional wisdom, by R. Freedman, et al. INTERNATIONAL FAMILY PLANNING PERSPECTIVES 7:3-15, March, 1981.

IRELAND
Attitudes, knowledge and the extent of use of artificial contraception in social classes IV and V in Ireland, by A. Moore, et al. IRISH MEDICAL JOURNAL 73(9): 342-347, September, 1980.

Irish women's eyes aren't smiling, by M. Wilson. OFF OUR BACKS January, 1981.

ITALY
Study of the use of contraceptives by a town and a country population of northern Italy, by G. G. Novelli, et al. ACTA EUROPAEA FERTILITATIS 11 (2):167-179, June, 1980.

JAPAN
The cultural context of condom use in Japan, by S. Coleman. STUDIES IN FAMILY PLANNING 12:28-39, January, 1981.

LEBANON
Breastfeeding and contraceptive patterns postpartum—a study in South Lebanon, by H. Zurayk. STUDIES IN FAMILY PLANNING 12:237, May, 1981.

CONTRACEPTIVES

PANAMA
Conocimiento y uso de métodos anticonceptivos: un
análisis comparativo con datos de los informes de
países en América Latina [Colombia, Costa Rica, the
Dominican Republic, Panama and Peru], by E.
Taucher. NOTAS DE POBLACIÓN 8:9-43, December,
1980.

PERU
Conocimiento y uso de métodos anticonceptivos: un
análisis comparativo con datos de los informes de
países en América Latina [Colombia, Costa Rica, the
Dominican Republic, Panama and Peru], by E.
Taucher. NOTAS DE POBLACIÓN 8:9-43, December,
1980.

POLAND
Contraception and abortion in Poland, by D. P. Mazur.
FAMILY PLANNING PERSPECTIVES 13:195-198,
July-August, 1981.

THAILAND
Thailand's Mr. Contraception [M. Viravaidya; director of
Family Planning Service]. TIME 117:67, March 23,
1981.

UNITED STATES
Blood pressure changes and oral contraceptive use: a
study of 2676 black women in the southeastern
United States, by B. A. Blumenstein, et al. AMERI-
CAN JOURNAL OF EPIDEMIOLOGY 112(4):539-
552, October, 1980.

Contraceptive utilization: United States, by K. Ford.
VITAL HEALTH STATISTICS 23(2):1-48, September, 1979.

Contraceptive utilization: United States, 1976, by W. D.
Mosher. VITAL HEALTH STATISTICS 23(7):1-58,

CONTRACEPTIVES

UNITED STATES
March, 1981.

The impact of the female marriage squeeze and the contraceptive revolution on sex roles and the women's
liberation movement in the U. S., 1960 to 1975, by D
D. Heer. JOURNAL OF MARRIAGE AND THE
FAMILY 43:49-66, February, 1981.

Use of cervical caps at the University of California at
Berkeley, by G. G. Smith. JOURNAL OF THE
AMERICAN COLLEGIATE HEALTH ASSOCIA-
TION 29:93-94, October, 1980.

ZAIRE
Characteristics of contraceptive acceptors in rural Zaire,
by J. E. Brown, et al. STUDIES IN FAMILY PLAN-
NING 11:378-384, December, 1980.

CONTRACEPTIVES: ADVERTISING
APHA: renew Title X, lift ban on radio, TV contraceptive
ads. FAMILY PLANNING PERSPECTIVES 13:47-48,
January-February, 1981.

Advertisements for contraceptives as commercial speech in
the broadcast media. CASE WESTERN RESERVE LAW
REVIEW 31:336-362, Winter, 1981.

Another blast at spermicide ads. CHEMICAL WEEKLY 12:
26+, January 14, 1981.

Should the media advertise contraceptives? by D. E. Greydanus. AMERICAN JOURNAL OF DISEASES OF
CHILDREN 135(8):687-688, August, 1981.

CONTRACEPTIVES: ATTITUDES
Attitudes, knowledge and the extent of use of artificial con-
traception in social classes IV and V in Ireland, by A.
Moore, et al. IRISH MEDICAL JOURNAL 73(9):342-

347, September, 1980.

Behavioral-social aspects of contraceptive sterilization, by
S. H. Newman, et al. HEALTH p217-268, 1978.

Can Joel Wells be wrong on contraception, by W. E. May.
OUR SUNDAY VISITOR 69:5, December 28, 1980.

Contraception—abortion lifeline, by G. E. Richardson.
HEALTH EDUCATION 12(2):37, March-April, 1981.

Contraceptive choices for lactating women: suggestions for
postpartum family planning. STUDIES IN FAMILY
PLANNING 12(4):156, April, 1981.

Contraceptive efficacy: the significance of method and motivation, by E. F. Jones, et al. STUDIES IN FAMILY
PLANNING 11(2):39-50, February, 1980.

Contraceptive knowledge: antecedents and implications, by
R. O. Hansson, et al. THE FAMILY COORDINATOR
28(1):29-34, January, 1979.

Does your contraceptive fit your personality? by G. A.
Bachman. MADEMOISELLE 87:52-53, June, 1981.

The influence of memory factors on contraceptive information acquisition and choice, by W. D. Hoyer. DAI 42(3),
1981.

A survey of attitudes towards permanent contraceptive
methods, by A. E. Reading, et al. JOURNAL OF BIO-
LOGICAL SCIENCE 12(4):383, October, 1980.

Various aspects of individual attitudes to irreversible contraception. Results of a survey, by G. Klinger, et al. ZEN-
TRALBLATT FUR GYNAEKOLOGIE 103(2):121-123,
1981.

CONTRACEPTIVES: BARRIER

Another blast at spermicide ads. CHEMICAL WEEKLY
12:26+, January 14, 1981.

CONTRACEPTIVES: COMPLICATIONS
Breast-feeding and contraception. PEDIATRICS 68(1):138-
140, July, 1981.

Carbohydrate metabolism with three months of low-estrogen
contraceptive use, by W. N. Spellacy, et al. AMERICAN
JOURNAL OF OBSTETRICS AND GYNECOLOGY 138
(2):151-155, September 15, 1980.

Cigarette smoking, oral contraceptives and serum lipid and
lipoprotein levels in children of a total community, by
G. S. Berenson. CIRCULATION 62(3):III-270, 1980.

Contraception and the etiology of pelvic inflammatory di-
sease: new perspectives, by P. Senanayake, et al. AMER-
CAN JOURNAL OF OBSTETRICS AND GYNECOLO-
GY 138(7 Part 2):852-860, 1980.

Contraception and the 'high-risk' woman, by S. K. Khoo, et
al. MEDICAL JOURNAL OF AUSTRALIA 1(2):60-68,
January 24, 1981.

Contraception and pelvic inflammatory disease, by P. Senanayake, et al. SEXUALLY TRANSMITTED DISEASES 8
(2):89-91, April-June, 1981.

Contraception in risk patients. Discussion, by K. Detering, et
al. MEDIZINISCHE WELT 31(49):1805-1806, Decem-
ber 5, 1980.

The contraceptive effect of breastfeeding. STUDIES IN
FAMILY PLANNING 12(4):125, April, 1981.

Contraceptive risk-taking in a population with limited access
to abortion. JOURNAL OF BIOLOGICAL SCIENCE 12
(4):373, October, 1980.

298

CONTRACEPTIVES: COMPLICATIONS

Gallstone risk, by J. Labreche. CHATELAINE 53:38, December, 1980.

Internal medicine problems regarding contraception. Part I, by M. Mall-Haefeli. SCHWEIZERISCHE MEDIZINISCHE WOCHENSCHRIFT 110(36):1314-1319, September 6, 1980.

Intestinal infarction caused by mesenteric venous thrombosis during contraceptive treatment, by G. Melodia, et al. CHIRURGIA ITALIANA 31(6):1132-1137, December, 1979.

Pelvic inflammatory disease and its consequences in the developing world, by D. G. Muir, et al. AMERICAN JOURNAL OF OBSTETRICS AND GYNECOLOGY 138(7 Part 2):913-928, 1980.

CONTRACEPTIVES: FEMALE
Contraception and female sterilization, by A. J. Penfield. NEW YORK STATE JOURNAL OF MEDICINE 81(2): 255-258, February, 1981.

Contraception for the insulin-dependent diabetic woman: the view from one clinic, by J. M. Steel, et al. DIABETES CARE 3(4):557-560, July-August, 1980.

Do OTC vaginal contraceptives face FDA ban? DRUG TOPICS 125:16, January 16, 1981.

On the dispersion capacity of an intra-vaginal contraceptive ovule. Results of an in-vivo study in sexually not stimulated women, by I. Schmid-Tannwald, et al. GEBURTSHILFE UND FRAUENHEILKUNDE 41(6):424-426, June, 1981.

Postcoital contraception, by J. Porter, et al. MEDICAL JOURNAL OF AUSTRALIA 1(2):68+, January 24, 1981.

299

An anti-spermatozoan contraceptive, the ST film. JOSANPU ZASSHI 35(2):138-142, February, 1981.

Ask a doctor (barrier methods), by C. Carver. CHATELAINE 54:24, February, 1981.

Barrier contraception: a comprehensive overview, by H. J. Tantum, et al. FERTILITY AND STERILITY 36(1):1-12, July, 1981.

The cervical cap: an alternative contraceptive, by P. A. Canavan, et al. JOGN NURSING 10:271-273, July-August, 1981.

The cervical cap: past and current experience, by B. Fairbanks, et al. WOMEN AND HEALTH 5:61-80, Fall, 1980.

Cervical caps—the perfect, untested contraceptive, by J. Willis. FDA CONSUMER 15:20-21, April, 1981.

Cervical cerclage, by I. A. McDonald. CLINICAL OBSTETRICS AND GYNAECOLOGY 7(3):461-479, December, 1980.

Combination of the ovulation method with diaphragm, by J. F. Cattanach. MEDICAL JOURNAL OF AUSTRALIA 2 (9):511-512, November 1, 1980.

Condoms and foam: traditional forms of contraception still going strong, by V. Wirth. ISSUES IN HEALTH CARE OF WOMEN 1(5):29-36, 1979.

Contraceptive foams and birth defects. SCIENCE NEWS 119: 229, April 11, 1981.

Contraceptive use of cervical caps [letter], by K. P. Zodhiates, et al NEW ENGLAND JOURNAL OF MEDICINE 304(15):915, April 9, 1981.

Customized cervical cap: evolution of an ancient idea, by C. Arthur. JOURNAL OF NURSE-MIDWIFERY 25:33-34, November-December, 1980.

Dalkon shields are out. FDA CONSUMER 15:31, May, 1981.

Diaphragm use instruction: time of insertion before coitus, by A. Mariella. JOURNAL OF NURSE-MIDWIFERY 25 (6):35-36, November-December, 1980.

Fitting of diaphragms, by E. Weisberg. MEDICAL JOURNAL OF AUSTRALIA 2(5):250-253+, September 6, 1980.

Medical news: are spermicides safe? by S. Katz. CHATE-LAINE 54'37, August, 1981.

Medical news: the twice-a-year pellet, by S. Katz. CHATE-LAINE 54:37, August, 1981.

Nonprescription vaginal contraception, by D. A. Edelman. INTERNATIONAL JOURNAL OF GYNAECOLOGY AND OBSTETRICS 18(5):340-344, 1980.

Norethisterone enanthate as an injectable contraceptive in puerperal and non-puerperal women, by G. B. Melis, et al. CONTRACEPTION 23(1):77-88, January, 1981.

Putting a lid on the cap [FDA restrictions on distribution of cervical caps]. PROGRESSIVE 45:13, March, 1981.

The rebirth of the cervical cap, by J. D. Capiello, et al. JOUR-NAL OF NURSE-MIDWIFERY 26:13-18, September-October, 1981.

Spermicidal saponins from Pittosporum nilghrense, by G. K. Jain, et al. INDIAN JOURNAL OF PHARMACEUTICAL SCIENCES 42(1):12-13, 1980.

The use of cervical caps at the university of California at

CONTRACEPTIVES: FEMALE: BARRIER

Berkeley, by G. G. Smith. JOURNAL OF THE AMER-
ICAN COLLEGIATE HEALTH ASSOCIATION 29(2):
93-94, October, 1980.

The use of intrauterine device inserted during the immediate
postabortion time, by R. L. Reynoso, et al. GINECOLO-
GIA Y OBSTETRICIA DE MEXICO 47(283):311-320,
May, 1980.

Warning on spermicides [risk of birth defects], by J. Seligmann. NEWSWEEK 97:84, April 13, 1981.

Government barriers against the cervical cap. OFF OUR
BACKS 11:12, January, 1981.

CONTRACEPTIVES: FEMALE: BARRIER: COMPLICATIONS
Barrier contraception and breast cancer, by A. N. Gjorgov.
CANCER DETECTION AND PREVENTION 3(1), 1980.

High rates of pregnancy and dissatisfaction mark first cervical
cap trial. FAMILY PLANNING PERSPECTIVES 13:48,
January-February, 1981.

Toxic-shock syndrome and the diaphragm [letter], by E. E.
Hymowitz. NEW ENGLAND JOURNAL OF MEDICINE
305(14):834, October 1, 1981.

CONTRACEPTIVES: FEMALE: CERVICAL CAP
(see ... CONTRACEPTIVES: BARRIER)

CONTRACEPTIVES: FEMALE: COMPLICATIONS
Breast cancer in women who have taken contraceptive
steroids, by P. N. Matthews, et al. BRITISH MEDICAL
JOURNAL 6266:774-776, March 7, 1981.

Breastfeeding and contraceptive patterns postpartum: a
study in South Lebanon, by H. Zurayk. STUDIES IN
FAMILY PLANNING 12(5):237, May, 1981.

Contraception with subcutaneous capsules containing ST-1435, by P. Lähteenmäki, et al. CONTRACEPTION 23 (1):63-75, January, 1981.

Contraceptive foams and birth defects. SCIENCE NEWS 119: 229, April 11, 1981.

Contraceptives and cancer. SCIQUEST 54:4, January, 1981.

Contraceptives in sickle cell disease, by H. W. Foster, Jr. SOUTHERN MEDICAL JOURNAL 74(5):543-545, May, 1981.

Quantitative morphological investigations in livers and liber tumors after taking contraceptives, by D. Kranz, et al. ZENTRALBLATT FUR ALLGEMEINE PATHOLOGIE 124(5):441-447, 1980.

Risk factors for benign breast disease, by L. A. Brinton, et al. AMERICAN JOURNAL OF EPIDEMIOLOGY 113(3): 203-214, March, 1981.

Serum high density lipoprotein cholesterol levels in women using a contraceptive injection of depot-medroxyproges-terone acetate, by J. Kremer, et al. CONTRACEPTION 22(4):359-367, October, 1980.

Side effects of using modern contraceptive methods for a period of 9192 cycles, by B. Nalbanski. SKUSHERSTVO I GINEKOLOGIIA 19(5-6):553-556, 1980.

Use, nonuse, and risk of pregnancy. POPULATION RE-PORTS 9(3):M-171, May-June, 1981.

CONTRACEPTIVES: FEMALE: DIAPHRAGM
(see . . . CONTRACEPTIVES: FEMALE: BARRIER)

CONTRACEPTIVES: FEMALE: IUD
Changing profile of IUD users in family planning clinics in

rural Bangladesh, by S. Bhatia, et al. JOURNAL OF BIO-
SOCIAL SCIENCE 13:169-178, April, 1981.

A comparison of the efficacy and acceptability of the Copper-
7 intrauterine device following immediate or delayed insertion after first-trimester therapeutic abortion, by P. G.
Gillett, et al. FERTILITY AND STERILITY 34(2):121-
124, August, 1980.

Discontinued intrauterine device use and spontaneous abortion, by D. W. Kaufman, et al. AMERICAN JOURNAL
OF EPIDEMIOLOGY 112(3):434, 1980.

Flower intrauterine contraceptive device, by L. Zilan. CHI-
NESE MEDICAL JOURNAL 93(8):528-530, 1980.

Four years of experience with the TCu 380A intrauterine
contraceptive device, by I. Sivin, et al. FERTILITY AND
STERILITY 36(2):159-163, August, 1981.

IUD advisory renews debate on health risk, by R. Alsop.
WALL STREET JOURNAL p25, March 30, 1981.

IUD maker wants former insurer to pay for claims, by M.
LeRoux. BUSINESS INSURANCE 14:9, July 7, 1980.

IUD update: is it the right contraceptive for you? by M. Newton. FAMILY HEALTH 13:56-57, May, 1981.

IUD users have fewer ectopic pregnancies than noncontraceptors. FAMILY PLANNING PERSPECTIVES 13:150,
May-June, 1981.

Immediate postabortion insertion of IUDs, by B. Backe, et al.
TIDSSKRIFT FOR DEN NORSKE LAEGEFORENING
100(25):1480-1482, September 10, 1980.

Intrauterine contraception with levonorgestrel: a comparative
randomised clinical performance study, by C. G. Nilsson,

CONTRACEPTIVES: FEMALE: IUD

et al. LANCET 1(8220 Pt 1):577-580, March 14, 1981.

Physiological method and intrauterine devices for contraception, by A. P. Kiriushchenkov. FEL'DSHER I AKUSHER-KA 46(1):55-57, 1981.

CONTRACEPTIVES: FEMALE: IUD: COMPLICATIONS
Bacterial infection from actinoymces, though rare, is found to be a problem among some IUD users. FAMILY PLAN-NING PERSPECTIVES 12:306-307, November-December, 1980.

Bacteriological colonisation of uterine cavity: role of tailed intrauterine contraceptive device, by R. A. Sparks, et al. BRITISH MEDICAL JOURNAL 6271:1189-1191, April 11, 1981.

Effect of long-term use of intrauterine contraception on the form of the uterine cavity and on the patency of the uterine tubes, by E. V. Derankova. VOPROSY OKHRAN-Y MATERINSTVA I DETSTVA 24(6):69, 1979.

Gynaecology: piercing pains . . . a woman admitted to hospital in an attempt to remove her intrauterine device, by E. Hawkes. NURSING MIRROR 152:41, April 2, 1981.

PID risk increased sharply among IUD users, British cohort, U. S. case-control studies affirm. FAMILY PLANNING PERSPECTIVES 13:182-184, July-August, 1981.

Pregnancies after ineffective interruption or intrauterine procedure in early pregnancy, by W. Hardt, et al. GEBURT-SHILFE UND FRAUENHEILKUNDE 40(7):654-657, July, 1980.

Risk of pelvic inflammatory disease among users of intrauterine devices, irrespective of previous pregnancy, by S. Osser, et al. AMERICAN JOURNAL OF OBSTETRICS AND GYNECOLOGY 138(7 Part 2):864-867, 1980.

CONTRACEPTIVES: FEMALE: IUD: COMPLICATIONS

Serum prolactin levels in women before and after the use of copper IUD, by R. S. Raikar. INDIAN JOURNAL OF MEDICAL RESEARCH 69:436-439, March, 1979.

CONTRACEPTIVES: FEMALE: IMPLANTED
Menstrual blood loss with contraceptive subdermal levonorgestrel implants, by C. G. Nilsson, et al. FERTILITY AND STERILITY 35(3):304-306, March, 1981.

CONTRACEPTIVES: FEMALE: ORAL
The benefit of the classification of oral contraceptives. Studies of 525 women taking oral contraceptives, by J. M. Wenderlein. MMW 123(23):957-961, June 5, 1981.

Biochemical-hormonal bases for the selection of contraceptives for oral use, by V. Cortés-Gallegos. GACETA MEDICA DE MEXICO 116(7):323-326, July, 1980.

Contraindications to the pill [letter], by S. J. Emans. PEDIATRICS 66(4):643-644, October, 1980.

Differences between women who begin pill use before and after first intercourse: Ontario, Canada, by E. S. Herold, et al. FAMILY PLANNING PERSPECTIVES 12:304-305, November-December, 1980.

Effect of a controlled exercise program on serum lipoprotein levels in women on oral contraceptives, by T. P. Wynne, et al. METABOLISM 29(12):1267-1271, December, 1980.

Effect of HR (O-(beta-hydroxyethyl)-rutosides) on the impaired venous function of young females taking oral contraceptives. A strain gauge plethysmographic and clinical open controlled study, by S. Forconi, et al. VASA 9(4): 324-330, 1980.

The effects of oral contraceptives in inducing changes in blood pressure in the African green monkey; the role of

CONTRACEPTIVES: FEMALE: ORAL

the renin-angiotensin system, by F. F. Vickers, PhD. DAI
42(5), 1981.

'Escape' ovulation in women due to the missing of low dose
combination oral contraceptive pills, by V. Chowdhury,
et al. CONTRACEPTION 22(3):241-247, September,
1980.

Exploring risks and benefits of the birth control pill . . . teaching ideas, by D. A. Dunn. HEALTH EDUCATION 12:35,
January-February, 1981.

Good news about the pill, by J. E. Rodgers. MADEMOISELLE
87:107-109, May, 1981.

Influence of fatty acids and an oral contraceptive on the eyes
of a nonhuman primate, by W. K. O'Steen, et al. EXPER-
IMENTAL AND MOLECULAR PATHOLOGY 34(1):43-
51, February, 1981.

Insulin receptors in circulating erythrocytes and monocytes
from women on oral contraceptives or pregnant women
near term, by J. C. Tsibris, et al. JOURNAL OF CLINI-
CAL ENDOCRINOLOGY AND METABOLISM 51(4):
711-717, October, 1980.

The interaction of phenobarbital and other anticonvulsants
with oral contraceptive steroid therapy, by D. J. Back, et
al. CONTRACEPTION 22(5):495-503, November, 1980.

Levonorgestrel, by S. J. Hopkins. DRUGS TODAY 16(6):
186-190, 1980.

Limited usefulness of the breath test in evaluation of drug
metabolism: a study in human oral contraceptive users
treated with dimethylaminoantipyrine and diazepam, by
A. Sonnenberg, et al. HEPATOGASTROENTEROLOGY
27(2):104-108, April, 1980.

Matter of blood, sweat and the pill, by P. De Vries. MAC-
LEAN'S 94:56-57, March 16, 1981.

More contraindications to the pill [letter], by J. P. Realini.
PEDIATRICS 66(4):644-645, October, 1980.

Morning after pill—both synthetic, natural estrogens are effective. FAMILY PLANNING PERSPECTIVES 13:148,
May-June, 1981.

Morphologic effects of oral contraceptives (Norinyle) on the
guinea pig liver, by C. S. Kim, et al. YONSEI MEDICAL
JOURNAL 21(1):43-51, 1980.

Normal fertility in women with post-pill amenorrhoea, by M.
G. Hull, et al. LANCET 1(8234):1329-1332, June 20,
1981.

Oral contraception and thromboembolism: the role of progestogens [editorial]. NEW ZEALAND MEDICAL JOUR-
NAL 92(665):98+, August 13, 1980.

Oral contraceptive and trisomy 21. A retrospective study of
730 cases, by J. Lejeune, et al. SEMAINES DES HOPI-
TAUX DE PARIS 55(43-44):1985-1990, December 18-
25, 1979.

Oral contraceptive steroids and atherosclerosis: lipogenesis in
human arterial smooth muscle cells and dermal fibroblasts in presence of lipoprotein-deficient serum from
oral contraceptive users, by P. V. Subbaiah, et al. ARTER-
Y 6(6):437-457, 1980.

Oral contraceptive steroids as promoters of hepatocarcinogenesis in female Sprague-Dawley rats, by J. D. Yager, Jr.,
et al. CANCER RESEARCH 40(10):3680-3685, October,
1980.

The pill at 20: an assessment, by H. W. Ory, et al. FAMILY

CONTRACEPTIVES: FEMALE: ORAL

PLANNING PERSPECTIVES 12(6):278, November-
December, 1980.

Pill revisited. SCIQUEST 54:26-27, September, 1981.

The place of oral contraceptives and pregnancy in the aetiology of amenorrhoea, a study of 188 cases of secondary
amenorrhoea lasting more than one year, by C.
Le Pogamp, et al. JOURNAL DE GYNECOLOGIE OB-
STETRIQUE ET BIOLOGIE DE LA REPRODUCTION
10(3):223-229, 1981.

Precursor stage of hepatocellular neoplasm following long ex-
posure to orally administered contraceptives, by S. N.
Thung, et al. HUMAN PATHOLOGY 12(5):472-474,
May, 1981.

Return of ovulation after abortion and after discontinuation
of oral contraceptives, by P. Lahteenmaki, et al. FERTIL-
ITY AND STERILITY 34(3):246-249, September, 1980.

Successful pregnancy soon after oral contraceptive-associated
malignant hypertension, by J. H. Silas, et al. POSTGRAD-
UATE MEDICAL JOURNAL 56(661):790-791, November, 1980.

Third report on oral contraceptives. THESA JOURNAL 20
(5):49-52, June, 1980.

Use-effectiveness of standard-dose and low-dose oral contra-
ceptives in Dacca, by A. R. Measham, et al. INTERNA-
TIONAL JOURNAL OF GYNAECOLOGY AND OB-
STETRICS 18(5):354-356, 1980.

Weighing the facts about oral contraceptives, by S. R. Cavanaugh. LIFE AND HEALTH 96:14-15, May, 1981.

Zinc and copper nutriture of women taking oral contraceptive agents, by S. C. Vir, et al. AMERICAN JOURNAL

CONTRACEPTIVES: FEMALE: ORAL

OF CLINICAL NUTRITION 34(8):1479-1483, August, 1981.

CONTRACEPTIVES: FEMALE: ORAL: COMPLICATIONS
Acute ischemic lesions in young women taking oral contraceptives. A report on 5 cases, by R. K. Danis, et al. JOURNAL DES MALADIES VASCULAIRES 5(4):273-276, 1980.

Amenorrhea following oral contraception, by N. Smiljanić, et al. ACTA OBSTETRICIA ET GYNECOLOGICA SCANDINAVICA 59(3):261-264, 1980.

Amenorrhoea following oral contraception. Pathophysiological problems, by G. Schaison. NOUVELLE PRESSE MEDICALE 9(41):3083-3086, November 1, 1980.

Angiography of cerebrovascular accidents in patients taking contraceptive pills. An analysis of 85 cases, by S. Hardy-Godon, et al. JOURNAL OF NEURORADIOLOGY 6 (3):239-254, 1979.

Antibiotic-oral contraceptive interaction? by R. C. Andersen, et al. DRUG INTELLIGENCE AND CLINICAL PHARMACY 15:280, April, 1981.

Antibiotics and oral contraceptives [letter], by D. F. Rubin. ARCHIVES OF DERMATOLOGY 117(4):189, April, 1981.

Are contraceptive pills teratogenic? by A Czeizel. ACTA MORPHOLOGICA ACADEMIAE SCIENTIARUM HUNGARICAE 28(1-2):177-188, 1980.

Atheromatous mesenteric occlusion associated with oral contraceptives and cigarette smoking, by W. R. Carlisle, et al. SOUTHERN MEDICAL JOURNAL 74(3):369-370, March, 1981.

Automatic assay of circulating immune complexes induced by oral contraceptives, by J. C. Buxtorf, et al. PATHOLO-GIE BIOLOGIE 29(1):62-64, January, 1981.

Basilar artery occlusion, two angiographically demonstrated cases in young women using oral contraceptives, by W. A. Nolen, et al. CLINICAL NEUROLOGY AND NEURO-SURGERY 82(1):31-36, 1980.

Benign hepatic tumours and oral contraception. Pathophysiology, by H. Bondue. ACTA GASTROENTEROLOGICA BELGICA 43(7-8):278-284, 1980.

Benign tumours of the liver and oral contraceptives, by F. Lesbros, et al. SEMAINES DES HOPITAUX DE PARIS 56(43-44):1823-1830, November 18-25, 1980.

Breast cancer and oral contraceptives: findings in Oxford-Family Planning Association contraceptive study, by M. P. Vessey, et al. BRITISH MEDICAL JOURNAL 282 (6282):2093-2094, June 27, 1981.

Breast cancer and oral contraceptives: findings in Royal College of General Practitioners' study. BRITISH MEDI-CAL JOURNAL 282(6282):2089-2093, June 27, 1981.

Breast cancer and the pill [letter], by P. L. Diggory. LANCET 1(8227):995, May 2, 1981.

Breast cancer and the pill—a muted reassurance. BRITISH MEDICAL JOURNAL 6282:2075-2076, June 27, 1981.

Breast feeding and oral contraceptives, by P. E. Treffers. NEDERLANDS TIJDSCHRIFT VOOR GENEESKUNDE 125(11):425-427, March 14, 1981.

British pill studies stress importance of relation between progestogen content and vascular disease. FAMILY PLAN-NING PERSPECTIVES 12:262-263, September-October,

CONTRACEPTIVES: FEMALE: ORAL: COMPLICATIONS

1980.

Budd-Chiari syndrome and oral contraceptives. Report of a case and review of the literature, by J. P. Lima, et al. ARQUIVOS DE GASTROENTERELOGIA 17(3):135-140, July-September, 1980.

Budd-Chiari syndrome following intake of oral contraceptives, by H. Gstöttner, et al. ZENTRALBLATT FUR GYNAE-KOLOGIE 102(3):146-150, 1980.

Budd-Chiari syndrome in women taking oral contraceptives, by S. H. Tsung, et al. ANNALS OF CLINICAL AND LABORATORY SCIENCE 10(6):518-522, November-December, 1980.

Cardiovascular side-effects of oral contraceptives with special regard to metabolism, lipoproteins and their role in the pathogenesis of vascular complications, by H. Ludwig. PRAXIS 70(13):549-553, March 24, 1981.

A case of multiple cerebrovascular and migraine episodes caused by the use of oral contraceptives, by G. Moretti, et al. ACTA BIO-MEDICA DE L'ATENEO PARMENSE 52(1):25-29, 1981.

Cerebral circulatory disorders while taking contraceptives, by D. Khadzhiev, et al. ZHURNAL NEVROPATOLOGII I PSIKHIATRII 81(1):64-67, 1981.

Cerebral thrombosis in woman receiving oral contraceptives: report of two cases, by I. Maruyama, et al. RINSHO KETSUEKI 21(6):822-827, June, 1980.

Cerebral vein thrombosis and the contraceptive pill in paroxysmal nocturnal haemoglobinuria, by M. L. Stirling, et al. SCOTTISH MEDICAL JOURNAL 25(3):243-244, July, 1980.

312

Cerebrovascular complications following intake of oral contraceptives [review of the literature apropos of a case], by K. Bouraoui, et al. UNION MEDICALE DU CANADA 109(2):284-288, February, 1980.

Changes in insulin receptors during oral contraception, by R. De Pirro, et al. JOURNAL.OF CLINICAL ENDOCRINOLOGY AND METABOLISM 52(1):29-33, January, 1981.

Changes in serum beta-thromboglobulin levels during oral contraception, cardiac valve disease and pulmonary embolism, by J. Conrad, et al. NOUVELLE PRESSE MEDICALE 10(16):1327-1329, April 11, 1981.

Cholestatic jaundice after triacetyloleandomycin and oral contraceptives. The diagnostic value of gamma-glutamyl transpeptidase, by I. Haber, et al. ACTA GASTRO-ENTEROLOGICA BELGICA 43(11-12):475-482, November-December, 1980.

Chorea induced by oral contraceptives [letter], by P. M. Green. NEUROLOGY 30(10):1131-1132, October, 1980.

Clomipramine and oral contraceptives: an interaction study—clinical findings, by M. Gringras, et al. JOURNAL OF INTERNATIONAL MEDICAL RESEARCH 8(Suppl 3):76-80, 1980.

Contraceptive pills and thrombosis [letter], by K. Helweg-Larsen, et al. UGESKRIFT FOR LAEGER 143(4):220, January 19, 1981.

Cystic disease, family history of breast cancer and use of oral contraceptives, by D. V. Vakil, et al. CANCER DETECTION AND PREVENTION 3(1), 1980.

Cytologic smear findings in oral contraceptive users: population screening in Jewish women, by A. E. Schachter, et al. ACTA CYTOLOGICA 25(1):40, 1981.

Diagnosis and management of post-pill amenorrhea, by R. Rojas-Walsson, et al. JOURNAL OF FAMILY PRACTICE 13(2):165-169, August, 1981.

Diet and oral contraceptive induced changes in bile acid pools in healthy women, by C. Williams. GASTROENTEROLOGY 78(5 Part 2):1327, 1980.

Does the 'pill' promote the development of tumors?, by C. Lauritzen. MEDIZINISCHE KLINIK 75(16):6-7, August 1, 1980.

Dosage of antithrombin III in women taking oral contraceptives, by N. Agoumi, et al. MAROC MEDICAL 2(3):309-315, October, 1980.

Effect of age, sex, oral contraceptive steroids and liver disease on the disposition of caffeine, by R. Patwardhan. CLINICAL RESEARCH 27(4):684A, 1979.

Effect of a combined oral contraceptive preparation on the dental pulp of experimental animals, by A. Cowie, et al. ORAL SURGERY 51(4):426-433, April, 1981.

Effect of oral contraceptive cycle on dry socket (localized alveolar osteitis), by J. E. Catellani, et al. JOURNAL OF THE AMERICAN DENTAL ASSOCIATION 101(5):777-780, November, 1980.

Effect of an oral contraceptive on uterine tonicity in women with primary dysmenorrhea, by O. Lalos, et al. ACTA OBSTETRICIA ET GYNECOLOGICA SCANDINAVICA 60(3):229-232, 1981.

Effect of oral contraceptives on the circulatory system, by T. Stasiński, et al. POLSKI TYGODNIK LEKARSKI 35 (19):713-715, May 12, 1980.

Effect of oral contraceptives on tryptophan and tyrosine availability: evidence for a possible contribution to mental depression, by S. E. Moller. NEUROPSYCHOBIOLOGY 7(4):192-200, 1981.

Effect of prolonged administration of oral contraceptives and psychotropic drugs on some ovarian adrenocortical functions, by M. T. Abdel-Aziz, et al. JOURNAL OF THE EGYPTIAN MEDICAL ASSOCIATION 61(11-12):703-709, 1978.

Effectivity and acceptability of oral contraceptives containing natural and artificial estrogens in combination with a gestagen. A controlled double-blind investigation, by J. Serup, et al. ACTA OBSTETRICIA ET GYNECOLOGICA SCANDINAVICA 60(2):203-206, 1981.

Effects of age, cigarette smoking and the oral contraceptive on the pharmacokinetics of clomipramine and its desmethyl metabolite during chronic dosing, by V. A. John, et al. JOURNAL OF INTERNATIONAL MEDICAL RESEARCH 8(Suppl 3):88-95, 1980.

Effects of angiotensin II analog on blood pressure, renin and aldosterone in women on oral contraceptives and toxemia, by T. Saruta, et al. GINECOLOGIA Y OBSTETRICIA DE MEXICO 12(1):11-20, 1981.

Effects of oestro-progestogenic oral contraceptives on blood coagulation, fibrinolysis, and platelet aggregation, by F. Ghezzo, et al. HAEMATOLOGICA 65(6):737-745, December, 1980.

Effects of oral contraceptive agents on copper and zinc balance in young women, by M. G. Crews, et al. AMERICAN JOURNAL OF CLINICAL NUTRITION 33(9): 1940-1945, September, 1980.

Effects of oral contraceptives containing 50 microgram

estrogen on blood coagulation in non-Caucasian women, by F. H. Tsakok, et al. CONTRACEPTION 21(5):505-527, May, 1980.

Effects of oral contraceptives on the liver [letter], by A. T. Coopland. CANADIAN JOURNAL OF SURGERY 23(6): 511, November, 1980.

Effects of subjects' sex, and intake of tobacco, alcohol and oral contraceptives on plasma phenytoin levels, by E. A. De Leacy, et al. BRITISH JOURNAL OF CLINICAL PHARMACOLOGY 8(1):33-36, July, 1979.

Elevated prolactin levels in oral contraceptive pill-related hypertension, by P. Lehtovirta, et al. FERTILITY AND STERILITY 35(4):403-405, April, 1981.

Endocrine, cardiovascular, and psychological correlates of olfactory sensitivity changes during the human menstrual cycle, by R. L. Doty, et al. JOURNAL OF COMPARATIVE AND PHYSIOLOGICAL PSYCHOLOGY 95:45-60, February, 1981.

Enzyme picture in the use of oral contraceptives, by R. Lorenz. SFA 56(32):2237-2240, November 20, 1980.

Erythema nodosum and oral contraception. Demonstration of an anti-ethinyl estradiol antibody [letter], by J. L. Touboul, et al. NOUVELLE PRESSE MEDICALE 10(9): 712, February 28, 1981.

Exercise, blood clots, and the pill [work of S. Pizzo], by G. B. Kolata. SCIENCE 211:913, February 27, 1981.

Exercise ECG and serum enzymes in women using oral contraceptives, by K. Ziesenhenn, et al. ZEITSCHRIFT FUR DIE GESAMTE INNERE MEDIZIN 35(15):619-623, August 1, 1980.

Failure of oral contraceptive with rifampicin, by K. C. Gupta, et al. MEDICAL JOURNAL OF ZAMBIA 15(1):23, December 1980-January 1981.

Family history and oral contraceptives: unique relationships in breast cancer patients, by M. M. Black, et al. CANCER 46(12):2747-2751, December 15, 1980.

Fibrinolytic response and oral contraceptive associated thromboembolism, by S. V. Pizzo, et al. CONTRACEPTION 23(2):181-186, February, 1981.

Focal hemorrhagic necrosis of the liver. A clinicopathological entity possibly related to oral contraceptives, by E. S. Zafrani, et al. GASTROENTEROLOGY 79(6):1295-1299, December, 1980.

Focal nodular hyperplasia of the liver and hepatic cell adenoma in women on oral contraceptives, by I. Bartók, et al. HEPATOGASTROENTEROLOGY 27(6):435-440, December, 1980.

For women aged 35 and under, little or no risk of circulatory disease death found from pill use. FAMILY PLANNING PERSPECTIVES 13:142-146, May-June, 1981.

Free thyroxine and free thyroxine index in women taking oral contraceptives, by M. A. Swanson, et al. CLINICAL NUCLEAR MEDICINE 6(4):168-171, April, 1981.

Further analyses of mortality in oral contraceptive users. LANCET 1(8219):541-546, March 7, 1981.

Hepatic angiosarcoma. Possible relationship to long-term oral contraceptive ingestion, by P. S. Monroe, et al. JAMA 246(1):64-65, July 3, 1981.

Hepatocellular adenoma. Its transformation to carcinoma in a user of oral contraceptives, by H. Tesluk, et al. AR-

CHIVES OF PATHOLOGY AND LABORATORY MEDICINE 105(6):296-299, June, 1981.

Hyperplastic lesions and benign tumours associated with oral contraception. Report of ten cases, by A. Dumont, et al. ACTA GASTROENTEROLOGICA BELGICA 43(7-8): 285-291, 1980.

Hypertension and oral contraceptive therapy, by M. Colliard, et al. SEMAINES DES HOPITAUX DE PARIS 56(33-36): 1407-1411, September 18-25, 1980.

Hypertension in 45 females on oral contraceptives, by M. Salvador, et al. REVUE DE MEDECINE INTERNE 1(2): 253-257, 1980.

Incidence of cerebrovascular lesions in users of oral contraceptives, by D. Borovaská, et al. CESKOSLOVENSKA NEUROLOGIE A NEUROCHIRURGIO 44(2):116-120, March, 1981.

An incremental-dose combined oestrogen-progestogen oral contraceptive: cycle control and endometrial changes, by S. K. Khoo, et al. AUSTRALIAN AND NEW ZEALAND JOURNAL OF OBSTETRICS AND GYNAECOLOGY 20(3):168-171, August, 1980.

The influence of a combined oral contraceptive pill and menstrual cycle phase on digital microvascular haemodynamics, by J. E. Tooke, et al. CLINICAL SCIENCE 61 (1):91-95, July, 1981.

Influence of oral contraceptives of differing dosages on alpha-1-antitrypsin, gamma-glutamyltransferase and alkaline phosphatase, by B. Herbeth, et al. CLINICA CHIMICA ACTA 112(3):293-299, May, 1981.

Is the pill dangerous? by H. Seiden. TODAY p21, December 13, 1980.

Jaundice and heaptic hemangioma after ten years of oral
contraception and recent administration of triacetyloleandomycin [letter], by D. Meyniel, et al. THERAPIE
35(6):754-755, November-December, 1980.

Liver cell carcinoma in young women possibly induced by
oral contraceptives, by F. Amtrup, et al. ACTA OB-
STETRICIA ET GYNECOLOGICA SCANDINAVICA
59(6):567-569, 1980.

Liver function tests and low-dose estrogen oral contraceptives,
by J. Dickerson, et al. CONTRACEPTION 22(6):597-
603, December, 1980.

Liver rupture after prolonged use of contraceptive, by G.
Böttger, et al. ZEITSCHRIFT FUR DIE GESAMTE IN-
NERE MEDIZIN 36(3 Suppl):226-227, February 1, 1981.

Measurement by isotope dilution mass spectrometry of 17
alpha-ethynyloestradiol-17 beta and norethisterone in
serum of women taking oral contraceptives, by L. Siekmann, et al. BIOMEDICAL MASS SPECTROMETRY 7
(11-12):511-514, November, 1980.

Mortality in oral contraceptive users [letter], by M. P. Vessey,
et al. LANCET 1(8219):549-550, March 7, 1981.

The neurological complications of the pill, by H. Damasio.
MEDICAL TIMES 109(6):84-86+, June, 1981.

Nutritional deficiencies and the "pill". NURSES DRUG
ALERT 5:42-43, May, 1981.

Nutritional effects of oral contraceptive use: a review, by J.
L. Webb. JOURNAL OF REPRODUCTIVE MEDICINE
25(4):150-156, October, 1980.

Nutritional effects of oral contraceptives, by B. H. Robinson,
et al. ISSUES IN HEALTH CARE OF WOMEN 1(1):37-

60, 1978.

Ocular side effects through oral contraceptives, by R. Rochels, et al. GEBURTSHILFE UND FRAUENHEILKUNDE 40(8):713-715, August, 1980.

Oestrogen containing oral contraceptives decrease prostacyclin production [letter], by O. Ylikorkala, et al. LANCET 1(8210):42, January 3, 1981.

Oestrogen containing oral contraceptives, decreased prostacyclin production, and haemolytic uraemic syndrome [letter], by D. Hauglustaine, et al. LANCET 1(8215): 328-329, February 7, 1981.

Oral contraception and congenital abnormalities, by P. N. Kasan, et al. BRITISH JOURNAL OF OBSTETRICS AND GYNAECOLOGY 87(7):545-551, July, 1980.

Oral contraception and myocardial infarction revisited: the effects of new preparations and prescribing patterns, by S. A. Adam, et al. BRITISH JOURNAL OF OBSTETRICS AND GYNAECOLOGY 88(8):838-845, August, 1981.

Oral contraceptive and coronary thrombosis. Two clinicopathological cases, by R. Loire, et al. ARCHIVES DES MALADIES DU COEUR ET DES VAISSEAUX 73(4): 432-437, April, 1980.

Oral contraceptive and physiological variables, by L. D. Ostrander. JAMA 244:677-679, August, 1980.

Oral contraceptive hazards—1981 [editorial], by J. W. Goldzieher. FERTILITY AND STERILITY 35(3):275-276, March, 1981.

Oral contraceptive history as a risk indicator in patients with pituitary tumors with hyperprolactinemia: a case compari-

son study of twenty patients, by L. Teperman, et al.
NEUROSURGERY 7(6):571-573, December, 1980.

Oral contraceptive—induced chorea, by N. Kaplinsky, et al.
AMERICAN JOURNAL OF OBSTETRICS AND GYNE-
COLOGY 138(2):237, September 15, 1980.

Oral contraceptive-induced hepatic adenoma and focal nodular hyperplasia, by C. J. Bryant, et al. AUSTRALASIAN
RADIOLOGY 24(3):289-292, November, 1980.

Oral contraceptive risk found negligible. CHEMICAL AND
ENGINEERING NEWS 58:6, October 27, 1980.

Oral contraceptive steroid plasma concentration in smokers
and non-smokers, by F. E. Crawford, et al. BRITISH
MEDICAL JOURNAL 282(6279):1829-1830, June 6,
1981.

Oral contraceptive use and blood pressure in a community-
based cohort study, by C. H. Hennekens, et al. CIRCULA-
TION 62(3):III-306, 1980.

Oral contraceptive use and diseases of the circulatory system
in Taiwan: an analysis of mortality statistics, by L. P.
Chow, et al. INTERNATIONAL JOURNAL OF GYNAE-
COLOGY AND OBSTETRICS 18(6):420-432, 1980.

Oral contraceptive use and early abortion as risk factors for
breast cancer in young women, by M. C. Pike, et al.
BRITISH JOURNAL OF CANCER 43(1):72-76, January,
1981.

Oral contraceptive use and prevalence of infection with
Chlamydia trachomatis in women, by G. R. Kinghorn, et
al. BRITISH JOURNAL OF VENEREAL DISEASES 57
(3):187-190, June, 1981.

Oral contraceptive use: its risks and benefits, by T. G. Skillman. HOSPITAL FORMULARY 15:622-623+, August, 1980.

Oral contraceptive use, sexual activity, and cervical carcinoma, by S. H. Swan, et al. AMERICAN JOURNAL OF OBSTETRICS AND GYNECOLOGY 139(1):52-57, January, 1981.

Oral contraceptives, by G. J. Petursson, et al. OPHTHALMOLOGY 88(4):368-371, April, 1981.

Oral contraceptives and benign tumorous conditions of the liber, by R. Lesch, et al. RADIOLOGE 20(12):565-576, December, 1980.

Oral contraceptives and birth defects, by R. W. Smithells. DEVELOPMENTAL MEDICINE AND CHILD NEUROLOGY 23(3):369-372, June, 1981.

Oral contraceptives and breast cancer, by H. Jick, et al. AMERICAN JOURNAL OF EPIDEMIOLOGY 112(5): 577-585, November, 1980.

Oral contraceptives and cardiovascular disease, by J. E. Dalen, et al. AMERICAN HEART JOURNAL 101(5):626-639, May, 1981.

Oral contraceptives and cardiovascular disease (second of two parts), by B. V. Stadel. NEW ENGLAND JOURNAL OF MEDICINE 305(12):672-677, September 17, 1981.

Oral contraceptives and cardiovascular diseases, by M. Aosaki, et al. NIPPON RINSHO 38(10):4187-4195, October, 1980.

Oral contraceptives and the decline in mortality from circulatory disease, by R. A. Wiseman, et al. FERTILITY AND STERILITY 35(3):277-283, March, 1981.

Oral contraceptives and depressive symptomatology: biologic mechanisms. COMPREHENSIVE PSYCHIATRY 20(4): 347-358, July-August, 1979.

Oral contraceptives and liver disease, by D. Lockhat, et al. CANADIAN MEDICAL ASSOCIATION JOURNAL 124 (8):993-999, April 15, 1981.

Oral contraceptives and liver tumors, by R. Cavin, et al. SCHWEIZERISCHE MEDIZINISCHE WOCHENSCHRIFT 111(22):804-806, May 30, 1981.

Oral contraceptives and oral candidiasis, by G. Krekeler, et al. FORTSCHRITTE DER MEDIZIN 99(7):230-232, February 19, 1981.

Oral contraceptives and post-molar trophoblastic tumours [letter], by R. S. Berkowitz, et al. LANCET 2(8197): 752, October 4, 1980.

Oral contraceptives and responsiveness of plasma renin activity and blood pressure in normotensive women, by F. H. Leenen, et al. CLINICAL AND EXPERIMENTAL HYPERTENSION 2(2):197-211, February, 1980.

Oral contraceptives and systematic lupus erythemtosus, by M. Garovich, et al. ARTHRITIS AND RHEUMATISM 23(12):1396-1398, 1980.

Oral contraceptives: effects on carbohydrate metabolism, insulin like activity and histology of the pancreas, by H. J. Kulkarni, et al. HORMONE AND METABOLIC RESEARCH 12(10):497-504, October, 1980.

Oral contraceptives. Liver diseases in 25 million women [news], by E. Roseau. NOUVELLE PRESSE MEDICALE 9(33):2296, September 20, 1980.

Oral contraceptives: misunderstood etiology of erythema

nodosum, by G. Beaucaire, et al. SEMAINES DES HO-
PITAUX DE PARIS 56(33-36):1426-1428, September 18-
25, 1980.

Oral contraceptives, side effects and drug interactions, by S.
E. Thomas. EAST AFRICAN MEDICAL JOURNAL 57
(12):816-821, December, 1980.

Oral steroid contraception in hyperprolactinemia, by W.
Völker, et al. GEBURTSHILFE UND FRAUENHEIL-
KUNDE 41(3):199-203, March, 1981.

Outcome of pregnancies following the use of oral contraceptives, by E. Alberman, et al. INTERNATIONAL JOUR-
NAL OF EPIDEMIOLOGY 9(3):207-213, September,
1980.

Periportal sinusoidal dilatation, inflammatory bowel disease,
and the contraceptive pill, by M. Camilleri, et al. GAS-
TROENTEROLOGY 80(4):810-815, April, 1981.

Pill's dangers don't go away, by J. Seligmann. NEWSWEEK
98:54, August 31, 1981.

Plasma tocopherol and lipid levels in pregnancy and oral contraceptive users, by V. Jagadeesan, et al. BRITISH JOUR-
NAL OF OBSTETRICS AND GYNAECOLOGY 87(10):
903-907, October, 1980.

Poll reveals mixed feelings on abortion in U.S. OUR SUN-
DAY VISITOR 70:7, June 21, 1981.

Possible association of angiosarcoma with oral contraceptive
agents, by E. C. Shi, et al. MEDICAL JOURNAL OF
AUSTRALIA 1(9):473-474, May 2, 1981.

Prevention of recurrent menstrual psychosis by an oral contraceptive, by A. Felthouse. AMERICAN JOURNAL OF
PSYCHIATRY 137(2):245-246, 1980.

Primary hepatocellular carcinoma developing in a female patient on long term oral contraceptives—a case report, by C. J. Oon, et al. ANNALS OF THE ACADEMY OF MEDICINE, SINGAPORE 9(3):402-404, July, 1980.

Primary malignant tumour of the liver associated with the ingestion of oral contraceptives, by J. Leclere, et al. NOUVELLE PRESSE MEDICALE 8(5):346-349, January 27, 1979.

Probable stenocardial effects of combined oral contraceptives, by G. Colucci, et al. MINERVA MEDICA 71(42):3123-3130, October 31, 1980.

Problem patients and the 'pill', by F. M. Graham. DRUGS 21(2):152-156, February, 1981.

Prolonged pill use, many sex partners may lead to cervical cancer or precursors, studies find. FAMILY PLANNING PERSPECTIVES 13:45-46, January-February, 1981.

'Prolonged pregnancy' after oral contraceptive therapy, by G. J. Ratten. MEDICAL JOURNAL OF AUSTRALIA 1(12): 641-642, June 13, 1981.

Prospective carbohydrate metabolism studies in women using a low-estrogen oral contraceptive for one year, by W. N. Spellacy, et al. JOURNAL OF REPRODUCTIVE MEDICINE 26(6):295-298, June, 1981.

Psychosis associated with oral contraceptive-induced chorea, by I. Sale, et al. MEDICAL JOURNAL OF AUSTRALIA 1(2):79-80, January 24, 1981.

Rapid fibrinolysis, augmented Hageman factor (factor XII) titers, and decreased C1 esterase inhibitor titers in women taking oral contraceptives, by E. M. Gordon, et al. JOURNAL OF LABORATORY AND CLINICAL MEDICINE 96(5):762-769, November, 1980.

Renin substrate, active and acid-activatable renin concentrations in human plasma and endometrium during menstrual cycles controlled by oral contraceptive preparations, by I. R. Johnson. BRITISH JOURNAL OF OBSTETRICS AND GYNAECOLOGY 87(10):883-888, October, 1980.

Rise in female-initiated sexual activity at ovulation and its suppression by oral contraceptives, by D. Adams. THE NEW ENGLAND JOURNAL OF MEDICINE November 23, 1978.

Risk of carcinogenesis among pill users, by N. N. Chowdhury. JOURNAL OF THE INDIAN MEDICAL ASSOCIATION 74(5):98-99, March 1, 1980.

Risk of myocardial infarction in relation to current and discontinued use of oral contraceptives, by D. Slone, et al. NEW ENGLAND JOURNAL OF MEDICINE 305(8): 420-424, August 20, 1981.

Ruptured benign hepatic tumors. Influence of oral contraception (apropos of two cases), by G. Grall, et al. LILLE MEDICAL 25(10):569-573, December, 1980.

Reversal of long-standing renal insufficiency by captopril in a patient with relapsing hemolytic uremic syndrome due to an oral contraceptive, by S. J. Hoorntje, et al. ANNALS OF INTERNAL MEDICINE 94(3):355-357, March, 1981.

Role of angiotensin II in oral contraceptive hypertension in anesthetized rats, by D. H. Stubbs, et al. LIFE SCIENCES 27(5):435-440, August 4, 1980.

Serum levels of ethinylestradiol following its ingestion alone or in oral contraceptive formulations, by P. F. Brenner, et al. CONTRACEPTION 22(1):85-95, July, 1980.

Side effects of oral contraceptives, by O. Blaskova, et al.

BRATISLAVSKE LEKARSKE LISTY 75(2):167-172, February, 1981.

Spontaneous resolution of oral-contraceptive-associated liver tumour, by R. R. Penkava, et al. JOURNAL OF COMPUTER ASSISTED TOMOGRAPHY 5(1):102-103, February, 1981.

Study of blood pressure in women taking oral contraceptives, by K. A. Bano, et al. JPMA 30(7):157-159, July, 1980.

A study of interaction of low-dose combination oral contraceptive with ampicillin and metronidazole, by J. V. Joshi, et al. CONTRACEPTION 22(6):643-652, December, 1980.

A study of interaction of a low-dose combination oral contraceptive with anti-tubercular drugs, by J. V. Joshi, et al. CONTRACEPTION 21(6):617-629, June, 1980.

A study of postpill amenorrhea, by R. Chatterjee, et al. INTERNATIONAL JOURNAL OF GYNAECOLOGY AND OBSTETRICS 18(2):113-114, September-October, 1980.

Teratogenic hazards of oral contraceptives analyzed in a national malformation register, by E. Savolainen, et al. AMERICAN JOURNAL OF OBSTETRICS AND GYNECOLOGY 140(5):521-524, July, 1981.

Tetracycline and oral contraceptives [letter], by R. J. Coskey. JOURNAL OF THE AMERICAN ACADEMY OF DERMATOLOGY 5(2):222, August, 1981.

Thrombin inhibitors in women on oral contraceptives, by E. Guagnellini, et al. ACTA HAEMATOLOGICA 65(3):205-210, 1981.

Thrombosis and oral contraception, by K. D. MacRae. BRIT-

CONTRACEPTIVES: FEMALE: ORAL: COMPLICATIONS

ISH JOURNAL OF HOSPITAL MEDICINE 24(5):438-440+, November, 1980.

Transient postoperative hypertension: role of obesity and oral contraceptives [letter] , by L. H. Honoré. JOURNAL OF THE ROYAL SOCIETY OF MEDICINE 72(7):543, July, 1979.

Two cases of benign liver tumour in women on oral contraceptives, by J. Dauplat, et al. JOURNAL DE CHIRURGIE 116(11):651-657, November, 1979.

Vascular thrombosis and oral contraceptives—a risk correlated study, by V. Beaumont, et al. JOURNAL OF MEDICINE 12(1):51-61, 1981.

Who says oral contraceptives are safe? [misleading claims of safety in drug industry press releases] , by B. O'Malley. NATION 232:170-172, February 14, 1981.

CONTRACEPTIVES: FEMALE: ORAL: THERAPEUTIC USE
Characteristics of lipoprotein metabolic disorders during treatment with oral contraceptives, by V. N. Titov, et al. FARMAKOLOGIYA I TOKSIKOLOGIYA 43(3):345-348, May-June, 1980.

Impairment of antipyrine clearance with low-dose oral contraceptive steroid therapy, by D. R. Abernethy. CLINICAL RESEARCH 28(3):621A, 1980.

Vaginal chemoprophylaxis in the reduction of reinfection in women with gonorrhoea. Clinical evaluation of the effectiveness of a vaginal contraceptive, by C. H. Cole, et al. BRITISH JOURNAL OF VENEREAL DISEASES 56 (5):314-318, October, 1980.

CONTRACEPTIVES: FEMALE: POST-COITAL
A-nor steroids as post-coital contraceptives in the hamster with special reference to the transport and degeration of

CONTRACEPTIVES: FEMALE: POST-COITAL

eggs, by Z. Gu, et al. CONTRACEPTION 20(6):549-557, December, 1979.

CONTRACEPTIVES: FEMALE: SUPPOSITORY
A clinical trial of Neo Smapoon vaginal contraceptive tablets, by S. F. Begum, et al. CONTRACEPTION 22(6):573-582, December, 1980.

CONTRACEPTIVES: FEMALE: TECHNIQUES
Injectable contraception [letter], by H. Ratner. MEDICAL JOURNAL OF AUSTRALIA 1(11):598-600, May 30, 1981.

Irreversible contraception in women: a supplementary method of family planning, by R. Sudik, et al. DAS DEUTSCHE GESUNDHEITSWISSEN 35(45):1785-1794, 1980.

CONTRACEPTIVES: HERBAL
(see . . . CONTRACEPTIVE AGENTS: FEMALE)

CONTRACEPTIVES: MALE
Contraceptives—return of the condom, by A. Benoist. INFIRMIERE FRANCAISE (219):27, November, 1980.

The cultural context of condom use in Japan, by S. Coleman. STUDIES IN FAMILY PLANNING 12(1):28, January, 1981.

The effect of condom use on squamous cell cervical intraepithelial neoplasia, by A. C. Richardson, et al. AMERICAN JOURNAL OF OBSTETRICS AND GYNECOLOGY 140(8):909-913, August 15, 1981.

The relationship between contraceptive sex role stereotyping and attitudes toward male contraception among males, by S. Weinstein, et al. JOURNAL OF SEX RESEARCH 15(3):235-242, August, 1979.

CONTRACEPTIVES: MALE

Relationship between condom strength and failure during
use, by M. J. Free, et al. CONTRACEPTION 22(1):31-
37, July, 1980.

The use of condoms by VD clinic patients. A survey, by Y.
M. Felman, et al. CUTIS 27(3):330-336, March, 1981.

CONTRACEPTIVES: MALE: ORAL
Male "pill" blocks sperm enzyme [gossypol inhibition of
lactate dehydrogenase X], by T. H. Maugh. SCIENCE
212:314, April 17, 1981.

Male pill [gossypol's inhibiting effect on lactate dehydrogenase X]. SCIQUEST 54:4, May-June, 1981.

Male "pill" seen as vaginal spermicide [gossypol]. MEDICAL
WORLD NEWS 22:21-22, May 11, 1981.

CONTRACEPTIVES: METHODS
An alternative contraceptive method: fertility awareness, by
E. A. Magenheimer. ISSUES IN HEALTH CARE OF WO-
MEN 1(6):39-50, 1979.

Billings method of contraception in adolescents [letter], by
T. J. Silber. PEDIATRICS 66(4):645-646, October, 1980.

Birth control methods: the choice is yours. AMERICAN
BABY 34:37-38+, May, 1981.

Clinical performance and endocrine profiles with contraceptive vaginal rings containing a combination of estradiol
and D-norgestrel, by S. Mehta, et al. CONTRACEPTION
23(3):241-250, March, 1981.

Depo-provera: a critical analysis, by S. Minkin. WOMEN
AND HEALTH 5:49-69, Summer, 1980.

Depo-provera: new developments in a decade-old controversy, by R. B. Gold, et al. FAMILY PLANNING PER-

SPECTIVES 13:35-39, January-February, 1981.

Experience in a series of fimbriectomies, by S. Oskowitz, et al. FERTILITY AND STERILITY 34(4):320-323, October, 1980.

Experiences with a tampon-spermicide device, by E. W. Page. CONTRACEPTION 23(1):37-44, January, 1981.

Injectable contraception [letter], by J. R. Edwards. MEDICAL JOURNAL OF AUSTRALIA 1(12):651-652, June 13, 1981.

—, by H. Ratner. MEDICAL JOURNAL OF AUSTRALIA 1 (11):598-600, May 30, 1981.

Medullary infarction—was it depo-provera? by C. J. Oon, et al. SINGAPORE MEDICAL JOURNAL 21(5):717-719, October, 1980.

Methods of contraception, with special reference to sterilization [letter], by L. Lampé. ORVOSI HETILAP 121(39): 2422, September 28, 1980.

Perception of methods of contraception: a semantic differential study, by P. K. Kee, et al. JOURNAL OF BIOSOCIAL SCIENCE 13:209-218, April, 1981.

Psycho-somatic considerations in surgical contraception, by F. Berger, et al. GEBURTSHILFE UND FRAUENHEILKUNDE 40(5):448-455, May, 1980.

Regulation of implantation as a contraceptive method, by J. J. Hicks-Gómez. GACETA MEDICA DE MEXICO 116(7): 318-323, July, 1980.

Researchers give evidence of safety for low-dose OCs. DRUG TOPICS 124:27-28, October 17, 1980.

CONTRACEPTIVES: METHODS

Ultrastructure of human spermatozoa in the presence of the spermicide nonoxinol-9 and a vaginal contraceptive containing nonoxinol-9, by W. B. Schill, et al. ANDROLOGIA 13(1):42-49, January-February, 1981.

What do lovers whisper when the sexometer's on? 'I'll check my chip, dear' [computerized thermometer that signals if sex without fear of pregnancy is possible]. PEOPLE 15:129, April 6, 1981.

CONTRACEPTIVES: PARENTERAL
You and contraceptives, by D. Edmondson. PARENTS 56: 67-74, July, 1981.

CONTRACEPTIVES: STATISTICS
The benefit of the classification of oral contraceptives. Studies of 525 women taking oral contraceptives, by J. M. Wenderlein. MMW 123(23):957-961, June 5, 1981.

Breast cancer and oral contraceptives: findings in Oxford-Family Planning Association contraceptive study, by M. P. Vessey, et al. BRITISH MEDICAL JOURNAL 6282: 2093-2094, June 27, 1981.

Contraception and liberal medical acts. The results of a national enquiry carried out by INSERM 1974-1975, by B. Garros, et al. JOURNAL DE GYNECOLOGIE OBSTETRIQUE ET BIOLOGIE DE LA REPRODUCTION 9(8): 835-841, 1980.

Contraceptive habits in women between thrity and fifty years of age. A comparison of two periods, 1967-1969 and 1972-1974, by E. Bostofte, et al. ACTA OBSTETRICIA ET GYNECOLOGICA SCANDINAVICA 59(3):237-243, 1980.

A cross-cultural study of menstruation: implications for contraceptive development and use. STUDIES IN FAMILY PLANNING 12:3-16, January, 1981.

CONTRACEPTIVES: STATISTICS

Development of contraceptive prevalence surveys. POPULA-
TION REPORTS 9(3):M-163, May-June, 1981.

From the N1H: the 'pill' receives mixed reviews in latest report of Walnut Creek study. JAMA 246(10):1071-1072,
September 4, 1981.

Further analyses of mortality in oral contraceptive users.
Royal College of General Practitioners' Oral Contraception Study. LANCET 1(8219):541-546, March 7, 1981.

The R.C.G.P. oral contraception study [letter], by E. C.
Grant, et al. LANCET 1(8231):1206-1207, May 30, 1981.

A randomized, double-blind study of two combined oral contraceptives containing the same progestogen, but different estrogens. World Health Organization Task Force on
Oral Contraception. CONTRACEPTION 21(5):445-459,
May, 1980.

Sexuality and contraception. Studies of 420 university students concerning correlation between menarche, beginning of sexual activity and contraception, by M. Conti.
ANNALI DI OSTETRICIA, GINECOLOGIA, MEDI-
CINA PERINATALE 100(4):233-238, July-August, 1979.

The Walnut Creek Contraceptive Drug Study. A prospective
study of the side effects of oral contraceptives. Volume
III, an interim report: a comparison of disease occurrence
leading to hospitalization or death in users and nonusers
of oral contraceptives, by S. Ramcharan, et al. JOUR-
NAL OF REPRODUCTIVE MEDICINE 25(6 Suppl):345-
372, December, 1980.

CONTRACEPTIVES: TECHNIQUES
Biodegradable microsphere contraceptive system, by L. R.
Beck, et al. ACTA EUROPAEA FERTILITATIS 11(2):
139-150, June, 1980.

CONTRACEPTIVES: TECHNIQUES

Choice in the womb [abortion performed on mongoloid fetus while preserving life of the healthy twin], by M. Clark, et al. NEWSWEEK 97:86, June 29, 1981.

Clinical evaluation of injectable biodegradable contraceptive system, by L. R. Beck, et al. AMERICAN JOURNAL OF OBSTETRICS AND GYNECOLOGY 140(7):799-806, August 1, 1981.

CONTRACEPTIVES AND COLLEGE STUDENTS
Contraceptive attitudes and practices; a comparison of non-pregnant college females and those with problem pregnancies, by K. E. Lelm, et al. HEALTH EDUCATION 11: 39-41, September-October, 1980.

Knowledge and use of contraceptive methods by university physicians and medical students, by G. C. DiRenzo, et al. ANNALI DI OSTETRICIA, GINECOLOGIA, MEDICINA PERINATALE 100(4):213-232, July-August, 1979.

Parental support, locus orientation, and self esteem as they relate to contraceptive behavior of unmarried college students, by L. P. Weiser. DAI 42(2), 1981.

Sexuality and contraception. A study of 548 female university students, by M. Conti. MINERVA GINECOLOGIA 32 (11):1013-1018, November, 1980.

Trends in contraceptive use at one university: 1974-1978, by S. M. Harvey. FAMILY PLANNING PERSPECTIVES 12: 301-304, November-December, 1980.

CONTRACEPTIVES AND HORMONES
Anovulation syndrome in nulligravidae following intake of hormonal contraceptives, by R. Müller, et al. ZENTRAL-BLATT FUR GYNAEKOLOGIE 102(1):33-41, 1980.

Behavior of Butanol-extractable jodine in serum, during and after long-time application of hormonal contraceptives,

by G. Klinger, et al. ZENTRALBLATT FUR GYNAE-
KOLOGIE 103(1):31-35, 1981.

Biochemical-hormonal bases for the selection of contraceptives for oral use, by V. Cortés-Gallegos. GACETA MED-
ICA DE MEXICO 116(7):323-326, July, 1980.

Breast cancer in women who have taken contraceptive steroids, by P. N. Matthews, et al. BRITISH MEDICAL
JOURNAL 282(6266):774-776, March 7, 1981.

British pill studies stress importance of relation between pro-
gestogen content and vascular disease. FAMILY PLAN-
NING PERSPECTIVES 12(5):262-264, September-
October, 1980.

Characteristics of the course of periodic disease in women
who use hormonal contraceptives, by K. B. Akunts, et al.
AKUSHERSTVO I GINEKOLOGIIA (9):44-46, September, 1980.

Chronic treatment with the gonadotropin-releasing hormone
agonist D-Ser(TBU)6-EA10-LRH for contraception in
women and men, by S. J. Nillius, et al. INTERNATION-
AL JOURNAL OF FERTILITY 25(3):239-246, 1980.

Coagulation studies in Asian women using injectable proges-
togen for contraception, by F. H. Tsakok, et al. INTER-
NATIONAL JOURNAL OF GYNAECOLOGY AND OB-
STETRICS 18(2):105-108, September-October, 1980.

Contraception by progestational agents administered in
sequential form, by J. Barrat, et al. NOUVELLE PRESSE
MEDICALE 9(21):1491-1494, May 10, 1980.

Contraceptive effects of an agonist of luteinizing hormone releasing hormone: a long-term study on the female stumptailed monkey, by H. M. Fraser. JOURNAL OF ENDO-
CRINOLOGY 85(2):13, 1980.

CONTRACEPTIVES AND HORMONES

Cytological studies in women using different types of hormonal contraceptives, by A. D. Engineer, et al. JOURNAL OF THE INDIAN MEDICAL ASSOCIATION 74 (5):88-91, March 1, 1980.

Detection of N-acetylneuraminic acid with long-time application of hormonal contraceptives, by G. Klinger, et al. ZENTRALBLATT FUR GYNAEKOLOGIE 103(1):36-40, 1981.

Determination of trace elements in serum (Fe, Cu, Zn) and urine (Fe, Cu, Zn, Mn) as well as carrier proteins in hormonal contraception, by G. Klinger, et al. ZEITSCHRIFT FUR AERZTLICHE FORTBILDUNG 74(22):1077-1084, November 15, 1980.

Effect of contraceptive steroids on serum levels of sex hormone binding blobulin and caeruloplasmin, by S. Limpongsanurak, et al. CURRENT MEDICAL RESEARCH AND OPINION 7(3):185-191, 1981.

Effect of a low dose estrogen-progestogen oral contraceptive on lipids and lipoproteins, by H. Taggart, et al. IRISH JOURNAL OF MEDICAL SCIENCE 150(1):13-14, January, 1981.

Effects and side effects of hormonal contraceptives, by W. Carol, et al. ZEITSCHRIFT FUR AERZTLICHE FORTBILDUNG 74(3):97-104, February 1, 1980.

The effects of hormonal contraceptives on lactation: current findings, methodological considerations, and future priorities. STUDIES IN FAMILY PLANNING 12(4):134, April, 1981.

Effects of hormonal contraceptives on parameters of lipid metabolism, by W. Carol, et al. ZENTRALBLATT FUR GYNEAKOLOGIE 102(22):1273-1282, 1980.

336

Effects of oral contraceptive steroids on the thickness of human cornea, by P. S. Soni. AMERICAN JOURNAL OF OPTOMETRY AND PHYSIOLOGICAL OPTICS 57(11): 825-834, November, 1980.

Estradiol implants for conception control, by C. Nezhat, et al. AMERICAN JOURNAL OF OBSTETRICS AND GYNECOLOGY 138(8):1151-1156, December 15, 1980.

Exogenous estrogens and carcinoma of the endometrium: a critical analysis of the literature, by S. Franceschi, et al. ANNALI DI OSTETRICIA GINECOLOGIA, MEDICINA PERINATALE 101(6):397-403, November-December, 1980.

Hormonal contraception—side effects and surgical aspects, by G. Göretzlehner, et al. ZENTRALBLATT FUR CHIRURGIE 105(24):1601-1616, 1980.

Hormonal contraceptives cause depression? by J. M. Wenderlein. MEDIZINISCHE KLINIK 76(10):288-290, May 8, 1981.

Hormonal contraceptives of differentiated composition—effects on thrombocyte function, by M. Brandt, et al. ZENTRALBLATT FUR GYNAEKOLOGIE 103(11): 631-643, 1981.

Hypertension and hormonal contraceptives, by U. Retzke, et al. ZEITSCHRIFT FUR DIE GESAMTE INNERE MEDIZIN 35(21 Suppl):138-141, November 1, 1980.

Immune reactivity of women on hormonal contraceptives. Phytohemagglutinin and concanavalin-A induced lymphocyte response, by G. Gerretsen, et al. CONTRACEPTION 22(1):25-29, July, 1980.

Impairment of antipyrine metabolism by low-dose oral contraceptive steroids, by D. R. Abernethy, et al. CLINICAL

PHARMACOLOGY AND THERAPEUTICS 29(1):106-110, January, 1981.

Increased synthesis of aortic collagen and elastin in experimental atherosclerosis. Inhibition by contraceptive steroids, by G. M. Fischer, et al. ATHEROCLEROSIS 39(4):463-467, July, 1981.

Influence of environmental chemicals on drug therapy in humans: studies with contraceptive steroids, by A. M. Breckenridge, et al. CIBA FOUNDATION SYMPOSIUM (76):289-306, 1980.

Initial action of synthetic sexual steroids on serum-haptoglobin concentration, by G. Klinger, et al. ZENTRAL-BLATT FUR GYNAEKOLOGIE 103(1):41-45, 1981.

Injectable and oral contraceptive steroids in relation to some neurotransmitters in the rat brain, by T. T. Daabees, et al. BIOCHEMICAL PHARMACOLOGY 30(12):1581-1585, June 15, 1981.

Interindividual variation and drug interactions with hormonal steroid contraceptives, by D. J. Back, et al. DRUGS 21 (1):46-61, January, 1981.

Low serum creatine kinase values in contraceptive steroid users [letter], by U. Gupta. CLINICAL CHEMISTRY 27 (9):1624, September, 1981.

Luteolytic activity of luteinizing hormone-releasing hormone and D-serine (*tert*-butyl)-6-deglycinamide luteinizing hormone-releasing hormone ethylamide: a new and physiological approach to contraception in women, by A. Lemay, et al. INTERNATIONAL JOURNAL OF FERTILITY 25(3):203-212, 1980.

Menarche of young girls and tolerance of hormonal contraceptives—results of a field study of 33,000 cases, by J.

M. Wenderlein. ZENTRALBLATT FUR GYNAEKOLO-
GIE 102(17):974-980, 1980.

Oncological aspects of hormonal contraceptives, by I. V.
Bokhman, et al. AKUSHERSTVO I GINEKOLOGIIA
(4):3-5, April, 1981.

Pill and IUD [intrauterine device] discontinuation in the
United States, 1970-1075, by E. F. Jones, et al. FAMILY
PLANNING PERSPECTIVES 12:293-300, November-
December, 1980.

A prospective study of the effects of the progestagen content
of oral contraceptives on measures of affect, automatization, and perceptual restructuring ability, by A. Worsley.
PSYCHOPHARMACOLOGY 67(3):289-296, 1980.

Skin changes from taking hormonal contraceptives, by H.
Zaun. MEDIZINISCHE MONATSSCHRIFT FUR PHAR-
MAZEUTEN 4(6):161-165, June, 1981.

The sluggish gallbladder of pregnancy [editorial] , by S.
Cohen. NEW ENGLAND JOURNAL OF MEDICINE 302:
397-399, February 14, 1980.

Steroid contraception and hyperprolactinemia, by W.
Voelker, et al. ACTA ENDOCRINOLOGICA 94(234):
8, 1980.

A study of the meachnism of weight gain in medroxyprogesterone acetate users, by K. Amatayakul, et al. CONTRA-
CEPTION 22(6):605-622, December, 1980.

Thrombosis and sex hormones: a perplexing liaison, by S.
Wessler. JOURNAL OF LABORATORY AND CLINI-
CAL MEDICINE 96(5):757-761, November, 1980.

Transitory ischemic attacks, migraine and progestogen drugs.
Etiopathogenetic correlations, by G. Moretti, et al.

CONTRACEPTIVES AND HORMONES

MINERVA MEDICA 71(30):2125-2129, August 25, 1980.

Urinary bile acids in women treated with contraceptive steroids. A study using computerized gas chromatography-mass spectrometry, by P. A. Thomassen. ACTA OB-STETRICIA ET GYNECOLOGICA SCANDINAVICA 60(2):173-176, 1981.

Venous thrombosis of the upper extremity after hormonal contraception, by M. Kohoutek, et al. CESKOSLO-VENSKA GYNEKOLOGIE 46(4):302-306, May, 1981.

CONTRACEPTIVES AND NURSES
Nursing protocol to improve the effectiveness of the contraceptive diaphragm, by E. Gara. AMERICAN JOURNAL OF MATERNAL CHILD NURSING 6:41-45, January-February, 1981.

CONTRACEPTIVES AND PHYSICIANS
Ask a doctor [barrier methods], by C. Carver. CHATE-LAINE 54:24, February, 1981.

Knowledge and use of contraceptive methods by university physicians and medical students, by G. C. Di Renzo, et al. ANNALI DI OSTETRICIA, GINECOLOGIA, MEDICIN-A PERINATALE 100(4):213-232, July-August, 1979.

CONTRACEPTIVES AND POLITICS
The socipolitics of contraception [news]. JAMA 244(13): 1415, September 26, 1980.

CONTRACEPTIVES AND RELIGION
Un contexte nouveau por L'enseignement sur la contraception, by J. R. Quinn. LA DOCUMENTATION CATHO-LIQUE 77:1054-1058, November 23, 1980.

Contraception in a new context, by J. M. Russell. AMERI-CA 145:182-183, October 3, 1981.

CONTRACEPTIVES AND RELIGION

Most dissent from church line on contraception [Irish students], by J. Walshe. TIMES HIGHER EDUCATION SUPPLEMENT 413:5, October 3, 1980.

U. S. bishops cite dissent: ask contraception review, by P. Hebblethwaite. NATIONAL CATHOLIC REPORTER 16:1, October 10, 1980.

CONTRACEPTIVES AND YOUTH
Acute ischemic lesions in young women taking oral contraceptives. A report on 5 cases, by R. K. Danis, et al. JOURNAL DES GALADIES VASCULAIRES 5(4):273-276, 1980.

The adolescent and contraception: issues and contraversies, by A. Rosenfield. INTERNATIONAL JOURNAL OF GYNAECOLOGY AND OBSTETRICS 19(1):57-64, March, 1981.

Adolescent contraception, by A. K. Kreutner. PEDIATRIC CLINICS OF NORTH AMERICA 28(2):455-473, May, 1981.

Adolescent girls and contraception, by R. Frydman, et al. ARCHIVES FRANCAISES DE PEDIATRIE 37(Suppl 1): XXV-XXVIII, 1980.

Adolescent health services and contraceptive use, by E. Mudd. AMERICAN JOURNAL OF ORTHOPSYCHIATRY 48 (3):495-504, July, 1978.

Adolescent pregnancy, by P. J. Goldstein. JOURNAL OF THE INTERNATIONAL ASSOCIATION OF PUPIL PERSONNEL WORKERS 25(2):124-129, Spring, 1981.

Adolescent sexuality and pregnancy, by N. J. Burton. ISSUES IN HEALTH CARE OF WOMEN 2:43-51, April, 1980.

Alternatives to adolescent pregnancy: a discussion of the contraceptive literature from 1960 to 1980, by D. E. Greydanus. SEMINARS IN PERINATOLOGY 5(1):53-90, January, 1981.

Analysis of attitudes of Oklahomas of voting age toward sex education, teen contraception and abortion, by N. L. Turner. DAI 42(5), 1981.

Antecedents affecting contraceptive behavior of teenage females, by C. R. Griffin, PhD. DAI 41(11), 1981.

Appeals Courts decision reverses former minors' contraceptive position, by A. S. Kerr. MICHIGAN MEDICINE 79 (17):331, June, 1980.

Basilar artery occlusion, two angiographically demonstrated cases in young women using oral contraceptives, by W. A. Nolen, et al. CLINICAL NEUROLOGY AND NEURO-SURGERY 82(1):31-36, 1980.

Billings method of contraception in adolescents [letter], by T. J. Silber. PEDIATRICS 66(4):645-646, October, 1980.

The choice of a method of contraception during adolescence, by U. Gaspard. REVUE MEDICALE DE LIEGE 35(9): 377-390, May 1, 1980.

A comparison of unwed pregnant teenagers and nulligravid sexually active adolescents seeking contraception, by L. A. DeAmicis, et al. ADOLESCENCE 16(61):11-20, Spring, 1981.

Contraception and adolescent pregnancy, by C. A. Burbach. JOGN NURSING 9(5):319-323, September-October, 1980.

Contraception and the under-16s [news]. BRITISH MEDI-

CAL JOURNAL 281(6235):318, July 26, 1980.

Contraception in adolescence, by R. Gagné, et al. UNION MEDICALE DU CANADA 110(3):197-200, March, 1981.

Contraception with Monogest in young women, by M. Chalupa. CESKOSLOVENSKA GYNEKOLOGIE 46(4): 300-301, May, 1981.

Contraceptive ban on under 16s in care condemned, by D. Spencer. TIMES EDUCATIONAL SUPPLEMENT 3369: 3, January 16, 1981.

Contraceptive bheavior in adolescence: a decision-making perspective, by M. J. Rogel, et al. JOURNAL OF YOUTH AND ADOLESCENCE 9:491-506, December, 1980.

Contraceptive embarrassment and contraceptive behavior among young single women, by E. S. Herold. JOURNAL OF YOUTH AND ADOLESCENCE 10:233-242, June, 1981.

Contraceptive services for adolescents: an overview, by J. G. Dryfoos, et al. FAMILY PLANNING PERSPECTIVES 10(4):223-233, 1978.

Coping with contraception: a cognitive behavioral approach to prevention of unwanted teenage pregnancy, by L. D. Gilchrist, PhD. DAI 41(1-2), 1981.

The distribution of contraceptives to unemancipated minors: does a parent have a constitutional right to be notified? by J. L. Rue. KENTUCKY LAW JOURNAL 69(2):436-452, 1980-1981.

Effects of oral contraceptive agents on copper and zinc balance in young women, by M. G. Crews, et al. AMERICAN JOURNAL OF CLINICAL NUTRITION 33:1940-1945, September, 1980.

The impact of early use of prescription contraceptives on reducing premarital teenage pregnancies, by L. S. Zabin. FAMILY PLANNING PERSPECTIVES 13:72-74, March-April, 1981.

The moral development of black adolescents and its relationship to contraceptive use, by B. Fawcett. DAI 42(5), 1981.

Parent and peer influence on sexual behavior, contraceptive use, and pregnancy experience of young women, by F. Shah, et al. JOURNAL OF MARRIAGE AND THE FAMILY 43:339-348, May, 1981.

Perceived side effects of oral contraceptives among adolescent girls, by E. S. Herold, et al. CANADIAN MEDICAL ASSOCIATION JOURNAL 123(10):1022-1026, November 22, 1980.

Self esteem, locus of control, and adolescent contraception, by E. Herold. THE HOURNAL OF PSYCHOLOGY 101 (1):83-88, January, 1979.

Sexual behaviour and contraceptive use among socioeconomic groups of young women in the United States, by K. Ford, et al. JOURNAL OF BIOSOCIAL SCIENCE 13 (1):31-45, January, 1981.

A study of adolescent attitudes toward sexuality, contraception and pregnancy, by J. J. O'Leary. DAI 41(9-10), 1981.

FAMILY PLANNING
Antifertility activity of Montanoa tomentosa (Zoapatle), by D. W. Hahn, et al. CONTRACEPTION 23(2):133-140, February, 1981.

Establishing linkages between women's literacy programmes, status issues and access to family planning by R. Chhabra.

INDIAN JOURNAL OF ADULT EDUCATION 41(4):
6-9, April, 1980.

Family building: a social psychological study of fertility decisions. POPULATION AND ENVIRONMENT 3(3-4):210,
Fall-Winter, 1980.

Family planning [letter] , by E. Elliott. BRITISH MEDICAL
JOURNAL 281(6250):1287-1288, November 8, 1980.

Family planning and immigrants, by P. Thornton. NURSING
1(16):704-708, August, 1980.

Family planning and tuberculosis, by M. Prasad, et al. INDI-
AN JOURNAL OF PUBLIC HEALTH 24(2):92-98,
April-June, 1980.

Family planning: a cautionary tale, by M. Norman. HEALTH
VISITOR 54:61-62, February, 1981.

Family planning centers strong in drug stores, by E. Cheney.
AMERICAN DRUGGIST 181:78+, March, 1980.

Family planning: helping men ask for help, by B. M. Rappaport. PUBLIC WELFARE 39:22-27, Spring, 1981.

Family planning in the postpartum period, by W. E. Fuller.
CLINICAL OBSTETRICS AND GYNECOLOGY 23(4):
1081-1086, December, 1980.

Family planning in the year 2000, by T. Standley, et al.
WORLD HEALTH p10, February-March, 1981.

Family planning—the pill or natural method of birth control,
by H. Janisch. WIENER KLINISCHE WOCHENSCHRIFT
92(16):555-558, August 29, 1980.

Family planning realities in the third world. PEOPLE 7(4):
12, 1980.

Family size and sex preference of children: a biracial comparison, by V. V. Ruo, et al. ADOLESCENCE 16(62):385-401, Summer, 1981.

Infant mortality and family planning, by S. Y. L. Arora. JOURNAL OF FAMILY WELFARE 26:73-78, June, 1980.

Multivariate relationships between modernity value orientations and family planning indicators, by B. N. Mukherjee. POPULATION AND ENVIRONMENT 4(1):24, Spring, 1981.

NFP and ecological mothering, by G. G. Sweet. MARRIAGE 63:21, September, 1981.

NFP: the facts, by J. Marshall. TABLET 234:1197-1198, December 6, 1980.

NFP programs provide consumer choice, benefit hospital, by K. D. Daly, et al. HOSPITAL PROGRESS 61:56-58, October, 1980.

Networks and resource sharing in family planning libraries and documentation centres, by S. C. Dhir. INTERNATIONAL LIBRARY REVIEW 12(3):259-267, July, 1980.

Normative pressures in family planning, by E. Fried, et al. POPULATION AND ENVIRONMENT 3(3-4):199, Fall-Winter, 1980.

Planned parenthood, by M. A. Walsh. OUR SUNDAY VISITOR 70:3-4, June 7, 1981; 70:8-9+, June 14, 1981.

Planned parenthood and active family planning, by W. Fijalkowski, et al. PIELEGNIARKA I POLOZNA (3):12-15, 1980.

Planning status of marital births, 1975-1976, by J. E. Anderson. FAMILY PLANNING PERSPECTIVES 13(2):62+, March-April, 1981.

The politics of fertility control, by M. Simms. NEW HUMAN-IST 96:73-75, January, 1981.

Population control: free choice or coercion, by V. Ortiz. CHURCH AND SOCIETY 71:78-80, March-April, 1981.

Postpartum family planning, by S. Walker. NURSING MIR-ROR 153(9):xxii-xxiv, September 9, 1981.

The process of problem pregnancy counseling, by J. Urman. JOURNAL OF THE AMERICAN COLLEGE HEALTH ASSOCIATION 28(6):308-315, June, 1980.

Psychosocial support of residents in family practice programs, by J. K. Berg, et al. JOURNAL OF FAMILY PRACTICE 11(6):915-920, November, 1980.

Sielkundige implikasies van gesinsbe-planning, by H. Viljoen. DIE SUID-AFRIKAANSE TYDSKRIF VIR SOSIOLO-GIE 18:53-65, September, 1978.

Sterilisation as part of a family planning service [editorial]. LANCET 2(8239):186, July 25, 1981.

Teaching family planning management and evaluation skills, by M. E. Gorosh, et al. INTERNATIONAL JOURNAL OF HEALTH EDUCATION 23(2):107-115, 1980.

Value orientation family planning, by A. Bhowmik. SOCI-ETY AND CULTURE July, 1975.

AFRICA
Campaign to encourage family planning in Tunisia and some responses at the village level, by K. L. Brown. MIDDLE EASTERN STUDIES 17:64-84, January, 1981.

FAMILY PLANNING

AFRICA

Family planning in Africa: a 1981 People wallchart. PEOPLE 8:1 folded sheet insert, 1981.

Opinions and beliefs regarding family size among a population of Nigerian undergraduate students, by O. Ikpormwosa. JOURNAL OF THE AMERICAN COLLEGE HEALTH ASSOCIATION 28(5):287-289, April, 1980.

ASIA

East Asia review, 1978-1979, by J. J. Clinton, et al. STUDIES IN FAMILY PLANNING 11:311-350, November, 1980.

East Asia review 1978-1979. Introduction, by J. J. Clinton, et al. STUDIES IN FAMILY PLANNING 11 (11):311-316, November, 1980.

BANGLADESH

Attitude towards introduction of abortion as a method of family planning in Bangladesh, by S. K. C. Bhuyan. JOURNAL OF FAMILY WELFARE 27:46, March, 1981.

Consumer demand and marketing action plans for family planning in Bangladesh, by R. I. Molla, et al. JOURNAL OF MANAGEMENT STUDIES 18:219-230, April, 1981.

Family planning in Bangladesh, by S. Saito. JOSANPU ZASSHI 35(3):181-185, March, 1981.

Health and family planning services in Bangladesh: a study in inequality, by O. Gish. INTERNATIONAL JOURNAL OF HEALTH SERVICES 11(2):263-281, 1981.

FAMILY PLANNING

BARBADOS
Metropolitan dominance and family planning in Barbados,
by H. R. Jones. SOCIAL AND ECONOMIC STUDIES
26(3):327-338, September 3, 1977.

CHINA
China. Family Planning. Interpersonal communication,
by A. Goonesekera. MEDIA ASIA 7(2):105-109,
1980.

Family planning in the People's Republic of China, by Z.
F. Zhang, et al. INTERNATIONAL JOURNAL OF
GYNAECOLOGY AND OBSTETRICS 18(5):345-
347, 1980.

Planned birth in Tianjin, by K. C. Lyle. CHINA QUAR-
TERLY (83):551-567, September, 1980.

Planning births in China: what confidence can be placed
in local data, by L. Bianco. POPULATION 36:123-
146, January-February, 1981.

Population trends, population policy, and population
studies in China, by A. J. Coale. POPULATION AND
DEVELOPMENT REVIEW 7:85-97, March, 1981.

Recent developments in China's population planning, by
J. M. Maloney. PACIFIC AFFAIRS 54:100-115,
Spring, 1981.

COLUMBIA
Comparative evaluation of two methods of natural family
planning in Columbia, by J. E. Medina, et al. AMER-
ICAN JOURNAL OF OBSTETRICS AND GYNE-
COLOGY 138(8):1142-1147, December 15, 1980.

DEVELOPING COUNTRIES
The Calabar rural maternal and child health/family planning project. STUDIES IN FAMILY PLANNING 12

349

FAMILY PLANNING

DEVELOPING COUNTRIES
(2):47, February, 1981.

The campaign to encourage family planning in Tunisia
and some responses at village level, by K. L. Brown.
MIDDLE EASTERN STUDIES 17:64-84, January,
1981.

Demographic impact of family welfare programme in the
area covered by Rural Health Training Centre, Harsola
Indore (Madhya Pradesh), by R. K. Patodi, et al.
INDIAN JOURNAL OF PUBLIC HEALTH 24(1):32-
34, January-March, 1980.

Family planning knowledge, attitude and practice in the
rural areas of Sarawak, by C. K. Lam. JOURNAL OF
BIOSOCIAL SCIENCE 11(3):315-323, July, 1979.

Family planning programs and fertility decline [based on
a World Bank study of 63 developing nations], by R.
Cuca. FINANCE AND DEVELOPMENT 17:37-39,
December, 1980.

Family planning programs and fertility decline [develop-
ing countries], by R. Cuca. JOURNAL OF SOCIAL
AND POLITICAL STUDIES 5:183-190, Winter,
1980.

EGYPT
Use of nutrition surveys for family planning program
evaluation. The case of the Arab Republic of Egypt
nutrition status, by H. E. Aly, et al. JOURNAL OF
THE EGYPTIAN PUBLIC HEALTH ASSOCIATION
54(5-6):290-312, 1979.

FINLAND
Family planning in Finland in the 1970s, by O. Riihinen,
et al. KATILOLEHTI 86(1):8-14, January, 1981.

GUATEMALA
Determinants of fertility in Guatemala, by J. E. Anderson, et al. SOCIAL BIOLOGY 27:20-35, Spring, 1980.

Ethnic differences in family planning acceptance in rural Guatemala, by J. Bertrand. STUDIES IN FAMILY PLANNING 10(8-9):238-245, August-September, 1979.

HONG KONG
East Asia review 1978-1979, Hong Kong, by P. Lam, et al. STUDIES IN FAMILY PLANNING 11(11):316-320, November, 1980.

Hong Kong. STUDIES IN FAMILY PLANNING 11(11): 316, November, 1980.

INDIA
Adopters and non-adopters of family planning in an Indian village: a case study, by S. A. S. C. Mouli, et al. JOURNAL OF FAMILY WELFARE 27:30-38, March, 1981.

Nutrition, health, and population in strategies for rural development, by B. F. Johnston, et al. DISCUSSION 29:401-405, January, 1981.

Population policy in India: recent developments and current prospects. POPULATION AND DEVELOPMENT REVIEW 6(2):299, June, 1980.

INDONESIA
East Asia review 1978-1979. Indonesia, by S. Surjaningrat, et al. STUDIES IN FAMILY PLANNING 11 (11):320-324, November, 1980.

Family planning in the 1980's: challenges and opportunities; recommendations of the International Conference on Family Planning in the 1980's, Jakarta,

FAMILY PLANNING

INDONESIA
Indonesia, April 26-30, 1981. STUDIES IN FAMILY
PLANNING 12:251-256, June-July, 1981.

Indonesia, by S. Surjaningrat, et al. STUDIES IN FAMI-
LY PLANNING 11(11):320, November, 1980.

Indonesia plans ten years ahead. POPULI 8(1):14, 1981.

ISRAEL
Family-size limitation and birth spacing: the fertility
transition of African and Asian immigrants in Israel.
POPULATION AND DEVELOPMENT REVIEW 6
(4):581, December, 1980.

KENYA
Family size and family planning in Kenya: continuity and
change in metropolitan and rural attitudes, by T. E.
Dow, Jr., et al. STUDIES IN FAMILY PLANNING
12(6-7):272, June-July, 1981.

KOREA
Determinants of fertility differential in Korea, by E. H.
Shin, et al. SOCIOLOGY AND SOCIAL RESEARCH
65(2):211-225, January, 1981.

East Asia review 1978-1979. Republic of Korea, by T. I.
Kim, et al. STUDIES IN FAMILY PLANNING 11
(11):324-330, November, 1980.

Republic of Korea. STUDIES IN FAMILY PLANNING
11(11):324, November, 1980.

LATIN AMERICA
Developing countries. Family planning. Latin America.
Media, by F. Risopatin, et al. JOURNAL OF COM-
MUNICATION 30(4):81-89, Autumn.

Power in families, communication, and fertility decision-

FAMILY PLANNING

LATIN AMERICA
making [based, in part, on data from Latin American fertility surveys and anthropological studies]. POPULATION AND ENVIRONMENT 3:146-173, Summer, 1980.

MALAYSIA
East Asia review 1978-1979. Malaysia, by N. L. Aziz, et al. STUDIES IN FAMILY PLANNING 11(11):330-334, November, 1980.

Malaysia. STUDIES IN FAMILY PLANNING 11(11):330, November, 1980.

MEXICO
Population and migration problems in Mexico, by M. Alisky. CURRENT HISTORY 80:365-369+, November, 1981.

Population policy and public goods, by F. Miller, et al. PHILOSOPHY AND PUBLIC AFFAIRS 8:148-174, Winter, 1979.

NIGERIA
The use of socio-economic and accessibility information for improving MCH/FP services—the Nigerian case, by A. A. Udo. JOURNAL OF TROPICAL PEDIATRICS AND ENVIRONMENTAL CHILD HEALTH 26(5): 203-208, October, 1980.

PAKISTAN
Family planning in Pakistan: an analysis of some factors constraining use, by I. Sirageldin, et al. STUDIES IN FAMILY PLANNING 7(5):144-154, May, 1976.

THE PHILIPPINES
East Asia review 1978-1979. The Philippines, by M. B. Concepción. STUDIES IN FAMILY PLANNING 11(11):335-340, November, 1980.

THE PHILIPPINES
The Philippines. STUDIES IN FAMILY PLANNING 11 (11):335, November, 1980.

Predictors relating to implementation of family planning policy in the Philippines, by P. Klobus-Edwards, et al. JOURNAL OF SOUTHEAST ASIAN STUDIES 11:335-347, September, 1980.

Status of family planning in the Philippines, by A. Sugiyama. JOSANPU ZASSHI 34(8):568, August, 1980.

SCOTLAND
The estimation of costs and effectiveness of community-based family planning services [experience in the Grampian Health Board Area, Scotland], by A. Chamberlain. INTERNATIONAL JOURNAL OF SOCIAL ECONOMICS 7(5):260-272, 1980.

SINGAPORE
East Asia review 1978-1979. Singapore, by S. Devi, et al. STUDIES IN FAMILY PLANNING 11(11):341-342, November, 1980.

Quantitative analysis of some decision rules for family planning in an oriental society, by T. N. Goh. INTERFACES 11:31-37, April, 1981.

Singapore, by D. Sivakami, et al. STUDIES IN FAMILY PLANNING 11(11):341, November, 1980.

TAIWAN
Cohort consistency in family size preferences: Taiwan, 1965-1973. STUDIES IN FAMILY PLANNING 12 (5):229, May, 1981.

Taiwan, Republic of China, by C. M. Wang, et al. STUDIES IN FAMILY PLANNING 11(11):343, November, 1980.

TAIWAN

Trends in fertility, family size preferences and family planning practice-Taiwan, 1961-1980, by M. C. Chang, et al. STUDIES IN FAMILY PLANNING 12: 211-228, May, 1981.

Verbal judgments of Taiwanese family planning field workers about induced abortion, by G. P. Cernada, et al. AMERICAN JOURNAL OF PUBLIC HEALTH 71:420-422, April, 1981.

THAILAND

East Asia review 1978-1979. Thailand, by S. Varakamin, et al. STUDIES IN FAMILY PLANNING 11(11): 347-350, November, 1980.

Thailand, by S. Varakamin, et al. STUDIES IN FAMILY PLANNING 11(11):374, November, 1980.

UNITED STATES

Evolution of Margaret Sanger's family limitation pamphlet, 1914-1921, by J. M. Jensen. SIGNS 6:548-555, Spring, 1981.

Family planning practices among Anglo and Hispanic women in U. S. counties bordering Mexico, by R. W. Rochat, et al. FAMILY PLANNING PERSPECTIVES 13:176-180, July/August, 1981.

Family planning services in the United States, 1978-1979, by A. Torres, et al.. FAMILY PLANNING PERSPEC- TIVES 13:132-141, May-June, 1981.

Legal abortion, family planning services largest factors in reducing U. S. neonatal mortality rate. FAMILY PLANNING PERSPECTIVES 13:84-85, March-April, 1981.

Legal regulations as an instrument of family planning, by

FAMILY PLANNING

UNITED STATES
B. Colaković, et al. JUGOSLAVENSKA GINEKOLO-
GIJA I OPSTETRICIJA 20(3-4):124-126, May-
August, 1980.

Planned and unplanned births in the United States (1)
Planning status of marital births, 1975-1976, by J. E.
Anderson. FAMILY PLANNING PERSPECTIVES 13:
62-69, March-April, 1981.

The role of nurse practitioners as family planning clinicians in Tennessee, by H. K. Atrash, et al. JOURNAL
OF THE TENNESSEE MEDICAL ASSOCIATION 74
(1):15-20, January, 1981.

Social work as an integral part of family planning service
for low-income families: an example of U. S. experience, by K. T. Sung. INTERNATIONAL SOCIAL
WORK 21(2):23-32, 1978.

Statewide family planning programs in Tennessee—a 1980
update, by B. Campbell, et al. JOURNAL OF THE
TENNESSEE MEEICAL ASSOCIATION 73(9):629-
634, September, 1980.

Trends in contraceptive method of use by California fam-
ily planning clinic clients aged 10-55, 1976-1979, by
B. M. Aved. AMERICAN JOURNAL OF PUBLIC
HEALTH 71(10):1162-1164, October, 1981.

FAMILY PLANNING: ATTITUDES
Attitudes of 110 married men towards family planning, by J.
T. Arokiasamy. MEDICAL JOURNAL OF MALAYSIA
35(1):22-27, September, 1980.

Contraceptive choices for lactating women: suggestions for
postpartum family planning. STUDIES IN FAMILY
PLANNING 12(4):156, April, 1981.

FAMILY PLANNING: ATTITUDES

The decline of unwanted fertility, 1971-1976, by C. F. West-off. FAMILY PLANNING PERSPECTIVES 13:70-72, March-April, 1981.

Moral theology and family planning, by M. Reidy. FURROW 32:343-361, June, 1981.

Some psychological correlates of family planning among women, by P. Kumar, et al. INDIAN JOURNAL OF SOCIAL WORK 42:81-86, April, 1981.

FAMILY PLANNING: ECONOMICS
The costs and benefits of government expenditures for family planning programs, by M. Chamie, et al. FAMILY PLANNING PERSPECTIVES 13:117-118+, May-June, 1981.

Toward efficient allocation of fertility reduction expenditures, by B. Berelson, et al. EVALUATION REVIEW 5: 147-166, April, 1981.

FAMILY PLANNING: LAWS AND LEGISLATION
Blocking family planning [possible effects of Reagan administration proposals to replace certain categorical health and social welfare programs with block grants to the states, by J. I. Rosoff. FAMILY PLANNING PERSPECTIVES 13:125-131, May-June, 1981.

FAMILY PLANNING: METHODS
Ovulation method of family planning, by E. B. Martinez. AMERICA 144:277-279, April 4, 1981.

FAMILY PLANNING: NATURAL
The Billings method: natural family planning that works, by C. M. Anthony. OUR SUNDAY VISITOR 70:3, July 19, 1981.

Natural family planning III. Intermenstrual symptoms and estimated time of ovulation, by T. W. Hilgers, et al. OBSTETRICS AND GYNECOLOGY 58(2):152-155,

August, 1981.

—. The identification of postovulatory infertility, by T. W. Hilgers, et al. OBSTETRICS AND GYNECOLOGY 58 (3):345-350, September, 1981.

Natural family planning: periodic abstinence as a method of fertility control. SOCIAL JUSTICE REVIEW 72:185-187, September-October, 1981.

Natural family planning study validates treatment's success; St. Vincent Hospital, Green Bay, Wisconsin, by L. Dolack. HOSPITAL PROGRESS 62:58-61, October, 1981.

Natural family planning: women deserve the truth, by H. Hart. JOURNAL OF THE AMERICAN COLLEGE HEALTH ASSOCIATION 29(6):311, June, 1981.

A pastoral application of natural family planning, by T. G. Morrow. HOMILETIC AND PASTORAL REVIEW 81: 54-63, June, 1981.

A prospective multicentre trial of the ovulation method of natural family planning. I. The teaching phase. FERTILITY AND STERILITY 36(2):152-158, August, 1981.

FAMILY PLANNING: STATISTICS
Contraceptive prevalence surveys: a new source of family planning data. POPULATION REPORTS Series M(5): M162-200, May-June, 1981.

Estimating the need for subsidized family planning in the U. S.: obtaining imput from a special tabulation of the 1970 census, by J. Dryfoos. REVIEW OF PUBLIC DATA USE 1(4):1-9, October, 1973.

A family planning survey, by C. J. Carr. IRISH MEDICAL JOURNAL 73(9):340-341, September, 1980.

FAMILY PLANNING: STATISTICS

Patterns of child-bearing: a report on the World Fertility Survey [recent findings concerning developing countries; eight articles]. PEOPLE 7(4):3-20, 1980.

FAMILY PLANNING AND COLLEGE STUDENTS
Role of the pharmacist in the delivery of family planning services to college students, by M. C. Smith, et al. JOURNAL OF THE AMERICAN COLLEGE HEALTH ASSOCIATION 29:292-294, June, 1981.

Study of registered ayurvedic practitioners in five M.O.H. divisions and the Kandy district,—on their role in maternal and child care and family planning, by C. Sivagnanasundram, et al. CEYLON MEDICAL JOURNAL 24(1-2): 21-28, March-June, 1979.

FAMILY PLANNING AND MALES
Men and family planning, by B. Stokes. WORLDWATCH PAPER 41:50, December, 1980.

FAMILY PLANNING AND NURSES
The community health nurse and family planning, by N. stockton. NURSING NEWS 3:7, August, 1980.

The nurse practitioner in Planned Parenthood clinics, by M. Manisoff. FAMILY PLANNING PERSPECTIVES 13(1): 19-21, January-February, 1981.

FAMILY PLANNING AND PHYSICIANS
The psychiatrist in a family planning center, by G. Maruani, et al. ANNALES MÉDICO-PSYCHOLOGIQUES 136(6-8): June-October, 1978.

FAMILY PLANNING AND POLITICS
Blocking family planning, by J. I. Rosoff. FAMILY PLANNING PERSPECTIVES 13(3):125-131, May-June, 1981.

FAMILY PLANNING AND RELIGION
Natural law, the teaching of the church, and the regulation of

FAMILY PLANNING AND RELIGION

the rhythm of human fecundity, by J. T. Noonan, Jr.
AMERICAN JOURNAL OF JURSIPRUDENCE 25:16-
37, 1980.

Population growth and global security [critical of the lack of
American leadership in this area and of the role of the
Roman Catholic Church] , by S. Mumford. HUMANIST
41:6-25+, January-February, 1981.

FAMILY PLANNING AND YOUTH
The impact of family planning clinic programs on adolescent
pregnancy, by J. D. Forrest, et al. FAMILY PLANNING
PERSPECTIVES 13(3):109-116, May-June, 1981.

Survey of family planning services provided to teenagers in
five public health projects, by H. G. Green. PUBLIC
HEALTH REPORTS 96:279-285, May-June, 1981.

Telling parents: clinic policies and adolescents' use of family
planning and abortion services, by A. Torres, et al.
FAMILY PLANNING PERSPECTIVES 12(6):284-292,
November-December, 1980.

FAMILY PLANNING CLINICS
Computerized patient-flow analysis of local family planning
clinics, by J. L. Graves, et al. FAMILY PLANNING PER-
SPECTIVES 13:164-170, July-August, 1981.

Contraceptive use among family planning clinic personnel.
FAMILY PLANNING PERSPECTIVES 13(1):22, January-February, 1981.

Films for family planning programs. POPULATION RE-
PORTS (23):J493-522, January-February, 1981.

Relationship-centered family planning services: role of the
family counselor, by C. Figley. AMERICAN JOURNAL
OF FAMILY THERAPY 7(2):64-68, Summer, 1979.

The role of nurse practitioners as family planning clinicians in Tennessee, by H. K. Atrash, et al. JOURNAL OF THE TENNESSEE MEDICAL ASSOCIATION 74(1):15-20, January, 1981.

Starting family life and sex education programs: a health agency's perspective, by E. Wagman, et al. JOURNAL OF SOCIAL HEALTH 51(4):247-252, April, 1981.

FERTILITY AND FERTILITY CONTROL
Antifertility activity of DMA in hamsters: protection with a luteotropic complex, by W. L. Miller, et al. PROCEED-INGS OF THE SOCIETY FOR EXPERIMENTAL BIOL-OGY AND MEDICINE 166(2):199-204, February, 1981.

Antifertility activity of Lygodium flexosum, by B. B. Gaitonde, et al. INDIAN JOURNAL OF MEDICAL RE—SEARCH 72:597-604, October, 1980.

Antifertility activity of N-protected glycine activated esters, by J. H. Drew, et al. JOURNAL OF PHARMACEUTI-CAL SCIENCE 70(1):60-63, January, 1981.

Antifertility properties of Embelia ribes: (embelin), by M. Krishnaswamy, et al. INDIAN JOURNAL OF EXPERI-MENTAL BIOLOGY 18(11):1359-1360, November, 1980.

Does the career woman face infertility? by A. B. Kapstrom. SUPERVISOR NURSE 12:54-55+, July, 1981.

Effects of child mortality on fertility in Thailand, by M. Ha-shimoto, et al. ECONOMIC DEVELOPMENT AND CUL-TURAL CHANGE 29:781-794, July, 1981.

An elective course in fertility control, by J. B. Modrak. AMERICAN JOURNAL OF PHARMACEUTICAL EDU-CATION 44(3):266-269, August, 1980.

Epidemiology of human fertility [editorial] , by D. Schwartz. REVUE D'EPIDEMIOLOGIE ET DE SANTE PUBLIQUE 28(1):7-12, April 30, 1980.

An evaluation of an adolescent family planning program, by N. Ralph. AMERICAN JOURNAL OF EPIDEMIOLOGY 112(3):434-435, 1980.

Female work status and fertility in urban Latin America, by M. Davidson. SOCIAL AND ECONOMIC STUDIES 27: 481-506, December, 1978.

Fertility impairment in females—present status, by M. Prashad, et al. ENDOKRINOLOGIE 76(2):192-201, May, 1980.

Fertility status of men following vaso-vasostomy, by M. L. Mehrotra, et al. INDIAN JOURNAL OF MEDICAL RE-SEARCH 73:33-40, January, 1981.

How gossypol inhibits male fertility begins to emerge, by R. Rawls. CHEMICAL AND ENGINEERING NEWS 59:36-37, March 23, 1981.

It's time to take male infertility seriously, by C. W. Cooke, et al. MS MAGAZINE 9:89-91, March, 1981.

Labor; fertility and the workplace, by J. W. Singer. ENVI-RONMENT 22:5+, December, 1980.

Law of fertility regulation in the United States: a 1980 review, by S. L. Isaacs. JOURNAL OF FAMILY LAW 19: 65-96, November, 1980.

Measuring potential fertility through null segments: an exploratory analysis, by R. G. Potter, et al. SOCIAL BIOLOGY 26:314-329, Winter, 1979.

Methodological kit: monitoring statistics relating to the control of fertility and the provision of abortion, by J. R. Ashton. COMMUNITY MEDICINE 3(1):44-54, February, 1981.

Modern methods of regulating fertility, by S. I. Sleptsova. AKUSHERSTVO I GINEKOLOGIIA (10):5-8, October, 1980.

More children from the fit; less from the unfit, by M. C. Schwartz. OUR SUNDAY VISITOR 70:5, June 14, 1981.

On control over fertility regulation, by M. Salo. SOCIAL PRAXIS 7:191-203, 1980.

Positive pregnancy tests at Stanford: a follow up study, 1978-1980, by J. M. Dorman. JOURNAL OF THE AMERICAN COLLEGE HEALTH ASSOCIATION 29(6):286-288, June, 1981.

Spasmogenic effects of the anti-fertility agent, zoapatanol, by J. B. Smith, et al. LIFE SCIENCES 28(24):2743-2746, June 15, 1981.

Structure and activity relationships of alpha-chlorohydrin-bis-nitro benzoates an antifertility agents in male rats, by F. R. Rooney, et al. IRCS MEDICAL SCIENCE: LIBRARY COMPENDIUM 8(11):817-818, 1980.

Studies on non-steroidal antifertility agents—synthesis and antifertility effects of 1, 1-diphenyl-2-naphthyl ethylenes, by Y. L. Hu, et al. YAO HSUEH HSUEH PAO 14(12):715-719, December, 1979.

Surgical fertility regulation among women on the Navajo Indian reservation, 1972-1978. AMERICAN JOURNAL OF PUBLIC HEALTH 71(4):403, April, 1981.

Vaginal administration of 15-methyl-PGF2 alpha methyl ester for preoperative cervical dilatation. Task force on

prostaglandins for fertility regulation: the World Health
Organization. CONTRACEPTION 23(3):251-259, March,
1981.

Program applications. POPULATION REPORTS 9(3):M-
183, May-June, 1981.

HYSTERECTOMY

Abortion-sterilization by abdominal hysterectomy [letter].
AMERICAN JOURNAL OF OBSTETRICS AND GYNE-
COLOGY 139(1):115-117, January, 1981.

Cesarean hysterectomy for sterilization [letter], by N. D.
Diebel. AMERICAN JOURNAL OF OBSTETRICS AND
GYNECOLOGY 140(3):351-352, June 1, 1981.

Induced abortion by means of vaginal hysterectomy. Studies
on the indications and risks of this method, by K. W.
Schweppe, et al. ZENTRALBLATT FUR GYNAEKOLO-
GIE 102(24):1431-1436, 1980.

Is a hysterectomy justifiable to prevent post-tubal ligation
syndrome? by R. Maheux, et al. UNION MEDICALE DU
CANADA

Peripheral blood volume pulse associated with hot flashes following a hysterectomy—a preliminary case report, by F.
S. Fehr, et al. JOURNAL OF SEX RESEARCH 17:152-
156, May, 1981.

Preventive hysterectomy versus paragraphs 224 and 225 of
the german penal code, by G. H. Schlund. GEBURT-
SHILFE UND FRAUENHEILKUNDE 41(5):382-383,
May, 1981.

A 34 year-old woman with pelvic pain not relived by hysterec-
tomy and salpingo-ophorectomy for endometriosis, by F.
Ingersoll. NEW ENGLAND JOURNAL OF MEDICINE
June 12, 1980.

MISCARRIAGES

Adjuvant anticoagulant therapy in repeated fetal loss, by R. Langer, et al. HAREFUAH 99(3-4):65-67, August, 1980.

Ask a doctor: what are my chances of having a miscarriage? by C. Carver. CHATELAINE 54:26, June, 1981.

Coping with a miscarriage, by H. Pizer, et al. AMERICAN BABY 43:42+, September, 1981.

Incidence of miscarriage. BRIEFS 44:131-132, November, 1980.

Miscarriage; excerpt from forthcoming book *When pregnancy fails, families coping with marriage, stillbirth, and infant death*, by S. O. Borg, et al. CHATELAINE 54:46+, May, 1981.

Miscarriage: putting the myths to rest, by L. A. Michel. LIFE AND HEALTH 96:16-18, February, 1981.

Parity, miscarriages and abortions in women with epilepsy, by J. J. Zieliński, et al. POLSKI TYGODNIK LEKARSKI 35(18):655-657, May 5, 1980.

Pathogenic therapy of miscarriage in leukocytic imcompatibility, by V. V. Shcherbakova, et al. VOPROSY OKHRANY MATERINSTVA I DETSTVA 25(9):64-66, September, 1980.

When something goes wrong: an estimated 15 to 20 percent of all pregnancies end in miscarriage, by A. Pappert. HOMEMAKER'S MAGAZINE 16:54-58+, May, 1981.

SEX AND SEXUALITY
Contemporary attitudes toward sex, by M. Shivanandan. MARRIAGE 63:18+, November, 1981.

Secret synod proposition's rule on sex, by P. Hebblethwaite NATIONAL CATHOLIC REPORTER 17:19, November

7, 1980.

Sex on the dole, by C. Doyle. OBSERVER p33, July 26, 1981.

Sex problems in practice. Training and referral. Institute of Psychosexual Medicine, Margaret Pyke Centre, and Brook Advisory Centres, by P. Tunnadine, et al. BRITISH MEDICAL JOURNAL 282(6277):1669-1672, May 23, 1981.

Study finds sharp rise in teen sexual activity. YOUTH ALTERNATIVES 8(4):14, April, 1981.

What do teens know about the facts of life? by R. G. Amonker. JOURNAL OF SCHOOL HEALTH 50(9):527-530, November, 1980.

STERILIZATION
Coalitions can end sterilization abuse, by H. Rodriquez-Trias. WITNESS 64:10-13+, January, 1981.

Comparison of laparoscopic sterilization via spring-loaded clip and tubal ring, by G. Argueta, et al. INTERNATIONAL JOURNAL OF GYNAECOLOGY AND OBSTETRICS 18(2):115-118, September-October, 1980.

The decision for male versus female sterilization, by M. P. Clark, et al. THE FAMILY COORDINATOR 28(2):250-254, April, 1979.

Medical and social indications of sterilization, by L. Gagliardi, et al. MINERVA GINECOLOGIA 32(6):459-464, June, 1980.

The personal dilemmas of sterilization, by S. Wernick. BOSTON 72:116+, December, 1980.

The problem of sterilization, by E. Robecchi. MINERVA GINECOLOGIA 32(6):445-448, June, 1980.

Psychological aspects of sterilization, by N. Kapor-Stanulović.
JUGOSLAVENSKA GINEKOLOGIJA I OPSTETRICIJA
20(3-4):172-175, May-August, 1980.

Recent trends in sterilization, by M. Bone. POPULATION
TRENDS 13:13-16, Autumn, 1978.

Refertilization by implantation of both tubes, by T. Bobscheff. ZENTRALBLATT FUR GYNAEKOLOGIE 102
(19):1100-1104, 1980.

The refusal to sterilize. PROGRESS IN CLINICAL AND BI-
OLOGICAL RESEARCH 50:133-154, 1981.

Request for sterilization reversal, by K. G. Metz, et al.
NEDERLANDS TIJDSCHRIFT VOOR GENEESKUNDE
125(11):409-412, March 14, 1981.

Reversal of tubal sterilization, by R. M. Winston. CLINICAL
OBSTETRICS AND GYNECOLOGY 23(4):1261-1268,
December, 1980.

Sperm hazard, by B. Dixon. OMNI 3:18, November, 1980.

Sterilization. A preventive method for both men and women.
LEKARTIDNINGEN 77(48):4499-4526, November 26,
1980.

Sterilization under discussion, by G. Tassinari. MINERVA
GINECOLOGIA 32(6):473, June, 1980.

Surgical sterilization: now more popular than the pill. FU-
TURIST 15:75, December, 1981.

What bioethics should be, by T. F. Ackerman. JOURNAL OF
MEDICAL PHILOSOPHY 5(3):260-275, September,
1980.

A year ago this week . . . a case for more counselling about sterilisation. NURSING MIRROR 152:26, March 26, 1981.

Tubal lesions subsequent to sterilization and their relation to fertility after attempts at reversal, by G. Vasquez, et al. AMERICAN JOURNAL OF OBSTETRICS AND GYNE-COLOGY 138(1):86-92, September 1, 1980.

ASIA
The Hong Kong experience in promoting sterilization, by P. Lam. ASSOCIATION FOR VOLUNTARY STER-ILIZATION 4TH INTERNATIONAL CONFER-ENCE, SEOUL p90, May 7-10, 1979.

The use of the laparoscope in rural Thailand, by K. Chaturachinda. INTERNATIONAL JOURNAL OF GYNAECOLOGY AND OBSTETRICS 18(6):414-419, 1980.

AUSTRALIA
Sterilization operations in Australia, by T. Selwood, et al. MEDICAL JOURNAL OF AUSTRALIA 2(9):499-501, November 1, 1980.

CANADA
Sterilization and mental deficiency: survey among obste-tricians and gynecologists in Québec, by A. Dupras. UNION MEDICALE DU CANADA 110(6):538-544+, June, 1981.

CHILE
Sterilization of women in Chile. Results of two samples of Valdivia and Santiago, by D. Menanteau Horta. RE-VISTA CHILENA DE OBSTETRICIA Y GINECOL-OGIA 44(1):27-33, 1979.

FLANDERS
Voluntary sterilization in Flanders, by R. L. Cliquet, et al. JOURNAL OF BIOSOCIAL SCIENCE 13:47-62,

STERILIZATION

FLANDERS
January, 1981.

GREAT BRITAIN
If sterilization is oversold, or offered without careful
counselling . . . it can blight a woman's life, by P.
Toynbee. GUARDIAN p10, May 18, 1981.

KOREA
The recent demographic history of sterilization in Korea.
INTERNATIONAL FAMILY PLANNING PERSPEC-
TIVES 6:136-145, December, 1980.

UNITED STATES
The impact of laparoscopy in tubal sterilization in United
States hospitals, 1970 and 1975 to 1978, by H. B.
Peterson, et al. AMERICAN JOURNAL OF OBSTE-
TRICS AND GYNECOLOGY 140(7):811-814, Au-
gust 1, 1981.

WEST INDES
Laparoscopic sterilization—the Trinidad experience, by S.
Roopnarinesingh. WEST INDIAN MEDICAL JOUR-
NAL 30(2):90-93, June, 1981.

STERILIZATION: ATTITUDES
Moral aspects of sterilization, by D. G. Arosio. MINERVA
GINECOLOGIA 32(6):453, June, 1980.

Present views on sterilization, by L. Andolsek-Jeras. JUGO-
SLAVENSKA GINEKOLOGIJA I OPSTETRICIJA 20(3-
4):103-107, May-August, 1980.

St. Rita says no, by P. B. Donham. ATLANTIC INSIGHT 3:
18-19, April, 1981.

STERILIZATION: COMPLICATIONS
Complications of laparoscopic sterilization [letter] , by M. D.
Birnbaum. LANCET 1(8210):43, January 3, 1981.

STERILIZATION: COMPLICATIONS

Juridical considerations on the problem of sterilization, by E.
Germano. MINERVA GINECOLOGIA 32(6):449-452,
June, 1980.

Zur problematik der operativen sterilisation in Katholischen
Krankenhausern, by J. Gründel. STIMMEN DER ZEIT
199:671-677, October, 1981.

Tubal torsion, a late complication of sterilization? by R. E.
Bernardus, et al. NEDERLANDS TIJDSCHRIFT VOOR
GENEESKUNDE 125(18):707-710, May 2, 1981.

Unusual complication of laparoscopy [letter], by D. C. Mc-
CORMICK 1(13):667-668, June 28, 1980.

Uterine perforation during sterilization by laparoscopy and
minilaparotomy, by I. Chi, et al. AMERICAN JOURNAL
OF OBSTETRICS AND GYNECOLOGY 139(6):735-736,
March 15, 1981.

STERILIZATION: ECONOMICS
Bringing surgical sterilization, the number one contraceptive
method for married couples, to a low income rural population, by C. N. Wells. JOURNAL OF THE ARKANSAS
MEDICAL SOCIETY 77(6):226-228, November, 1980.

Eugenic sterilization: great for what ails the poor, by R.
Fleming. ENCORE 9:17-19, June, 1980.

STERILIZATION: FEMALE
Aspects of female sterilization, by P. Bhatia. EASTERN AN-
THROPOLOGIST 32(2):107-115, 1979.

Contraception and female sterilization, by A. J. Penfield.
NEW YORK STATE JOURNAL OF MEDICINE 81(2):
255-258, February, 1981.

Contraception by female sterilisation [letter], by A. F. Wright.
BRITISH MEDICAL JOURNAL 280(6231):1618-1619,

STERILIZATION: FEMALE

June 28, 1980.

The effects of sterilisation: a comparison of sterilised women with the wives of vasectomised men, by E. Alder, et al. CONTRACEPTION 23(1):45-54, January, 1981.

Elective sterilization in childless women, by L. Benjamin, et al. FERTILITY AND STERILITY 34(2):116-120, August, 1980.

Female sterilization, by J. M. Emens. PRACTITIONER 224 (1349):1177-1183, November, 1980.

Female sterilization: a centennial conference, by D. Wulf. FAMILY PLANNING PERSPECTIVES 13:24-29, January-February, 1981.

Female sterilisation—no more tubal coagulation [letter], by M. Sutton, et al. BRITISH MEDICAL JOURNAL 281 (6254):1564, December 6, 1980.

Follow-up of 375 sterilised women—the view from a general practice, by A. F. Wright. HEALTH BULLETIN 38(5): 194-198, September, 1980.

Indications for female sterilization in our surgical records, by D. Novaković, et al. JUGOSLAVENSKA GINEKOLO-GIJA I OPSTETRICIJA 20(3-4):148-152, May-August, 1980.

Laparoscopic and minilaparotomy female sterilisation compared in 15,167 cases, by S. D. Mumford, et al. LANCET 2(8203):1066-1070, November 15, 1980.

Recanalization and fistulization of the fallopian tubes are thought to be the causes of pregnancies following female sterilization [letter], by A. M. McCausland. AMERICAN JOURNAL OF OBSTETRICS AND GYNECOLOGY 139 (1):114-115, January, 1981.

STERILIZATION: FEMALE

Reversal of female sterilization, by C. F. Pill, et al. BRITISH
JOURNAL OF OBSTETRICS AND GYNAECOLOGY
88(3):314-316, March, 1981.

Reversal of female sterilization: comparison of microsurgical
and gross surgical techniques for tubal anastomosis, by
S. R. Henderson. AMERICAN JOURNAL OF OBSTE-
TRICS AND GYNECOLOGY 139(1):73-79, January,
1981.

Reversing female sterilization. POPULATION REPORTS 8
(5):97, September, 1980.

A review of women requesting reversal of tubal sterilization,
by J. Murray. AUSTRALIAN AND NEW ZEALAND
JOURNAL OF OBSTETRICS AND GYNAECOLOGY 20
(4):211-213, November, 1980.

Surgical sterilization in women, by V. Lehmann. MEDI-
ZINISCHE KLINIK 75(21):747-750, October 10, 1980.

STERILIZATION: FEMALE: COMPLICATIONS
Complications in sterilized women in Ljubljana, by D. Kos-
Gril. JUGOSLAVENSKA GINEKOLOGIJA I OPSTE-
TRICIJA 20(3-4):145-147, May-August, 1980.

Deaths following female sterilization with unipolar electrocoagulating devices. MMWR 30(13):149-151, April 10,
1981.

Ectopic pregnancy and tubal ligation [letter], by N. H.
Wright, et al. AMERICAN JOURNAL OF OBSTETRICS
AND GYNECOLOGY 139(5):611-612, March 1, 1981.

Endometriosis and the development of tuboperitoneal fistulas
after tubal ligation, by J. A. Rock, et al. FERTILITY
AND STERILITY 35(1):16-20, January, 1981.

Hemorrhage and cardiac arrest during laparoscopic tubal ligation, by J. W. Chapin, et al. ANESTHESIOLOGY 53(4): 342-343, October, 1980.

A retrospective survey of female sterilisation for the years 1968 to 1973. Analysis of morbidity and post-sterilisation complications for 5 years, by J. R. Newton, et al. CONTRACEPTION 22(3):295-312, September, 1980.

STERILIZATION: FEMALE: FAILURE
Extrauterine pregnancy after sterilization, by S. Ulbak, et al. UGESKRIFT FOR LAEGER 143(5):276, January 26, 1981.

Failure of an Irving tubal sterilization, by A. C. Wittich. OBSTETRICS AND GYNECOLOGY 57(6 Suppl):50S-51S, June, 1981.

Morphology of Fallopian tubes removed from a patient after failure of clip sterilization, by K. A. Walz, et al. ARCHIVES OF GYNECOLOGY 230(2):123-135, 1980.

Physician's liability for sequelae of failed sterilization, by H. J. Rieger. DEUTSCHE MEDIZINISCHE WOCHEN-SCHRIFT 105(33):1141, August 15, 1980.

Regeneration processes in human oviducts following sterilization procedures, by E. Philipp. MEDIZINISCHE KLINIK 76(1):15-19, January 2, 1981.

STERILIZATION: FEMALE: TECHNIQUES
Comparative morbidity following tubal ligation by abdominal and vaginal routes, by I. Gupta, et al. INDIAN JOURNAL OF MEDICAL RESEARCH 72:231-235, August, 1980.

Ectopic pregnancy after correct application of Hulka-Clemens clips [letter], by G. O'Neill, et al. MEDICAL JOURNAL OF AUSTRALIA 2(10):573, November 15, 1980.

Endoscopic tubal ligation, by M. Oliver. SURGICAL TECH-
NOLOGISTS 13:21-25, September-October, 1981.

Laparoscopic sterilization with the Falope ring: experience
with 10,100 women in rural camps, by P. V. Mehta. OB-
STETRICS AND GYNECOLOGY 57(3):345-350, March,
1981.

Late tubal patency following tubal ligation, by G. M. Grunert.
FERTILITY AND STERILITY 35(4):4-6-408, April,
1981.

Methods of female sterilization, by A. Omahen. JUGOSLA-
VENSKA GINEKOLOGIJA I OPSTETRICIJA 20(3-4):
135-139, May-August, 1980.

Methods of the sterilization of women in Norwegian hos-
pitals, by P. E. Bordahl, et al. TIDSSKRIFT FOR DEN
NORSKE LAEGEFORENING 100(34-36):2030-2032,
December 10, 1980.

Microscopic study of human fallopian tubes after laparo-
scopic sterilization, by J. Donnez, et al. JOURNAL DE
GYNECOLOGIE OBSTETRIQUE ET BIOLOGIE DE LA
REPRODUCTION 9(2):193-199, 1980.

Microsurgical reanastomosis of the fallopian tubes for reversal
of sterilization, by G. M. Grunert, et al. OBSTETRICS
AND GYNECOLOGY 58(2):148-151, August, 1981.

Microsurgical reversal of female sterilization [letter], by W.
W. Hurd, et al. FERTILITY AND STERILITY 36(1):122-
123, July, 1981.

Microsurgical tubal reanastomosis—the role of splints, by D.
R. Meldrum. OBSTETRICS AND GYNECOLOGY 57
(5):613-619, May, 1981.

New laparoscopic sterilization with exteriorization of tubes (cauterization, ligation): a preliminary report, by D. Muzsnai, et al. EUROPEAN JOURNAL OF OBSTE-TRICS, GYNECOLOGY AND REPRODUCTIVE BIOL-OGY 11(4):281-289, February, 1981.

Outpatient laparoscopic sterilisation: comparison between electrocautery and clip application, by G. Hughes, et al. AUSTRALIAN AND NEW ZEALAND JOURNAL OF OBSTETRICS AND GYNAECOLOGY 20(2):119-121, May, 1980.

Patient counseling model key to successful mini-lap [inter-view], by L. R. Levy. SAME DAY SURGERY 5(3):34-36, March, 1981.

Pregnancy risk following laparoscopic sterilization in non-gravid and gravid women, by I. C. Chi, et al. JOURNAL OF REPRODUCTIVE MEDICINE 26(6):289-294, June, 1981.

Quinacrine hydrochloride pellets: preliminary data on a non-surgical method of female sterilization, by J. Zipper, et al. INTERNATIONAL JOURNAL OF GYNAECOLOGY AND OBSTETRICS 18(4):275-279, 1980.

Stromal and epithelial changes in the fallopian tube following hormonal therapy, by S. E. Mills, et al. HUMAN PA-THOLOGY 11(5 Suppl):583-585, September, 1980.

A study of menstrual patterns following laparoscopic sterili-zation with silastic rings, by T. H. Goh, et al. INTERNA-TIONAL JOURNAL OF FERTILITY 26(2):116-119, 1981.

Surgical procedures for the sterilization of females (vaginal approach), by F. Rio. MINERVA GINECOLOGIA 32(6): 469-472, June, 1980.

Technical failures in tubal ring sterilization: incidence, perceived reasons, outcome, and risk factors, by I. Chi, et al. AMERICAN JOURNAL OF OBSTETRICS AND GYNECOLOGY 138(3):307-312, October 1, 1980.

The titanium/silicone rubber clip for female sterilization, by G. M. Filshie, et al. BRITISH JOURNAL OF OBSTETRICS AND GYNAECOLOGY 88(6):655-662, June, 1981.

Tubal anastomosis after tubectomy, by R. Chandra. JOURNAL OF THE INDIAN MEDICAL ASSOCIATION 76 (3):41-43, February 1, 1981.

Tubal ligation: good medicine? Good morality? by J. R. Connery. LINACRE 48:112-114, May, 1981.

Tubal occlusion by laparoscopy with unipolar current, by J. D. Ortiz Mariscal, et al. GINECOLOGIA Y OBSTETRICIA DE MEXICO 48(287):191-197, September, 1980.

Tubal patency following 'uchida' tubal ligation, by R. J. Stock. OBSTETRICS AND GYNECOLOGY 56(4):521-525, October, 1980.

Tubal ring sterilization: experience with 10,086 cases, by S. D. Mumford, et al. OBSTETRICS AND GYNECOLOGY 57(2):150-157, February, 1981.

Tubal sterilization by bipolar laparoscopy: report of 232 cases, by J. S. Seiler, et al. OBSTETRICS AND GYNECOLOGY 58(1):92-95, July, 1981.

Vaginal tubal ligation, by D. B. Stephens. SOUTHERN MEDICAL JOURNAL 73(12):1578-1580, December, 1980.

STERILIZATION: LAWS AND LEGISLATION
Damages for wrongful conception: Doiron v. Orr, by J. E. Bickenbach. UNIVERSITY OF WESTERN ONTARIO LAW REVIEW 18:493-503, December, 1980.

STERILIZATION: LAWS AND LEGISLATION

The importance of clinical investigation in laparoscopy, by
L. Keith. JOURNAL OF REPRODUCTIVE MEDICINE
24(6):236-238, June, 1980.

Legal statutes on sterilization, by K. Zupančič. JUGOSLA-
VENSKA GINEKOLOGIJA I OPSTETRICIJA 20(3-4):
108-111, May-August, 1980.

Sterilization of men and women according to present regulations with particular emphasis on the Vojvodina region,
by B. Berić, et al. JUGOSLAVENSKA GINEKOLOGIJA
I OPSTETRICIJA 20(3-4):117-120, May-August, 1980.

Sterilization of the mentally retarded: a decision for the
courts, by G. J. Annas. HASTINGS CENTER REPORT
11:18-19, August, 1981.

The status of sterilization in proposed legislation in Serbia,
by M. Husar. JUGOSLAVENSKA GINEKOLOGIJA I
OPSTETRICIJA 20(3-4):112-116, May-August, 1980.

STERILIZATION: MORTALITY AND MORTALITY STATISTICS
Mortality risk associated with female sterilization, by J. M.
Aubert, et al. INTERNATIONAL JOURNAL OF GYY-
NAECOLOGY AND OBSTETRICS 18(6):406-410, 1980.

STERILIZATION: RESEARCH
Effect of chemical sterilization on the sexual functions of
male mosquitoes, by N. F. Zakharova, et al. MEDITSIN-
SKAIA PARAZITOLOGIIA I PARAZITARNYE
BOLEZNI 50(3):56-62, May-June, 1981.

Immunological sterilization of male dogs by BCG, by R. K.
Naz, et al. INTERNATIONAL JOURNAL OF ANDROL-
OGY 4(1):111-128, February, 1981.

Morphological alterations of rabbit oviducts after ligation of
the isthmus or ampulla, by D. Bernhardt-Huth, et al.
ARCHIVES OF GYNECOLOGY 229(3):167-176, 1980.

STERILIZATION: RESEARCH

Morphology of rabbit oviduct after microsurgical techniques
for reanastomosis of the isthmus or ampulla, by D.
Bernhardt-Huth, et al. ARCHIVES OF GYNECOLOGY
230(3):251-262, 1981.

Preliminary results of experimental reanastomosis of uterine
horns of laboratory rats after sterilization, by M. Bujas, et
al. JUGOSLAVENSKA GINEKOLOGIJA I OPSTETRICI
JA 20(3-4):157-162, May-August, 1980.

STERILIZATION: RURAL
Bringing surgical sterilization, the number one contraceptive
method for married couples, to a low income rural population, by C. N. Wells. JOURNAL OF THE ARKANSAS
MEDICAL SOCIETY 77(6):226-228, November, 1980.

STERILIZATION: STATISTICS
CDC's surveillance of surgical sterilization: objectives and
methods of data collection, by J. C. Smith. PUBLIC
HEALTH REPORTS 96:357-362, July-Agust, 1981.

Tubal ligation via laparoscope: report of 84 cases, by G. Y.
Fan. CHUNG HUA FU CHAN KO TSA CHIH 15(2):
110-111, 1980.

Views on sterilization of the Stage I Commission on Abortion
in Ljubljana, by M. Maček. JUGOSLAVENSKA GINE-
KOLOGIJA I OPSTETRICIJA 20(3-4):127-131, May-
August, 1980.

STERILIZATION: TECHNIQUES
Clip sterilization [letter], by C. S. Vear. MEDICAL JOUR-
NAL OF AUSTRALIA 2(2):96, July 26, 1980.

Experiences with 3120 outpatients sterilized by laparoscopic
tubal bipolar coagulation, by H. J. Lindemann, et al.
GEBURTSHILFE UND FRAUENHEILKUNDE 41(7):
500-503, July, 1981.

STERILIZATION: TECHNIQUES

Laparoscopic sterilization under local anesthesia, by O. H. Jensen, et al. TIDSSKRIFT FOR DEN NORSKE LAEGEFORENING 100(34-36):2036-2037, December 10, 1980.

Laparoscopic sterilization using tubal rings and clips, by E. Borko, et al. JUGOSLAVENSKA GINEKOLOGIJA I OPSTETRICIJA 20(3-4):140-145, May-August, 1980.

Laparoscopic sterilization with Falope rings [letter], by H. J. Orford. SOUTH AFRICAN MEDICAL JOURNAL 59 (11):361, March 14, 1981.

Laparoscopic sterilization with the Hulka-Clemens clip. Review of 215 cases, by C. Lecart, et al. JOURNAL DE GYNECOLOGIE OBSTETRIQUE ET BIOLOGIE DE LA REPRODUCTION 9(2):253-259, 1980.

Laparoscopic sterilization with room air insufflation: preliminary report, by M. O. Diaz, et al. INTERNATIONAL JOURNAL OF GYNAECOLOGY AND OBSTETRICS 18(2):119-122, September-October, 1980.

Optimal terms for sterilization, by M. Ribič-Pucelj. JUGOSLOVENSKA GINEKOLOGIJA I OPSTETRICIJA 20 (3-4):132-134, May-August, 1980.

Results of refertilization with end-to-end anastomosis following microsurgical sterilization, by H. Hepp, et al. THERAPEUTISCHE UMSCHAU 37(6):473-478, June, 1980.

Spontaneous recanalization of tubes after surgical sterilization, by S. Bojović. JUGOSLAVENSKA GINEKOLOGIJA I OPSTETRICIJA 20(3-4):153-156, May-August, 1980.

Sterilization by minilaparotomy, by M. Beckmann. MEDIZINISCHE WELT 31(17):633-635, April 25, 1980.

Sterilization with Hulka clips, by E. Qvigstad, et al. TIDS-SKRIFT FOR DEN NORSKE LAEGEFORENING 100 (34-36):2033-2035, December 10, 1980.

STERILIZATION: TUBAL

The declining length of hospitalization for tubal sterilization, by P. M. Layde, et al. JAMA 245(7):714-718, February 20, 1981.

The effectiveness of different methods of laparoscopic tubal sterilization, by H. Frangenheim. GEBURTSHILFE UND FRAUENHEILKUNDE 40(10):896-900, October, 1980.

Failure of an Irving tubal sterilization, by A. C. Wittich. OB-STETRICS AND GYNECOLOGY 57(6 Suppl):50S-51S, June, 1981.

The impact of laparoscopy on tubal sterilization in United States hospitals, 1970 and 1975 to 1978, by H. B. Peterson, et al. AMERICAN JOURNAL OF OBSTETRICS AND GYNECOLOGY 140(7):811-814, August 1, 1981.

Laparoscopic tubal electrocoagulation for sterilization: 5000 cases, by K. Limpaphayom, et al. INTERNATIONAL JOURNAL OF GYNAECOLOGY AND OBSTETRICS 18(6):411-413, 1980.

Laparoscopic tube sterilization. Methods and their safety, by H. Frangenheim. GYNAEKOLOGISCHE RUNDSCHAU 20(Suppl 1):142-143, June, 1980.

Luteal function after tubal sterilization, by J. Donnez, et al. OBSTETRICS AND GYNECOLOGY 57(1):65-68, January, 1981.

Objections to tubal sterilization: what reversibility can and cannot overcome, by R. N. Shain. CONTRACEPTION 22(3):213-225, September, 1980.

STERILIZATION: TUBAL

The 100th anniversary of tubal sterilization, by A. M. Siegler, et al. FERTILITY AND STERILITY 34(6):610-613, December, 1980.

The potential impact of reversibility on selection of tubal sterilization, by R. N. Shain. CONTRACEPTION 22(3): 227-240, September, 1980.

Reversal of tubal sterilization, by R. M. Winston. CLINICAL OBSTETRICS AND GYNECOLOGY 23(4):1261-1268, December, 1980.

Surgical procedures for tubal sterilization (by abdominal approach), by G. Ferraris. MINERVA GINECOLOGIA 32 (6):465-468, June, 1980.

STERILIZATION: VOLUNTARY

The health implications of voluntary sterilization, presented at Association for Foluntary Sterilization, 4th International Conference, Seoul, May 7-10, 1979. p54.

Legal trends and issues in voluntary sterilization. POPULATION REPORTS 9(2):73, March-April, 1981.

Psychological aftermath of female voluntary sterilization: a comparison of client and agency perceptions, by E. Bisconti, PhD. DAI 41(9), 1981.

Voluntary sterilization. HUMANIST 41:57, January-February, 1981.

Voluntary sterilization. Medico-legal considerations, by M. Portigliatti-Barbos. MINERVA GINECOLOGIA 32(6): 454-458, June, 1980.

Voluntary sterilization, non-injury, justified injury or offense, by M. Del Re. GIUSTIZIA PENAL 85(1):50-63, 1980.

Voluntary sterilization of women and men in Croatia, by P.

STERILIZATION: VOLUNTARY

Drobnjak. JOGOSLAVENSKA GINEKOLOGIJA I OP-
STETRICIJA 20(3-4):121-123, May-August, 1980.

STERILIZATION AND CRIMINALS
Chapman would cut rapists off at the pass. LAW ENFORCE-
MENT NEWS 7(4):4, February 23, 1981.

Very troubling search, by R. Dolphin, et al. ALBERTA RE-
PORT 8:22-23, April 24, 1981.

STERILIZATION AND HOSPITALS
Discussion of 'Laparoscopic sterilization in a community hos-
pital with a two-year follow-up' given by Dr. Joshua
Tayloe, by A. C. Christakos. NORTH CAROLINA MEDI-
CAL JOURNAL 41(9):583-584, September, 1980.

The impact of laparoscopy on tubal sterilization in United
States hospitals, 1970 and 1975 to 1978, by H. B. Peter-
son, et al. AMERICAN JOURNAL OF OBSTETRICS
AND GYNECOLOGY 140(7):811-814, August 1, 1981.

Laparoscopic sterilization in a community hospital with a
two-year follow-up, by J. Tayloe. NORTH CAROLINA
MEDICAL JOURNAL 41(9):581-582, September, 1980.

Lincoln hospital: the sterile solution, by J. Conason. VIL-
LAGE VOICE 26(2):1+, February 18, 1981.

Tubal sterilization and later hospitalizations, by P. A. Poma.
JOURNAL OF REPRODUCTIVE MEDICINE 25(5):
272-278, November, 1980.

STERILIZATION AND THE MENTALLY RETARDED
In re Grady [NJ 405 A 2d 851] : the mentally retarded individual's right to choose sterilization. AMERICAN JOUR-
NAL OF LAW AND MEDICINE 6:559-590, Winter,
1981.

Law and the life sciences—sterilization of the mentally retarded: a decision for the courts, by G. Annas. HAST-ING'S CENTER REPORT 11:23-24, April, 1981.

New Jersey Supreme Court drafts strict guidelines for sterilization of mental incompetents: hospitals should require court authorization, by R. L. Schwartz. HEALTH LAW VIGIL 4(10):6-7, May 15, 1981.

The position of the Association of French Language Physicians of Canada on the sterilization of the mentally-deficient, by D. Robillard. CANADIAN MEDICAL ASSOCIATION JOURNAL 124(9):1214, May 1, 1981.

Sterilization and mental deficiency: survey among obstetricians and gynecologists in Québec, by A. Dupras. UNION MEDICALE DU CANADA 110(6):538-544+, June, 1981.

Sterilization and the retarded female: another perspective [letter], by L. S. Crain. PEDIATRICS 66(4):650-651, October, 1980.

Sterilization of the mentally retarded: a decision for the courts, by G. J. Annas. HASTINGS CENTER REPORT 11:18-19, August, 1981.

Sterilization of mentally retarded minors [letter]. BRITISH MEDICAL JOURNAL 281(6250):1281-1282, November 8, 1980.

Sterilization of mentally retarded minors [editorial]. BRITISH MEDICAL JOURNAL 281(6247):1025-1026, October 18, 1980.

Sterilization of the mentally retarded: position of the Committee of Deontology of the Association of the French Speaking Physicians of Canada [editorial]. UNION MEDICALE DU CANADA 110(3):280-281, March, 1981.

STERILIZATION AND THE MENTALLY RETARDED

Sterilization of the retarded [editorial], by L. E. Karp.
AMERICAN JOURNAL OF MEDICAL GENETICS 9
(1):1-3, 1981.

Sterilization and the welfare of the retarded [letter], by R.
Sherlock. HASTINGS CENTER REPORT 10(3):4+,
June, 1980.

STERILIZATION AND NURSES
Female sterilization: the nurse's role, by M. T. Stone. IS-
SUES IN HEALTH CARE OF WOMEN 1(5):45-60, 1979.

Is it right? 12,500 nurses speak out. How do your colleagues
view abortion, sterilization, and birth control? by R.
Sandroff. RN 43:24-30, October, 1980.

STERILIZATION AND YOUTH
Problems of sterilization in younger women—results of a ques-
tioning of patients wanting refertilization after steriliza-
tion within one year, by R. Grosspietzsch, et al. OEF-
FENTLICHE GESUNDHEITSWESEN 42(4):175-179,
April, 1980.

VASECTOMY
Behavioral response to vasectomy, by R. L. Vaughn. AR-
CHIVES OF GENERAL PSYCHIATRY 36(7):815-821,
1979.

Comparative popularity of vasectomy and tubectomy, by S.
D. R. Devi. JOURNAL OF FAMILY WELFARE 26:79-
93, June, 1980.

Contraceptive behavior of vasectomy acceptors, by S. S. R.
Grover. JOURNAL OF FAMILY WELFARE 27:3-15,
March, 1981.

Counselling for vasectomy, by B. Spencer, et al. PATIENT
COUNSELLING AND HEALTH EDUCATION 2:47-50,
2nd Quarter, 1980.

Doubts about vasectomies. TIME 117:63, February 9, 1981.

The effects of sterilization: a comparison of sterilized women with the wives of vasectomized men, by E. Alder, et al. CONTRACEPTION 23(1):45-54, January, 1981.

Factors influencing the outcome of vasectomy reversal, by H. A. Bagshaw, et al. BRITISH JOURNAL OF UROLOGY 52(1):57-60, February, 1980.

Folding-approximating clamp to simplify microvasovasostomy, by B. Strauch. UROLOGY 16(3):295-296, September, 1980.

Improved results of vasovasostomy after sparing of nerves during vasectomy, by P. C. Esk, et al. FERTILITY AND STERILITY 35(3):363-364, March, 1981.

Microsurgical reversal of vasectomy, by D. C. Martin. AMERICAN JOURNAL OF SURGERY 142(1):48-50, July, 1981.

Microsurgical two-layer vasovasostomy. Simplified technique using hinged, folding-approximating clamp, by A. M. Belker. UROLOGY 16(4):376-381, October, 1980.

Microsurgical vasovasostomy: immunologic consequences and subsequent fertility, by A. J. Thomas, Jr., et al. FERTILITY AND STERILITY 35(4):447-450, April, 1981.

Reversal of vasectomy and the treatment of male infertility. Role of microsurgery, vasoepidedymostomy, and pressure-induced changes of vasectomy, by S. J. Silber. UROLOGIE CLINICS OF NORTH AMERICA 8(1):53-62, February, 1981.

Reversal of vasectomy. A simple procedure, by G. D. Burfield, et al. AUSTRALIAN FAMILY PHYSICIAN 10(2):94-95, February, 1981.

VASECTOMY

Rhesus monkey study links vasectomy and atherosclerosis.
FAMILY PLANNING PERSPECTIVES 12:311-313,
November-December, 1980.

Social and emotional aspects of voluntary childlessness in
vasectomized childless men, by R. H. Magarick, et al.
JOURNAL OF BIOSOCIAL SCIENCE 13:157-168, April,
1981.

A study of twenty-three cases of postvasectomy sterility
operated for recanalization, by D. K. Paliwal, et al. IN-
TERNATIONAL SURGERY 65(2):165-169, March-
April, 1980.

A study on motivational factors influencing sterilization
(vasectomy) in a mass family planning camp, by S. T. D.
Gopala Krishnan. JOURNAL OF FAMILY WELFARE
27:16-24, March, 1981.

Vasectomy [letter], by H. Klosterhalfen. DEUTSCHE MEDI-
ZINISCHE WOCHENSCHRIFT 105(22):786, May 30,
1980.

Vasectomy counseling and clinical social work, by H. Y.
Smith. HEALTH AND SOCIAL WORK 6:64-70, August,
1981.

Vasectomy reversal [letter], by E. LeBeck, et al. JOURNAL
OF UROLOGY 125(4):604, April, 1981.

—, by L. Taylor, et al. MEDICAL JOURNAL OF AUSTRAL-
IA 1(2):94, January 24, 1981.

Vasectomy reversal [editorial]. LANCET 2(8195 pt 1):625-
626, September 20, 1980.

La vraie nature de la vasectomie, by P. Sormany.
L'ACTUALITÉ 6:60, January, 1981.

VASECTOMY

Use of exteriorized stents in vasovasostomy, by F. S. Shessel, et al. UROLOGY 17(2):163-165, February, 1981.

Vasovasostomy: four year experience at Ochsner Medical Institutions, by H. A. Fuselier, Jr., et al. JOURNAL OF THE LOUISIANA STATE MEDICAL SOCIETY 132(12): 195-196, December, 1980.

Vasovasostomy—is the microscope necessary? by H. Fenster, et al. UROLOGY 18(1):60-64, July, 1981.

VASECTOMY: RESEARCH
Autoantibodies from vasectomized guinea pigs inhibit fertilization in vitro, by T. T. Huang, Jr., et al. SCIENCE 213 (4513):1267-1269, September 11, 1981.

AUTHOR INDEX

Bancroft, J. 61
Bano, K. A. 153
Barrat, J. 42
Barrett, F. M. 31, 145
Barson, A. J. 64
Bartók, I. 71
Baum, F. 148
Beaucaire, G. 113
Beaumont, V. 168
Beazley, J. M. 114
Beck, L. R. 25, 35, 163
Becker, J. 54
Becker, W. 12
Beckman, M. 151
Begum, S. F. 35, 116
Belker, A. M. 99
Benedetti, A. 65
Benjamin, L. 61
Bennett, R. W. 8
Benoist, A. 46
Bercovici, B. 100
Berelson, B. 160
Berenson, G. S. 34
Berg, J. K. 131
Berger, F. 131
Berić, B. 151
Berkowitz, R. S. 112
Berliński, B. 37
Bernardus, R. E. 163
Bernhardt-Huth, D. 101, 139
Bernstein, A. H. 92
Bertrand, J. 63
Betts, K. 22
Bhatia, P. 21
Bhowmik, A. 168
Bhuyan, S. K. C. 21
Bianco, L. 26, 119
Bickenbach, J. E. 49
Bird, H. W. 152
Birnbaum, M. D. 39
Bisconti, E. 131
Black, M. M. 66

Blake, J. 104
Blašková, O. 146
Blocher, C. 142
Block, R. A. 138
Blum, M. 11
Bobscheff, T. 134
Boes, E. G. 99
Bojović, S. 149
Bokhman, I. V. 108
Bondue, H. 24
Bone, M. 134
Bordahl, P. E. 98
Borg, S. O. 99
Borko, E. 89
Borovská, D. 82
Bostofte, E. 44
Bosworth, M. 13
Böttger, G. 93
Bouraoui, K. 31
Bourgault, R. 88
Bowen, D. A. 47
Brandt, M. 76
Breckenridge, A. M. 84
Breen, J. P. 42
Brenner, P. F. 144
Breo, D. L. 88
Breu, G. 20
Brewer, C. 36, 37, 125
Briel, R. C. 25
Brinton, L. A. 139
Brodsky, J. B. 155
Bromboszcz, A. 43
Brosseau, K. D. 167
Brown, J. E. 32
Brown, K. L. 29
Brudenell, M. 73
Brunt, L. 91
Bryant, C. J. 110
Bryce, E. M. 134
Bryson, A. M. 78
Buckley, W. F., Jr. 108, 139
Budner, S. 168

397

402